*Wage Labor and Guilds
in Medieval Europe*

WAGE

& LABOR

GUILDS IN

MEDIEVAL

EUROPE

Steven A. Epstein

The University of North Carolina Press

Chapel Hill and London

The paper in this book meets the guidelines for permanence and
durability of the Committee on Production Guidelines for Book
Longevity of the Council on Library Resources.

98 97 96 95 94   6 5 4 3 2

Library of Congress Cataloging-in-Publication Data

Epstein, Steven, 1952–
    Wage labor and guilds in medieval Europe / by Steven A. Epstein.
       p.   cm.
    Includes bibliographical references and index.
    ISBN 0-8078-1939-5 (cloth : alk. paper)
    ISBN 0-8078-4498-5 (pbk. : alk. paper)
    1. Guilds—Europe—History. 2. Wages—Europe—History.
  I. Title.
    HD6456.E67   1991
    331.2'94—dc20   90-40427
                                                         CIP

Portions of chapter 3 appeared earlier in somewhat different form as
part of Steven A. Epstein, "Labour in Thirteenth-Century Genoa,"
Mediterranean Historical Review 3 (1988): 114–140, and are reproduced
here by permission of Frank Cass & Co. Ltd.

Contents

Tables

Acknowledgments

In the course of writing this book, I have piled up a number of debts, and it is a pleasure for me to record my thanks. One convention of this genre is to absolve one's friends and colleagues from any responsibility for the errors and omissions that persist in any work. This formulaic ritual is not satisfactory in my case because I have added and subtracted many examples and views, in the process going against what may very well have been good advice. But still, I want to thank my colleagues Fred Anderson, Robert J. Ferry, Boyd H. Hill, Jr., Robert Hohlfelder, Patricia Nelson Limerick, and Marjorie K. McIntosh for reading parts of the drafts and making valuable suggestions. I am also grateful to another colleague and friend, Dean Charles R. Middleton, for his interest in my work.

John P. Powelson scrutinized the whole work and with his skill in all matters economic saved me from some big mistakes. James B. Given has been a valuable critic of my writing ever since he suffered through my first draft of a Ph.D. thesis longer ago than either of us care to remember. And also once again, David Herlihy improved my work through his painstaking reading. He also encouraged me to persist with what at times seemed an intractable subject, and his optimism kept me going.

I could not have written this book without the help of the interlibrary loan staff of the University of Colorado. The vast majority of titles in the Bibliography came to me through this office from libraries too numerous to mention. Patricia Murphy prepared the manuscript several times, and I am very grateful for her patience and high standards. Gabriella Airaldi put me on the track of some Genoese evidence and listened to my earliest ideas on the subject of labor and guilds, and the director and staff of the Archivio di Stato di Genova helped me find and use some fresh material.

I owe particular thanks to people at the University of North Carolina Press: to Lewis Bateman for his many courtesies and encouragement, to Ron Maner for skillfully handling the editorial process, and to Mary Repaske for perceptive and expert copyediting. I count myself fortunate to have benefited from their high standards.

My wife, Jean, lends me her expertise in what is today called "human resources," and I often wish the people I study had her help as well.

*Wage Labor and Guilds
in Medieval Europe*

In the sweat of thy face shalt thou eat bread.
—Genesis 3:19

For the laborer is worthy of his hire.
—Luke 10:7

*Friend, I do thee no wrong, didst not thou
agree with me for a penny? Take that thine
is and go thy way.*
—Matthew 20:13–14

Introduction

This book is my answer to two simple questions—why did wage labor appear in medieval Europe, and what sort of rules and traditions governed the causal and dynamic relationship between employer and employee? At first glance wages might not seem to rank with the Gothic cathedral or the university as important legacies to us from the Middle Ages. Yet everyone who has received a pay envelope, eaten in the company cafeteria, punched a time clock, taken a paid or unpaid holiday, and witnessed unfairness on the job has occasionally wondered how this strange inheritance—wage labor—came into being. Wage labor is an old idea, and its roots are deep in a society not traditionally credited with shaping its essential and durable features. Medieval employers devised an institution with a long and tangled history—the guild—as well as a system of regularly obtaining extra hands and defining their own status—wage labor. Hence this history of labor must treat wages and guilds as two sides of the same coin, subjects comprehensible together but incomplete when studied separately.

The reader is entitled to know what is in this book and what is not. I have not attempted to write a general history of the medieval guild, but this abstraction merits a preliminary definition. The medieval guild was an association of employers who banded together to foster their self-interest. These guilds existed in various political, regional, and economic settings, had a wide range of standings in law, and contained members who pursued almost every conceivable means of earning a living. Generations of intelligent people across Europe applied themselves to elaborating upon or changing whatever original rules guided the masters in the earliest years of the guild's existence. A biologist might see the medieval guild as a rapidly spreading organism with a high mutation rate and also be surprised at its spontaneous generation in different places. Historians try to account for parallel development by seeking a common cause, and the self-interest of employers is an obvious one. Yet as will be seen below, this self-interest, even among the payers of wages, was by no means self-evident.

The earners of wages in the Middle Ages are historically elusive subjects because of the long time before they developed, or were permitted to have, lawful organizations devoted to self-help. Hence employees mostly appear as items in records (guild statutes, apprenticeship and work contracts, court cases) generated by people who hired them, and so the great mass of evidence concerns things done to workers rather than by them. Therefore, a history of wage labor appears to be a subcategory of the history of employers, but the sources should not dictate such an asymmetrical analysis. Employers in a sense created employment, and they also caused a market for labor to come into being. Some of the new traditions of this market helped to redress the inherent imbalance between employers and employees. Bargaining for apprentices and journeymen was at the heart of this market and provides yet another good reason for looking at both sides.

Wage labor also required societies practicing it to have two other features—ready cash and a respect for contracts. Without denigrating the possibilities of a barter economy, we can accept the fact that extensive use of wage labor necessitated a means to pay it. Unless employers chose to assume all of the responsibilities for maintaining workers, cash was the sine qua non for wage labor. The fluctuations over time in the supply of reliable currency provide some useful benchmarks in the history of labor. The idea of contract occupied a central role in many aspects of medieval society, and we can place it one rung lower than the noble or merchant classes in the social hierarchy—the pact between employer and employee.[1] The takers of wages had some rights under the prevailing concepts of contract, and they were free, at least as day laborers, to take their capacity for work where it suited them. Work rules illustrate how employers modified competition among themselves and how they intended to employ labor. Work contracts, and the customs and laws that shaped and grew out of them, reveal what wage labor was like at its beginnings.

The organization of this book also requires an explanation. Much of the first chapter concerns the urban economy in the late Roman state. Several reasons point to starting in antiquity a study of medieval guilds and wage labor. Rome provides a perfect example of how several systems of labor (free, enslaved, and state-coerced) could exist in harmony for a long time, and Rome certainly knew both wage labor and a guild—the *collegium.* Since the extent of wage labor, as opposed to the other forms of labor in the empire, remains a point of contention, the question of whether or not wages and guilds survived the collapse of the empire in the west is an intriguing one. The balance of the chapter explains why they did not. The Romans bequeathed to posterity a body of law containing within it certain ideas about contracts and a rigorous sense of the state's right to intervene in the economy. When this law began to count for something in Europe, corporatism had a cogent jurisprudence for anyone with the desire to be like a Roman emperor.

Chapter 2 takes up the twelfth- and thirteenth-century sources for the appearance of guilds and wage labor: rare foundation charters for guilds, early statutes, and the apprenticeship and work contracts from the notarial records of southern Europe. I have added to this chapter a short section on the Humiliati, a religious movement in northern Italy with some interesting connections to the new guilds and system of labor. Close scrutiny of these sources lays the foundation for chapter 3, where I discuss the internal workings of guilds and the perfecting of the apprentice and journeyman system. This chapter concentrates on the thirteenth century, broadens the scope of examples, and explains some changes taking place in the economy. Its last section treats the issue of status and the variety of trades. In chapter 4, I argue that, in the same way in which guilds and wage labor developed in tandem, this system itself played a part in a wider world. Many features of medieval society impinged upon urban work; religious views on labor and associations, and the broader field of politics as it related to municipal government, offer the clearest and most important cases. The status of Jews in the economy helps to tie together some previous themes as well. In chapter 5, I carry these themes into the fourteenth century in order to illustrate the durability of the guild and the system of wage labor. This chapter makes no claim of comprehensiveness, but some important changes in this century demonstrate that the system was flexible or obdurate enough to survive. In the aftermath of the Black Death, I have found a logical terminus for this study.

The geographical scope of the work—western Europe—is more the product of necessity than audacity. I have had to take my evidence where I could find it. Some regions and cities are a complete blank. I have concentrated my efforts on England, France, and northern Italy, with the Rhineland and the Low Countries receiving less attention. Although wages were not exclusively an urban phenomenon, I have had to exclude the difficult question of rural wages, at least agricultural ones, in all periods. One reason for this is practical: I had enough to cover. But more importantly, I am interested in tracing the relationship between landless laborers and their masters working at crafts and businesses in the cities. The men, women, and children who form the principal subjects of this book were city people, by birth or by choice, and the destinies of these who were out of the agricultural mainstream, who had no option but to live by paying or taking wages, comprise the part of labor history I want to explore. Although by the end of the period under review some people in the countryside were certainly landless and living by casual employment or as sharecroppers, the increasing numbers living by what once were urban trades suggest that the cities were the incubators of the part of wage labor's history with the greatest import—the crafts and business. Genoa receives what might appear to be more than its fair share of attention, but I hope the readers will find these parts to be something fresh. I am greatly in the debt of those nineteenth- and twentieth-century scholars who devoted themselves to the patient and unglamorous work of editing source materials, and I have tried to go back to the sources wherever possible.

What in other fields is called labor history remains for the Middle Ages largely unwritten, and hence apart from Sylvia Thrupp's still-definitive chapter in the *Cambridge Economic History of Europe*, little recent work in English, and not much more in the continental languages, exists.[2] Many of the dates in the Bibliography cluster in the period from the late 1870s to the First World War, the last era when medievalists apparently took their cue from contemporary labor turmoil and looked to the past for some guidance. Since the 1920s, labor history has found a place in the histories of modern Europe and America and, through the work of pathfinders like M. I. Finley, even appeared in ancient history. With few exceptions—particularly Bronislaw Geremek and Gunnar Mickwitz—medievalists, who seldom hesitate to generalize about the Church, family, nobility, or the high economy, have been reluctant to take on urban labor history. In part, this gap may result from respect for the great works of the last century, a respect in the main justified. The greater obstacle is that medieval labor history, if the subject flourished, would require putting the guild at the center; and ever since Adam Smith, guilds have seemed to be a part of medieval history best consigned to the now proverbial rubbish heap. Even occasional fits of nostalgia for the medieval guild, for example in the work of Émile Durkheim, failed to take root. Antony Black's recent fine study of guilds and the idea of *civil society* concluded on the dire thought that modern fascism probably owes a great deal to medieval corporatism.[3] This observation is not likely to stir up interest in "what everyone knows" is a dull and dead-end subject—the medieval guild. The guild by itself is a collective history of the Chambers of Commerce, or, as Smith would have it, the study of conspiracies to defraud the public. But the Genoese work contracts and apprenticeship agreements reveal that the guild was only half the story. And so I incorporate both sides of the equation, labor and its masters, into this account of a dynamic and evolving relationship. Durkheim, no believer in class warfare, called the work contracts "treaties between belligerents," and these long truces marked by mutual suspicions and slow changes in the balance of forces constitute the raw materials of this book.[4]

Wages and guilds have much to do with the history of the division of labor, and this term obligates me to acknowledge some debts to social theory. Although Durkheim misunderstood the role of corporations in antiquity and guilds in the Middle Ages because his authorities did not sufficiently emphasize the status of these societies as associations of employers, he reminds us that guilds existed for good reasons, and looking closely at those reasons and the environment that brought them into being will be helpful. His constant emphasis on the moral character of work makes particular sense for the Middle Ages, when people were consciously operating in a religious framework that was relevant to, and had something to say about, every aspect of life. Durkheim also believed that the division of labor was potentially a force for social solidarity and hence an antidote to anomie—that malaise produced by the breakdown of civilizing ties and values necessary to the proper and moral functioning of society.[5] Convinced that a corporate society furnished no panacea for social ills, Durkheim still considered the division of labor to be a potential force for good because it could produce institutions that would support the individual and the family in ways a state (or indeed civil society) could not.[6] In the Middle Ages, the guilds were such institutions operating as a force for social solidarity. Durkheim envisioned a progression from mechanical, or prescribed, solidarity to an organic one, characterized by just, humane, and more completely voluntary ties.[7]

The history of the division of labor in this period reveals no neat or even predominant pattern but instead the proliferation of divisions. In short, many divisions of labor appear. Within crafts, distinctions of age, wealth, and experience helped to produce the continuum of master, journeyman, and apprentice; but gender frequently made a hash of these ostensibly clean lines. Specialization in the crafts and business caused a splitting off of jobs and tasks that were at an earlier stage performed by one person or under one roof. The rise of employment itself produced a pervasive division of labor that was quick to stimulate a sense of solidarity among employers but slow to inculcate the same sense of common purpose among laborers. Thus we will have to keep in mind that the division of labor can mean many things depending on what perspective is taken. Nevertheless, the period under review here constitutes a crucial and neglected stage of the history of the division of labor, whether by craft or by the age or sex of the employers and employees.

Employers were bound to have power over those who had no choice but to live by wages. United employers were in an even more advantageous position since they enjoyed the benefits of solidarity. But employers were not the only center of power in medieval society, and so the concept of power does not prove to be any clearer than the division of labor. Hence I have divided the discussion of guilds and labor into two parts, found in chapters 3 and 4. The internal structure of the wage market reveals the expected advantages employers enjoyed, but in the setting of the wider economic and social world of medieval Europe, the power of employers faced some challenges, and employees acquired unexpected patrons. Specialization in the crafts and business enabled some highly skilled journeymen and -women to extract higher wages from employers, but these workers were in no position to translate their competence into power in the guild.

A history of wage labor and guilds in medieval Europe, in addition to providing a means to test existing social theory and supplying grist for the mills of future theorists, can serve as a healthy reminder that historical development has been contingent; it has depended on individuals driven by unfathomable impulses and circumstances beyond the control of the most powerful and efficient people. Two vignettes illustrate this point. My favorite example is a local one with no consequences whatsoever, yet it illustrates that this general study rests on many local experiments and that the relative economic success or failure of regions and cities depended in part on quirky oddities. The master dyers of Tournai in 1356 decided to pay their journeymen wages of four sous four pence on Monday, three sous eight pence on Tuesday, and two sous eight pence a day for the rest of the workweek.[8] Practical experience, in 1356 or today, suggests that this was a marvelous idea, a way to counteract absenteeism on Monday, one of the absolute constants of labor history. Some nimble mind in Tournai actually thought to carry the premium over to Tuesday as well. Whether this wage scale was simply too clever, cumbersome, or caused problems of its own (perhaps on Wednesday), as far as I know, it was unique to Tournai, and I have found elsewhere only uniformity of wages for workdays. But the local exception adds force to the general rule because it proves that some of the paths of development not taken were tried and rejected. If for some reason this plan of wages had produced spectacular results, it might have been imitated across Europe. This small scale example underscores the theme of competition and the role it played in determining which innovations would survive.

The second vignette is more somber. In one of the earliest surviving *commenda* contracts from Barcelona, dated 3 January 1236, Guillem d'Espina committed his Saracen slave Cassim to Bernat Calafat for one year.[9] Cassim was supposed to work for Bernat as a caulker, and Guillem, his owner, received three-quarters of the profit; Bernat kept the remainder. Guillem also retained the right to recall Cassim to caulk his own ship, and he would not have to pay for this service. Medieval slavery was not limited to Barcelona, and the ancient world had proved that slavery was capable of solving the problems of recruiting and training a labor force. The contract for Cassim's work reminds us that wage labor was not the only way to acquire a person's services. With Durkheim's admonitions about work and morality fresh on the page, it is difficult to put the more recent debates about slavery aside for a moment and ask—what features of wages made them more reliable and profitable than slavery? Back in the thirteenth century, Bernat was capable of calculating the expenses and profits of an enslaved caulker. For us, the lesson is that nothing was inevitable about wage labor.

In the famous long run, wage labor triumphed over slavery, and the masters usually preferred the guild to unbridled competition. But the result might have been different, and this book's purpose is to explain why.

1

Roman and Early Medieval Guilds

Ancient Guilds in Rome

A study of the medieval guild system must begin with a brief survey of the ancient Roman guild because a line of argument will always be in favor of a continuity, however tenuous and ill-defined, between the Roman college and the medieval guild. In the eastern Mediterranean, the argument for a continuous tradition is more appealing, and the Byzantine guild system would be incomprehensible without some explanation of Roman practice. However, the Roman college merits attention in its own right and provides an example for testing the hypothesis of spontaneous development of social and economic institutions. Many of the problems associated with the study of Roman guilds relate to the quality and type of source materials available for research, and separating the historical questions involved from the problem of the sources is difficult.

The ancient historians, past and present, have not lavished attention on the Roman guild. A few snippets of information are in the narrative sources, principally in Livy, Cassius Dio, and Plutarch, but social and economic history were not central concerns of the classical authors, and collectively their comments mainly reveal how little is known. The Theodosian Code of the fifth century A.D. and the Code of Justinian from the sixth century are informative about guilds. The law's concern was the radically different relationship between the colleges and the state that resulted from "reforms," discussed below, enacted by Diocletian and Constantine. Justinian's *Digest* of Roman law contains excerpts about colleges from the great jurists of the Severan period (third century), when the Roman colleges were voluntary and spontaneous associations. So, most of our information about the earlier periods has been selected by Justinian's jurists, who were not interested in voluntary guilds and who were mainly trying to organize the body of law that affected guilds as quasi-public bodies with obligations to the state. Since most of our information about previous legal arrangements comes from the sixth century, we are looking into the early empire and republican-period colleges with a measure of distortion. The legal sources pose problems of their own. The tension between the prescriptive generality of the law and the vagaries of actual practice is a familiar one, and a history of the guild in any period written from the point of view of the rules would overlook many important practical realities. A few late classical writers such as Libanius of Antioch and Cassiodorus provide some useful details about colleges, and inscriptions are particularly valuable sources, especially for the colleges of Rome and Ostia. Still, the sources are not good, and they confine us to a narrow view of the Roman guild. New inscriptions, discovered every year, hold forth the hope for more knowledge, but we will have to make the best of what we currently have.

Roman guilds are known by a variety of names, but the most common is the classic *collegium* (*conlegium*), emphasizing in its etymology a group of persons bound together by common rules or laws. The words *corpus* (body) and *corporatio* (extension of the same word) were also used, especially by the Severan jurists, as synonyms for *collegium*, but not every body or association was in fact a college. *Sodalitas*, the most common word for social club, also described religious brotherhoods, which were in turn termed *collegia*, and referred to secret societies and political conspiracies. For our purposes, the sodalities, as they are known in English, are special colleges, religious in nature, that have little to do with the artisan or professional colleges.[1] The Romans used *collegium* to describe these organized groups comprised of people in a particular craft, trade, or line of business. *Corporatio* or *corpus* was sometimes reserved for the upper levels of these associations—for example, the *corpus naviculariorum*, the college of long-distance shippers at Ostia, the port of Rome. The Romans also used the word *collegium* to describe what are today called burial societies—private groups whose sole function was to guarantee, in return for dues, an honorable interment for the members. These colleges took their names from various gods or temples, and although in certain social respects they resemble the artisan or professional colleges, the absence of any common economic interest clearly distinguishes them from groups with the same name.

The origins and early history of the Roman colleges are subjects that later Roman and Greek authors embellished with received myth or invention. Plutarch wrote that Numa, the second king of Rome, was responsible for organizing eight artisan trades into colleges.[2] The first eight colleges were for musicians, goldsmiths, carpenters, dyers, shoe-makers, tanners, braziers, and potters. The source Plutarch took this information from is unknown, and Livy does not attribute this innovation to Numa. The supposed early foundation of colleges is imaginary and reflects a desire of colleges under the empire to place their origins in a distant and honorable past. Livy says that Numa did institute the priesthoods, a credible if not proved assertion, and perhaps the beginnings of the religious colleges encouraged later writers to believe that Numa had established other colleges as well.[3] Plutarch's comments suggest two useful conclusions about the colleges. As Jean-Pierre Waltzing observed, the origins of colleges as Plutarch related them are legendary, but the list of artisan trades is a good summary of a Bronze Age economy and represents what are likely to have been the earliest trades practiced in a small Italian market town.[4] Although Plutarch's facts are in this case suspect, he does offer an interesting analysis of Numa's motives. Plutarch was in no position to fathom these motives, but he may have drawn on his own reading of first-century Greco-Roman social thought to project into the past a plausible explanation. The relationship between the state and the private college was always a complex question, and Plutarch attributes to state initiative something that more likely developed from private and voluntary aspirations. Plutarch goes beyond the question of Numa's initiative to claim that the colleges were a good thing for society since the existing social distinctions "would be lost among the lesser ones."[5] The idea that minute social divisions produce social harmony both justifies a state interest in colleges and is itself a social theory worthy of note. Plutarch's reflections are more relevant to his own age than they are to the origins of colleges. In the context of the struggles of the orders in the early republic, the idea that social and presumably economic divisions among the artisanal classes promoted social peace requires us to ask—harmony among whom? The internal structure of the college, unknown in this period, provided the members with the opportunity to participate in a social institution in which they were full and equal members. This political experience, not available in the Centuriate Assembly or elsewhere in the state political process, gave artisans an acceptable outlet for political talent and the social experience of equality. The harmony resulting from these experiences was apparent within the particular trades, but not necessarily among them, and also freed the artisans to pursue interests beneath the notice of the traditional elites of Roman society.

If we put aside the evidence Plutarch supplies, is it safe and reasonable to assume a voluntary and spontaneous origin for the Roman college at some early date in the republic and to view the colleges as private associations? A piece of evidence in favor of this assumption comes from the *Digest* of Justinian, whose compilers observed that the Twelve Tablets—the mid-fifth-century B.C. Roman code of law—confirmed the existence and rights of private associations.[6] The law jumbled together colleges and other private groups, but the Twelve Tablets definitely point to a private- and not state-inspired origin for guilds. Waltzing believed that the silence of the sources suggests that the state had little interest in colleges, except when some public religious cult was invested in an existing college.[7] The silence of the sources may inspire in its listeners some confidence in their own preconceived ideas. The inclusion of the colleges in the list of private associations sanctioned in the Twelve Tablets strongly supports the idea that the colleges were voluntary and spontaneous groups whose members shared the interest of a common trade. Nothing is known about the internal organization or purpose of these colleges in the republican period.

Colleges emerged from obscurity when they played a role in the political disorders of the first century B.C. Cassius Dio records that all colleges were suppressed in the aftermath of the Catilinarian Conspiracy in 64 and that Clodius reestablished them in 58.[8] The principal problem for the state was the existence of political gangs and their role in factional strife. Artisan colleges may not have been involved in political violence at all, but the ban on private "clubs" was absolute, if brief. Memories of these political problems endured; Suetonius writes in his biography of Julius Caesar that the dictator dissolved all artisan guilds except the ancient ones.[9] Presumably Caesar, who had witnessed the earlier ban, attempted to distinguish the colleges from the gangs this time and banned the more recent, and hence suspicious, associations. Augustus modified the ban by again proscribing all artisan guilds except the ancient ones or those carrying on legitimate business—a clear sign that the government was prepared to recognize new colleges, so long as they were not, in Suetonius's words, "in reality organizations for committing every sort of crime."[10] Here again no evidence exists that artisan colleges were engaging in seditious activities, but their private nature made them at times hard to separate from the old gangs. At some time in the early empire, the colleges needed official permission in order to exist and obtained this privilege from the emperor or the senate. The government was not overly concerned about illicit colleges, as long as they remained innocuous. The law itself granted a form of toleration to illicit colleges if they caused no trouble, recognizing a difference between the merely illegal and the dangerous.[11] Colleges, whether they were artisan, professional, or burial associations, were proud to obtain sanctions in the law, and surviving inscriptions indicate that official approval merited a permanent memorial.[12]

Little is known about colleges in the early empire. Tacitus records in the year 59 A.D. the story of a riot in Pompeii that broke out between the citizens of Nuceria and Pompeii at a gladiatorial show. The emperor Nero turned the matter over to the senate, which banned such shows in the city for two years and dissolved the colleges that had been established contrary to the law.[13] Inscriptions and graffiti from Pompeii reveal that the colleges endorsed candidates for municipal office and therefore had a minor role in politics.[14] The illicit colleges that Tacitus mentions may have had more in common with the gangs of the previous century or have been a local variant of the circus factions developing in Rome itself. Tacitus mentions this incident after his long and carefully crafted description of Agrippina's murder, and the events in Pompeii begin a catalog of lesser, but noteworthy, examples of political corruption under Nero. Pompeii gave Tacitus evidence of municipal turmoil outside Rome, and Caesar and Augustus apparently had not succeeded in eliminating a role for colleges in politics. Artisan and professional groups, however, were probably not permanently suppressed in Pompeii.

The colleges had the right to petition the emperor for legal recognition, and the gray area that the illicit colleges occupied marked them as obvious candidates for repression after public disturbances. Pliny's letters to the emperor Trajan in the early years of the second century A.D. concerning the status of carpenters in Bithynia reveal that colleges in the provinces came under the same set of rules that applied to Italy.[15] Colleges everywhere caused the government some concern, and Trajan rejected Pliny's suggestion for using a college of carpenters as part-time firefighters. Pliny's concerns, and Trajan's doubts, also provide a rare piece of information about the development of colleges in the Greek east. The ill-charted history of the Greek guild remains to be studied, but Roman law and edicts on colleges were enforced in the east, and the status of licit and illicit colleges appears in Pliny's letters to be in force in the eastern provinces. Pliny singled out the carpenters as a useful and logical source for the local fire brigade, a function the carpenters occasionally fulfilled in other cities. Carpenters constructed buildings, and their knowledge would be helpful in fighting fires. Fire brigades, public and private, are a permanent concern in cities, and Pliny's ideas for Bithynia are one of the first signs that someone in government service recognized that colleges could be useful to the state. As will be discussed below, the chronology of this interest is difficult to determine. Legal recognition was a privilege obtained from the state, and evidently, at least in Pliny's time, some public service in return for this favor was deemed reasonable.

For the other colleges, like the shippers, the question was public service in return for special privileges, and the colleges were in a position to bargain with the government for immunities and concessions. The second century witnessed the gradual realization on the part of men in colleges and the government that closer cooperation could be mutually beneficial. Again, this development is seen principally through the eyes of the Severan jurists, as excerpted in the sixth century, a century in which state involvement loomed larger than it did in the second. The law suggests that the "divine brothers" Marcus Aurelius and Lucius Verus (161–169) were the first to look closely at the colleges and the way they might assist the state. The empire faced wars and financial pressures in these years, and the situation encouraged the emperors to look in new places for resources to serve the war efforts.

The *Digest* of Justinian offers the first extended glimpse of the state's interest in the colleges. Under Marcus Aurelius (161–180), the empire began to define more sharply the corporate rights and responsibilities of the colleges. As private associations, the colleges came under a general rubric that included all sorts of groups, and much of this legislation by edict defined the status of corporations as persons at law. For example, Marcus Aurelius granted to all colleges the rights to manumit slaves and to receive lawfully executed legacies.[16] The slaves that colleges owned presumably took care of the meeting hall (*scola*), and no evidence suggests that the colleges as groups employed slaves in the course of the work or business of the members or, in fact, engaged in any corporate business activities. The ability to receive legacies, however, was more important to the colleges; charitable acts toward members and the expenses of social occasions created a need for money and, hence, a hope for bequests. Some inscriptions record legacies by testament that members of colleges made to each of the surviving members, usually in the form of small gratuities (*sportulae*) to be distributed once or endowed for every year.[17] The jurist Ulpian also observed that the property rights of colleges were the same as those of persons, and the ability to buy and sell property, as well as to litigate over property matters, buttressed the position of colleges as legitimate, permanent associations.[18] The need for these concessions from the state may reflect the aftermath of the colleges' original, suspicious social role, at least from the point of view of the early imperial state. These modest privileges represent a regularizing of the status of colleges in Roman society.

Other edicts affecting the colleges deal more specifically with the place colleges occupied in the economy. The Roman jurists were careful to distinguish the corporate rights of the colleges from the personal liabilities of the members (*collegiati*). The colleges did not assume any liability for the personal business of the members and did not behave as companies with joint ventures including all or some of the members. This personal liability for business contracts extended to agreements made between members or transferred from one to another. Ulpian attempted to sort out the liabilities of a shipper (*navicularius*) who transferred cargo to another carrier whose vessel sank.[19] Resolution of the claims varied, depending on whether the second shipper was suitable or whether a pilot was present, but the key point is that the college of shippers was not liable at law. The jurist Gaius emphasized that the right to have a college was a special concession from the state, not casually granted to any group, and that the petitioner must follow the proper form for an imperial edict or senatorial decree. He singled out certain colleges that were closely connected to the public welfare, those involved with the public food supply—most notably the corn merchants and factors (*frumentarii*). In the same context he mentioned the operators of gold and silver mines and the salt works.[20] The mines were crucial to the economic health of the state, and the dietary and financial rewards from the salt works were also vital. Gaius put the urban colleges in a different category, since colleges like the bakers (*pistores*) appeared in Rome and in the provinces and had a clearly defined but purely local significance. The shippers were important in Ostia and Alexandria, with their successes and failures reverberating throughout the empire.

To portray the *Digest*'s compilers as very interested in or concerned about the status of colleges would be a mistake. The one chapter devoted to the colleges is brief, and the references to colleges in the rest of the text are scattered and discuss colleges in the context of their ability to behave as legal persons.[21] The principal interest the jurists had in colleges concerned this one interesting feature the colleges enjoyed in the law, as well as their special duties and their subsequent immunities from other burdens the state imposed. Membership in colleges vital to the provisioning of Rome and the legions entailed special responsibilities, and hence the colleges gradually obtained exemptions from other civic duties. The best-documented colleges in this regard were food suppliers. The shippers received some privileges as early as the reign of Trajan (98–117), an emperor whose activities in Ostia testify to his awareness of keeping Rome supplied with food.[22] The *Digest* mentions exemptions given to the corn merchants and the measurers of corn from legal obligations attached to their land or possessions.[23] The obligations of the municipal classes included being responsible for tax collecting and serving on town councils. The exemptions that the law allowed from these services represent state efforts to foster the business of certain colleges, and the exemptions tangibly benefited traders who might otherwise have found themselves elevated to decurion status. Various second-century emperors legislated on these immunities: Antoninus Pius (138–161) was careful to make sure that people claiming the privileges of the shippers were actually engaged in the trade; Pertinax (193) allowed the *navicularii* to refuse decurion status and its liabilities;[24] and most importantly, Marcus Aurelius decreed that a person could belong to only one guild, this rule presumably intended to prevent anyone from claiming more privileges than deserved.[25] Evidence from Ostia suggests this rule was not widely followed.[26]

All the edicts link the immunities to the performance of other public service—in the case of the shippers, the provisioning of Rome and the armies. The state was, of course, the principal customer of some important colleges, and the more formal relationship between the state and these colleges benefited both parties. Septimius Severus (193–211) and Caracalla (211–217) formalized this phase in the development of Roman colleges.[27] The jurist Callistratus described the system of immunities as fixed under these two rulers.[28] In the difficult years of the third century, this system of privileges managed to survive, and doubtful evidence suggests that Severus Alexander (222–235) organized all the artisans and merchants of Rome into official colleges.[29] The third century, especially after the Severan emperors, offers little information about colleges, but the numerous surviving inscriptions suggest that the situation remained basically the same until Diocletian and Constantine changed it.

The colleges had a history apart from what the legal sources reveal, and most of this knowledge comes from inscriptions of the second and third centuries. As Russell Meiggs observes, "Inscriptions do not tell the whole story, and it is the things that were taken for granted and were not worth recording that we most want to know."[30] Waltzing was not prepared to reach into the Middle Ages for some comparisons to fill in the gaps in his description of Roman colleges. I will also avoid any references to the medieval guild and instead try to summarize what is known from inscriptions about the social and economic functions of the colleges in urban life. Perhaps the most important feature of the college is that it was a voluntary association of traders or employers devoted to a specific line of commerce or commodity production. In the early empire, merchants or artisans were free not to join colleges, but the system of immunities made it likely that the eligibles became members. The colleges possessed halls that served as headquarters and gathering places for social and religious activities. All the colleges had divine patrons, and Minerva, for obvious reasons, was the most popular patroness. The day of the inauguration of her temple was March 19, the *artificium dies* (Labor Day) for artisans.[31] The colleges included illustrious citizens, not likely to have engaged in active trade or a craft, to serve as patrons who lent their influence in the state to the colleges in exchange for the social prestige of the title of patron.[32] The patron was useful when the time came to seek some favor from the emperor or those who had influence with the emperor. The colleges in turn commemorated the generosity of the patrons, whose gifts added some luster to social occasions. The members of the colleges, except for the patrons, were actively engaged in their business, or else they were not able to claim any immunities. The benefits derived from enrollment in a college required an accurate list of members, and verification of status was important both to the colleges and the state. Slaves were members of the artisanal colleges, and this mix of free plebeians, freedmen and -women, and slaves is a useful example of a blurring of legal and social distinctions in Roman society.[33]

Although the law granted the colleges corporate legal status, it did not recognize any specific economic functions of the colleges, other than service to the public good. The Roman colleges did not regulate competition among their members or establish any work rules or production standards. Doubtless some informal agreements among members fostered exchanges of technical innovations, and in some instances the *collegiati* may have informally divided up markets. General prosperity may have been an aim of the colleges, but no signs point to any concrete economic steps taken to influence the personal business fortunes of the members. The social atmosphere of the colleges promoted at best some sense of social solidarity among the members, and perhaps honest dealing and fair competition were more likely to happen among people who passed some social time together. More importantly, the system of officers and responsibilities gave some men with an aptitude for politics an outlet for their talents and ambitions. The chief official, the *quinquennalis*, so-called for his five-year term of office, served along with treasurers to run the affairs of the college.[34] These offices and the way members filled them allowed men to participate in politics on a scale that was admittedly narrow, but still more than they experienced in any other setting. The political life of the college, and the system of patronage that came to envelop this internal system, gave the members some power in the face of a bureaucratic and increasingly intrusive state.

The religious character of the Roman college has already been mentioned, and the social atmosphere of the college derived first from religious observance and second from frequent meetings and banquets. Since the colleges were primarily associations of employers, the people engaged in particular trades did not perform the heavy labor, for that was usually left to slaves. The members of the Roman colleges were small-time entrepreneurs, at the low end of the scale, but for some tradesmen, such as shipowners and corn merchants, great fortunes could be made. In the small provincial towns, the more modest artisan trades, like baking, fishing, and barbering, might have a few wealthy patrons in the college, but these colleges were thoroughly plebeian, as were the majority of members of most colleges. Meiggs's study of the colleges of Ostia convinced him that, before the colleges became hereditary, "it had long been customary for sons to follow fathers in the guilds."[35] This traditional approach to occupations is not surprising and indicates a firm basis for the social ties among members. By the 200s, many of these colleges had existed for centuries, and the habit of sons replacing their fathers lent additional weight to the social cohesion in the various trades and professions.

Waltzing was one of the first to observe that no trace of an apprenticeship system for free labor in the colleges appears in Roman law.[36] Apprenticeship agreements from Roman Egypt reveal that some slave and free youths received training under a contract establishing a rental agreement, the *locatio-conductio rei.*[37] In this type of contract, the master was not paid for his services as an educator; when he was, the contract, a *locatio-conductio operarum,* was a straight service-for-hire deal. W. L. Westermann believed that apprenticeships must have existed in other parts of the empire, but generalizing on the basis of this unique evidence from Roman Egypt or assessing the degree to which artisans utilized apprentices by contract who were free rather than slave is difficult. The law and the colleges did not regulate apprenticeship contracts between slaves or free persons, and the complete silence of the law on this subject suggests that the training and education of the next generation were private matters in which the state took no interest. Again, since much of the manual labor of the artisan trades was performed by slaves, the experienced slaves would simply train, on the job, younger slaves destined to work at the craft, or masters would contract for someone else to train their slaves. Slavery removed one of the principal reasons for having extensive free apprenticeship, since slaves could not presume to make a contract for service in exchange for education with their own masters. But some masters arranged for their slaves to be trained by others.[38] Sons succeeding their fathers would provide some, but not all, members with replacements; for the rest, a replacement might be a son-in-law, a purchaser of the shop or business, or even second husbands for their wives. Some slaves were members of colleges, and particularly in the manual trades, this would not have struck the free members as incongruous. The children of slaves succeeded their fathers as well. The family workshop was the norm, and entrance to the college was so easy as to make any restrictive practices useless.

The eras of Diocletian (284–305) and Constantine (306–337) revealed the profound flaws in the social and economic fabric of the later empire, and to their credit, these emperors attempted to put in place a wide range of reforms.[39] Two keys to the survival of the empire were that the government had to maintain the cities and to keep a large army in the field. Those colleges that had been brought into the system of immunities devised by the empire in previous centuries found themselves transformed into official corporations. The process by which the colleges became compulsory and hereditary bodies is not well understood; the main evidence for these changes comes from fourth-century inscriptions and the fifth-century legal compilation known as the Theodosian Code. The Christian emperors did not often cite Diocletian's reign as a model of good government, so it is difficult to know what credit to assign to Diocletian and to what extent Constantine simply built on what his predecessor had begun. The Roman college is seen to be operating, as early as the legislation of Constantine, in a way quite different than in previous centuries. One clear example of this is the collection of edicts concerning the bakers. In 319, Constantine wrote to the prefect of the corn supply about the "detestable falsification" some bakers practiced to avoid their obligations. Some bakers were transferring landholdings to others so that they might claim to be too poor to provide the service of breadmaking. The emperor ordered such bakers "to remain in the service of breadmaking without any claim for exemption."[40] The obligation to perform this vital service is attached to the person of the baker and in a way to his land, since immunities from other services relieve the baker from other fiscal liabilities.

All the emperors were aware of the importance of feeding the urban population, and regulating the grain supply and baking is a constant thread through Roman history. Later edicts supply more details about the relations between the bakers and the state. An edict by Valentinian and Valens mentions a regulation by Constantine that required various officials throughout the empire to send bakers to Rome or Constantinople.[41] The colleges of these two main cities of the empire needed reenforcements from the provinces, and despite all the subsequent regulations, they clearly found it difficult to maintain their numbers through hereditary service alone. In 355, Constantius ordered that anyone marrying the daughter of a baker should also take up a share of the duties of the college of bakers. Constantius also sorted out the obligations of patrons and wanted those of the bakers' college to "be freed from other compulsory public service" so that "with the exertions of undisturbed minds they might perform only this service."[42] This edict illustrates the degree to which the state regulated colleges and also indicates that the office of patron, once largely honorific, became for the state a means to hold prominent citizens responsible for the conduct of the colleges. The connection between taxes and public service, as well as the system of immunities to colleges in exchange for service, helped to spread the policy toward colleges throughout the empire. Although at one time Rome's interest in the provincial colleges may have been minimal, the issue assumed a greater importance when the notion of general public service took root.

Later emperors continued to define the system of hereditary public service. Valentinian and Valens regulated the transfer of property by bakers and insisted that nothing should interfere with heirs who "were forced by right of succession to assume compulsory public services of breadmaking."[43] The same emperors allowed the minor sons of deceased bakers to put off assuming their duties until they were twenty, provided that they supplied suitable substitutes to meet their obligations.[44] Later, the emperors made leaving the college impossible, even if all the bakers agreed to the departure, and they even directed that no one be allowed to move from one bakery to another.[45] These emperors had a great interest in the bakers, and they continued to insist that obligation to serve went with property, however it was acquired, and that anyone who had enrolled in another college to escape service "shall be unhesitatingly dragged back and assigned to the compulsory public service to which he has been attached by this law."[46] No one was allowed to escape service by entering the Church. At some date before 364, the state had repealed an exemption for members of the clergy.[47] The weight of legislation on the backs of the bakers was heavy but not unique to them; other colleges attracted the scrutiny of fourth-century emperors as well. Constantine the Great decided to repopulate the college of pig collectors and ordered that a public meeting should determine who owned the property of the pig collectors so that the new owners might learn of their obligations and fulfill them.[48] Pork was an important part of the Roman diet, and the emperors wanted to make sure that urban meat supplies remained adequate. Valentinian and Valens later indicated that the business of collecting herds of pigs to transport to the capital was fraught with difficulties. The government closely regulated the details of this trade and issued orders that the hogs should not eat the day before they were weighed for sale.[49]

Most of the legislation concerns specific colleges, and the details in some imperial edicts suggest that the law did not apply to all colleges. Constantine's edict on bakers supplied to Rome by the provinces presumes that these colleges existed in the provinces. The provincial colleges often had obligations to regional centers that resembled the situation in Rome, and the law applied to their duty to perform public service as well. The colleges mentioned in the fourth-century legislation played an important part in the urban economy and had some ability to contribute to military needs. Other colleges, largely catering to luxury trades, attracted no apparent notice from the government. However, even as early as Constantine, the state ordered the wood haulers to be included in the college of ragmen and artisans, in order to sustain the numbers in these colleges.[50] Usually the state was interested in colleges because of their public obligations, but to all appearances the demands of public service were spread so widely through society that few artisans or professionals escaped. By the end of the fourth century, imperial legislation took on the desperate note of repetition. As the internal and external pressures on the empire mounted, members of colleges took increasingly to flight to avoid their duties. In 397, the officials running the empire during the reigns of Arcadius and Honorius made the earliest surviving general edict on colleges, and here the concerns were again to recall guild members to their own towns so that they might discharge their obligations and also to reemphasize the old rule that in free marriages the sons inherit the services of the fathers and in marriages between persons of different status the children inherit the status of the mother.[51] The escape from duty became a characteristic feature in the decay of fifth-century urban society, and how the official colleges fared in the eastern cities during the early years of the Byzantine state will be examined briefly below.

Government control seems to have worked best during the fourth century. Little evidence exists that shows how tighter rules affected the artisans and professionals who became so closely tied to the state. As the empire became more and more a Christian state, the old religious aspects of the college changed, but the adoption of patron saints to replace the patron deities, although a profound shift in religious sensibility, in practice disturbed only the actual generation that witnessed the removal of an altar and the arrival of a new statue or mural. The social functions of the colleges remained intact, though it would be interesting to know if the feasting and drinking abated with the advent of Christianity. Free apprenticeship, practiced to an unknown extent under the old system, had no reason to develop further when the government took steps to insure that the colleges remained up to strength. The sources do not supply enough information to determine whether the tax immunities made up for the increased demands for service, but it is hard to conclude that they did; the repeated orders to drag members back to their duties strongly suggest that the compulsory services were onerous. The government closely regulated the colleges and hence changed their original status as voluntary associations. Now that a collection of artisans was responsible for a particular service, the college and the state wanted no potential member to escape sharing the burden.

In at least one case, the pig collectors, the government attempted to regulate both the price paid to farmers and the conditions of sale.[52] In

367, the state tried to compensate the pig collectors for the loss in weight their stock suffered during transport.[53] In 359, the state set a scale of bonuses for the limeburners—an amphora of wine for three wagon loads of lime—and in 365, this was increased to one solidus for each wagon load of lime.[54] The state estimated the needs for the public buildings and aqueducts in Rome at three thousand loads and protected the monopoly granted to the college of limeburners from any attempt to usurp their right to this business. These examples illustrate the economic effects on the guilds that the new system of regulation created. Diocletian's efforts to set general price levels had an impact difficult to determine, but his successors continued, at least in some areas, his economic policies. The demands for services in lieu of taxation certainly distorted the market and upset work schedules. The edict of 365 on limeburners noted, for example, that the decurions of Tuscany were not obligated in that year to supply nine hundred loads of lime, but the state left open the possibility that it might renew this demand.[55] If the demand were renewed, the decurions would have to turn to the limeburners for the lime, and these state needs would be hard to anticipate. The decurions would offer the limeburners some sort of tax break, and hence the need for services would percolate through the economy, down to the local level, turning more and more work into duty remunerated with tax immunities that powerful members of society acquired with less effort.

The economic consequences of state supervision are hard to fathom, but the outcomes for the colleges seem to have been negative ones. The lack of narrative sources and contemporary comment makes the portrait of Roman colleges sketchy and vague. One bright spot in the sources is Antioch, where the prolix and perceptive Libanius gives some indication of the realities the colleges faced under the later empire. J. Liebeschuetz has used Libanius's speeches and correspondence to develop a picture of state burdens on the local level. He cites the duty of the college of innkeepers to provide, as their compulsory service, the hostel for the imperial post. "Their contribution included couches, tables, mugs, cooks, cleaners, grooms, pimps, and if need be, doctors."[56] Even colleges that might appear to be safe from public service found themselves bound to some task devised by an imaginative bureaucracy; in Antioch, the shopkeepers became transporters of pillars and also had some charitable obligations to beggars. Libanius also supplies unusual detail about the bakers' guild.[57] The supervisor of this college set the price of bread and determined the size of loaves.[58]

This supervisory function, while not eliminating competition among bakers, established rules for the trade that colleges in previous centuries had never tried to set. These public supervisors took the place of the patrons and also protected the colleges under their authority.[59]

Liebeschuetz believed that "the indispensability of the services provided by the shopkeepers, combined with a hundred-per-cent guild membership, should have greatly increased the guilds' ability to further the interest of their members," and he cites an impressive array of evidence, from Antioch and elsewhere in the east, to support this conclusion.[60] In this view, the end of competition, occasional grants of monopolies, the solidarity of the guild and its ability to negotiate with the government, and greater stability in prices—all benefited the colleges and more than balanced out any disadvantages in the new arrangements. Most of the evidence for the colleges in the later empire comes from the east, the more urbanized half of the empire and the half that after all survived and preserved more of its sources.

However, set against these gains are liabilities to consider. The advantages of a controlled market need to be weighed against its inefficiencies, corruption, shortages, and the tendency to create unofficial markets for the powerful. The bakers of Antioch were able to change government policy by threatening to leave the city, but more instances of this behavior are required to prove that the colleges were better able to bargain with the state in the fourth century than they were before.[61] In the old days of voluntary associations, the state was interested in fostering certain vital trades and services and used a system of immunities to accomplish its purposes. The colleges were recipients of favors. The new ability in the fourth century to negotiate with the government resulted, it must be remembered, from the question of levels of compulsory service. The basic issue was, What set of economic and political circumstances would benefit the colleges? The Roman state did not ask this question; instead, it wanted to know how the colleges might serve the financial and supply needs of the government. The flight of people from their obligations, so characteristic of both urban and rural society in the late empire, suggests that the government failed to create a favorable economic climate for the colleges or, indeed, for any social or economic group. Especially in the western part of the empire, the wreckage of the fifth century proved to be a difficult environment for the colleges, whether in Rome or the provinces.

The legacy of the Roman college depended in large measure on the extent to which the college managed to hang on as an economic institution in the western half of the empire. The unbroken tradition in the east allowed the Byzantine guild to retain many of the features of the late Roman college. Roman law on the college had little or no relevance in the west, and by the time the study and knowledge of this law revived in the west in the late eleventh and twelfth centuries, the medieval guild had developed its own structure and rules without the benefit of Roman examples. As will be seen below, some medieval governments may have gleaned from Roman law a way to justify their ambitions to subordinate the guilds to a central authority, but even here the value of the example of Roman practice was limited. Waltzing, the most thorough student of the Roman college, saw many good things in the college during its day as a voluntary and private association. He believed that the college did not inhibit economic growth because it did not share the restrictive and monopolistic practices of the medieval guild—apprenticeship and various restrictions on the liberty of work.[62] The value of the college in this period primarily derived from its role in fostering social solidarity among the artisan and commercial classes. Once the state, under Constantine and his successors, incorporated the college into what Waltzing called a "detestable economic system," the freedom of work vanished and the colleges became empty shells.[63] With the best of intentions, the emperors "only succeeded in precipitating a ruin that became inevitable."[64]

Waltzing's gloomy assessment concentrated primarily upon the social functions of the colleges. More recent work has followed his example and continued to focus on the colleges and urban life. The sources for the empire as a whole—the laws—do not permit any extended analysis of the role of the colleges in daily economic life. The problem is that the empire is not an appropriate unit for looking at the balance between free and enslaved labor in the various trades or at other issues of local significance. Peter Orsted has emphasized the heterogeneity of the Roman economy with the need to investigate regions as the only appropriate basis for generalizations.[65] For example, there is evidence from second-century Dacia for wage labor by contract (the *locatio-conductio rei*), and the daily wage for work in the gold mines can be calculated.[66] Balanced against this specific evidence is G. E. M. de Ste Croix's point that "there is no evidence at all for *regular* hired labour of any kind in Rome."[67] The rare contracts from Dacia suggest that mining was a seasonal occupation there and hence not a regular form of employment, so the local evidence and the general view are not at second glance incompatible. However, Diocletian fixed wages in 301 for a broad cross section of trades, and this complex and interesting edict implies that wage labor was common enough to regulate across the empire. The edict's effectiveness was short-lived at best, but in any case it cast no light on the prevalence (as opposed to existence) of wage labor.[68]

Most scholars seem to accept M. Rostovtzeff's view that craft manufacture "was chiefly, though not exclusively, in the hands of slaves."[69] But again, this generalization applies to some regions and trades more than others, and entire areas of the economy, like mining or agriculture, might count as exceptions. The sayings of Jesus—the parable of the vineyard owner, remarks about laborers and their hire, references to coins—leave the impression that the Roman east, at least, was familiar with wage labor. The casual workers in the vineyard, certainly an early group of complainers about their wages, were told to take their pay and go home (Matthew 20:1–16). One literal lesson of this parable, that upholding agreements is best, was fundamental to establishing a level of trust necessary for wage labor to work. But clearly, the heavy burdens placed on the shoulders of slaves and other coerced workers were equally familiar parts of daily life.

Since broad statements about the Roman economy are perilous, its legacies are equally difficult to pin down. With this caveat, I offer some cautious assessments. The Roman colleges were associations of employers whose dominant source of labor was coerced. Pervasive slavery did not, however, exclude apprenticeship, and even some free people received training by contract. These apprentices and other free persons could find a place for themselves in the pool of wage laborers, expansive in some trades and completely absent in others. Slavery was the dominant engine in this system of labor. Other methods of recruiting a work force, apprenticeship and wage labor, were also present; hence, as is so often the case in real economies, other forms of labor are capable of existing in the shadow of the most characteristic method—in the Roman case, slavery. The law reflects these realities; copious on the subject of slaves, it was succinct on hired labor and virtually nonexistent on apprentices.

What lived in the shadows would thrive when artisanal slavery along with the empire and the Roman college began to fall apart. This mechanistic view of historical change suggests that, when the barbarian tribes arrived and swept away much of the Roman economy, wage labor and apprenticeship would have a chance to come into their own, albeit very slowly. Many problems exist with this interpretation. The collapse of the empire in the west left behind two enduring achievements—the Church and the law—and these legacies had a lingering influence on work and contracts. The end of Roman rule meant the end of small change, an apparently trivial fact, but one with an important sequel. Wage labor cannot exist on a regular basis without a reliable and abundant coinage. Barter for labor evolves in a different direction, as will be seen. The tribes brought with them some original types of social organization and their own customs on slavery and work. At least in Italy, greatly diminished cities and manufacturing continued to exist for a time under foreign rule, and how they fared in these new circumstances reveals the fate of the Roman colleges and crafts and of those who worked.

Early Medieval Guilds in the West, ca. 450–1000

The sources on Roman colleges were not abundant, yet the historian of guilds in the early Middle Ages would still envy the classicist's breadth of material. The collapse of Roman authority in the west produced a number of barbarian kingdoms that had a sense of being successor states to Rome, and some kings like Theodoric in Italy made a serious attempt to govern in the Roman style. Whatever tribal kings aspired to accomplish, the economies of the west in these centuries were not able to sustain the close relationship that had existed between the Roman state and colleges. The fifth and sixth centuries witnessed, among other calamities, a rapid and fundamental depopulation of the principal cities in the west, principally in Italy and southern France. The cities had formed the basis for artisan and merchant life, and without the markets and supplies that cities created, the colleges lost at the same time both state supervision and an economic reason for existing. The Visigothic (410) and Vandal (455) sacks of Rome and the disastrous, from the point of view of Italian cities, campaigns that Belisarius and others waged on behalf of Justinian in the sixth century left the urban centers of Italy and Sicily a shadow of their former selves. The Visigoths had pillaged their way across southern France in the early fifth century, and the late-arriving Burgundians and Franks further weakened towns along the Rhine and at places like Lyons, Arles, and Nimes. The Rhineland cities—modern Cologne, Trier, and others— were the first to suffer from the invasions across the Rhine. The emperor Honorius simply withdrew legions from Britain to reinforce the hard-pressed armies in Gaul. Spain and North Africa, among the least-urbanized parts of the western empire, fell to the Visigoths and Van-dals—the latter quickly taking to the sea, with devastating conse-quences for central Mediterranean ports.

The barbarian tribes, a convenient shorthand expression used when considering these diverse peoples as a group, were unfamiliar with urban life, but even the most destructive of them wanted to take advantage of what they found and to preserve as much of the produc-tive capacities of the Roman economy as they could. The new arrivals were a minority nearly everywhere they settled, and a constant theme of theirs was the effort to maintain the tax system and other sources of state income, since these were still partially in place and relatively easy to tap. As discussed above, the colleges provided an important part of the Roman state's income in kind, and the habit of public service was also a useful one. The new kingdoms might have substituted them-selves for the old state and continued the ordinary relationship with what was left of urban society. Several problems, however, frustrate this expectation; in some places, almost nothing was left of urban society, and the colleges collapsed without a trace.

The tribes also brought with them different conceptions of the exchange of goods and services. Philip Grierson notes that thefts, gifts, bribes, and tribute characterized the circulation of goods and gold in the early Middle Ages.[70] Payments in gold required some western kings to mint gold coins in the sixth century, but this gold coinage had a special role in the economy and little significance for artisans. Georges Duby has concisely described this gift and pillage economy so charac-teristic of tribal societies, but the tribes, especially those like the Goths who had participated in a functioning Roman economy for genera-tions, did not find themselves in a mysterious new environment.[71] The Roman emphasis on public service in fact fit well with notions of gift exchanges through a hierarchy, and here the tribal kings had little difficulty in taking the emperor's place. However, most tribal kingdoms did not have the ambitions or supply requirements of the Roman state. In particular, the tribes had devised their own methods for equipping and supplying warriors; none of these methods seem to have involved payments in kind other than food, and all of them initially required as much cash as possible and not services from colleges. So on the one hand the colleges had a difficult time merely surviving, and on the other the new states had no need for their services. In these circumstances, one might expect the colleges to revert to what they had been before Diocletian—free associations that also provided convenient categories for taxation. In general, the balance tipped against the colleges and their chances for survival, and the key ingredient in this development was not the state but depopulation and the scarcity of markets—what Theodahad, king of the Ostrogoths in Italy, called in 535/536 "the sterility of present times."[72]

The best place to look for any colleges that survived is Italy, where a number of sizable towns like Milan, Naples, and Rome were fortunate enough to fall for a time under Ostrogothic rule. In the period before the Lombard invasions (568) and Byzantine efforts at reconquest, the able Theodoric (493–526) created a kingdom known for its conscious efforts to preserve elements of Roman civilization. One of the main witnesses to this reign, the Roman Cassiodorus, is also an important source of information, and thus Theodoric's Roman officials and secretaries can be expected to preserve more flavor of the past than actually existed in their time. Sometime between 493 and 500, Theodoric issued a comprehensive edict of laws for Italy. In title 64, the law addresses the ways to find and punish debauchers of virgins and other heinous criminals. Buried in these details is one of the rare references to a college in the surviving documents from this kingdom. The college simply supplied a way for determining the proper venue for a trial concerning a murder committed "most basely with cudgels."[73] Theodoric's law refers to an earlier edict of Valentinian III that is not extant, but the general drift of Valentinian's proclamation appears to be that a member of a college was entitled to have his killer tried, not where the murder took place, but in the victim's town. Being but small consolation to the members of colleges, this rule does not say much for the safety of travel. More importantly, the college survives in the law only as a category of persons, and perhaps only for merchants, since most artisans did not spend much time on the road.

Cassiodorus made an extensive collection of his letters and some Ostrogothic state papers—a collection called the *Variae*—and it contains few references to a *collegium*. Twice royal correspondence refers to the Roman senate as a college, an old and inappropriate use of the term.[74] The only other reference to a *collegium* concerns the status of public criers, certainly a useful profession, but not evidence of any economic activity.[75] Some of the old corporations were still active, and the state took an interest in their prosperity. The scope of economic endeavor had considerably diminished, and the steps Theodoric took in his kingdom to encourage trade reflect the decayed position of Italy. Merchants engaged in the silk trade from Antioch merited the king's attention and support.[76] The whole tone of the letter suggests that what had once been a routine matter became a risky business, and Antioch was after all still part of an empire in the east that found Theodoric's position in Italy and his rights there problematic. The king's government was attempting to preserve at least part of the public grain distribution (*annona*), and a few references are to merchants buying grain for the public in Apulia and Calabria.[77] Theodoric also gave the *navicularii* of Campania, Lucania, and Tuscany permission to trade with Gaul, where scarcity had driven up grain prices and hence created opportunity for his subjects.[78] Our purpose is not to survey the economy of Ostrogothic Italy but to show that the colleges survived the fall of the empire in the west and that, apart from the always important issue of the food supply, the colleges seem to have been left alone.

Whatever low level of economic activity characterized Italian cities, the devastation and wars during Justinian's efforts to conquer the peninsula, along with the subsequent Lombard invasions, accelerated the process of urban depopulation and decay. The Lombard kingdom at Pavia eventually controlled most of northern Italy; Lombard warlords and Byzantine officials struggled over the south; and in central Italy and Rome itself, the papacy occupied the uneasy middle ground. The popes found themselves increasingly isolated from Byzantine protection and also forced to assume some purely secular administrative burdens in central Italy. Hence the correspondence of Pope Gregory I contains some of the most revealing notices of guilds in this disordered period. In 599, Gregory wrote a letter to the bishop of Naples concerning grievances brought to the pope by the guild (*corpus*) of soapmakers in Naples.[79] That the bishop of Rome was dragged into this dispute is symptomatic of conditions of the time. The soapmakers complained that John, count of the sacred largess (a Byzantine treasury official), damaged and oppressed them and interfered with the oath of their art by extorting benefits for himself from the soapmakers who wanted to join the guild. Count John had attempted to install himself as patron of the guild without the consent of the members. Gregory wanted the bishop to solve this problem and make sure that whatever oath was taken by the soapmakers should not be used against their interests. The oath was an appropriate pretext for the Church to involve itself in the dispute, and this issue of the oath will remain an important one. Gregory also spoke to the prefect of Italy about Count John, and the

pope thought that would be sufficient. In any case, Gregory wanted no
one to be kept from their work because of this controversy. Almost
every specific in this letter points to the decay of the Roman system of
colleges and the difficult circumstances of the contemporary guilds.
The soapmakers were an organized body with rules and standards for
admission. It is interesting that the compulsory aspects of guild membership had fallen away and that soapmakers outside the guild wanted
to join. Count John inserted himself into the guild in the guise of patron
and created for himself, by means of an oath, a formal role and, more
importantly, unspecified but nevertheless tangible rewards. Gregory's
letter suggests that oaths among the soapmakers were not unusual but
in this case that they had sworn against their will and best interests. A
treasury official was in a good position to tyrannize the soapmakers,
and unfortunately whether the prefect of Italy or the bishop of Naples
were able to help them is unknown.

In the same year Gregory wrote to his official in the city of Otranto
about a young man named Pietro, who had been sent to Rome as a
servant under contract (*mancipus*) of the bakers' guild (*ars pistoria*).[80]
The pope wanted the local official to find this "boy" (*puer*), who might
be located through his wife or children, and return him and all his
possessions to Rome. The pope refers to the bakers as an art (*ars*), and
clearly bakers still maintained some corporate identity. Pietro's status is
ambiguous; he was probably not a slave—the word *mancipus* did not
have that meaning in the sixth century—but the classical uses of this
word are inapplicable here as well. The context of the letter focuses
attention on Pietro's flight and the fact that he did not have the right to
run away from his obligations. The text is not clear on the question of
Pietro's legal status; he may in fact have run away from the pope's own
brother. Gregory was in a position to write a letter to papal officials
requesting their help in finding Pietro, but that he bothered to do so is
remarkable. A long personal story may be behind this runaway and the
reasons for such lofty attention to him. These two chance references in
Gregory's letters suggest, as noted by Gennaro M. Monti, that, although the Roman colleges still existed, they were decayed institutions
beset by violence on all sides.[81] Count John probably found that op-
pressing the soapmakers as a collectivity was easier than having to seek
out individual victims. The pope might have been able to help these
soapmakers and to track down a runaway baker, and the nature of
papal correspondence may be that it brings more local failures than
successes to light. On balance, nothing in the sources indicates a

thriving urban environment or happy days for artisan and professional associations.

Elsewhere in western Europe, the sources are completely silent about the colleges or anything else that might relate to the survival of any corporate bodies with common economic interests. The great encyclopedist Isidore of Seville, who found time to comment upon and define many ideas and words in use in his age (ca. 570–636), did not bother to define *collegium* in his fairly comprehensive *Etymologia*. He did offer a curious definition for *collegiatus* (a member of a college). Isidore rightly defined that term as a person from a college, but he went on to remark that these colleges were associations devoted to crime and that a member was a real bastard—"for he is the most sordid type of man born of an unknown father."[82] Isidore must have had before him some old source that used the word *collegium* for a political club or conspiracy. He knew nothing more about it.

Gregory of Tours, the historian of sixth-century Gaul, never used either word, which is not surprising given his portrait of the decay in urban life and trade. Gregory does record that King Guntram, in a harangue against a pretender in 584, commented that the pretender's father was a mill operator and also spent time carding wool. Gregory observed that one could pursue both these trades (*unius homo utriusque artificii magisterio subderetur*), and the defenders of this pretender made a clever reply.[83] The purpose of relating this vignette in detail is to show how Gregory described crafts (*artificii*) and artisanal skill (*magisterio*), one of the rare instances in which he employed technical terms for crafts or even mentioned them. Alfons Dopsch, who believed that guilds had a continuous if low-level existence in these centuries, cited this very passage as proof for his assertion that "Gregory of Tours shows that there was an organization of industries (*artificia*) according to *magisteria* or offices."[84] The context of the story reveals nothing of the kind, and the arguments in favor of a continuous tradition between the Roman college and the medieval guild tend to rely upon this kind of selective and hopeful reading of the sources. Mills were still in operation in Merovingian Gaul, and people carded wool, and a king was able to demean a rival by associating his father with these ignoble trades. To see these trades as anything more than a convenient insult is to see what one wants.

After around 500, apart from a few pieces of evidence from Italy that will be discussed further below, nothing was left of the Roman system. The seventh century was not a time of economic revival in Italy, and the two odd notices from Pope Gregory I's letters were not to be repeated. References to another kind of association—the *gilda*—and the historical controversies that surround this and similar terms in the written record appear in the eighth and ninth centuries and in the laws and writers of the Carolingian era. Tribal society and economy had no need for artisan or professional groups. What little knowledge is known about tribal life comes from the views of outsiders, beginning with Tacitus and continuing on through the church authors of the early Middle Ages. Anthropologists studying modern tribal societies have provided some French historians with a useful conceptual framework, and the sources supply enough details so that we can make some use of social theory.[85] Two features of tribal society stand out as relevant to a discussion of guilds— peer associations and the system of compensation for crime known as the wergild. The tribe and the collection of families that sustained it were not the only forms of social organization, and observers as early as Tacitus took note of the human tendency to associate in age groups. Roman society was of course familiar with this phenomenon too, which was viewed as a source of rowdiness and trouble. The German *comitatus*, according to Tacitus, was a warband with a charismatic leader at the center.[86] This collection of peers provided the education and experience necessary for assuming a mature role in the tribe. German society did not make heavy social or economic investments in its young, and the reliance on the peer group was a practical adjustment to the problems of growing up in a culture that offered little of what is today known as institutional support. The primary economic activity in this society, apart from farming, was warfare. The raids the peer groups conducted, in terms of practical experience, may not have been the safest way to train the young, but they were an effective way. These peer groups are significant because they provided a primitive division of labor, and that this society was inclined to group people by age and experience and had some means of determining which people merited advancement is important to remember when examining guilds, with their rigid system of apprentices, journeymen, and masters. The hierarchy within the guild structure and the way the masters limited membership to what was in general a peer group are unlike anything seen in the Roman college. This fact again argues against any continuity between the college and the guild and also suggests that early medieval society merits our attention. The purpose of the peer group was to provide what the family and the tribe did not supply. One of the contributions that Christianity made to this society was the idea of the parish, a large geographical unit that cut across other social divisions. The Church's efforts to convince the laity to think of themselves as parishioners was something new. Although urban parishes and the neighborhood are problems for the future, the habit of thinking of loyalty to a church as a basis for social divisions will also play a part in the evolution of guilds. These questions will be examined in more detail when guilds, religion, and the division of labor are studied below.

The tribes had traditional rules for governing conduct, and fairly early the barbarian kings issued written codes of law for their subjects. The laws of Theodoric for the Ostrogoths were one of the first such codes; and the famous laws of the Visigoths, the Burgundians, the Salian Franks, the Lombards, and particular kings—the laws of Ine for the West Saxons in England—or even the later capitularies (royal commands and regulations) issued by Carolingian rulers in the eighth and ninth centuries are all a tribute to the enduring value the Romans placed on written law. The codes recognized, at least in southern Europe, that a Roman law and a population that was entitled to the benefits of this law still existed. Not much Roman jurisprudence was relevant to or even survived the early Middle Ages in the west. A common thread through all these law codes is the idea that victims of criminal acts, or their surviving relatives in cases of homicide, were entitled to compensation and that the king himself often deserved some payment when a malefactor broke his peace. In turn, blood feuds extended liability beyond the actual perpetrators of a crime to one's relatives. This system of compensating victims with money or cash equivalents is conveniently called the wergild. When the word *gilda*, related to *gelt* in its various spellings, first appeared, it was intimately associated with this concept of mutual obligation.[87] That the later guild shares its name with money is no accident. The connection between money and social organization is not solely a linguistic one. Only a few hints in the later sources suggest a hypothesis as to how the forms of the word *gilda* came to mean more than money.

In one of the early capitularies of Charlemagne's reign, the word *gildonia* appears for the first time on the continent: "Concerning oaths made through guilds by members [*coniurantibus*] to one another, that no one should presume to make them."[88] When Charlemagne conquered the Lombard kingdom of northern Italy and extended his authority to those areas, he issued a similar set of laws, and for his new subjects the term *gildonia* was defined as a "violent conspiracy."[89] These stark prohibitions do not clearly indicate whether Charlemagne objected to the formation of these groups, their activities, or both. The Capitulary of Heristal went on to condemn sworn associations made for the purpose of almsgiving, fire, or shipwreck. In these cases the law clearly intended to prevent such groups from forming by stating that no one should presume to swear an oath for these purposes. The mention of almsgiving suggests the classic religious confraternity, and the clergy probably drew Charlemagne's attention to the dangers inherent in such groups. The Church had its doubts about lay associations and their oaths. But from the limited point of view of the Carolingian state, the objections to sworn groups devoted to almsgiving were a small price to pay for the Church's support. Rights over shipwreck and fire were of more interest to the king, since he wanted to emphasize the regalian rights over loot from disasters. It might be argued that, in the narrowest sense, the guilds mentioned in this capitulary did have an economic interest common to the members if they were joined together to plunder shipwrecks. Lawless bands whose principal business was organized theft did exist. The evidence in the capitulary suggests that the guild was either a kind of confraternity that the Church did not favor and the law condemned or that the word *gildonia* was also applicable to sworn criminal associations. As seen above, the Latin *collegium* suffered in the early part of its history from a similar ambiguity. The fate of lay groups at the lower end of a social hierarchy may be to endure obloquy at their beginnings, or afterward. If the categories of church and state were not yet clearly defined, in terms of jurisdiction and the ability to impose penalties, in the Carolingian period, they both were deeply suspicious of private sworn associations, whatever their purposes. The Carolingian legislation provides the first documentary evidence on the continent that these groups existed, outside the law, and owed their formation to private concerns, whether religious or criminal.

The Church's attitudes toward these lay groups received their first sustained definition in the legislation Hincmar of Rheims promulgated for his archdiocese in 852.[90] This legislation, intended to instruct the parish clergy, defined the guild (*gildonia*), as it was called in the vernacular, as a confraternity (*confratria*). Hincmar thought there was an appropriate sphere of activity for these guilds, one in which they conformed to authority and were useful and reasonable, but beyond this such parish groups were wrongful. These parish guilds had a role in the observance of religion; for them to participate in almsgiving and funerals, to provide candles for churches, and to make offerings on behalf of their members (*omnibus conjunctis*) and associates (*familiari*) was permissible. Hincmar disapproved of the banquets the guilds might have, and he completely forbade the holding of these unseemly events because they were contrary to the teachings of divine authority and might lead to dissensions and homicides. For the guild to meet was lawful, but any discord within the confraternity was to be brought before a priest or an assembly of priests for resolution. The members were entitled to break bread and have a single drink together and then depart with the Lord's blessing. The guild was in Hincmar's eyes a useful buttress to the Church, but one prone to excess if not carefully regulated. The legislation does not mention any oath, and given the scope of the guild's proper activity, no need for any oath existed. These guilds were not craft or professional associations; instead, they were groups of lay persons who had in common the fact that they lived in the same parish. The confraternities had a legitimate role in fostering the charitable activities of the parish, and the legislation acknowledged that the effectiveness of local piety depended on the proper function-ing of these lay bodies. However, the laity was inclined to extend their social activities into drunken feasts, and here Hincmar laid down ex-plicit rules of conduct to control such tendencies.

The problem of the guild and confraternity remained with society for some time. Confraternities have a history of their own, and some will always be purely religious lay associations. Other confraternities formed the basis for craft or professional groups that emerged follow-ing the Carolingian period. Already in place at the local level was the habit of coming together, based on the neighborhood, for religious and also social purposes. In ninth-century Carolingian Europe, no parish in the small urban centers like Rheims would have contained a suffi-cient number of people in the same line of work to make the parish and the craft neighborhood coterminous. Even if anyone was capable of thinking of the economic interests of the parish, these interests would, at this stage, have been so diverse as to make any common design impossible. Of all the acts of piety Hincmar mentioned, almsgiving merits the most attention for its possible role in encouraging people to think about the causes and amelioration of poverty. The plight of those who lack food, clothing, and shelter produces, in those who bother to think about it, a policy of relief but also some ideas about how to avoid poverty in the first place. At this stage, the parishioners were simply accepting a responsibility to their neighbors in a way the Church carefully circumscribed. The members were capable of defining self-help at the local level more broadly than Hincmar or his clergy thought necessary.

One other accomplishment of the Carolingian state, its silver coinage, raises again the thorny problem of small change and wage labor. Philip Grierson observed that the Carolingian silver pennies "provided a standard for value and a means of storing wealth, but they did not yet play anything like the same role as a medium of exchange that coins were to do in the later middle ages."[91] The high exchange value of the pennies and their generally excellently preserved state argue against the idea that coins circulated rapidly through this society or that they served the needs of a wage economy.[92] Alexander Murray blamed inertia, short supplies of silver, and the brevity of vigorous and reform-minded government in the empire for the small role that coinage played in the Carolingian economy.[93] Supply is, however, only one-half of the equation; the demand for money, particularly in small denominations, seems to have been minor or nonexistent. Barter, coercion (in the form of slavery or labor dues), gift, and pillage continued to provide mechanisms of exchange that served the needs of the marketplace. Regular wage labor in the Carolingian state was unknown because no apparent need for it existed in light of the readily available alternatives. Here a comparison with antiquity is instructive. Rome had an elaborate currency supply, including small-denomination coins of copper and bronze, so it had a money economy without regular wage labor. The Carolingians, by definition, had a money economy of sorts, but they utilized barter when a Roman might have used small change, and no one lived by wages. The lack of money was remediable if the traditional forms of exchange failed. But the change in systems of currency from the Roman to the Carolingian period in this case can obscure a variable that remained constant by its virtual absence—wage labor. The system for supporting the Carolingian army and bureaucracy, to the extent that the latter existed, suggests that, if anything, wage labor was even less important in this period than it had been under Rome.

For a time in the ninth century, Carolingian practices and laws dominated most of Christian Europe. Looking at the other Germanic society that has left traces of actual practices—Anglo-Saxon England—is also useful. This is not the place to rehearse the ethnic history of the British Isles, but the wave of tribal invasions that engulfed England in the fifth and subsequent centuries left it with a mixed legal and social tradition. The tribes in England and on the continent were ethnic cousins, but their practices were not identical. Nevertheless, some rough similarities should exist in social organization, and Anglo-Saxon England preserved in its own language precious information about local custom. Anglo-Saxon law in the vernacular permits a glimpse of these customs without the inevitable distortions that the Latin language imposed on most of the evidence from this early medieval period. Despite the well-known relationship between Anglo-Saxon kingdoms and the Carolingian state, the exchanges of scholars and gifts, a kind of rudimentary diplomacy, England still represents an authentic and independent development of tribal society.

In one of the first law codes issued for a British kingdom, King Ine of Wessex in 688–694 gathered together existing customs and set forth a typical system of crimes and punishments. F. L. Attenborough translated the relevant passage as follows: "He who kills a thief shall be allowed to declare on oath that the man he slew was guilty. The associates [*gegildan* (variant: *glydan*)] of the slain man shall not be allowed to proceed to an oath."[94] Dorothy Whitelock notes the difficulties of translating this rule and turns the translation around: "He who slays a thief may declare with an oath that he slew him as a guilty man, by no means the associates [*gegildan*]," hence implying that "the thief's associates have no right to swear to his innocence."[95] The problem is that either the associates of the thief or the slayer would have grounds for trying to clear by oath either one of them. The word *gegildan* emerges in ambiguity. Scholars differ on the way they translate this word, and this vague word may be simply another term for kin. Oath helpers, who were able to clear the accused by swearing to their innocence, were originally the nearest kin, and whether or not this function had extended beyond the kin to include neighbors does matter. The laws of Ine do not suggest an answer to this question. The distinction between kin and nonkin is not a neat one in this period, and the *gegildan* may hark back to some basic tribal affinities that subsume both categories.[96] The oath mentioned in Ine's laws is also an old religious tradition with which Christianity had not yet come to terms.

The laws of King Alfred of Wessex, dated to 892–893 or a few years earlier, are more informative about the *gegildan*. Again, the context is murder and the wergild—the compensation required for the crime. By Alfred's time, if not during Ine's, the *gegildan* is clearly a group of associates who were not related by blood. The clearest example of this is in chapter 31 of the laws: "If a man in this position is slain—if he has no relatives (maternal or paternal)—half the wergild shall be paid to the king, and half to the *gegildan*."[97] No information exists on the purpose of the *gegildan* other than its role as a substitute for kinship ties for those without any relatives. These associates, who presumably were bound together by an oath for mutual protection, if only to identify who was responsible, would benefit anyone, whether the person had relatives or not. The support of the kinship group was a good idea in the abstract, but the size and composition of families and whether they existed in the first place would make some sort of alternative network of protection desirable. Although the evidence from the laws of Ine may be read either way, the *gegildan* seems to be an old social institution. As seen more clearly in the tenth and eleventh centuries, it acquires additional functions—a policing role and a religious character.

The nobles, clergy, and commoners of London agreed upon a series of regulations for the city, with the encouragement and approval of King Athelstan, who caused the rules to be set down some time in the late 920s or 930s. The primary purpose of these ordinances was to maintain peace and security in the city, and all those supporting these goals had solemnly pledged themselves to this *gegildan*.[98] This type of inclusive guild, sometimes referred to as a peace guild, was an attempt to create one more additional level of social responsibility to support the king and his officials in keeping the peace. This social group of every responsible person in London is a broad one, and the law does not use the term *gegildan* to describe the association in general. It is significant that the Londoners themselves referred to the association as a guild when they promised to honor deceased members with gifts for the soul and commemorative singing of the Psalms. In these ordinances issued under Athelstan, the Anglo-Saxon guild takes on for the first time in the record a religious character that in part makes it appear to be a kind of confraternity. The peace guild of London had many policing functions, but this important spiritual obligation connects the oath the members took to a religious brotherhood that reinforced the social purposes that lay behind the institution.

The idea of a guild to keep the peace was not limited to London, and a document from the late tenth century contains the rules and duties of the thegn's guild in Cambridge.[99] This guild appears to have been a private association, and no king or noble is mentioned as assenting to or encouraging this group. Most of the rules concern the principal purposes of this guild—the security of the members, which receives the most attention, and the spiritual benefits of membership itself. The guild performed the tasks of the old *gegildan*: the members were obliged to defend one another, collect the wergild, and take up vengeance against anyone refusing to pay compensation. The members also swore an oath of loyalty to each other, promising to bring the body of a deceased member to a chosen burial site and supply half the food for the funeral feast. For the first time, another category of help was made explicit—the guild bound itself to common almsgiving for departed members—and the oath of loyalty the members swore included both religious and secular affairs. Although in many respects this guild resembles a confraternity along the lines Hincmar established for the archdiocese of Rheims, the older purpose of the group—mutual protection with its necessary threat of vengeance—makes the Anglo-Saxon guild something more than a prayer meeting. To include almsgiving to members in distress would be a small step, given the scope of activities this guild established. There is no sign that the thegns cooperated in any economic endeavors, but older rules of rural society had already determined methods of sharing responsibility in the villages, and the thegns cooperated on everything that was important in their lives. The thegns of Cambridge had a guild that resembles in some important ways the communal oath, that will be discussed below, of some Italian cities in the next century.

This type of local guild was not unique to Cambridge; other roughly contemporaneous sets of rules survive from Exeter, Bedwyn, and Abbotsbury.[100] The guild in Exeter placed particular stress on its religious duties. In Bedwyn, according to the fragmentary text, the members made gifts to the priest who celebrated mass for them, and they also contributed building materials when a house burned down. None of the Anglo-Saxon guilds, except perhaps for the one of Abbotsbury, seem tied to a specific parish. The latest of the guilds, the early eleventh-century guild in Abbotsbury that was specially created to honor God and St. Peter, was the only one to mention a guild hall—a place for the social meetings. The one distinctive feature of this guild is this stipulation: "And he who undertakes a brewing and does not do it satisfactorily is to be liable to his entrance fee, and there is to be no remission."[101] That membership now entailed a price is not surprising, but why should the guild be interested in upholding the quality of local brewing? To consider the guild in Abbotsbury to be a collection of brewers would be a distortion, but this rule is certainly not typical of a religious confraternity either—one need only note the reputation for drunkenness the continental guilds had. The religious reason for proper brewing is not obvious. Someone cared about the matter, perhaps on grounds of health or aesthetics. On balance the Anglo-Saxon guild was partly religious confraternity and partly keeper of the peace, but in Abbotsbury, at least, there is a sign that the guild was a flexible institution and that the line between social and economic interests was undefined.

The one other area of Europe that merits attention as a place where a tribal society established its own institutions or adapted older ones to its own purposes is the Lombard kingdom in northern and central Italy. The Lombards were relative latecomers to Italy (568), and some two centuries later Charlemagne acquired the iron crown of Lombard Italy. When the Lombards came under laws emanating from the heartland of the Carolingian empire, the word *geldonia* had to be explained to them, presumably because it was not in use in Italy. Urban society was in a baleful state in the sixth century and continued to deteriorate under both the Lombards and Carolingians. However, certain areas of Italy— most notably in the northeast, where Ravenna fell to the Lombards only in 751, and in most of southern Italy, the Mezzogiorno—remained in Byzantine hands. If any argument can be made that the Roman college somehow clung to a precarious life in Italy or that guilds were reestablished as a result of imitating Byzantine practices in the south, Rome, Pavia, and Ravenna are the best places to look.

A document, the *Honorantiae Civitatis Papiae*, prepared in the early eleventh century to describe the older rights of the royal household in Pavia describes organizations of artisans (*ministeria*) and the obligations they had to the king.[102] The boatmen, fishermen, and soapmakers all performed various services and supplied goods, and these collective duties imply some sort of corporate status. The merchants also had leaders, an organization, and the protection of the king. The *ministeria* of Pavia may have owed their existence to the presence of the royal court, and in turn these obligations may reflect some dim and distant knowledge of the late Roman or Byzantine practice of liturgies. It is presumed that these practices date back to Lombard times and were resurrected when Italy slipped out of Carolingian domination, but no evidence appears for these *ministeria* before the tenth century. These *ministeria* are probably older than the later notices of their existence, but their only apparent function is a relic of their royal service, and no evidence exists that they did anything else. Soap is an interesting commodity because it represents one of this society's most complicated industrial processes, and the soapmakers receive a fair amount of attention. In 744, King Ildebrand of the Lombards promised the bishop and cathedral of Piacenza, in a general confirmation of the Church's rights and privileges, thirty pounds of soap per year to be used to bathe paupers.[103] The soap was to come from the royal palace, and the soapmakers must have been providing the king with a certain amount of their product every year—good evidence for the continuing practice of liturgies. The soapmakers had to decide among themselves how to apportion their collective duty, and it was in their interest that no soapmaker avoid sharing the burden. The obligation to provide soap forced them to act in concert, in effect to act like a guild. This external stimulus undercut the voluntary and spontaneous reasons for coming together that characterized both the early Roman college and the medieval guild of the late eleventh and twelfth centuries. All of this left the soapmakers with no reason of their own for acting in harmony, and without the order imposed from outside, they would have resembled their unorganized neighbors.

On the other side of the peninsula in Ravenna, a document from 943 relates an agreement between the archbishop and the *scola piscatorum* about local fishing rights.[104] The word *scola*, as discussed above, was used by the Romans as the name for the meeting hall of the college, and in the intervening centuries the word acquired a broader meaning; in this case, the word means some sort of association. The Italian *scuola* became a popular term for a religious confraternity in northeast Italy, and in Venice the *scuola* took on a life of its own. The fishermen of Ravenna had *ministeriales*, probably officers of their association. They promised to make some fixed payments of fish to the archbishop, obligations to pass on to their sons, nephews, and colleagues. Again, these services to the archbishop imply that the fishermen had a traditional way to divide up the burden and that they would not want anyone outside their group to take fish out of the river. That their descendants inherited their status and rights is also clear. This was a guild of fishermen, but it had much in common with contemporary Byzantine practices in Constantinople. A *schola* of gardeners was also in Rome in 1030, but in this case the purpose behind the organization seems to have been simply to form a joint farming venture. These institutions appeared in areas of Italy familiar with Byzantine practices, and yet the *scola* seems to have evolved in a unique way. The *scola* was not the late Roman college, and since the state, such as it was in tenth- or eleventh-century Italy, had no apparent tie to these *scolae*, Gennaro M. Monti sensibly concluded that these groups, with their emphasis on ad hoc arrangements and family ties, owed nothing to the Roman college, owed a little to the Byzantine guild, and did not influence the later development of the Italian craft guilds.[105]

Ludo M. Hartmann, who collected most of these documents from various archives for the first time in the late nineteenth century, expressed some disappointment that his thorough investigations yielded so little evidence for a continuous tradition or a Roman origin for the medieval guild.[106] The paucity of evidence will never permit a definitive resolution of this question, and Hartmann considered the silence of the sources something of a gain, in the sense that the burden of proof remained with the supporters of continuity. The fishermen of Ravenna are the only plausible piece of evidence in favor of continuity, yet even the well-trained notary who redacted the agreement with the archbishop used all the wrong words to describe the organization of fishermen, which in turn may only have existed because the church of Ravenna had rights over the river. Advancing this argument, however, is possible. The rest of Europe did not look to Pavia or Ravenna for social innovation, and there the gradual development of the guild as a species of the lay confraternity is the significant event. When the rise of guilds in Italy are examined below, the important areas will be not in the northeast or in Rome but instead the ports of the west coast and the interior market towns of Milan and Florence. These guilds did not come into existence in order to face entrenched rights, as in Ravenna, or to cooperate on a common venture, as in Rome.

Byzantine and Muslim Guilds to 1000

The purpose of this study is not to investigate Byzantine or Muslim guilds in any detail, but their histories provide a useful point of comparison at this juncture. To the extent that medieval, Byzantine, or Muslim systems might draw upon a common cultural and economic experience—classical antiquity—the comparison is an apt one. Opinions on the history of the medieval guild have influenced the ways scholars have looked at developments in the eastern Mediterranean. The lack of data is another common theme uniting these three fields; historians working in one field tend to assume that the generalizations about the other two rest on sound evidence unavailable to them. This optimism is unwarranted, and inferences about Byzantium, medieval Europe, and Islam have proved unhelpful in studying guilds or city life in the Middle East. A few cautions are in order. Every notice of merchants or craftsmen is not evidence for the existence of a guild system, even when people appear to act in common in specific instances of political or economic agitation. Greek words for the Latin *collegium* or *corporatio* are well known, and Justinian's jurists worked out a common vocabulary, but no similarity exists between these two languages and Arabic. Filling in gaps in one particular field by appealing to some bit of evidence from another is inappropriate. There is no justification, for example, for the belief that Byzantine guilds would continue to exist under Muslim rule in eastern cities or the theory that the failure of the college system to survive in the west proves that it did not survive under the Arabs. The spontaneous and distinctive ways in which the three societies evolved, without much reference to one another, make a brief comparison more instructive than if they were continuously borrowing from each other's experiences.

In the Byzantine state, which remained in spirit a Roman empire, the corporation (*somateion*) or college and the government for a time continued to operate under the rules set forth in the Code of Justinian.[107] In the seventh century, the spread of Islam in the east and the crisis of the Byzantine state profoundly changed the size of the empire and its internal economic structure. The state retained an interest in supervising the corporation, which in turn looked to the state for regulation. The classic source for the Byzantine guild, *The Book of the Prefect*, also known as *The Book of the Eparch*, is a handbook of regulations for the eparch of Constantinople issued in the reign of Leo VI the Wise (880–912).[108] These regulations reveal that the relationship between the state and the guilds had continued to evolve and was no longer what it had been under Justinian. The book mentions twenty-four professions and crafts: notaries, jewelers, bankers, silk-garment merchants, importers of Syrian silks, raw-silk merchants, silkspinners, silkweavers, linen merchants, perfumedealers, candlemakers, soapmakers, victualers (grocers), leathercutters (saddlers), butchers, porkdealers, fishmongers, bakers, innkeepers, joiners, plasterers, marbleworkers, locksmiths, and painters; and it implies that others exist. The regulations closely define work sites, rules, market practices, production standards, and other aspects of particular trades; and *The Book of the Prefect* has been used to analyze the workings of the important silk industry.[109] The prefect or eparch was a kind of grand market inspector, with a staff to look into trade. The fishmongers were supposed to report to him every morning on the "size of the night catch of tunny fish, so that the sale to the people in the city may be made according to his instructions."[110] The porkdealers were required to make their purchases at the great market in the city, and dire penalties were imposed on anyone caught sneaking out of the city to meet the swine collectors to steal a march on competitors.[111]

The Byzantine state closely regulated the economy in a way that Diocletian would have envied; this aspect of the law remained in full force and seems in fact to have become more rigorous. The prefect kept lists of members of the guilds and supervised the admission of new ones. The noticeable changes in the system since the time of Justinian are the absence of hereditary service and any direct comment on liturgies, or public duties, with two exceptions. The edict explicitly states that "the bakers shall be exempt from all liturgies, both they themselves and their animals, so that they may prepare their bread without interruption."[112] The bakers enjoyed this specific exemption, and the public burdens, once the centerpiece of the state's interest in the guilds, receive one further notice—the leathercutters, who performed their public liturgies under the prefect's direction.[113] The leathercutters presumably provided the army with leather gear, and theirs is the only guild mentioned that had any possible role to play in equipping the army. The state's principal interest in the guilds was a clear desire to protect customers and ensure that contracts were fulfilled.

The rules for the other guilds rest on the assumption that the prosperity of the capital depended upon wise and careful state intervention. The state intended to regulate the guilds down to the smallest detail: "Any spinner [of silk] . . . showing himself to be gossiping, a boaster, troublesome, or noisy, shall be expelled from the corporation with blows and insults, to prevent his selling the silk."[114] The punishment is also interesting since in previous centuries the state's main concern was to keep people in the corporations in order to exact services from them. Despite the high degree of regulation, rules for entering or leaving the corporations reveal that membership benefited tradesmen and artisans and excluding them was a severe penalty. The edict is silent on the question of compulsory hereditary service, and this suggests to most observers that the earlier strictures had disappeared. The prefect determined whether new members were qualified or not, and this procedure at least raises the possibility that some applicants would be turned down. Without official access to the marketplace, the applicant would not be able to pursue the desired trade or craft.

The Byzantine guilds of Constantinople may not reflect conditions elsewhere in the empire, and nothing is known about the position of guilds in other cities. The one theme that links the eras of Diocletian, Justinian, and Leo the Wise is the pervasive role of the state. No ruler in the west had a city the size of Constantinople, a ready bureaucracy, or a level of economic activity comparable to the east, so the system of state-supervised artisan and professional associations survived, with some fundamental changes, only in the east. Guilds also played a part in urban political disturbances and court ceremonies in the tenth and eleventh centuries.[115] In the west, religion had a role in the social activities of the Roman college and seemed the basis for the guilds of the early Middle Ages, yet *The Book of the Prefect* has little to say on the subject. The guild of notaries received the most scrutiny because of its key role as the producer of legal records. The edict required notaries to participate in a deceased member's funeral "so that the pomp of his burial may be in keeping with that of his election," and a fine was imposed on any notary who missed the funeral "without good cause."[116] The guild must have initiated this requirement, which is the only one that hints at a tenuous connection to religion. The members of all the guilds may have had social or religious ties, but the authority of the state was their principal motive for coming together as guilds and their principal incentive for remaining intact. By the time of Leo the Wise, little remained of the pre-Islamic Byzantine state. In the west, Sicily was lost and the Lombards were enjoying the height of their domination in southern Italy. North Africa and the Middle East were no longer ruled from Constantinople. Under the special circumstances of continuous rule in the southern Balkans and Asia Minor, the Roman colleges continued to exist, but nowhere in the west had this happened. No evidence suggests that Byzantine practices, as revealed in *The Book of the Prefect*, had the slightest impact in the west, or even, ironically, on the subsequent history of Constantinople. "During the twelfth century, traditional forms of corporate organization were gradually lost; guilds in Constantinople vanished."[117] This is precisely the time when craft and professional guilds gradually appeared in the west.

Guilds in Islamic societies in North Africa and the Middle East have an equally complex history. Despite assumptions that some kind of craft groups must have maintained the traditions of the Roman college, particularly in the large cities of Alexandria and Antioch, no evidence has been found for the existence of guilds. S. D. Goitein, in his famous studies of the communities of Old Cairo (Fustat), concluded: "The assertion that, in early Islam, corporate life found a refuge in the guilds of artisans and merchants, although reiterated with strong emphasis by some scholars, cannot be upheld, for these guilds, as far as any term may be applied to them at all, developed only in the Late Middle Ages"—which for Goitein meant the Turkish period beginning in the thirteenth century.[118] Claude Cahen investigated the *futuwwa*, a youth association characteristic of Muslim urban society; and he also concluded that these groups, whatever they were, had nothing to do with guilds, at least before the period of the Ottoman Turks.[119] The most common word for guild (*sinf*, pl. *asnaf*) was only used in this sense in the later periods. Ira Lapidus found that "there were no guilds in Muslim cities in this period [Mamluk Egypt, 1250–1517] in any usual sense of the term," and Lapidus's sense of the term was quite broad.[120]

Instead of asking, as is usually the habit, why no guilds existed, it is more useful to look briefly at some of the distinctive features of Muslim cities in the Middle East. There were, of course, large and prosperous cities with a variety of merchants and artisans, and states often contained a high degree of centralization, certainly closer in experience to Byzantium than early medieval Europe. The common legal framework for the Islamic world in this period, the Koran—while containing some guidelines on business practices, work, and honest dealing—offered neither support for state interest in organizing artisans or professionals nor a rationale for these groups to form on their own. Muslim cities had social divisions and a sense of neighborhood and, most importantly, the central focus of the marketplace, where the state reaped taxes and enforced what rules it desired. When these cities were still under Byzantine rule in the seventh century, they may have had guilds, but the new rulers had no interest in this aspect of local tradition, and the compulsory and hereditary organizations disappeared without a trace. In this sense, early medieval Europe and Islam had more in common with each other than either had with Byzantium, but guilds will emerge in Europe centuries before they appear in the Muslim cities of the eastern Mediterranean.

This rapid survey of a millennium necessarily raises up for scrutiny only one thread from the complex tangle of political, social, and economic developments in the Roman and early medieval worlds. That thread is labor and its users. Scholars have intensively debated the "known facts" for over a century, and specialized studies continue to ratify or to controvert the established interpretations. Regions experienced change in various ways; at first glance, it may appear absurd that any hypothesis can range over such diverse places as Antioch, Pavia, and Abbotsbury without distorting the local trends and imposing on change an artificial and meaningless uniformity. Labor is, however, one common variable, and it is presented here as the critical one for understanding the economy. All these societies required labor. Marx recognized this and offered his model both of ancient or slave and of feudal modes of production in order to explain the transition in the economy from classical antiquity to the Middle Ages.[121] This line of reasoning suggests, in brief, that the most important change described here may be in the style of coercion; in the absence of regular wage labor, however, slavery or some other more refined type of dependent labor remained the basic ways of making people work. This continuity in coercion is a valuable insight but, by itself, will not explain why a market for labor ever developed. Wage labor might be argued to be simply more refined coercion, but I will show in the next chapter that it represented an improvement over previous terms for those who must work.

The experiences of Rome and the early medieval kingdoms point the way to a few clear trends to keep in mind as we turn to the first signs of associations of employers. Freeing *employer* from its modern con-notations and seeing the word as ambiguous and open-minded about the different ways to profit from labor is necessary. In other words, we have seen employers without regular wage labor, and this situation did not seem to depend solely on the supply of money but also on the effectiveness of coercion. Coercion is the enduring theme, but where is the solvent to loosen up a thousand years without regular wages? Why did wage labor again appear? These are questions to take up in the next chapter.

2

Early Craft and Professional Guilds

As discovered so often in the study of medieval history, the twelfth-century sources provide the first documentary evidence for the existence of wages and craft and professional guilds in the west. These sources are scattered and fragmentary, with very few documents indicating the moment when a group of people formed a guild. Most of the testimony picks up the story of a guild that already existed and hence leaves the question of origins shrouded in the forgotten past. Another difficulty that obscures the earliest traces of guilds is that innovation would sometimes be disguised in order to allay the suspicions of secular authorities. Guilds occasionally pretended to an antiquity they did not possess. Investigating a broad selection of urban guilds across medieval Europe remains worthwhile. This effort again runs the risk of imposing an artificial similarity on what in some cases were clear regional variations that should not be minimized. The problems of terminology must be kept in mind; local societies devised words and forms to suit regional purposes, and the Latin language, used everywhere, itself glosses over these distinctions.

Some common traditions and contemporary economic developments affected the ways craft and professional groups came into being. The standard interpretations are by now commonplace and require only a brief mention here.[1] Trade and urbanization brought people in the same line of work into close proximity with one another, creating rivalries but also the first reasons for cooperation. The increased study and availability of Roman legal texts served as a reminder to any secular authority that it had the right and the responsibility to regulate such groups. The desire to protect the vested interests of a king or aristocracy did not wait upon the revival of Roman law, and in fact a public role in this regard, be it from a king, other secular ruler, or communal government, arose before the elaboration of a framework that justified this intervention. The craft and professional guilds first appeared in the cities and small towns along the newly thriving trade routes of medieval Europe.

Yet I want to do more here than show that guilds and wage labor simply reflect the rise of trade all over again. Macroeconomic changes taking place in the late tenth and eleventh centuries certainly fostered an environment in which handicrafts and trade would eventually flourish. But nothing about these grand trends dictated the precise role of labor in the marketplace. At this juncture, a close look at the idea of the market is useful. Exchange had continued throughout the bleak centuries before the revival; local markets always existed; and barter worked well up to a certain point. The institutions of slavery and dependent labor suggest that barter for services functioned well enough when the need was for manual labor or domestic service.[2] In other words, the economic structures of Carolingian Europe, for example, were adequate for supplying maintenance in its basic form—food, clothing, and shelter—in exchange for continuous service. Substantial organizations like the monarchy and great monasteries were capable of supporting a person whose specialized, full-time work did not permit him or her to raise food, build shelter, and do all the rest. On a smaller scale, some households devoted to handicraft production had already solved these supply problems, presumably through barter, and hence they could augment their production by taking on additional hands. But choices about how to do this were available. In the eleventh and twelfth centuries, slavery and serfdom still had the potential to solve the problem, not just on the farm, but also in handicraft manufactures. A market for labor as such did not yet exist. The place to look for such a market is among the potential employers in the cities, in the initially small group of self-sufficient artisans and traders whose enterprises succeeded to the point of requiring help beyond the means of the family group to supply. And yet, for some reason, wages became the preferred way to achieve this goal.

These potential employers in the cities had other problems besides the need for additional labor. Many of the cities were also busy trying to acquire some measure of self-government from the local feudal lord or, in the German and Italian areas, the often hard-pressed emperors. The rise of cities and communal forms of government is not the subject here, but at times it is impossible to disentangle the liberty of cities from the liberty of employers within them to form guilds for mutual protection and benefit. In some places the town council itself may have initiated the organization of trades; in others the trades sought this right from the city. This same period also witnessed a dramatic increase in the number of religious confraternities. These groups, often utilizing the terminology and social forms of guilds, complicate the search for craft and professional guilds. The fraternities or confraternities, organized along parish or neighborhood lines, contained the kinds of people who lived in particular parts of a town. As neighborhoods increasingly reflected some specialization by trade, the confraternity, for reasons having little or nothing to do with the original religious impulse to form it, might count as members a high proportion of people in the same craft or business.

Let us begin with the employers. The sources from this period survive in a random and fortuitous fashion, and some of the most interesting or important cities left behind almost no trace of their earliest guilds. Five cities provide a useful starting point for this analysis, since together they encompass the range of local circumstances, quality of evidence, and, most importantly, the different paths of development. These cities are the two important German towns of Cologne and Worms, St. Omer in Flanders, and two capitals, one on the way to becoming much more than it had been—London—and one that had seen its best days—Pavia.

Cologne's position on the Rhine and its tenacious clinging to existence through centuries of trouble, and its string of important and frequently powerful archbishops, in effect guaranteed that the city would be able to foster and to take advantage of the increased Rhineland trade of the eleventh and twelfth centuries. Something is known about commerce in Cologne because rare documents of practice survive from this northern European town.[3] This city shared in the growth of the prototypical medieval industry, the manufacturing of wool cloth. The charter of the weavers of Cologne, from 1149, is one of the earliest genuine notices of craftsmen actually forming a guild.[4] This particular charter announces the intention of the weavers of mattresses and pillows (presumably the covers) to form what they call a *fraternitas,* a brotherhood, for their own common good. These Cologne weavers almost never receive their proper identity in the literature; they were not all of the weavers in the city. Precisely four weavers, along with unnamed and uncounted others, distinguished themselves clearly and repeatedly as confined to the business of making mattress and pillow covers. This kind of work required some tailoring ability, since the covers needed to be fitted with seams. These weavers practiced a narrow specialty work within the broader category of weaving. I think it likely that other guilds existed for other kinds of weavers, and this document illustrates a common practice and a reason why the origin of a guild is so hard to pinpoint. Many of the guilds that have such clear beginnings formed by splitting off a branch of a craft or trade from a previously broader and less-defined sphere of work. These specialities suggest the kind of division of labor that prosperity engendered. The sources indicate that this was the first guild in Cologne, but these specialist weavers cannot have been the first group in Cologne to ask for a legal sanction.

What these weavers wanted is interesting and important. They asked nearly everyone to confirm their brotherhood—the advocate, the count, the senators, and the better people of the city—and the people (*vulgus*), not having a confirming power, were limited to applauding in approval. As will be seen, guildsmen in later periods were to make much of their voluntary and spontaneous origins and would claim the legal right to form private associations. However, the twelfth-century examples all include this element of petition to a higher authority. These weavers of Cologne wanted corporate status, and long before this idea received a thorough legal and theoretical analysis, they knew that their own common good would only benefit from the formal recognition of the established powers in the city.

A similar element of petition is present in a privilege that the bishop of Worms granted to twenty-three fishermen in 1106 and in which they received the corporate hereditary right to control the wholesale market in fish.[5] The charter contains no word to describe the group of fishermen; it refers to them by their names, an awkward procedure perhaps indicating that the bishop was doing something new. The fishermen's corporate status is apparent in their right to pass on membership in the group to their closest relative (*proximus eius*), and in default of an heir, the other fishermen would choose someone to take the place. The charter does not take away from other people whatever rights to fish they may have possessed, but they had to sell fish to one of the twenty-three. The bishop imposed penalties on those who tried to circumvent the rights of the group. In turn, the fishermen promised to give two salmon a year to the bishop and one salmon to the local count. The bishop made one specific rule about the time of sale; he ordered that none of the fishermen should buy any fish before prime (dawn).

This charter shares some features with the other forms of grants made in Lombard Italy, in the sense that the bishop and count represented public authority in Worms. They had the right to concede such a privilege to the fishermen, who in turn were petitioners acknowledging their authority. What the bishop granted them appears to be in one way a traditional hereditary tenement, in this case a bundle of rights concerning fish. Some historians have noted the absence of any word for a guild or corporation and do not regard this charter as the oldest evidence for a guild in northern Europe.[6] However, the fishermen approached the bishop, and clearly they asked him to regulate the market in particular by prohibiting predawn sales. Documents about fish frequently reveal a concern about the enterprising retailer who might purchase all of the fish, or just the best and freshest, before the other retailers had a chance. Without a rule, retailers might scurry around to haggle with other fishermen as soon as their boats hit dock. The fishermen of Worms wanted a more orderly market and perhaps as well simply to make their purchases in the clear light of day, always an advantage when buying fish. Whatever the motive, the fishermen were acting together to foster their common economic interest by setting rules for how they would compete among themselves, and in this they acted like a guild, albeit in all but name.

The special interests of one trade might prompt a request for legal recognition, yet often a general demand for a measure of self-government subsumed these narrow goals. The trades and professions had divergent interests, but at the same time that particular groups sought privileges, whole communities requested, demanded, purchased, or extorted a charter granting them rights of self-government—the right to have a commune. The two most urbanized areas of Europe, the Low Countries and northern Italy, witnessed the rise of the commune in the late eleventh and twelfth centuries.[7] The long and interesting story of how some cities acquired a degree of self-government, the right to have a commune, is related to the history of the guilds in several ways. This connection is clear in the famous charter that William of Normandy, Count of Flanders, granted to the burghers of St. Omer in 1127.[8] The burghers sought a complex of legal rights that involved their concept of justice—they wanted personal liberty, the ability to adjudicate merchant disputes according to law (and not by duel), good money, and freedom from vexatious tolls and duties. The count conceded rights and confirmed old customs; he gave the burghers control over those aspects of their town that affected their ability to engage in peaceful and profitable business. The early twelfth century witnesses considerable strife between the burghers and the aristocracy of Flanders, and this charter for St. Omer was one step in the long struggle by the Flemish towns to free themselves from feudal jurisdiction.[9]

The townsmen swore an oath of association and created an institution that was a kind of superguild, in part devoted to fostering the general economic interests of the whole community. Where one particular trade or business emerged as paramount, a particular guild or group of them might end up dominating local government, but in other cities the commune itself took a strong hand in regulating guilds or even bringing them into existence. The commune and the guild had no obvious or standard relationship; local circumstances determined the ways in which different trades participated in or controlled town government. In the histories of most towns in Europe, a moment occurred when the burghers achieved a corporate status and some kind of charter of liberties, although for some lucky ones like Venice that moment was already in a distant past by the twelfth century. Other cities found acquiring or keeping these rights to be difficult—the repeated struggles by the townspeople of Rome against the pope are a case in point. Every town had a putative lord—a king, count, bishop, or pope—and these figures, maintaining some tenuous or quite real rights in the town, were hence in the enviable position of entertaining appeals against the tyranny of the commune. For example, a guild might make an end run around the town government and attempt to secure justice or recognition from the lord.

All of this analysis suggests the complex and variable ties that existed among traditional rules, communes, and guilds. In the case of St. Omer, the guild of merchants emerged as the dominant guild in town, and it rode to this power with the charter the burghers secured in 1127. Count William granted freedom from all tolls in Flanders to those in the guild. This is a merchants' guild, which in St. Omer meant a guild of those in the business of buying and selling wool and woolens.[10] Some burghers, those sworn to the commune, were not members of this guild, and this particular concession is the only one that Count William made to a subgroup of the general class of burghers. The merchants involved in regional or long-distance trade constituted the backbone of St. Omer's prosperity, and they benefited from all of the other liberties the count granted. The weavers of St. Omer also benefited from some of these provisions, but unless they had sworn to the commune, they were not burghers. Humble weavers did not receive any specific advantage other than the indirect boon to their employment that resulted from their employers being exempt from some tolls. Louis VI, king of France and Count William's lord, witnessed this charter and assented to it. The king had also found himself drawn into the conflict in Bruges in 1127, when the previous count of Flanders was murdered in a local dispute.[11] That Count William granted this charter to his townspeople of St. Omer is significant, but Louis was learning something by observing the troubles his vassals had with these towns of the Low Countries. The French monarch seldom granted such sweeping jurisdiction to the towns in the royal domain and, in particular, never gave Paris the right to have a commune. A guild might have preceded Count William's recognition of communal liberties; a certain Hugh, styled head of the guild (*Major de gilda*), had witnessed a charter of Balwin of Flanders for Arras in 1111.[12] The fact that Hugh occupied this office suggests that a guild had achieved some recognition from the counts of Flanders before towns acquired their charters of liberties. The guild of merchants in St. Omer also came into being sometime before 1111, but exactly when is not known.

Cities like Cologne, Worms, and St. Omer all fell under the jurisdiction of a lord, but they did not serve as capitals of great lordships or kingdoms. In the period under review here, monarchies in particular were in the process of establishing bureaucracies and permanent residences that decisively shaped the ways cities like London and Paris would develop and that in turn affected the level of supervision trades or guilds were likely to receive. The ancient town of Pavia in the northwest corner of Italy, the principal place of residence for the Lombard kings and hence their capital, retained an administrative importance long after the kingdom was incorporated into first the Carolingian and then the Salian and Hohenstaufen states. Pavia seldom hosted its distant later monarchs and was not destined to emerge as the dominant city of its region; nearby Milan and Genoa came to dominate, in turn, the upper Po Valley and the Ligurian coast, leaving Pavia a circumscribed territorial and economic ambit.

For a time under the emperor Frederick I, Pavia regained some political stature as it became the administrative headquarters for the emperor's chancellor Rainald of Dassel, Archbishop of Cologne. Frederick's reign witnessed a renewed German effort to consolidate its position in northern Italy, and the rights of the old Lombard kings provided an occasional pretext for Frederick's acts and ambitions.[13] All of this provides the context for understanding the record of a dispute in 1179 between the monastery of Morimond and what appears to be a guild of fishermen over fishing rights in the Ticino.[14] The consuls of the commune of Pavia had representatives collect evidence on the question, and the notarial document recording their findings contains a record of testimony by various monks and fishermen. The masters of the fishermen claimed that the monks had no right to put boats in the Ticino for the purpose of fishing. The monks unsuccessfully asserted that they had received exclusive rights from the emperor Conrad and that the present emperor Frederick had confirmed these privileges. The consuls of the commune, a recent innovation in Pavia (1164), had stepped into the supervisory role formerly exercised by the emperor or his agents, and they were able to impose a compromise settlement on the parties.[15] The fishermen had two officials (*magistri*) and a formal organization, called in their charter a *misterium*, a word derived from the older *ministerium*. Arrigo Solmi believed that the traces of guild structures he found in twelfth-century Pavia, concerning the fishermen, moneyers, and merchants, traced their origins back through the *Honorantiae Civitatis Papiae* of the tenth century, to the period of Lombard rule, and finally back to the Roman colleges of Ticinum in the late empire.[16] Solmi based his argument on the philological continuity in the use of words like *misterium* and also on the way guilds legally depended on a higher authority, whether the emperor or his local delegates, the consuls of Pavia. More importantly, the revival in the study of Roman law, one of the most significant intellectual accomplishments of the twelfth century, provided the emperor Frederick in particular with a conceptual framework that justified his idea of empire and added luster to it. By this century, the emperor's lawyers were familiar enough with the jurisprudence of Justinian's era to claim imperial rights that no one had exercised for centuries—in particular rights over associations of artisans and professions. However, two arguments weigh against Solmi's case for continuity. The use of classical words to describe these institutions was commonplace throughout Europe and cannot justify any specific argument for continuity in Pavia.[17] The fact that the leaders of the commune called themselves consuls is no case for the durability of the Roman consulate. The consuls of Pavia, standing in place of their emperor by a recent grant, were not the continuers of old and dim traditions but were innovators at the leading edge of an effort to reestablish public authority over all sorts of private jurisdictions.

London provides the final example of how the complex play of different forces—a central authority, in this case the Anglo-Norman monarchy, and town government, the eventual commune of London—determined the economic and political role guilds would have in London. By the thirteenth century, the mayor and aldermen of London had acquired the right to regulate to the most minute detail the activities of the crafts, whether through the well-known Assizes of Bread and Ale or through the ordinances and articles they conceded to the various crafts. In turn, these crafts managed to gain in some cases the rights to have their own courts and to supervise members.[18] The rich and detailed history of late medieval London will be considered below; for the present purposes, an earlier part of the story merits attention. The earliest documents on guilds in London reveal a connection between the crown and the guilds. The later history is in part the tale of how the municipal authorities interposed themselves between the king and the crafts. Apart from the slender possibilities considered in the last chapter, the Anglo-Saxon guilds did not provide the basis for the establishment of craft or professional guilds in thirteenth- and fourteenth-century England. The first evidence for such a guild comes from a charter Henry II (1154–1189) granted to weavers of London.[19] The king gave the weavers the right to have a guild (*gilda*), with all of the liberties and rights they enjoyed in the time of his grandfather, Henry I (1100–1135). No charter from Henry I exists, but it does not seem possible that the weavers would have been able to invent one out of whole cloth in order to acquire a confirmation from Henry II, who made it a policy to return to the good customs of the reign of his grandfather, at least where it suited his larger purposes. Unfortunately, Henry II's charter offers no details on these liberties and customs. The king granted the weavers the exclusive right to practice their craft in London, and no one outside the guild was able to engage in this craft (*ministerium*)—all according to the customs of the reign of Henry I. In exchange for these privileges, the weavers were obliged to pay the king two marks of gold at Michaelmas.

The only specific right the weavers certainly possessed was an important one—legal control over membership and a corporate monopoly. The charter does not mention any officials of the weavers' guild, nor does it list the individual members who might claim some of the privilege. The document portrays the weavers as a guild, a legal entity. The king addressed the charter: "Bishops, justiciars, sheriffs, barons, and all his servants and liegemen of London, greetings. Know that I have granted. . . ."[20] The king informed the leading figures of London; he did not require their consent, and the weavers petitioned the king alone. The charter of liberties Henry II granted the citizens of London in 1155 conceded them a measure of self-government and various liberties but contained nothing about guilds or any rights the city had over such organizations.[21] What the weavers gained from Henry II could be taken away by another king, and the *Book of Customs* records that King John (1199–1216) annulled this charter. However, in 1243, the guild of weavers presented their old charter to Henry III (1216–1272), who in turn issued a charter confirming all of the rights granted by his grandfather, Henry II.[22] The new charter adds nothing to the scope of the original, but the fact that the weavers, denied their legal status, nevertheless retained their charter and were able to present it to another king at least twenty-seven years after John's annulment of it is important. Perhaps only a single copy survived in the hands of one obstinate weaver, yet this episode highlights the durable impulse to form a guild. At the time that Henry III confirmed the old charter, the city of London still had no role to play in the matter, but this situation would soon change. The English evidence on the weavers suggests that their guild was created from the ground up and represented what in the discussion of Roman colleges was called a voluntary and spontaneous association. Once the king conceded the right to have a guild, the guild was no longer voluntary, in the sense that one had to join in order to practice the craft in London. The London weavers were not the only group to approach the king seeking legal recognition; Henry II had confirmed the rights of the merchant guilds in Lincoln and Winchester and granted a charter to the corvesars and cordwainers (cobblers) of Oxford.[23] In England, the earliest evidence for craft and professional guilds does not indicate that the active monarch or city governments brought the guilds into existence, but the balance among these forces would change.

Examining the guilds in Languedoc, in its broadest definition a vast region of southern France, provides examples of all of the different circumstances we have considered thus far and also helps to tie together the various ways guilds came into being. The study of the Languedocian guilds has benefited from the only regional study of guilds, the first-rate monograph by André Gouron.[24] In the twelfth and early thirteenth centuries, Languedoc lacked a strong central authority, since most of it remained outside of even the nominal reach of the Capetian kings in Paris; and the most important feudatory, the Count of Provence, exercised his authority over a bewildering array of jurisdictions. The economy of the region played a role in the contemporary revival of Mediterranean commerce, and Languedoc had a number of small but important towns that supported notaries who had some knowledge of Roman law and Italian business practices.[25] Gouron investigates the rise of communes in Languedoc and how they, along with the feudal lords of the region, regulated both guilds and the urban

economies. In some towns like Toulouse, the commune, in the form of a
city government headed by the familiar consuls, emerged just before
the first notices of guilds appeared; elsewhere, as in Montpellier, the
guilds preceded the commune.[26] (The same diverse pattern holds true
for guilds and communes in northern Italy.) However, Gouron emphasizes that the consuls came from the ranks of prominent merchants,
while the guilds were the domain of artisans who were not often
influential in town government. The communes of Languedoc were
actively intervening in commerce, the artisan trades, and the guilds in
Toulouse as early as the late twelfth century.[27] As examples of public
authority, these communes, generally in the hands of the merchant
elites, were in a position to develop a rudimentary economic policy and
impose it on the guilds. Communes tested their abilities to regulate the
guilds, and these rules provide another glimpse of early guilds in
action.

The pace of economic and political development in Languedoc
raises a complex and crucial question about the early evidence for
guilds that the rich documentation provides: is it possible that the
activities of communes brought forth organizations of artisans, that the
communes created guilds in a sense as a by-product of efforts to
regulate artisans? Different examples of how the earliest European
guilds came into existence have already been discussed, and this possibility of creation from above requires a closer look. For example,
Gouron cites the efforts that the consuls of Toulouse made to regulate
the profits of the millers and bakers.[28] In 1152, the consuls fixed the
profits of the millers at one-sixteenth of what they milled and for the
bakers set a maximum profit of four pennies per measure of grain, after
they deducted their expenses. Almost everywhere secular authorities
attempted to control the prices of key commodities like grain and
bread, but this evidence from Toulouse is very early and displays a
precocious economic policy. Gouron's thesis is that this type of regulation came from on high; the consuls devised these restrictions on prices
and profits. But there are two sides to the question of cui bono—just
who would benefit from the consuls' regulating of profits?

Perhaps the consuls, as Gouron suggests, did have a developing
vision of consumer interests, and maybe a conscious desire to ensure a
cheap and plentiful supply of the necessities of life endured. Times of
crisis amply justified any efforts to control the price of food in the city.[29]
The self-interest of the bakers and millers must also be kept in mind.
The maximum profit for the bakers allowed some leeway for those who

were willing to accept a smaller profit margin, so that bakers might continue to compete for business. Yet only a baker would possess the expertise necessary to determine the exact profit, and what outsider would be able to calculate with any accuracy the expenses of baking? Whatever the benefits, intended or otherwise, to the consumer, the bakers may have sought both a narrower base for competing among themselves and the formal recognition that their profit was guaranteed and always above the fluctuating price of grain. Even if the consuls inspired this regulation, the bakers still had the important prerogative of estimating their own expenses. The millers had a more obvious definition of appropriate income, a straight fee for service that did not include any allowance for the costs of maintaining a mill.[30] If the millers committed themselves to observing the one-sixteenth fee, no amount of competition would ever reduce the prices for the consumers, whom the consuls were presumably eager to protect. The fact that the city government issued rules for particular trades is not proof that these trades had developed any sort of organization. Even in instances where the trade had the burden of enforcing the rule, a guild need not result from this obligation.

Gouron is on surer ground when he points to the statutes the consuls of Toulouse issued for the innkeepers in 1205.[31] In this case, the consuls wanted to protect the lucrative pilgrim trade from abuse, and the links between higher authority and the public interest are clear. Many instances of town officials, feudal lords, or monarchs intervening in guild activities occurred throughout Europe, but no clear case is known where any group or individual summoned artisans and told them to form a guild. Gouron considers the more subtle point that the public authorities may have created some guilds as a by-product of intervention in the rules of the local economy. The idea that the guilds arose in the communal and feudal milieu is well taken, but just as some vassals took themselves to a lord and as some cities sought legal recognition of their liberties, the earliest guilds we have seen appear as petitioners for permission to exist. One cannot rule out the possibility that the guilds, in the examples Gouron cites, benefited from consular direction, and hence the guilds might just as well be the ones who asked for advantages like fixed prices or monopolies.

These five examples are "bolts out of the blue" and hence are frozen in time; no trail of records explaining the formation of these early guilds exists. At the end of this chapter, we will look closely at the formation of one association, the wool guild of Genoa, but this case is later and perhaps not typical of the circumstances in the twelfth century. The merchants and artisans involved in the earliest guilds seem to have been self-employed, and there was as yet no sign of regular wage earners. (This last observation may result from a simple gap in the documentation.) Whatever reasons people had for creating these guilds, the motives appear to have nothing to do with wage labor. Kinship groups may possibly have supplied the need for extra hands on the fishing skiff or the loom, but again, the problem of recruiting a work force was not the thing that brought people into these early guilds. The common theme in these examples is the way in which the artisans and merchants sought both legitimacy and the personal liberties so necessary in their eyes to the success of their own labors. Their aspirations were something new in a society with its sense of three orders and little understanding of those who did not fight, pray, or farm.[32] The artisans and merchants sought security in numbers and usually approached some superior in the safe and anonymous garb of "the weavers." Only the fishermen of Worms had their names put down in the bishop's charter. One common weakness of the histories under review thus far is that they do not say anything about the motives behind the desire to cooperate on the part of the guilds or the reasons why other entrenched groups in society found it useful or necessary to permit guilds to exist. Medieval charters seldom tell the whole story behind the manner in which artisans negotiated and compromised in order to get a charter. A look at how guilds actually functioned in the urban economy and at the documents their members produced in the course of ordinary business will help elucidate more clearly how guilds came into being in the first place.

Early Guilds in Action

The foundation document discussed above is very rare, and the vast majority of guilds do not appear for the first time in the historical record in this unambiguous manner. The guild statutes or sets of regulations that survive in considerable numbers tend to reflect the circumstances of later development; revisions of statutes rendered older versions obsolete and hence reduced their chances of survival. For example, the first extant statutes of the important guild of money changers (*cambio*) in Florence date from 1299 and were revised in 1300, 1313, and 1316 in the existing copy.[33] The guild had existed for a long time before 1299 and presumably had formal written rules, but the 1299 revision was so extensive as to make preserving older copies pointless. Old provisions are buried in later sets of rules, and the constant tinkering with the statutes shows changes in principal concerns and business conditions. The older practices are difficult to distinguish from the newer rules without some other source to indicate what the "ancient customs" might have been. The notarial records of southern European cities are a good place to look for documents of practice and early notices of guild activity. These documents pose problems of their own, but they do have the advantage of revealing how practical institutions and customs worked on a daily basis. The notarial records, from a variety of cities in France and Italy, also show in passing how much older the guilds are than other sources indicate.

A word or two on the notarial record is necessary in order to explain what kind of information is found there.[34] Notaries were in the business of drawing up commercial contracts and other personal matters like marriage agreements and wills, all of this an invaluable service in a basically illiterate society. Notarial cartularies, the large books into which notaries copied what in many cases was the formal and legal copy of a contract, contain a broad cross section of all types of medieval business practices and are a vital source for medieval economic and social history. The way society relied on notarial documents, or acts, reveals what M. T. Clanchy concisely describes as the shift from memory to record in medieval society.[35] Oral contracts and agreements were replaced in a slow and incomplete manner and naturally remained more prevalent in some spheres of activity than others. The shift to a greater reliance on written records varies from place to place, and even person to person. Most of the notarial acts concern title to property and the lending or investing of money. Robert Lopez's idea of the commercial revolution of the Middle Ages, involving changes occurring simultaneously in northern and southern Europe, rests on the necessity and usefulness of records as all types of business activity became more and more complex.[36] Legal knowledge kept apace of these economic changes, and merchant law and courts increasingly relied on records to settle disputes, hence helping to spread a reliance on written records.

All these changes in medieval society profoundly affected the ways in which some employers began to hire labor. Most work in this period remained in agriculture, the slowest sphere to enter the domain of written contracts. This whole question of labor in the countryside, specifically how the conditions of this work changed over time, is one of the most important and intensively studied subjects in medieval history. Here the concern is with what was at first a tiny percentage of the general population who lived in towns and did not earn their livelihood in farming. The obligations of feudal society, and in particular the services expected from a subject peasantry, did not prove to be the model for organizing the work of craftsmen or merchants. Where the aristocracy had been successful in imposing itself on rural society, the lords believed, in terms that they did not often articulate, that they had a right to the labor of peasants who lived on their land. The labor of these peasants might be bought, sold, bartered away, or simply allowed to lapse through disuse. What Michael Postan called the chronology or changes over time in these labor services is the story of how lords chose to live off their peasants.[37] To do justice to these themes here is not possible, but they are all fundamental to any consideration of how lawyers and employers could think of labor as a property right. The clearest instance of this was slavery, where the property rights of one person over another were virtually complete. One obvious method of employing labor was to enslave it, and this possibility was one of the principal challenges to the guilds of southern Europe and an alternative to the guild method of recruiting workers. The point here is to establish that labor, like other forms of property, might be bought and sold or rented, and to the extent that it was, the notarial record should reveal how the methods of contracting work developed and changed over time. Since guilds were at bottom associations of employers, one should expect to see members out in the market employing people, and the guilds existed in part for the purpose of regulating competition. The record bears traces of this regulation of an activity that contemporaries thought crucial to the survival of any craft or profession where the work required more hands than the family workshop alone was able to provide. The rise and division of labor within the family seldom became a matter requiring a formal written contract, but early on, the family alone did not meet the need for extra hands.

A small percentage of notarial documents concerns the employing of workers, principally as helpers in the artisan trades, but also as companions for merchants or crews for ships. The form of these contracts varies from town to town, and such records did not survive at all in some parts of Europe. The notarial practices of southern Europe are here a distinct advantage, and examples of contracts from Genoa, Venice, Siena, Marseilles, and Montpellier, primarily from the thirteenth century, will be considered. Genoa supplies the great bulk of examples because the quality and quantity of the early notarial cartularies preserved in this city are unmatched by any other in Europe.

Employers, and hence notaries, divided up the labor market into several broad categories and treated potential employees in different ways. The clearest issues were the duration of the contract and the age of the worker. Apparently everywhere, three general classes of workers, and hence worker contracts, existed—apprentices, seasoned mature workers employed for long periods of service, and casual workers taken on for brief periods of time, usually measured in days, for specific tasks. Apprentices generally worked for long periods of time, reckoned in years, that varied according to two factors: (1) the age of the apprentice as he or she entered into the agreement and (2) the level and complexity of skill required in a particular craft. The word *apprentice* is an Old French term that slipped into English usage, with numerous examples in the fourteenth century. In the Latin generally used in the earliest contracts and statutes, the apprentice is often called a *discipulus*, a student. We are looking here at a form of work contract in which the master was obliged to teach, and the apprentice to learn. These duties define an apprenticeship and distinguish it from all other forms of work contracts.

In the second category of worker contracts, the parties assumed that the newly employed worker possessed the skills necessary to practice the trade. This emerging group of journeymen and -women, not full members of the guild, since they themselves employed no one and had no apprentices, were skilled workers often commanding a high wage. These journeymen preserved in their names both in Italian and French (and hence in English) their distinctive characteristic—day work, in the sense that they were paid normally by the day. Almost never did a master actually employ a journeyman on a day-by-day basis, and the notarial contracts reveal a preference for terms of employment measured in months. The pay, however, remained fixed at so much per workday. Four Latin words for a wage—*locarium* (variant *loquerium*), *merces*, *salarium*, and *stipendium*—appear in the earliest worker contracts. The first two preserve the tie between a wage and a rent, since they can mean either; the last two strictly refer to a wage. All of these words have descendants in the vernacular languages of western Europe.

The third category is a kind of leftover collection of various contracts for work that did not involve any obligation to teach or learn skills, and such contracts usually ran for a brief period of time or were limited to a specific task. This kind of work is the least likely to creep into the written record, and usually some sort of special circumstance accounts for why an oral agreement did not suffice. Two examples from this heterogeneous group will be helpful in understanding its catchall nature. In August 1226, Enrico de Vedario of Genoa contracted with a French doctor practicing in Genoa, Maître Jean de Paris, and promised to pay the doctor the sum of two lire fifteen days after he was completely freed of a stone that he had in his bladder.[38] Enrico was no doubt wise to delay payment until after he had remained free of symptoms for a while, and this agreement is a typical work contract—payment in exchange for a specific service. Most services thus acquired were ordinary; two Genoese in 1214 agreed to break stones for a bridge, and their employer promised to retain them for a month and pay a daily wage.[39] As is apparent from these examples, this last category of worker contracts has little to do with guilds, although most physicians later had one as did the notaries employed for the few minutes to write down these agreements. It is useful to keep an eye on this casual labor because it was always there, ready to act as a check on the ways apprentices and journeymen and -women found themselves employed.

The apprenticeship contracts display considerable variability and do not fall neatly into a stock-in-trade form of contract.[40] Notarial formularies or handbooks existed in part to provide notaries with sample forms of agreements that they could adapt to specific circumstances. Most notaries used for this purpose the most general form of available contract, the *promissio et conventio*—the promise and agreement, in its most simple form. A contract beginning "I promise and agree that . . ." produced a very flexible document. It is revealing that one author of a notarial handbook, Salatiele of Bologna, put this promise in the master's mouth, whereas practice suggests that in the vast majority of cases the parent, guardian, or the future pupil made the promise and agreement to the master.[41] In the typical apprenticeship contract, some adult, usually the father or mother if living, was the one who had to make the promise because the apprentice had not reached the age of majority and often was not even old enough to swear to abide by the terms of the contract. In short, the adult guaranteed that the apprentice would observe the terms of the contract, almost invariably under a serious cash penalty. The standard conditions were that the apprentice would serve for a specified term for the purpose of learning and working at the art, in good faith without any fraud. Details, depending on the particular craft or professions, often described what kinds of services this work entailed. The agreement bound the apprentice not to run away or to marry without the permission of the master. Only in a few cases was the family of the apprentice obliged to pay the master for taking on the apprentice or to provide some material support for the pupil during the term of service.

The master in turn promised to teach the apprentice and keep him or her for the agreed-upon number of years. The master was also obliged to feed, clothe, and house the apprentice for the term, although this requirement varied according to place and economic conditions. In addition, the master promised not to place any insupportable burden on the apprentice but at times specifically reserved the right of correction. The same cash penalty applied to the master if he or she failed to fulfill the terms of the agreement. In practice, considerable variation existed in details according to which city, trade, legal tradition, or time period the contract concerned. These variations will be explored in detail below because they help to establish crucial facts about the labor market.[42]

Some notaries preferred to use, or their clients for some reason demanded, another form of contract—the rental agreement. In this form of contract, the general outline remained the same, but the act began with the simple phrase "I rent and concede. . . ." Placing a son or daughter with a master in this case became an ordinary rental; the parent handed over to the master quasi-parental authority and rented a child in the same way that one might rent a house or a mule. Salatiele included this type of contract in the formulary called the *instrumentum locationis puerorum* (instrument of the renting of children); in the example he used, a parent rented a son to a shoemaker for five years.[43] Many examples can be found of young men or women of seventeen or eighteen years of age committing themselves to an apprenticeship through a contract, but rarely in the form of a rental agreement.

Although some work contracts took on exotic forms, most of them involved standard trades and conditions, with fixed terms of service. The worker received a daily salary, most of the time paid on Saturday, the payday of the six-day workweek. Occasionally, and especially in the cloth trades, one might be paid by piecerate. These journeymen and -women made the conventional promise to work for the stipulated term and agreed to the traditional penalty for failure to comply with the conditions of hire. The employer promised to provide work on every day that was not a Church feast and, in turn, expected to have the sole right to the worker's labor in the agreed period, usually measured in months, but sometimes as long as one or two years. The daily wage included in these contracts provides a key indicator of prevailing wage rates, as well as some contrast to, and a means to evaluate, the work of apprentices. Changes over time should reflect the ebb and flow of the labor market in urban areas.

As other sources indicate, little tangible evidence is available for the existence of guilds before the first surviving set of statutes. The rich collection of Genoese notarial documents, as well as some comparisons with the less numerous sources from other cities, suggests that many trades had organized themselves long before the first statutes. Apprenticeship and work contracts give hints of this organization in a variety of ways. These hints are often blatant. For example, in a work contract dated 24 October 1231, a woolcarder committed himself to work for two years at six pennies a day for the first year and eight pennies a day for the second. This agreement went to the unusual length of defining the workday: "from the morning of San Andrea [the ringing of the bells of one of Genoa's prominent churches] to the evening according to the customs of the *lanerii* [woolworkers in general, including all the trades associated with the manufacture of thread and cloth]."[44] This custom of the woolworkers was no accident; they had agreed to do this, and precisely this kind of collective decision is expected from an organization. The contracts, however, rarely mention details about the internal structure of the trade.

When the members of a trade appear to be acting as a group, they seem implicitly to assume certain things that only make sense if a guild existed to define and enforce these rules. First, what was a *dies laboratorius* or *dies non festivus*—a workday? Later guild statutes generally include a list of the days honored as festivals or feasts on which members of the guild did not work.[45] A core group of holy days and feasts of the principal saints is always recognizable, and particular guilds also celebrated the days of their own patron saints or the ones honored in the church that was the focus of the members' corporate devotion. Since these holidays varied from guild to guild or even among neighborhoods, any guarantee in a contract that work would be forthcoming on all days *non festivus* presupposes that a generally recognized list of feasts existed and that the masters of a trade adhered to it. Second, the fixed penalties for failing to keep to the terms of an agreement were commonplaces of later guild statutes, and the apprenticeship contracts reflect an early consensus on the size of the penalty. Third, the terms of service likewise seem to assume a body of conventions, as in the length of the workday for the woolworkers. Fourth, the masters of some crafts always gave a set of tools to the apprentice at the end of his or her service; every single blacksmith in Genoa promised to give such a set, from the first surviving apprenticeship record in 1186 through those of the thirteenth century.[46] A hammer, an anvil, and a pair of tongs were the basic set of tools for the *ferrarii,* and other trades practiced similar customs. The smiths must have agreed to this gift; otherwise the bargaining between the master and the family of the apprentice would have at least occasionally produced a contract without the tools. These four features of contracts suggest that the historian of guilds need not seek out the first formal statute of a guild in order to prove that it existed but, instead, should search for signs of collective action or adherence to rules in other kinds of documents.

Notarial records provide a special kind of evidence that shows guild officials in action and other collective acts by craftsmen. The earliest surviving notarial cartularies from Siena contain two fortuitous notices of the *mercantia pizicariorum*—the guild of porkbutchers and vendors. In 1222, a certain Benvenuto de Terraccio promised to follow the orders of the consuls of the pork guild and, in particular, agreed to make all future contracts according to the use and custom of the *mercantia.*[47] The officials of the guild were clearly enforcing their rules on Benvenuto, who managed to escape without fine. Whatever he was doing, the consuls must have considered it injurious to the interests of the other pork vendors, and the most obvious kind of infraction would be one of the oldest—perhaps Benvenuto was going to the countryside to make deals with the pig farmers instead of waiting for the pigs to appear at the city gates. Another notary, in 1228, recorded a quitclaim by apparently injured parties in which they ceded their claim to the chief of the merchants of Siena and the rector of the swine-merchants' guild, in this case both acting on behalf of the commune of Siena.[48] André Gouron has shown that town officials in various cities of Languedoc took an interest in the activities of victualers, and he has convincingly demonstrated that concerns for public health constituted the principal reason for intervening in their activities.[49] Guilds played a part in Siena's communal government, and in this case the rector was most likely an official of the commune as well as of the guild and was charged with looking into the swine-merchants' business with an eye toward sanitation. If the more detailed evidence is any guide, the rector was most probably a member of the *mercantia,* since no outsider would possess a sufficient knowledge of the business. These early notarial cartularies from Siena, together containing less than one thousand acts of business, make no reference to any other guild. Only a tiny percentage of the hypothetical original mass of notarial records survive from any town, and finding any references to guilds or their activities is difficult. The swine merchants did not have the only guild in Siena, but these two references tell something about how the guild functioned and suggest a useful comparison with Languedoc.

The indications of guild activities in the Genoese documents are more numerous but, by chance, are later than the ones from Siena. The hints about the existence of guilds in the apprenticeship agreements are confirmed in an important document that the notary Matteo de Predono drew up on 2 October 1244. A group described as *lanerii* agreed among themselves that for five years none of them would weave or beat cloths at night.[50] The masters did not offer any explanations for why they prohibited night work. A similar agreement by the *batifolii* (metalworkers) in 1248 contains the observations that making mistakes was easier and that working was simply more dangerous at night.[51] Both these reasons apply to the heavy work of beating cloth and to the problem of finding adequate light for any work at all. The woolworkers also agreed that the consuls of the guild should impose the modest fine of ten solidi for each offense, with half to be paid to the commune of Genoa and half to the *misterium*—the word used to describe the guild. Nineteen more *lanerii*, including at least three women, joined this compact the next day, bringing the total membership to sixty.[52] The population of Genoa in this period is not easy to determine, but a conservative estimate would be twenty-five thousand. The analysis of apprenticeships in the next chapter will reveal that the general category of *lanerii* was the largest single one in the work force, so Genoa likely contained more than the sixty *lanerii*. These people seem to have been concentrated in Rivoturbido, just west of the city walls at that time, and some of the signers were residents of the city. As discussed earlier, the custom of the *lanerii* in 1231 was not to work at night, so at first glance this accord of 1244 seems redundant. If we turn to a similar kind of agreement about three-and-a-half years later and look at a broader political and economic climate, the agreement not to work at night makes more sense.

On 22 May 1248, all of the master armorers of Genoa agreed to terms for employing armorers from outside the city and also to set prices on various pieces of armor that they would make for the next five years.[53] The 1240s, in general, offered a favorable market to manufacturers of weapons; Genoa found itself dragged into the papacy's struggle with the emperor Frederick II and faced imperial fleets on its shores, Ghibelline-inspired revolts in subject towns along the Riviera, and troubles with Venice over trading rights in the eastern Mediterranean. In July 1244 alone, Genoa sent twenty-two galleys to Portovenere to rescue Pope Innocent IV and escort him to safety. Meanwhile, supporters of the emperor were attacking Genoese shipping off Tunis, and the important town of Savona was in full-scale revolt.[54] Not many peaceful years appear in Genoa's history; in 1244, a heavy demand for galleys must have disrupted normal commercial ventures and the labor market in the city. In 1248, a similar strong need for ships and crew occurred; a larger number of Genoese galleys and sailors had accompanied King Louis IX of France on his crusade to Egypt.[55] Local squabbles in the Tyrrhenian forced the commune to impose a levy of thirty-two ships on the city, four per ward. The pace of naval and military activity in these years certainly provided the armorers with work, and the way in which they decided to regulate their trade must be understood in this context of boom times.

The early months of 1248 had witnessed the efforts of various agents of Louis IX to recruit soldiers and ships in the city, and here again the armorers benefited from international warfare. All of these circumstances created a shortage of skilled labor and hence the need to contract for armorers to come from outside Genoa to work. The master armorers recognized that agreeing on the terms on which they would bring recruited labor into the city was in their best interests, since individual masters, free to strike their own deals, could easily steal a march on competitors and undermine any consensus on prices. So, the masters agreed to offer comparatively long terms of employment—five years—presumably in order to prevent foreigners from looking for better terms once they were in place in Genoa, and also to make immigration more attractive to these prospective armorers. The Genoese probably also thought that current wars would last for a while, and five years turned out to be an accurate estimate. The masters paid for piece-rate production, so much per shield and other pieces of armor, rather than a daily wage. The question of a daily versus a piece-rate wage will be considered in more detail below, but in this context of abundant work, the foreign armorers might have found piece-rate pay to be more attractive since it would have provided them with the best opportunity to make as much money as possible out of Genoa's market for arms. This letter announcing the intentions of the Genoese masters does not state that the armorers had a formal guild, but in its emphasis on *all* masters adopting a certain course, it again points to the type of common action that was the rationale for a guild.

One final example of the kind of evidence notarial cartularies provide concerns the guild (*ars*) of the *batifolii*—generic metalworkers, beaters of foil, who in Genoa worked most frequently in gold. Genoa was famous for this trade; in 1205, a Walter of London contracted to work for a Genoese master.[56] An act dated 23 January 1248 reveals that the *batifolii* had a guild with officials (*consules*) and thirty-three members in the city, including a William the Englishman and several Frenchmen.[57] The agreement concerned the prohibition of night work already mentioned, and the *batifolii* prefaced their accord with the view that the ban was for the good of the trade or guild of the *batifolii*, as well as for the general advantage of the city and for maintaining and serving the law. Besides providing the trade with safer work that is more error-free, the promise not to beat foil with hammers at night was clearly to the benefit of everyone in the city. The accord directed the consuls to select four men, with the consent of the majority, who were to make sure that the members observed the prohibition. The *batifolii* reserved to themselves the right to set a penalty for anyone found working at night and held the masters responsible for their employees. This pact was enforced in the city and the district, that area of the countryside Genoa directly controlled. The guild wanted to extend its authority beyond the confines of the city and knew that the mountainous rural areas surrounding Genoa offered possible places for *batifolii* to practice their craft away from the eyes of guild officials. In Genoa, where the city government thoroughly dominated the nearby countryside, the guilds had the chance to extend their jurisdiction, but in other places, as will be seen, the countryside posed one of the most significant threats to the guild's ability to regulate urban crafts or professions.

The apprenticeship and work contracts are the most useful and numerous kinds of documents in the notarial records that reflect the behind-the-scenes activities of guilds—the marshaling of labor for specific tasks. Masters made these contracts with the employees, and when viewed in aggregate, the deals reflect both the common concerns of the masters and the realities of the market for labor. Legal traditions, in this case the laws of indentures and contracts, also shaped the kinds of agreements made. These contracts presuppose the right of free people to enter into binding arrangements, and the desire to do this was precisely the impetus that in the past brought about the rise of the commune. Parents or guardians enjoyed this right when making agreements on behalf of minors, but the principal of free entry remained in force. Marc Bloch suggested that feudalism left as one of its enduring legacies to European civilization the idea of contract and that the voluntary tie of mutual dependence between fighters would eventually dispose the entire society to value and respect contracts.[58] In this view, those who did not fit into the feudal hierarchy, the townspeople and traders, simply wanted the same personal rights enjoyed by the lords: in this case, the right to make a contract.

Roman law also supplied a coherent framework for apprenticeship and work contracts, but the connection seems a bit stretched. The body of Roman law most relevant to the guilds, the laws on colleges described in chapter 1, emphasized hereditary status and had nothing to say about the medieval idea of apprenticeship. Salatiele of Bologna, in compiling a notarial handbook, subsumed apprentices into the category of rental agreements, a close and interesting analogy.[59] He conceived that the parent or guardian might rent a child (*puer*) to a master in much the same way that someone might rent a horse—with the customary safeguards of proper care and feeding for the rented animal. Selling land was a continuous tradition from antiquity through the early Middle Ages, and presumably beasts of burden were rented as well, though without the benefit of written contract.[60] The buying and selling of human flesh, in the form of slaves, never ended either, and this method of recruiting labor had a significant impact on the apprenticeship system. Apprenticeship, however, appeared to be something new, without an appropriate model or precedent, and rental contracts offered a somewhat useful model. Two important issues to resolve concerned the renting of children. First, a uniform set of terms would not have suited the particular demands of different trades, so we should expect some variety and inquire as to whether or not these different terms result from decisions made in the guild. Second, renting or hiring a person placed a special set of obligations on the parties, and we should look carefully at the demands of this relationship, which shares elements of fostering and hence might also draw on the habits and customs of the lordly class.[61]

The records of the notaries of several cities provide the earliest examples of apprenticeship and work contracts, but significantly, the earliest cartulary to survive, that by Giovanni Scriba of Genoa from the 1150s and 1160s, containing over thirteen hundred pieces of business, has no apprenticeships and only one work contract—oddly, between brothers.[62] The oldest document resembling a work contract, redacted by an unknown notary in 1155, relies on no known models and reveals an ad hoc arrangement.[63] A certain Sergius, a physician (*medicus*), promised a certain Romualdo food, clothing, and employment for four years. Sergius agreed to place any disputed burden or injury to Romualdo before some good men who would arbitrate the matter, and he stipulated the penalty of fifty solidi if he failed to fulfill the agreement. For his part, Romualdo promised to stay for the four years, to give Sergius everything he acquired above the expenses of his service, and to serve Sergius and safeguard his goods in good faith without fraud or ill will. Romualdo accepted the same penalty, and Sergius promised him work according to his availability—presumably whether Romualdo was able or not to do certain work.

The general class of work contracts includes some domestic servants of both sexes, but in this instance Romualdo's duties go beyond what was expected from the typical servant. Sergius did not offer him any education or training, as was normally a part of later apprenticeship agreements. One might learn to be a *medicus* as an apprentice, but this was one of the three professions for which the schools and universities trained people. Since Romualdo's abilities were to regulate the degree to which he was able to participate in the work, he was likely Sergius's assistant in his medical practice. Romualdo received food and clothing, not typical features of later work contracts, but no lodging, and although the document and probably the contract itself are vague about just what Sergius offered to pay him, Romualdo probably earned something beyond his expenses. How Romualdo incurred these costs is unknown. This rudimentary work contract presents the bargain in its starkest terms. The contract fixed the period of service, set a compensation, and addressed the issue of what later documents called an "insupportable burden"—what to do if the employee recoiled in the face of a task. One reason why the parties committed these contracts to writing is that they were intended to last, and the more casual or shorter periods of service did not require the good offices of a notary. Romualdo was not the first employee in the history of Genoa, but he appears early in the written records of the city. The decision to put this contract in writing points to the increasing sense of legality in this society and a deep respect for the written word. The names in this contract, Sergius and Romualdo, were rare in Genoa, and they suggest a southern Italian origin for the pair, possibly Salerno, a city with strong medical traditions. If the two were foreigners, this might account for the written contract. Finally, Sergius agreed to place any dispute before arbiters, an unusual procedure, again with respect to later contracts. The guilds would eventually make rules to help define the proper terms of service and settle disputes about them. At this time there was no sign of a guild of physicians in Genoa, so Sergius took the traditional path of relying on arbiters.

One of the earliest surviving apprenticeship contracts from all of Europe again comes from Genoa. On 7 April 1180, a certain Giovanni apprenticed himself to Guglielmo Buscarono, turner (*tornator*), for five years.[64] Giovanni swore to stay in Guglielmo's service and to commit no fraud beyond 18 pennies a year, all under the penalty of L3 Genoese. Guglielmo promised Giovanni food, clothing, and 12 solidi a year for his salary (*feudum*)—an interesting word to use in the twelfth century to describe the pay of an apprentice turner. Most importantly, he undertook to teach Giovanni the art of being a turner and to give him some iron tools appropriate to the trade at the end of the term. The obligation to teach defines the apprenticeship contract; the long term of service is also typical. Giovanni made this agreement himself, and even though his father was still alive, he did not employ him as a guarantor of the terms or the penalty. As the apprenticeship contract became more complex, a parent, other relative, or friend assumed the role of guarantor, but in this case the form of the agreement indicates that Giovanni had reached the age of majority, at this time in Genoa eighteen years of age. Almost all subsequent apprenticeships include a promise to commit no fraud and contain, as well, the nice touch of a small sum that allowed for the vagaries of human nature. The masters seemed to close their eyes to petty pilfering or gray areas rather than to raise the accusation of theft over derisory sums. The earliest guild statutes always address the question of apprenticeships, and the apprenticeship contracts are useful when looking for the earliest indications of guild activities. These contracts, by their uniformity and terms, suggest some common decisions by masters that, if not proving the existence of a guild, at least point to a necessary precondition—the desire for some form of common action. In this case the tools point to a policy of sorts. In 1214, a master turner promised to give his apprentice all of the tools "with which he will be able to work well" ("cum quibus bone poterit laborare"), and in 1226, another master also supplied tools and a small cash sum at the end of the term.[65] Other trades had similar customs about tools, one almost invariably honored, but still other trades never included a gift of tools as part of the deal. These and other provisions suggest that masters were capable of taking common action and that they most likely had guilds. This assumption, made necessary by the absence of foundation documents and early statutes, helps to explain the orderly recruitment procedures apparent in the earliest apprenticeship contracts.

Genoa's notarial record preserves the largest number of early apprenticeship records, and the first surviving cartularies from other cities also contain apprenticeship contracts. Early guild statutes, as for example those the cotton guild of Bologna promulgated in 1288, ordered the masters to make sure that they recorded any pact with a student before a notary.[66] In addition to the legal protection afforded by a written record, these pacts also discouraged masters from stealing one another's apprentices. The earliest contract from Siena, in 1227, clearly resembles the rental agreement Salatiele described in his formulary.[67] In this contract the pupil rented himself out for two years to a locksmith in order to learn the trade.

The apprenticeship contracts contained in the earliest surviving notarial cartulary from Marseilles are also in the form of a rental agreement. The notary Almaric seems to have passed much of his time and found his clients near the tables of the money changers of Marseilles, and two of the handful of apprenticeships he drew up concern budding money changers. On 12 May 1248, Jean de St. Maximin apprenticed his son Guillaumet to Jean Cordier, and the father agreed to pay the master fifty solidi for the term of two years and also to provide a quantity of wheat for his son's board.[68] In a similar agreement, a father promised to clothe his son while the son was the pupil of another money changer.[69] On a more humble level, when Pierre Boire placed his son Etiennet with a canvasmaker, the master provided Etiennet with food, clothing, and other expenses.[70] When we look at apprenticeships in more detail, we will see that, although a common format existed for the contract, whether it was in tone a rental or a promise, the agreement still left room for individual circumstances. The Marseilles apprenticeships suggest a common theme: the more lucrative the trade, the more difficulty an outsider had placing a son or daughter within it. Hence, the terms were more favorable to the employer, at least in the short run. The canvasmaker could not expect the same sort of bargain that the more prestigious money changer could obtain.

The earliest legible apprenticeship in Montpellier comes from the cartulary of the notary Jean Grimaud.[71] In March 1294, Marie the daughter of Adalasia, with her mother consenting and cooperating, rented herself to Durante the tailor (*corduraruis*) for three years. Marie was fourteen years old and needed her mother to make this contract legal. The form of the agreement resembles the earlier rental apprenticeships from Marseilles and presumably springs from the same legal tradition. Marie placed herself *in scolarem seu discipulam*, as a student, so the emphasis was clearly on education. Marie wanted to acquire the necessary skills to be a seamstress, or her mother wanted this for her. Durante and his wife agreed to teach her the craft, feed and clothe her, and keep her in sickness or in health, and in return for all of this teaching and food, they expected one livre for at least the first year. This single contract does not provide any information on how the guild of tailors may have functioned, but it does point to the anomalous position of women in this system of labor. Durante found himself dealing with three women in this matter. His nameless wife was an active partner in his craft. Adalasia, exercising parental authority, made the decision to place her daughter in this trade and guaranteed the contract. Marie was to receive training in a craft that was most unlikely to permit her to assume the status of master tailor. Most guilds seem not to have prevented their members from taking on female apprentices, despite the potential problems of mature women exercising their skills without being a member of the guild. In some cases women had official status, either as widows or mistresses in their own right, but for someone like Marie, the status of day laborer or wife to another tailor was the highest position she was likely to achieve.

The earliest surviving apprenticeship contract from Tournai in Flanders is dated 1264, and the document displays some distinctive features of northern notarial practices.[72] Written in Old French, this contract, as well as the subsequent ones, took the form of a chirograph—one medieval method of producing two (or more) legal copies. The notary wrote the copies seriatim and then cut across some common words or symbols to indicate authentic copies. In Tournai, the city government in 1280 had banned all guilds and confraternities among the artisans.[73] This rule had unknown consequences in the city, but the effort was typical behavior by the patriciate, which did not like métiers. An apprenticeship contract for a weaver in 1288 reveals that the terms were set "according to the use and custom of the métier"—a sign that, even when a formal guild did not exist, the trade itself still had certain traditions that the masters observed.[74] Artisan guilds in Flanders had a troubled history, and many of these contracts prove that apprenticeship could exist, because of its advantages, without the benefit of a guild. In the first contract, the master promised to take care of the apprentice "like his own child," and this type of obligation, as well as the contract itself and its legal ramifications, provided some of the same reasons for trust between the parents and a master that a guild statute on the subject might also have provided.[75] But in Tournai, as will be seen in chapter 5, the artisans would literally have to fight for their guilds.

A final example of an apprenticeship is from the Venetian colony on the island of Crete, and even in this distant area of medieval culture, the idea of contract had set deep roots. In 1271, Folco Trevisan placed his son with Viviano Penna the tailor for four years in order that his son learn the art.[76] Viviano was to feed, clothe, and shoe his apprentice, but Folco agreed to supply the tailor with a quantity of grain for the term. The document does not suggest that the tailors of Crete had a guild, and certainly the apprenticeship system could exist without one. The contract contained a sizable penalty clause, and both parties had copies made, a highly unusual request to the notary Pietro Scardon. Since the law enforced contracts like this one by compelling payment of penalties, apprenticeship was able to thrive without a guild. In places where only a few craftsmen or professionals pursued their avocations, there would be few students and no need for an elaborate structure of self-protection.

The work contracts comprise the most ubiquitous and diverse category of notarial acts. Wherever records of private business survive, some signs of work for hire exist among the other types of business. This basic type of contract provided for the exchange of a service for some kind of remuneration and also stipulated a penalty if one of the parties did not fulfill the terms. Older than the guild or the apprenticeship system, the work contract existed in oral form for centuries before the first one appeared in writing. These contracts evoke all of the different kinds of work, and for present purposes their significance rests in the ways these contracts begin to coalesce around practices or patterns of behavior that indicate the common decisions of employers or the rules of guilds. Most of the urban work contracts were agreements between masters and journeymen and -women—that group of former apprentices without the experience or capital to set up shops of their own. Since apprenticeship determined the eventual number and quality of journeymen and -women, the guilds were interested in the number of apprentices of a master and their terms of service. Journeymen, though excluded from full or even partial membership in a guild, were also the subjects of debate and legislation. The ways in which masters treated their journeymen reveal something about a guild in that critical period before the first set of surviving statutes. How a work contract might make some overt reference to a common pattern has already been seen in the case of the customs of the woolworkers of Genoa. General patterns of behavior are more interesting and only become apparent when a sufficient number of work contracts exist to make examining them in aggregate useful.

In the early period under review here, few collections of work contracts are substantial enough to warrant investigation, so once again the Genoese records provide a rare glimpse of this kind of contract. The contracts for woolcarders demonstrate a pattern; from one of the earliest in 1203 through those of the thirteenth century, all of the employers paid by the piece and never by the day.[77] Woolcarding was difficult and tedious work with little social prestige, but there is no inherent reason why the carders received so consistent a form of pay. The members of the wool guild, the *lanerii*, were the most frequent employers of the carders and had a clear standard of a given number of pennies per pound of carded wool. The output was easy to measure, and the trade had one of the more objective indices of output. But this fact alone cannot account for consistent pay, since the dyers, also dealing in discrete units of production, almost always received a set salary for a term of service and not a daily or piece-rate wage.[78] Dyers made more money than carders, and because their work either added considerably to the value of the cloth or had the potential to ruin it, their skills commanded more in the labor market. The woolcarders were not in an enviable bargaining position, and perhaps this accounts for why they always received piece-rate wages—presumably the least desirable form of remuneration. Since they always worked for the same form of wages, more than market forces may have been at work; otherwise, some variation in the form of wages would have occurred. A strong force of custom was governing the way employers paid carders. These market customs may reflect rules of the *lanerii*, but even if they do not, these are precisely the kinds of forces that encouraged people in the same line of work to cooperate in the first place. The work contracts, the subject of further examination below, demonstrate that the market for labor had an order, in part imposed by guild statutes, but also reflecting the pervasive tendency to survive new market conditions by relying on tradition, in this case the ingrained habit of conforming to common practices.

Statutes and Early Guilds

For reasons that concern how members of guilds used and preserved their regulations, the statutes are generally not the best means
to use in establishing the origins of guilds. For example, the earliest
statutes of the dyers' guild in Genoa date from 1426, and many cities
only preserved the latest or last redaction of the statutes.[79] A few cities,
most notably Bologna, London, Paris, and some French towns, have
old thirteenth-century statutes that are close to, and in some cases are,
the first set of rules. From the fourteenth century a considerable number of statutes, mostly in the vernacular, as well as particular ordinances or complete statutes for English and German guilds, exist. The
same phenomenon occurred in southern Europe as trades abandoned
the Latin language for French and Italian. In Italy, the cycle completed
itself when in the fifteenth century some guilds recorded their laws in
good Renaissance-Latin style. Primordial rules and ancient traditions
are embedded even in late statutes, but in the absence of explicit
statements about particular old customs, the only way to establish
these layers of practice is to find other documents that prove certain
customs to be older than the given set of statutes. These statutes were
not self-conscious historical documents, and their framers did not
pause to provide a resume of their craft's history.

Jurists, however, did comment extensively on the guilds and their
place in legal systems. The Roman law on colleges, as indicated by
Justinian's legislation, subordinated the guilds to the larger interests of
the state. Where a knowledge of Roman law remained alive or where it
suited the purposes of secular rulers to revive it, the guilds of the
twelfth and thirteenth centuries could have found themselves in the
unenviable position of late Roman colleges—if any secular ruler or arm
of government was capable of enforcing its rights in Roman law. The
communal statutes of Milan, redacted in 1216 and among the earliest in
Europe, reflect the deep influence of Roman law and the wide scope of
authority that the consuls of the commune arrogated to themselves.
The commune, however, recognized even by this early date that the
merchants and their consuls had special customs that had been observed in Milan since "ancient times."[80] The merchants emerge from
these statutes as a strong force in Milan, and the commune above all
wanted to remain at peace with them. This concord rested on the
commune's promise to leave the merchants undisturbed in their proper
sphere of business. The consuls of the commune relied on their mer-

chant colleagues to regulate weights and measures and to enforce good conduct in the marketplace. They did not, however, concede to the consuls of the merchants any status as officials of the commune, nor did they tolerate any interference in the exercise of their own offices. This compromise between a guild and the city government reflects the usual way communes, whose officials were often themselves prominent members of important local guilds, stepped away from completely subsuming the guilds into some grander concept of government on the Roman model. Quentin Skinner has demonstrated that the teachers and commentators on Roman law, particularly Bartolo of Sassoferrato, elaborated a theory of sovereignty that permitted communes to exercise the authority of a Roman emperor.[81] This Roman sovereignty had lapsed and therefore might appropriately devolve upon lesser jurisdictions. Responsibility for the economy was part of this ancient concept of sovereignty, and Gouron has shown in some cases in Languedoc that communes did take up part of this role. Most medieval guilds did not become creatures of the state, but their degree of independence required an intellectual framework that supported their right to have private associations. The masters forming guilds wanted more than the right to have a club; they needed what the Milanese commune conceded, a jurisdiction entailing some scope for statutes—a kind of private law.

Guilds found canon lawyers to be unexpected but strong allies in defending the legitimacy of corporate status. Antony Black has carefully explored the connection between guilds and what he terms civil society, and his search of canon law texts has turned up several important lines of reasoning put forward by canon lawyers and commentators on Roman law in support of the right of guilds to self-incorporate.[82] Black is surprised that one of the most eminent canon lawyers of the thirteenth century, Sinibaldo Fieschi, Pope Innocent IV, was one of the strongest advocates of the rights of guilds. This pope, from the Fieschi of Lavanga on the Italian Riviera, came from a family long active in Genoese business and politics, and he understood the realities of urban economics and once depended, as previously discussed, on the active intervention of merchants and seamen to save his life.[83] Innocent IV, as Black notes, wrote that "it seems that men in any profession (such as grammar), or business (such as food suppliers), or office (such as bakers), can come together and set up their own ruler or syndic and common chest by their own authority if they wish, provided they enter partnership or form a college for some cause."[84] This cause rested on the moral right that the craftsmen and professionals had to pursue justice, which in their case meant the right to protect their self-interest by collective means.[85]

Innocent IV's idea that they had the right to do this by their own authority was not the view of those early guilds who took themselves to some higher authority for a charter; nor was it a generally accepted legal opinion in the thirteenth century. The clergy had reasons of their own for defending private associations and liberties that did not flow down from the state or secular authority. The common law claims that some guilds made to support their right of self-incorporation did not overawe the communes. Jurisprudence lent its voice, in a small way, to defending the guild as a spontaneous institution, and by legitimizing self-interest as somehow just, some jurists provided a counterargument against those who claimed that self-interest was base and often harmed a more noble common good. Guildsmen had their own reasons for forming guilds and promulgating statutes, and though they did not often preface their rules with grandiose justifications, the statutes reveal some assumptions that offer another perspective on why the institution of the guild was created.

The guild statutes from Bologna derive from a number of different trades and date from the middle of the thirteenth century. Bologna, the home of the oldest and most prestigious law school in Europe, was also a center for the notarial profession, and many learned legal commentaries and formularies came from the pens of scholars active in the city. The members of guilds turned to lawyers and notaries for help in making laws, and the commune took an interest in these groups as well. These early statutes conform to no prescribed pattern; the statutes begin with various issues that seem to have been the major concerns of particular trades. The statutes of the tailors' guild (in Bologna called a *societas*) are typical specimens of the genre. The members of the guild made these rules in the church of Santa Croce in 1244. Then their consuls, four in number, put them in proper form, and their notary translated them into a businesslike Latin not on the lips of the tailors of Bologna.[86] By the end of this process, the final product was quite remote from the original discussions, and the statutes do not reveal the authentic voice of the tailors.

First, the tailors set up their administrative structure, in this case the four consuls, and then they set out an elaborate oath that all of the members would take to obey the rules and the consuls. The oath made clear that the statutes and consuls of the commune of Bologna took precedence over any rules or officials of the guild. The statutes regulated the kinds of commercial relations that the tailors had among themselves and set some rules on employing journeymen (*laboratori*) and apprentices (*discipuli*). If the apprentice was less than ten years old, the term had to be at least five years; if more than ten, three years. The statutes prohibited various types of injuries, financial and physical, that masters might commit against one another or their employees. The masters agreed to keep these rules for five years, and only longer if that were the wish of the majority; this interesting feature allowed for changes in the statutes and probably reflects the old idea that these agreements on procedures were not necessarily permanent. The consuls had the right and the duty to require anyone who was doing the work of a tailor in Bologna or the suburbs to join the guild. A newcomer had to pay an entry fine of ten solidi and put on a meal for the guild officers—but the son, brother, or nephew of a member paid no entry fine. No tailor who was a member of the merchants' or furriers' guild could serve as an official or advisor to the tailors' guild because, in the words of the statutes, "there was discord between the guilds of merchants and furriers and the guild of tailors."[87] The masters agreed to a list of feast days on which they did not work and set up a common place, presumably a block of shops in a neighborhood, where the tailors could work and keep an eye on each other.

This cursory examination of these statutes reveals some of the major concerns of the tailors, and all of these regulations point to why the tailors benefited from having a guild. Exactly when the tailors first established their guild is not clear; this set of statutes does not betray any signs of novelty or innovation and is not the first set of rules. These statutes highlight tensions present in Bologna and other cities. The guild of merchants, the wealthy long-distance traders who did not disdain local wholesale and retail business, posed an economic threat to the tailors, since some of the merchants imported cloth and clothing into the city. The merchants probably did not look with favor on the tailors' guild. Relations with the furriers' guild seem to have been no more amicable, and only a fine line separated the production of fur or fur-lined or -trimmed garments and the tailors' stitching of wool and cotton clothing. The interests of these two guilds overlapped. The commune, always solicitous toward the merchants, made sure that the tailors recognized that they always remained under its authority. The master tailors also faced some difficulties from below, hence the great deal of attention paid to recruitment policies. Few of the apprentices and journeymen not related to current masters would ever acquire enough capital to open their own shops, even though tailoring was not as capital intensive as some other types of manufacturing. As early as 1244 the tailors' guild was already giving preference to relatives of members; in future years, as the pace of the medieval economic boom slackened, guilds would increasingly turn to methods of limiting access to crafts. The most important feature of these statutes is that the tailors had the right to compel membership in their guild. None of the other provisions would work well if some tailors remained outside the fold. The ability to draft members does not conform to the view of guilds as private associations; the modest level of legal thought devoted to the theory of private groups does not seem to sanction this important privilege. Here again, the questions of public interest and the rights of the commune surface, and in Bologna with its international reputation for legal studies, lawyers knew that only a public authority, in this case the commune, could empower the guilds in this way. The *lanerii* of Genoa met to make a rule and then sought out other wool manufacturers to convince them to join in the agreement. The tailors of Bologna had the ultimate economic weapon—a monopoly.

A brief summary of certain features found in the statutes of the blacksmiths, or workers in iron (*fabri*), indicates some useful comparisons between these statutes and those of the tailors.[88] The blacksmiths made their statutes in 1252, and the initial ordinances prohibited members from injuring fellow smiths, their shops, work, employees, and apprentices. It was also illegal, except under limited conditions, for members to help smiths outside the guild, either by giving or renting them tools or by working with them. The masters were allowed to employ workers outside the guild for a period of up to four months, but after that the *laboratores* had to join the guild, or else no master could employ them. This rule also applied to apprentices. The masters were free to pay their workers any wage. The guildsmen made sure that the various parts of the craft were represented among the officials, and these rules reveal that makers of razors, knives, pots, and larger iron items were included in the general category of *fabri*. (The members agreed that none of them would make keys or burglar tools.)

The officials of the guild (*ministrales*) had various duties and rewards, but their special tasks were to control entry into the guild and to keep a list of apprentices of all masters. New members had to pay twenty solidi to join the guild; sons of members entered for free. The officials were to have a mass sung on the first Sunday of every month, as was the custom of the guild, to benefit the souls of the members. (This religious observance indicates that the guild was older than this set of statutes.) If anyone had more charcoal than he or she needed, it was to be sold only to members of the guild, at a fixed price, and no one was to purchase more than the work required. Apprentices were obligated to give the master quantities of wine and grain in the first five years of the term and a yearly ration of meat (*amisscere*). The master in turn supplied clothing and shoes to the apprentice for seven years. No master was to have more than two apprentices, and no master was permitted to own a slave. All of the masters had to put their sons in the guild at age fourteen, under penalty of a fine. The statutes do not explicitly state which members of the guild participated in the election of its officials; these laws required the *ministrales* to have resided in the city for ten years before their election.

The distinctive feature of these statutes is the inclusive nature of the guild. The masters wanted everyone to join the guild, but whether or not they extended any real power to their laborers and apprentices is not clear.[89] The masters devised their own method of forcing people into the guild; by means of their four-month rule, they made working for long outside the guild impossible. No legal power compelled workers to join—the masters relied on their own weight as employers to enforce the rule. In common with the other guilds in Bologna and elsewhere, the masters used a system of fines to enforce their rules. Collecting these fines depended on the ability of city officials to coerce people, and the common interest in fines provided guilds and communes with another reason to cooperate. Metalworkers outside the guild seem to have hampered the guild's ability to monopolize the local market, hence the necessary prohibition against renting tools to outsiders. Two features of the statutes relate to the specific circumstances of the metalworking trade. The rules about charcoal point to the vital role fuel played in their work, and the guild made an effort to ensure that no one hoarded charcoal or manipulated the market for personal advantage. The simple ban against owning a slave masks what must have been a complicated and difficult aspect of recruiting labor—the ready availability of slaves in the thirteenth-century Mediterranean world.[90] The metalworking trades involved a fair amount of heavy, dirty work, and for some masters a slave might have appeared to be the easiest solution to the problem. The guild's prohibition meant in practice that the masters agreed to rely upon free labor to meet their requirements, and some must have recognized that employing slaves would have disrupted the system and perhaps given an unfair advantage to those with the money to buy a number of slaves. The guild did not distinguish slaves as craftsmen from slaves as domestic servants; the ban was absolute. Slavery represented, at least in potential, a serious challenge to master craftsmen, since it added a new dimension to the problem of how to regulate competition among themselves. From the point of view of the ordinary workers, slavery spelled unemployment and no hope for economic advancement. The Mediterranean region teemed with potential slaves and eager purveyors of human beings, and a guild prohibition did not end the challenge.

The early guild statutes from northern Europe provide another perspective on the earliest guilds. At the same time that the Italians codified their rules and laws, their contemporaries in Cologne, London, and Chartres also produced statutes that suggest, as do the Italian examples, that the guilds were already in existence before the statutes appeared. These statutes reveal some distinctive features of the northern guilds and also some broad areas of parallel development. The economic benefits of cooperation existed in northern European cities as well as in the south, and there is no reason to look south for models of guild structures.[91] The artisans of Chartres or London were capable of responding to the challenges of competition and a commercial revolution by strategies of their own devising.

The statutes of the clothiers (*pannatores*) of Cologne, redacted in 1247, are one of the earliest sets of comprehensive statutes to survive in northern Europe.[92] These retailers of cloth called themselves *fratres* (brothers) and collectively a *fraternitas* (brotherhood), and the later statutes of the guild used the vernacular *bruderschaft* as the exact equivalent of the Latin term. These words already had a long history in northern Europe, and since religious confraternities used the same terms to describe their groups, the northern guilds require a close look in order to distinguish them from associations with a purely or predominantly spiritual purpose. The clothiers of Cologne did not include in this document any common religious observances, not even the standard feast days or the obligation to attend funerals. Probably the brothers observed these practices, but the impetus behind the statutes did not involve these matters. The clothiers recognized that they had the power to regulate their trades by the authority of the city government of Cologne.[93] Their principal concern, as the statutes state, was to control the guild's membership. New clothiers had to pay two marks to join, but only one mark if a father had been a member. The guild was an alliance of various trades—brothers were mainly cutters of whole cloth, with smaller subgroups of those who made linen (*linwatmengre*), those who cut clothing (tailors), and those who sold whole cloth. The brothers wanted the tailors to practice their craft in a specific location, and tailors were allowed to join for one mark, or for free if the father was a member.

The most important feature of the statutes was the rule that the brothers should only buy and sell among themselves. Since the guild was in effect a combine of the entire cloth industry, the rule effectively shut out anyone in Cologne who hoped to enter the business without joining the guild. The tailors had to buy cloth from their brother cloth-iers, who in turn found their only market among the tailors. By conced-ing the guild this privilege, the city government gave the brothers the desired monopoly, and since the members simply enforced their rule by their exclusive business practices, the statutes do not mention any fines for failure to comply with this provision. Presumably no brother would ever do business with one who broke rank. The officials of the guild, the *domini*, had the power to admit any citizen or guest of the fraternity to the privileges of membership. One sign of how the city government regulated this guild is the provision that no brother was to bring to the court of the guild any outsider who was not nor had ever been a brother. If a member violated this rule, that member had to provide the officials with a quantity of wine. The framers of the statutes used the words *ex antiqua constitucione* to place this rule in the guild's distant past, and thus the statutes suggest, as they usually do, that the guild was older than the rules at hand.[94] The members established rules by which they dealt with debts among the brothers, and they included in these statutes a list of the various brothers engaged at the time in several crafts—clothiers (56); linenmixers (23); tailors (22); sellers of whole cloth (23); others, listed by their names, the guests and citizens associated with the guild; and the brothers called "Schorren." This last category included some obvious foreigners like Jean of Flanders and Lambert of Brussels.[95] This guild had no women members and pre-sumably did not permit widows to participate in the business of their late husbands, an assumption based on the large sample of names included in the statutes and the likelihood of some widows of members being in Cologne.

The *Liber Custumarum* contains a wealth of documents about the social and economic life of London in the thirteenth and fourteenth centuries and includes a number of ordinances that the mayor and aldermen conceded to various crafts. One early and fairly typical set of ordinances is the Articles of the Cappers from 1270, with one amendment made in the early years of the reign of Edward II.[96] A useful aspect of these statutes is the additive nature of the revisions; this method of amplifying or changing existing intentions preserves both the original language and subsequent emendations. These ordinances took the form of concessions from the city government, in this case in the public forum of the London hustings, and the city retained through its bailiffs the right to enforce the rules. The cappers did not win the right to have their own court, and the city officials seem to have been primarily interested in protecting the consumers from fraudulent practices the cappers might commit. The craft received the most minute attention: caps were to be black, gray, or white, and the latter two colors were not to be dyed black, since the deception was great and rain caused the black dye to run. (A later rule suggests that the black dye might have been charcoal, hence its impermanence.) The city government banned night work with the unusual observation that such a prohibition was intended to benefit the many poor members of the craft.[97] The statute offers no explanation as to how this provision helped the poor cappers. Perhaps since the statute emphasizes the number of poor members, keeping the better-off members from working at night might have meant more work for the others. The ordinances also prohibited members from taking another's servant without permission; in effect this rule sanctioned the apprenticeship system. The cappers were permitted to have six officials to make sure that the members observed these ordinances, and the guild was to pay the commune of London half a mark per year.

In the early fourteenth century, the mayor and aldermen again turned their attention to the plight of the cappers. Once more the problem was caps of low quality made from scrap wool, but the real issue was the merchants from Germany who were importing "false caps" from overseas "to the greatest detriment of the people of the whole kingdom."[98] These foreign merchants were injuring both the wholesalers of caps and the cappers, presumably because the imported caps were priced low and outsold well-made London ones. The mayor and aldermen ordered the foreign merchants to withdraw their caps from all of the markets in the kingdom and to offer security for any future breach of this ban. Merchants in London had to take these caps off the market, or the city government would burn them. Anyone in the future who made such caps would face a fine and the burning of the caps.

Both the original ordinance and this addition raise the question of why the mayor and aldermen of London found it necessary to involve themselves in the business of the cappers. This particular trade represents an advanced division of labor, in the sense that the cappers were not among the first group of artisans to have guilds. This trade is not a trivial one, but it depended on a sufficient market and what modern economists call disposable income. The sources do not indicate whether the cappers themselves or the government instigated the ordinances; the emphasis on fraud might suggest a government intending to protect customers, but it might equally suggest a group of cappers attempting to safeguard the reputation of their products. The same reasoning holds for the later amendments, though the cappers were more likely to bring the threat of foreign competition to the notice of city officials. On balance, this guild made no claims to old customs, and the ordinances of 1270 might reveal the way this guild was formed. The ordinances named the first set of six officials and gave them the right to choose their successors, another sign that these six may have been the first. Even in this case, where the strong possibility exists that the ordinances come from the earliest days of the guild, the rules are not a good source for proving this assumption. These ordinances also raise the question of the role played by foreign competition in the early days of the guild. By the time the cappers complained about German caps, the growth of trade in the North Sea and Baltic region had been vigorous for at least a century, so this competition did not influence, in this case, the decision to create a guild.

The final example of an early guild statute comes from Chartres, a city in north-central France that the counts of Blois and Chartres considered to be thoroughly in their hands. Chartres was a market town of some importance and a center of the wool industry. Chartres seems typical of the many towns in this region that were not destined to rival Paris or Bruges but nevertheless enjoyed a period of prosperity before the difficult years of the mid-fourteenth century. Chartres was, like London, part of the commercial network of northern Europe, but it was also tied directly to the Mediterranean world because of the cloth trade and the city's position near the important fairs of Champagne. The oldest sign of a guild in Chartres is contained in a charter that Count Thibaut IV issued to the innkeepers in 1147 before he departed on the Second Crusade. At this early date the innkeepers had a chief official (*magister*), and the count stated that he had established their corporate status, presumably at some previous date.[99] Count Thibaut ordered the innkeepers to give up their annual feast and instead donate the money to lepers; he may have been thinking about his spiritual state and the level of piety in Chartres before risking his life in the East. This charter provides no other details on how innkeepers functioned as a unit, and it addresses them by their occupation and supplies no term for their collectivity.

In 1268, Count Jean de Châtillon issued, at the request of the drapers' guild (called *le bourgeoisie de la rivière*), a general confirmation of privileges that his predecessors back to 1214 had granted the drapers. The count also relied upon the evidence of old men as well as old charters to pull together a general list of rules for the drapers.[100] So far as the document reveals, the count was the dominant force in Chartres, and these privileges resulted from an act of grace on his part. The twelve sworn-in officials of the guild of drapers exercised authority over the four principal trades (*métiers*)—the combers and carders (*archonneurs*), the weavers (*tessiers*), the makers and/or finishers of woolens (*laneurs*), and the dyers (*tainteurs*)—and had a measure of control over the fullers and the carters who conveyed cloth to the mills. The ordinances prohibited any of these trades from forming their own community in Chartres without the assent or command of the count. This rule enforced a broad and vertical guild that included all of the important aspects of production, and it also confirmed how involved the count and his official in Chartres, the chatelain, were in the city's economic affairs.

The most interesting features of these ordinances are the easy entry to the trades and the absence of overt compulsion. Anyone could join the guild, and perhaps more importantly, anyone could become an apprentice upon paying a modest fee, two deniers, for wine for the members (*compaignons*).[101] The ordinances compelled no one to join the guild, but the general tenor of the rules suggests that participation in the cloth business while remaining apart from the guild would be impossible. A concern for quality of cloth permeates the rules, and above all the drapers wanted the reputation of Chartres cloth to remain high. An elaborate system of fines awaited anyone who sold substandard cloth. The easiest way for any weaver or dyer to make sure that one's work met the local mark of quality was to be a member of the guild in good standing. An inferior product was not allowed to be sold as the cloth of Chartres. The provision for public sale in a fixed spot guaranteed that passing off bad cloth would be difficult, and anyone violating the standards would come under the count's authority.

These ordinances reveal that the guild was already old in 1268 and that the alliance of trades was no longer among equals; the dyers in particular seem to have been in a slightly subordinate position to the rest. Since the ordinances made no provision for choosing the twelve officials, the count or his deputy may have appointed them. Where a strong central authority existed, in this case a feudal lord, and not a town council of fellow merchants, the guild depended on the pleasure of that authority. The drapers were not powerless in the face of the count; they were after all the main source of wealth in the region. In this guild, the burdens and benefits of membership seem less extreme than in the Bolognese examples. This guild remained purposefully open to newcomers, *sanz contredit des autres*, while still allowing a slight advantage to the sons and daughters of current or past members. The guild also anticipated that both men and women might rise to the status of master (*mestre ou mestresse*).[102] The count created a system of fines and placed his own authority behind enforcing the rules. These ordinances placed considerable importance on the oath that the members took upon entrance. In large part the oath itself was the main burden of membership, because this guild relied heavily on that oath to compel adherence to the rules. The ordinances gave the drapers a subtle monopoly, not by restricting membership or raw materials, but by giving the drapers a high standard of quality and the power to enforce it. The count as well as the drapers of Chartres knew that the Italians coming to the fairs of Champagne valued cloth by the town of its origin, and the common interest in having a fine reputation in the marketplace was in turn the significant benefit the drapers derived from their association.

The Humiliati

The medieval guild thrived in the economic and social circumstances that resulted from the increased prosperity of the central Middle Ages. The exact chain of events that led to the formation of a guild is often difficult to determine. The guilds were not the only popular response to increased wealth and trade, and in some of the other movements, glimpses can be found of the motives behind the decision to form a guild, as well as criticism, tacit or overt, of the guild system. The great age of journeymen protests and blatant attacks on guilds by varying social groups lay in the fourteenth century. At the time that guilds came into existence in the twelfth century, those who objected to them were usually critics of broader trends—as in the case of writers who attacked greed, avarice, the mercantile life, a surly peasantry, or grubby craftsmen who did not know their place. These writers did not care whether or not the merchants or cobblers had guilds but simply that the old social order faced challenges from these upstarts. Alexander Murray has looked carefully at social risers, their self-justification, and the ways the nobility found to defend, among other things, "a high class monopoly of church office" against the claims of merit.[103] Social and economic mobility had its defenders and detractors; wage labor occupied an ambiguous position, since it solidified the gains of the masters while it seemed to erect formidable obstacles to others who had the modest ambition to improve their situation. Those most likely to object to guilds, the journeymen and -women and apprentices, did not often find their way into medieval records, and only in the late fourteenth century are their views expressed and recorded.[104] When the masters began to close ranks around their children and relatives as special candidates for guild membership and when the capital requirements for operating an independent business were beyond the means of the hardest-working journeymen, the apprentices and day laborers became discontented with the guild. For the earlier period, the best way to find those who did not favor guilds or who wanted some way to combat guild influence is to look for a group that had different members and tried to organize and regulate production on some level. The Italian scholar Luigi Zanoni thought he found such a group in the Humiliati, and the case is worth reexamining in order to see how the same set of economic conditions was able to evoke a different response, one that posed a serious challenge to the wool guilds of northern Italy.

The Humiliati were a religious movement that Lester Little includes with the Waldensians, Beguines, and Cathars as one of the popular groups that responded to the threat that the new profit economy of the twelfth century posed to traditional spiritual values and practices.[105] These humble people appeared in various Italian towns, first around Milan, in the second half of the twelfth century. Their long history in which they moved from a fringe group with the taint of heresy to a perfectly respectable religious order in the medieval church is not a concern here; the significance of the Humiliati rests in the way they chose to support themselves. Some Humiliati, the first order, were priests; the second order lived in common with a vow and an informal rule; and others, the third order, were members of the laity, still married or with family commitments, who did not live in common but observed certain rules and injunctions.[106] Since poverty or at least the absence of ostentatious living was one of the main goals of the Humiliati, they chose to work for a living. Their communities were urban, so they took up what work was at hand, in their case the weaving of cheap wool or wool- and cotton-blend cloths. This business offered the Humiliati some advantages; the Italian towns were a ready market for inexpensive cloth, weaving could be done in small groups or at home where some Humiliati always remained, and weaving was an easily transportable skill that could be practiced anywhere.

The two drawbacks that the Humiliati faced were acquiring and paying for adequate supplies of raw wool in an area not noted for sheep rearing and, of course, the competition from the wool guilds and workers in the various towns. Zanoni found that the bulk of the Humiliati came from the ranks of the manual workers and not from the entrepreneurs of the wool guilds.[107] Herbert Grundmann challenges this view. He cites Jacques de Vitry's observation that the Humiliati clergy and laity were almost all literate; hence their members were not likely to be from the lower classes of urban society.[108] At the present time no answer exists to the question, Who were the original Humiliati? The one certainty remains that this urban religious movement was from its earliest stages associated with the wool-cloth industry. People from different social groups had their own reasons for participating—the appeal of voluntary poverty struck a responsive chord in all groups above the level of the involuntarily poor, the paupers. So perhaps, as well as the unquestioned religious impulses of some weavers who became Humiliati, the desire to chart an independent economic course motivated members of the group.[109]

Not all of the Humiliati were weavers, and ultimately this movement never posed much of a threat to the powerful Italian guilds. The Humiliati first appeared at roughly the same time as the earliest wool guilds, and Grundmann concludes from this that it was simply too soon to see in the Humiliati signs of worker protest, since the humble weavers could have no idea what the development of the wool industry had in store for them.[110] Weavers without capital soon figured out what their long-term ties were to the entrepreneurs in the nascent wool industry. As a group, the Humiliati had to establish some kind of relationship to the official church, the commune, and the guilds. The Humiliati did manage to obtain formal recognition from Pope Innocent III in 1201.[111] The fact that they supported themselves through the cloth industry was not so unusual; various Cistercian houses in the north actively produced raw wool, and monasteries throughout Europe had a reputation as centers of weaving. The Humiliati, however, needed capital, and this requirement was met. Where the Humiliati found their resources is difficult to say; some brothers and sisters may have brought wealth with them to the order. Pious donations and testamentary legacies may also have been helpful.

Two wills bring to life the world of the Humiliati and their place in the commercial economy. The testament of Giovanni de Vilmercato, *lanerius*, supplies a first step into the third order and the circle of people who lived and worked there. Brother Giovanni, as he styled himself, made his will near vespers on 20 August 1244.[112] He left one lira for his soul and charged his wife, Sofia, and Brother Anselmo, prior of a Humiliati house of the second order, to use most of the money for his funeral. The longest portion of the will describes Giovanni's business affairs and debts and provides a snapshot of a humble artisan's life. As guardian for two sets of heirs, he acknowledged that he had L22 belonging to Lanfranchino, the son of the late Giovanni the furrier, and L7s.10 belonging to the children of the late Maffeo. Giovanni's other debts, amounting to L5s.8d.7, were mostly to fellow *lanerii* (including Brother Anselmo) or to members of the closely allied craft of dyers. It is unusual that no one seems to have owed Giovanni anything. These accounts represent the state of his business at that time, and two features merit attention. First, to be a guardian was an honorable responsibility and a token of someone's esteem, and two men trusted Giovanni to perform this sensitive task. Second, the sums Giovanni had in trust comprised the greater part of his capital, and presumably he was putting this money to work in his wool business on behalf of the wards.

Giovanni named his wife, Sofia, as principal heir to the estate. Unfortunately, the amount Sofia received is unknown. The will reveals, however, that the couple had no living children, and the absence of masses for the souls of deceased offspring suggests that they never had children. Perhaps they lived in a chaste marriage in the style of some Humiliati. On 3 March 1247, Sofia, called the wife of the late Giovanni, made her own will.[113] The widow's statements provide a rare glimpse into a family and its work over time. More importantly, Sofia was as free as a woman in the thirteenth century could be—a widow with no trace of a living father, father-in-law, brother, or son. Sofia's last will should therefore express her own desires.

The will confirms Sofia's continuing activity in the wool business. One Bergamo had L26 in a *commenda* contract with her. This investment required Bergamo to use the capital for a time and then return it to Sofia along with one-quarter of the profit. Sofia noted that L8s.13 of this money belonged to the heirs of the late Brother Maffeo and that she wanted them to have it. Thus this Maffeo was a fellow member of the third order, and Sofia remained responsible for the children. The L8 of 1244 was in 1247 only L8s.13, a poor rate of return, but most likely the heirs had drawn out some of the money along the way for their maintenance. Sofia left her apprentice Guglielmino all of her household goods and implements and many tools of her craft. For a woman in Genoa to have an apprentice of either sex was rare, and rarer still to have a male for a pupil.[114] Sofia was presumably teaching Guglielmino how to weave. Sofia also had a skill worth passing on to the next generation, and she worked and managed her own affairs well enough to leave behind a debt (only 13 solidi) considerably smaller than her husband's. The principal heirs to the estate were her sisters Giovanna and Agnesia, and they counted on the money invested with Bergamo as their main inheritance. Sofia did not mention any nieces or nephews in her will and, as significant, no brother-in-law either. These three women were all apparently childless and supporting themselves as contract weavers in their own homes, and at least Sofia had a strong tie to the Humiliati. They were remarkable people in any age, especially in the thirteenth century.

Giovanni and Sofia may be placed in a broader context by looking at their fellow *lanerii* in order to see how lay members of the third order fit into the emerging guild system in Genoa. First, the inventory of the estate of Maffeo the *lanerius* happens to exist, and back on 27 February 1238, Giovanni had appeared before a notary and accounted for the property of his late friend.[115] Maffeo owned his own home (Giovanni and Sofia did not) but not the land under it, and he seems to have had the usual possessions of a modest household, among which were assorted kitchen utensils, bedding, two shirts, and four chickens. The guardian of the children recorded no cash or documents in the house, items that often appear in inventories. Giovanni, however, ended up as custodian for what amounted to L7s.10 in 1244, money perhaps derived from the sale of Maffeo's wool and looms. If an inventory of

Giovanni's estate were available, it would resemble Maffeo's except that Giovanni and Sofia seem always to have lived in rented housing. As Zanoni suspected, these Humiliati were not wealthy entrepreneurs in the wool industry; they were instead people of modest means living by working in their homes at a loom, their most expensive possession.

In order for the Humiliati to remain in the wool business and not be journeymen, they needed capital, access to wool, and markets for their products. They met these requirements and soon were able to raise capital in the same manner as their secular competitors did. On 27 April 1235, Brother Anselmo, prior of the house of the Genoese Humiliati in Murtedo, acknowledged that he had in a partnership (*societas*) with Gisla, the wet nurse (*mama*) of Simonetto Guercio, the sum of L22.[116] The Humiliati had the use of this money for one year and the right to keep three-quarters of the profit, with the other quarter reserved for Gisla. The normal *societas* required both parties to put up capital and divided profits according to proportion of capital invested, with an extra portion to the party who actually did the work. In this case the Humiliati acquired capital in a favorable way and presumably put the money to good use with the house's cloth manufacturers. Gisla was not a distinguished or wealthy member of Genoese society; she owed what she had to nursing a member of one of the city's most prominent families. Gisla might have derived some comfort from the spiritual merit attached to her investment, and the brothers did not shy away from the necessity of making a profit. The ordinary weavers must have been alarmed at the prospect of competing with the austere sisters and brothers in producing cloth, let alone the more attractive terms than they could manage in which the Humiliati raised money.

In Genoa the people in the wool industry were beginning to think of themselves as a trade, and they were taking the first steps toward forming a guild. About sixty people had subscribed to the compacts of 1244 not to work at night, yet none of them figured in the circle close to Giovanni and Sofia. Perhaps the Humiliati of the third order were not willing to promise, an act resembling an oath and hence one they denied themselves. Those agreeing not to work at night did not comprise the entire wool trade in Genoa, but they did represent the nucleus of it in the neighborhood in which this couple lived. Another place to look for *lanerii* is among the witnesses that gathered around the dying testator in order to confer legal validity on the will. The law required that five people—any sane males who were not beneficiaries—be present as witnesses. The collection of witnesses might include friends, neighbors, or people dragged off the street. The names of these witnesses reveal something about the world in which the testator lived. Of the ten witnesses to the two wills, nine were *lanerii*, and four were subscribers to the pact of 1244. So, none of the business associates and friends mentioned in either will were parties to the agreement among the *lanerii*, yet some of the witnesses were. This fact suggests that Giovanni and Sofia were part of two separate worlds in the wool industry, one inhabited by secular folk and the other by brothers and sisters of the third order. These two groups did not coalesce in the forming of a wool guild. The Humiliati confined their business ties in the main to fellow members of the third order.

A later document from the wool guild demonstrates how the relationship between the Humiliati and the guild developed over time. On 8 July 1274, the members of the wool guild of Genoa, in order to augment the honor, usefulness, and good state of their association, agreed not to purchase certain kinds of raw, washed, or carded wool from anyone who had acquired such materials for the purpose of reselling them.[117] This rule reflects a common desire of many guilds to cut out intermediaries and deal with suppliers on an equal footing. After the officials and masters of the guild promised to obey the rule, a Gianono de Castro promised the same for himself and for Brother Fulcone. Later in the document he again promised that Brother Fulcone and a Contino would make sure that Oberto Rapallino observed the agreement. This Brother Fulcone was recorded in 1278 as a *lanerius* and the seller of Humiliati cloth.[118] He was a kind of business agent for the Humiliati. The members of the guild knew that their rules would not be effective if the Humiliati remained on the outside. Despite whatever desire the Humiliati had to insulate themselves from the secular world, their work inevitably drew them closer to their fellow weavers and hence into the life of regulations.

The wool guilds were in a position to contain the potential damage that the Humiliati were capable of doing to guild business. The statutes from various cities imposed on members the obligation to buy and sell only among themselves. If the Humiliati remained outside the guild, purchasing raw wool or finding a retail outlet for their cloth would be difficult, if not impossible. The statutes of the wool guild of Bologna exempted Humiliati from holding offices in the guild, but these rules also imply that the Humiliati were members and had the duty to observe all of the other rules.[119] The Humiliati still had economic advantages over the other members, but they had to comply with any agreements on fixed prices. Ironically, this would only enrich the Humiliati, who presumably had the lowest costs. Zanoni surveyed the wool statutes from a number of Italian towns and found that only in Pisa did the commune step in and exempt the Humiliati from any guild regulation, and Pisa was never a notable center of weaving.[120] The mechanism by which the Humiliati in some towns joined the guild is not clear—presumably the house paid the entry fee for the brothers and sisters of the second order engaged in weaving. The third order became enmeshed in the rules when its agents bought and sold wool and cloth. Thus a religious order facilitated the entry into a guild of some people, who, if they had remained in secular life, would have been mostly the simple employees of guild members. As Little observes, "In lieu of a guild, that religious brotherhood offered them [the poorest workers] some measure of economic and social security."[121] Whatever the religious motives or social origins of the founders might have been, the humbler brothers and sisters in the thirteenth century found themselves put to work, probably in safer circumstances and with a better diet, but still in a manufacturing scheme not all that different from what they may have hoped they had left behind with their employers. The Humiliati did not even escape the guild, and the masters could be content that a potential challenge had been subsumed. Once again, the guild demonstrated that its value lay in the ability to mediate problems among different social groups and at the same time to protect the interests of the masters.

This survey of early guilds and the various sources for studying them is not comprehensive, and the geographic scope of examples suggests that caution about extracting general trends from the disparate sources is warranted. Guilds, known by a variety of names, appeared in twelfth-century towns across western Europe and by the thirteenth century developed a complex set of rules and practices. Although the political context varied from place to place, artisans and merchants everywhere found themselves in a social setting of competing forces. Even in an area where a lord or institution had defined the local structure of authority, overlapping areas of jurisdiction fostered the growth of an institution, the guild, that was capable of mediating on behalf of its members among these sources of local authority. The feudal hierarchy and often the town government were older than the guilds, whose members needed legitimacy and protection from entrenched powers. The urban economy and the ways interurban and international trade affected it were also important stimuli to the creation of guilds, especially for those crafts like the cloth trades that quickly became small parts of a wider, uncontrollable market. All of these factors external to the daily lives of merchants and artisans produced strong incentives to band together for mutual support. Although assigning a clear chronology to these broad trends in the European economy is not easy, the Low Countries, southern France, and northern Italy were in advance of other regions, but the other areas soon felt the hot breath of competing products from their neighbors. A social trend also existed that Pierre Michaud-Quantin has characterized as an "associative movement" throughout medieval society.[122] This tendency of people to coalesce into groups is a distinctive feature of medieval social life.

External competition and group theory do not by themselves explain the phenomenon of guilds on so broad a scale. Cogent internal reasons also motivated the townspeople to form guilds. Inside the crafts and professions competition existed, whether for raw materials or customers, and it was an equally strong incentive to cooperate. The guildsmen wanted local monopolies in part to allow survival of their crafts in the face of long-distance trade but also to provide for an orderly division of the local market. This emphasis on monopoly struck later observers like Adam Smith as damaging to free markets, innovation, and economic growth, but we must try to understand this original, strong impulse to regulate competition.

Gunnar Mickwitz proposed that the guild was, in the beginning, a special kind of monopoly—a cartel—on the grounds that competition within the "privileged circle" still existed.[123] In his view, masters were initially concerned about markets, and so they had good reason to band together against their customers, workers, and suppliers of raw materials.[124] Mickwitz attributed these characteristics to the economic reasons for the guild's existence, yet attempts to limit competition certainly occurred before the guild emerged.[125] For Mickwitz, the best sign of an ingrained desire to stifle competition was the habit of the fixed or customary price.[126] Rents and prices in the eleventh and twelfth centuries frequently reflected a traditional level, one that people continued to honor regardless of the changing values of money or commodities. According to this interesting argument, the quickening pace of economic life brought home the need for a more systematic way to counter the damages resulting from competition. A pervasive fear of competition could account for the phenomenon observed in this chapter—the spontaneous and independent appearance of guilds across medieval Europe.

The strength of Mickwitz's interpretation rests in his appeal to custom, a concept dear to the hearts of medieval people. But this particular custom, the desire at least to diminish the competitive aspects of commerce and craft production, requires us to accept two premises. First, an instinctive aversion to competition existed. Second, the founders of medieval guilds intended that the new institutions limit only external competition. Both suppositions seem to me to be wrong. The love of custom could just as easily go hand in hand with a zest for competition. Guild statutes regulated some matters but left ample scope for individual success or failure, and plenty of work remained outside any guild. Masters stood together and faced the outside world in unison, for the purpose of enhancing their ability to make a living, for the good of the trade. At the same time, however, the guild statutes indicate that the masters were just as concerned about competing among themselves as they were interested in protecting themselves from foreign goods. As discussed in this chapter, this self-help frequently took the form of a monopoly.

At first glance this emphasis on monopoly might seem typical of the precapitalist spirit, but theorists have always extolled the virtues of competition more than people faced with palpable risk have. Modern experience does not support the idea that monopoly and capitalism are antithetical concepts. A guild did not guarantee that all members would thrive in their businesses, but neither did it license unrestricted competition. The masters did not provide much testimony on how they viewed the question of competition; the calculus of different factors seems to have weighed in favor of emphasizing quality and individual craftsmanship at the expense of competing on the basis of price. In Chartres the drapers valued the reputation of the cloth of their town, but not all hands were equally skilled. A weaver might hope to establish a personal level of expertise that would command customers when other considerations were equal. Even the most restrictive guild practices prescribed rules for competition rather than abolish it. Throughout Europe, groups of artisans and professionals chose this middle way that granted a measure of security and at the same time rewarded individual effort. This compromise was important where membership in the guild was compulsory. On balance, the external reasons for having a guild were compelling, but the internal benefits to association had a more tangible importance in the daily life of a shoemaker. For many of the crafts not affected by the sweep of international trade, the local security gained by having one's place in a market guaranteed was the decisive advantage from having a guild. These local considerations will become clearer when we look into the question of how masters recruited labor through the apprenticeship system.

As discussed thus far, merchants and artisans had good reasons to band together without wage labor entering into the calculus. The Roman example renders this outcome comprehensible; associations of employers easily accommodated themselves to slave labor. In the thirteenth century, guilds and a system of training and employing free labor (apprentices and journeymen) seem to emerge in tandem. Early sources like the Genoese notarial record and the London charters and statutes do not link up well; the law and documents of practice do not often come together neatly for the historian in one place. The masters, however, competed against and cooperated with one another, and so difficult questions arose for the first time—how to define master status and, at least in Italy, how (or whether) to use slaves. The undisputed growth in the economy offered potential employers on the one hand the chance to increase the scale of their operations and on the other a pool of potential free laborers, the fruit of increased productivity and population growth in the countryside. In order to determine why masters availed themselves of the opportunity to establish a market for labor while treating this new phenomenon with the same leeriness that possible competitiveness always provoked, we need to examine in detail the actual mechanics of what we will call the apprentice and journeyman system. Masters had broad rights to regulate internal aspects of their crafts and professions, and in these innovations are seen the origins of that novelty—regular wage labor.

3

Internal Organization of Guilds and the Labor Market

The self-interest of the masters becomes clearer in the context of how they decided to control the internal aspects of their trades and professions. At this point we can go beyond the early statutes and foundation charters and look more closely at the process of ongoing development. These changes are first apparent in the thirteenth century when documents of practice became more common and widespread. Masters, that complex group of independent producers and employers, have been the focus thus far. The reality for masters included the possibilities that they might rise or sink in status, that some of them inevitably would work for others and not simply the abstract consumers; eventually, the labor market included some of them. Hence the competition for labor became, as early as the thirteenth century, not solely the market for apprentices and journeymen and -women, but also a question of the master's own place in a network of business connections. Guilds proved to be durable institutions because they became effective ways for a group of people to promote their own interests while still competing against one another. In order to explain why guilds lasted for so long, one must argue against the impression that their longevity resulted from changeless rigidity. The world around the guilds certainly changed in the thirteenth and fourteenth centuries, and in chapter 4 this problem will be more closely examined. For now, the emphasis is on that part of the environment the masters were capable of controlling—the internal aspects of the guilds and the market for labor.

Five issues that concern how masters organized their guilds and, in turn, how these guilds functioned in the economy will be explored here. (1) Masters everywhere defined the apprenticeship and journeyman system, and hence they had to recruit and educate a work force. (2) Regardless of how their particular guild came into existence, the masters desired to regulate how they competed with one another, and so they often planned to adhere to standards of production. (3) The merchant guild, the group that in some instances dominated long-distance trade as well as town government, often held, where it existed, the fates of the craft guilds in its hands. The presence of a merchant guild can help to explain regional variations and different paths of development. (4) How the masters or some other authority selected officials reveals something about the internal political life of the guild. In this arena the masters cooperated in an equal manner while facing demands for equality from their employees. (5) The artisan or craft guilds did not often share a sense of joint equality. Some guilds commanded more prestige and subordinated others in the social and economic world. As the crafts proliferated and new industries founded guilds of their own, this division of labor produced a clear hierarchy in which some trades became noble and others vulgar. Attitudes about trades reflect opinions about work and those who did it. These aspects of the daily lives and concerns of medieval professionals and craftsmen enable us to examine just how the guilds shaped the work of the counting house or the loom.

Apprentices and Journeymen

Masters of a guild cooperated at least in part in finding and training apprentices, most of whom would go on to the status of a day laborer hoping for something better. The term *apprentice* itself evokes the guild system, but of course the status of pupil or trainee was older than the medieval guild and remains in use today, despite the fact that the word has lost most of its official and formal meaning, except in some branches of the trade-union movement. This is a recent phenomenon; as late as 1811, when the fifteen-year-old John Keats became an apprentice for five years to a surgeon, the idea of apprenticeship retained much that a young man or woman of the thirteenth century would have recognized and often loathed. Keats himself, surely an articulate apprentice, had almost nothing to say about his experience, except a memory of a "hand that clench'd itself against Hammond," presumably his master.[1] This kind of rare comment, balanced against centuries of apprentices who toiled away without leaving a record of their feelings, evokes many similar clenched fists or muttered curses. The most common experience in the Middle Ages was to be a farm boy or girl, a model of work that lasted until and through much of the Industrial Revolution. Away from the farm, more people experienced the lot of apprenticeship than were ever priests, nuns, or knights. The very broadness of apprenticeship as a social category has probably been an obstacle to its study, but why the topic has been so neglected is still not easy to see. Part of the reason must be that apprenticeship contracts and statutes often only create a vague and static portrait of what was, for many people, a brief interlude in their lives—but for Keats, one sixth of his life. In chapter 2 the standard features and conditions of the apprenticeship contract were discussed; here, this stage of life, along with the relationship between master and apprentice, will be analyzed more deeply.

Apprentices fell into two natural groups based on the age at which they began service. One type of apprentice started to work between the ages of ten and thirteen or fourteen. These boys and girls generally faced longer periods of training and passed their early years of apprenticeship as helpers in a craft or shop, or as glorified servants. The tailors of Bologna stated in their official rules that "a little apprentice less than ten years of age" served for at least five years, while one older than ten could serve for as little as three years.[2] Even the fourteen-year-old who had completed this kind of apprenticeship was not immediately going to become a master; long years of low journeyman wages awaited such a person. The statutes of the sword dealers (*fornitori spadarum*), also from Bologna, declared that an apprentice had to be at least eight years old, and this age represents the bottom line for lawful apprenticeship.[3] The older group of apprentices came into their training between about fourteen and twenty or twenty-one years of age. These young men and women, older, larger, stronger than the children they worked alongside, frequently served long years of training, but they were also likely to receive some sort of stipend in at least the concluding years of their term. In a sample of 169 thirteenth-century Genoese apprentices, only 22 supplied their ages, and the youngest were fifteen years old.[4] The major difference between apprenticeships of older and younger children was that in the late teens a person was legally capable of taking an oath to keep to the terms of the contract. A parent or guardian had to swear to enforce the agreement if the apprentice was from the point of view of the law still a child. Real differences existed between the kinds of work performed by apprentices eight or eighteen years of age; the masters, however, placed great emphasis on the oath to keep the agreement, and thus their older apprentices had a different relationship to them. In the small Genoese sample cited above, most of these older apprentices were seventeen (10) or eighteen (7) years old, and these ages seem to have been something of a watershed for starting a son or daughter in an artisan career.

These two age groups reflect a more profound distinction in the general class of apprentices—those who followed in a parent's footsteps and those who did not. A master's own children were the most obvious pool of labor to tap, and a strong tendency pushed some sons and daughters to begin learning a skill at a young age in the family workshop. The guild members were eager to accept sons in particular into the crafts, and sons invariably paid less, or nothing at all, than strangers were expected to pay to enter the guild.[5] The smiths of Bologna insisted that the masters put in the guild sons or brothers working at the craft at age fourteen.[6] In general, many of the younger apprentices were related by blood to their masters and had been destined to work at a particular craft since infancy. Some of the younger apprentices were not relatives, but most were. Where apprenticeship contracts survive, they support this conclusion. When the training took place in the context of the family, no need for formal written contracts existed, since the master as parent already possessed the necessary legal authority over his or her own son or daughter. The written contracts, preserved in the notarial records of southern Europe, invariably concern master and pupil who were not father or mother and child. The requirement to put sons in the guild at a certain age, along with the rule to register all apprentices with the guild, did not fix a terminus to their service. The apprentice by contract always had a fixed term of service, but a son or daughter might languish in the family workshop for a long time, in some cases literally waiting to succeed to a parent's estate and trade. The weavers of Chartres had a rule that a son or daughter might take a deceased father's place, or be a master like one's father, by displaying to the guild six cloths woven by his or her own hand.[7] This kind of rule was common and helped to insure that new masters maintained local standards of quality. It also, however, gave the offspring a tangible goal and the assurance that an objective standard, beyond a parent's approval, existed for establishing competence at a craft.

In many workshops children by blood, rented or hired children, and young adults worked together. Often these apprentices also lived together as a kind of family unit because the master offered by contract bed and board to the apprentices. A certain percentage of masters would have no sons or daughters to follow them, and in these cases the quasi-parental nature of apprenticeship might have assumed a close emotional tie as well.[8] Some guilds had rules on the number of apprentices a master might have at any one time, but close blood relatives always had the right to receive training.[9] Thus the apprentices were a mixed bag of relatives—sons, occasional daughters and younger brothers, the odd nephew—and strangers. Any given master would have had this potential pool of labor on which to draw. The apprentices by contract mostly entered crafts or trades that differed from their parents. In the work contracts are many cases in which the age of the employee suggests that the particular job in question may have been the first work experience outside the home. In other words, the apprentices by blood became visible when a parent or guardian placed this person with some skills at gainful employment with another master. The sources on the family workshop, without outsiders present, are not good, but some of these trained sons and daughters appear later in the work-force records with the same skills as their parents. For the older apprentices, the parent had often placed the son or daughter in a different kind of work than the one the mother or father practiced. In these cases, the childhood and early teens of the apprentice may have been passed as an unofficial helper at home, or in some form of rudimentary schooling in reading, writing, and numbers, or perhaps in simple idleness.

The central obligation between master and apprentice was to teach and to learn. This was the most pervasive method of education the premodern European world ever developed. A mystery or art, be it cobbling or the law, required years of patient practice and instruction. The amount of time required to become proficient at a trade depended on the difficulty of the craft and the kinds of skills required. The statutes frequently set minimum terms of service that in turn reflect common assumptions about the ease or rigor of particular trades. The lorimers of London (makers of the metal parts of harnesses and other small specialty metal products) expected apprentices to serve fourteen years.[10] A decade was usually the longest time that apprentices served in the most demanding trades, but the apprentices served for at least twelve years in the specialized guild of Parisian masters who made religious artifacts out of coral and shell.[11] At the other end of the spectrum, the tailors of Bologna wanted apprentices who were over ten years old to work at least three years; the weavers of cotton expected apprentices to work at least one year.[12] In Paris the length of the apprenticeship in many trades depended on whether or not the pupils paid their masters. The locksmiths who made locks for small boxes normally required an apprenticeship of at least seven years and a payment of twenty sous, but if the apprentice worked for eight years, the parents did not pay anything.[13] The masters could count on a skilled and informed servant in the last year of a long term, so they would forgo an initial cash payment, at a small risk, for a year's labor down the road.

The Genoese apprenticeship contracts suggest that in some towns no hard-and-fast rules about the length of service existed. The smiths, for example, were willing to take an apprentice for ten years, but six to eight years was the most common length of the term. The woolweavers and -workers served as apprentices from five to eight years, and the novice shoemakers studied their craft from four to five years.[14] The statutes of the guilds of London, Bologna, and Paris and of others throughout western Europe suggest that terms of service fixed by rule were the exception, and masters preferred a minimum term with the right to adjust the period of training to fit the age and previous experience of the apprentice. The surviving contracts have another common denominator; the masters always fixed the term of training for some definite amount of time. The statutes of the clothfinishers of Toulouse required that no one could become a master until completing two years with a master, and apprentices were also instructed to be "prudent and wise."[15] The guild reserved for itself the right to determine who was capable of practicing a craft, and nothing guaranteed that a particular number of years would insure that the apprentice had acquired the requisite skills. A young person hoping to enter the guild as a journeyman was occasionally asked to produce a masterpiece to demonstrate competency. The word of his or her master did not usually suffice, nor did simple years of work.

A wide variety of guild statutes set rigorous and specific standards of production, but such rules only raise the presumption that the task of the master was to teach the pupil the actual manual skills or learning necessary to maintain quality.[16] The statutes left the content of the training to the experience of the master. To judge from the number of words devoted to apprenticeship, the masters were primarily concerned about pupils who ran away or whom other masters enticed away by offering better terms. Since the guild was intended to regulate the relations among masters, they were properly anxious that no one of their number should lure away another's apprentice. So the statutes generally insisted that no apprentice should depart from a master's service without the express permission of that master. The statutes also condemned runaways, but if the apprentice simply returned to his or her own family, a natural impulse in children, or just disappeared, it was the master's personal difficulty; the guild was not able to give much help. In order to make sure that apprenticeship was a public and binding contract, guild members devised various ways to make it a legal and recorded fact. In Bologna with its notarial culture, the statutes required that apprenticeship contracts be recorded *in carta*, in a written agreement, before a public notary or in some cases the official notary of the guild.[17] The mayor and aldermen of London required that the names of apprentices be recorded and displayed to the officials at a public meeting of the hustings.[18] These types of legal strictures enforced the public obligations of apprenticeship and supplied force to the penalties for failure by either party to observe the terms.

Some of the Genoese apprenticeship contracts provide a more concrete sense of what the actual conditions of individual apprenticeships were and how these agreements affected the lives of young people. Particular contracts contained special terms only appropriate to individual cases, but in aggregate the contracts reveal some common assumptions about the years of work and education the documents prescribed. The master promised to teach the apprentice, in the words of one contract, "as is the custom," but such contracts seldom reveal just what traditional skills the master was to impart. This master carpenter promised as well to teach diligently the art of working wood as best he knew how.[19] A necessary part of this education was the right of correction—the *ius corrigendi*. One master smith promised to inflict no intolerable punishment on his apprentice beyond what was necessary to teach him, and those were the standard words; all masters assumed that some form of corporal punishment was an inevitable part of education.[20] The actual skills transmitted depended on the craft in question. One blacksmith promised to teach his apprentice, in addition to the art of shoeing horses, how to care for the health of horses and how to prepare unguents for them. (In turn, the apprentice agreed never to practice this art in the same spot or land where his master worked.)[21] A master weaver assumed the difficult job of teaching his pupil how to weave left-handed; other masters taught the art in both hands.[22] (Most contracts did not mention any hand, but presumably in these cases only the right was used.) These examples invoke the daily rhythm of chores, instruction, occasional beatings, and the acquisition of specialized knowledge that marked the life of the apprentice. For his or her part, the apprentice promised to learn—no easy task—and perform any and all services the master might require, in some cases day and night. Apprentices could also serve as part-time domestic servants expected to help in household duties not related to the official purpose of the contract. For some women apprentices, the contracts themselves made this very clear. Part of the reason why the master or mistress accepted a female apprentice was to acquire a domestic servant as well.

The kind of training the apprentice received was connected to the questions of where the apprentice should live and of whether the master offered some payment to the apprentice, or whether the family of the pupil should pay the master. Occasionally the guild statutes had a clear answer to these questions. The smiths of Bologna required their apprentices to supply rations of wine, grain, and meat every year, while the masters assumed the expenses of clothing and shoes. The sword dealers (*fornitori spadarum*) simply declared that their apprentices should serve for five years at their own expense or seven years at the master's expense. These masters allowed themselves two additional years of presumably trained labor, paying only the cost of maintenance, to balance their expenses for the first five years.[23] The different ages and skills of apprentices must have made these sorts of rules difficult to enforce, and by all signs most guilds managed without rules or remuneration for apprentices. Food and clothing were the minimum compensation the masters offered for service. Even in the cases where families paid masters to take on an apprentice, the masters usually obligated themselves to provide these minimal requirements. The makers of straps and belts in Paris had the unusual rule that an apprentice who married during the term of service could no longer dine three times a day at the master's table. In recompense, the apprentice received for each workday four deniers, a sum perhaps close to the actual cost of three square meals.[24]

Shelter is the important question because it helps to identify the apprentice either as a full-time resident in the master's establishment or as a kind of day laborer returning to his or her own family every night. Some masters explicitly promised, in unambiguous terms, to provide shelter. The promise by the apprentice not to run away, a universal feature of contracts, holds equally for those who lived with the master and those who did not. A few contracts allowed apprentices to return home occasionally. An interesting local example is the custom in Genoa that permitted some apprentices to return home in October to collect the chestnut harvest.[25] This favor meant something to those apprentices whose families were in the countryside—and generally in those cases, the apprentice lived with the master. The promises to work by day and by night or to provide services in and out of the house, as the master wished, also implied that the apprentice was on the spot. In the sample of 169 Genoese apprenticeship contracts, 120 masters offered the apprentices food and clothing, and almost always one feature or another of the contract suggests shelter as well. A few of these masters still provided food and clothing for their apprentices even when they extracted a fee for the training. One enterprising Genoese master weaver received one goat and forty eggs at Easter and a capon at Christmas from the country family that supplied his apprentice—but the master still provided food, clothing, and shelter.[26] Forty-nine other masters offered their apprentices a different deal; they paid them a wage or gave them a cash gift at the end of the term. Of these, only 13 also provided food and clothing, so perhaps most of the apprentices earning a wage stayed at home with their own families. Still, these apprentices comprised a small minority (21 percent) of the pool of apprentices. At least for thirteenth-century Genoa, shelter was part of a master's obligation to most apprentices.

The other, or literal, side of the coin is that only a minority of masters felt obligated to pay apprentices anything at all in Genoa. The situation elsewhere is not clear and would have depended on the supply of labor—a factor presumably not uniform throughout Europe.[27] Journeymen and -women by definition received a wage, and payments to apprentices are best understood in the context of overall wages, an issue that will be addressed below. The most important form of remuneration that all apprentices received was their training and implied ability to become a journeyman or master. The minority of apprentices who also received some form of cash payment could usually count on an increase in wages over the term that reflected their higher levels of skill. The kinds of wages apprentices earned also depended on what trades they were pursuing, as well as their own age and skill. The masters allowed themselves considerable freedom in setting the terms of individual apprenticeships, and they took advantage of the supply of labor as the occasion warranted. Once a master had taken on apprentices, the guild had some appropriate rules. But apart from the issues of minimum age and runaways and a few limits on the number of apprentices, guilds left the matter of apprenticeship to the individual decisions of the masters.

The guild was also a social and charitable institution, and the masters took a natural interest in the moral welfare of the apprentices. This role partly sprang from the quasi-parental authority of the master, who housed, fed, clothed, and trained the young people; hence the master assumed some overall responsibility for the apprentice. Those parents allowing the young boy or girl to leave home, probably for good, expected the master to foster the well-being of their children. Many contracts contain the master's promise to keep the apprentice "in sickness and in health"—an assurance to the parents that a sick child would not lose a haven or his or her training. Some cagey masters insisted that days lost to illness be added to the end of the term, but all masters accepted some level of caring for the physical health of their charges. The parental role of the masters extended to other spheres of activity. Marco de Frascario swore to his master smith that, in addition to his ordinary obligations, he would not play at dice.[28] The most frequent promise of a moral nature, however, was not to marry without the permission of the master. This stipulation became such a standard feature of Genoese contracts that a few absent-minded notaries had women apprentices promising not to take a wife without permission.[29] Apprentices, male and female, invariably made this undertaking, not to their parents or guardians, but to their masters. Assuming that most apprentices lived with their masters, the arrival of a husband or wife, and potentially children, would disrupt the master's own domestic life, and so the master had a veto over any marriages. The notary Lanfranco Cazano in the 1290s extended the normal promise not to marry, and the apprentices in his contracts also agreed not to know a woman carnally in the master's house.[30] The emphasis seems to be more on the location (the master's house, and perhaps the daughters in the family) than on the act, and again the masters' own interests are evident. Most of the spiritual and social activities of the guild that involved the apprentices and journeymen concerned common religious observances and processions, which will be considered below.

The statutes and the work contracts are also able to explain how the journeymen, the day laborers, fit into the guild system of work. These former apprentices, already trained in their craft or business, could be as young as seventeen or eighteen or up to middle-aged or older with families of their own. The statutes of the cobblers of Paris suggest that some journeymen were in fact former masters who because of poverty had reverted to the status of journeyman.[31] From the point of view of the masters, journeymen were the readily available pool of extra labor, to be dipped into when necessary. The masters had to decide, however, just what part, if any, the journeymen should play in the guild and, more importantly, what kind of jurisdiction the masters would have over their employees. Most guilds allowed journeymen to be members, largely for the purpose of keeping track of them and collecting in some cases an annual fee for carrying them on the books. The journeymen were not eligible to serve as officials of the guild. The masters did not attempt to limit the number of journeymen anyone might employ, and the statutes say little about them. Instead, the masters took an active interest in journeymen when dealing with the questions of wages and the length of the workday.

The economic prosperity of the masters rested upon an adequate supply of labor and upon an implicit or explicit agreement among the masters as employers not to step over a line in competing for workers. The family workshops and enterprises were only capable of absorbing a limited number of employees, so the need for labor was more significant in aggregate than it was for any particular employer. Still, some guilds and occasionally city and later national governments attempted to fix the wages of journeymen. A document from London dated in the time of Edward I is the clearest example of this practice. The Ordinances of the Carpenters, Masons, Plasterers, Daubers, and Tilers included all of the basic facets of the construction business.[32] The mayor and aldermen of London addressed themselves to the question of wages of the *overours*—the workers by day, the journeymen. The masters, as the contractors of these trades and people of some prominence in London, were not included in the wage limits. The authorities, probably at the request of the master contractors, developed a complex scheme of wages for the carpenters that depended on the season of the year and whether or not the worker received meals (table 3-1). The masters offered a wage or wage and table, as they wished.

This scheme has several interesting features. Setting wages at so much per day throughout the year would have been simpler. The same ordinances set the wages of the less prestigious pavers at the clear rate of 2 pence a day, and the carters of raw materials earned the piece-rate wage of 1 penny per cartload.[33] The carpenters, however, received their highest wage in the summer when the days were long and their lowest in the dead of winter, and the difference amounted to a two-thirds increase in those months traditionally suited to heavy outdoor work in England. The premium the employers paid in the summer months balanced the lower wages of winter, when presumably construction did not cease but was at a seasonal low. The rule succinctly stated,

Table 3-1. Wages of London Carpenters per Day

Time of Year	Wage
St. Michael–St. Martin (Sept. 29–Nov. 11)	4d. or 1-1/2d. and table
St. Martin–Candlemas (Nov. 11–Feb. 2)	3d. or 1d. and table
Candlemas–Easter (Feb. 2–Easter)	4d. or 1-1/2d. and table
Easter–St. Michael (Easter–Sept. 29)	5d. or 2-1/2d. and table

Source: Riley, *Munimenta Gildhallae Londoniensis,* 2:100.

"when no work, no pay" ("quant rien ne oevre rien ne preigne"), so the journeymen would be expected, or at least well advised, to husband their resources from the busier summer months.[34] (The general price of labor likely was higher in the summer months.) The builders seem also to be employed for short terms on specific jobs. The ordinances do not specify the exact meaning of "table." This sizable charge against the daily wage was 2½ pence, except in the November to February quarter when it was only 2 pence. The table amounted to half the wages in summer and a larger percentage in the other quarters, so it provided (one hopes) two or three square meals, enough to replenish the energy of an adult male. If the laborers were receiving honest value for the table charge, how these wages would have kept anyone's family above bare subsistence is difficult to see. If the table charges were excessive, laborers would have flocked to those employers who offered cash money. These ordinances also set the wages for the workers called *serjauntz*—sergeants—who were clearly builders' helpers since the rules describe them as principally fetchers of mortar and carriers. These helpers received 2 pence a day, except for the time between Easter and Michaelmas when they received 3 pence. The employers did not offer them table, which implies that 3 pence a day were subsistence wages in late thirteenth-century London.

At the end of the ordinances, the mayor and aldermen stipulated the heavy fine of forty shillings to be imposed on anyone who paid workers more than these rules permitted.[35] The fine fell on the employers, an astute choice, since they alone were presumably able to pay a sum amounting to ninety-six-days' wages at the high summer rate. What effect, if any, this attempt at regulating wages had in the real market for labor is unknown. Masters had every reason to police themselves in this matter, since, apart from the fine, employers paying more would attract all of the best workers and might be able to supply superior work in a shorter time span. Even if this ordinance had no effect at all, it reveals that contemporaries had a clear sense of the seasonal nature of work and that a mix of wages and payment in kind provided the rigid system of fixed wages with some flexibility. Those employers supplying a first-rate, generous table would have seen their fame spread, and probably some masters thought that the kind of food and drink permitted a small degree of competition.

The information on the London builders does not include any sign of the length of employment. The journeymen, or valets, or *compagnons,* were in the strictest sense employees at will, and in seasonal trades like construction or shipping, the duration of a contract for hire might be only as long as a particular project or voyage. Most types of medieval business experienced a seasonal demand, but perhaps not as pronounced as builders and mariners; only a few trades, like baking, could count on the most regular of demands. The journeymen did not enjoy the security of long, fixed terms of service or generally a reliable bed and board. Their situation was not quite as precarious as that of the day laborer of today who turns up at a hall hoping to be called to work. The journeymen worked by contract, often an oral agreement that many social and religious pressures validated and enforced. In southern Europe, many would have the benefit of a written contract. In the sample of 112 Genoese work contracts from the thirteenth century, only 3 committed the journeyman to work as long as the master wished.[36] All of the rest contained fixed terms of service. These terms were invariably shorter than apprenticeships and typically lasted from six months to two years. For some women "apprenticed" as domestic servants but in effect contract workers, the term might last for as long as fourteen years. Six months represented a threshold below which the contract may simply not have been worth the cost of committing it to writing. The master and worker both promised to observe the terms of the agreement, which presumably were the length of employment and the rate of pay. The journeymen and -women also promised to work faithfully and well, and the masters obligated themselves to supply work. The consent of both parties was necessary to abrogate the agreement, but the issues of diligence and quality allowed both sides to attempt to break the contract for cause. No master had to keep on a lazy worker, and no journeyman had to bear intolerable burdens. Disputes of this kind would find their way to a committee of arbiters, always masters, so journeymen were at a disadvantage if they hoped to escape from a contract.

The relationship between master and journeyman was not the same as the one between master and apprentice. The masters usually did not supply food and clothing to the journeymen, most of whom, by the same test applied to apprentices, seem to have lived elsewhere than their master's home. The ties between master and employee were complex and involved more than the exchange of labor for money. Since the journeymen had all served a period of apprenticeship, they were usually enrolled in the guild and hence subject to its jurisdiction. The authority of the masters extended beyond the workshop into the social and religious parts of guild life. Some journeymen must have continued to work for the same masters under whom they had served as apprentices, and in these cases the quasi-familial relationship would have been difficult or undesirable to shed. Unless the journeymen were able to count on a substantial inheritance or a fortunate marriage, their primary interest, if they wanted to better their position, was to amass capital for opening their own shop or business.

The number of women working as day laborers in the urban trades is not easy to ascertain, but they seldom had the opportunity to become independent masters in the crafts, except in those industries in which they comprised the majority of the work force. Some women married men in the same line of work, and the couple would offer themselves on the labor market as a team. Other women married men who were in a different line of work and rarely might take on an apprentice of their own. The tanners of Paris expressly prohibited daughters who were not married to men in the craft from taking on apprentices, even though the tanners had ruled that their own daughters were the only women eligible to be apprentices in the first place.[37] Journeyman status was the great dividing line of labor—only a minority of men ever joined the ranks of independent masters, but for women this was an unusual and increasingly rare feat. Not surprisingly, the work contracts left the journeymen free to marry as they wished, and these marriages served to consolidate and pass on what wealth existed in the artisan classes.

The journeyman and casual laborer worked and lived for his or her wages, computed by the day but usually paid by the week. These wages were not the incentives or rewards for learning that they were for the apprentices. Journeymen wages meant starvation, subsistence, or social mobility. Few reliable statistics are available on wages before the fourteenth century, but the data on wages thicken after midcentury and the devastation of the bubonic plague. In the changed economic and social environment, the question of wages prompted occasional legislation and social protest.[38] For the thirteenth century, there are only a few indications of prevailing wage rates, and these are scattered and difficult to compare. Guilds rarely tried to set wages for journeymen, and again the effort in London to control wages of artisans was the exception and not the rule. Since the masters agreed upon common standards of production, price structure, and often methods of access to raw materials, limited flexibility existed on the question of journeymen wages. The masters may have recognized this fact and also that the effort to fix wages was troublesome and unnecessary. The market allowed for bargaining and small variations in journeymen wages, and perhaps more importantly, the difference between piece-rate and a daily wage provided all of the parties with the opportunity to reward skill and hard work.

The structure of the labor market seems to have favored wages by the day for journeymen. In some trades, however, most notably the cloth industry, piece-rate pay provided an objective standard of output that was conducive to paying by the amount of wool carded, thread spun, and cloth woven. Adam Smith later observed that "workmen . . . when they are liberally paid by the piece, are very apt to overwork themselves, and to ruin their health and constitution in a few years."[39] Smith thought that piecework was more prevalent "wherever wages are higher than ordinary," so he assumed that employers preferred piece-rate wages because in the end this payment method worked to their favor.[40] This favorable outcome for employers might result from either the incentives of piece-rate pay that produced more work by fewer hands or the decrease in general wages that resulted from a minority of laborers overworking themselves. The actual calculations by masters and journeymen remain elusive. Two important chronologies of labor need to be kept in mind: the general wage rate and changes in the balance between piecerate and a daily wage. An apparent paradox here is that two prestigious and well-rewarded guilds of professionals, physicians and attorneys, received what were in effect piece-rate wages. Some of these professionals worked on salary for kings or bureaucracies, but at their level of remuneration, no stigma was attached to fee for service, and no sign appears that this form of wage reduced the income of the masters or broke their own health.

E. H. Phelps-Brown and Sheila Hopkins present in two classic articles the most comprehensive set of data on wages and prices for

England from the thirteenth to the twentieth century.[41] The analysis of wages rests on a series of wages for those in the building trade and contains no information on wages before 1264. The authors conclude that falling wages were the exception, that wages had a tendency to remain constant for long periods of time, and that the difference between the wages of craftsmen and laborers was generally stable.[42] They find a wage in the fourteenth century of three pence a day for the vague category of craftsmen, a pay less than that of contractors or master builders.[43] The most notable decline in wages for craftsmen was in the 1330s, and the most rapid advance, in any century before the twentieth, followed the plague of 1348. The ratio of the difference between the wages of craftsmen and laborers, except in the fourteenth century when the market favored laborers, remained at two to one in favor of the craftsmen.[44] This is the same differential the mayor and aldermen of London tried to legislate for the builders in the reign of Edward I. These conclusions rest on the wages of one particular craft—construction—and do not take piece-rate work into account. When the authors analyze the prices of consumer items, they find considerable yearly fluctuations and a tendency in the late thirteenth century for wages to remain flat despite increases in the cost of living.[45] The volatile prices of food and the other necessities of life forced those working for a fixed wage to make some desperate choices; those on piece-rate pay had the opportunity, observed by Adam Smith, to exhaust themselves prematurely to maintain a constant standard of living.

The Genoese work contracts from the thirteenth century permit an inspection of journeymen wages from a narrower perspective. The contracts necessarily draw attention to certain features of the market for labor not emphasized in an aggregate analysis. The work contracts concern dozens of different trades and are limited in number, so they do not permit a close inspection of any one particular craft, except the wool business. Some useful insights can be gained from the analysis of these contracts.[46] The journeymen contributed to the apparent stability of wages by working for long periods of time for the same wage, and the piece-rate wages were especially conservative over time. The relatively short length of a typical contract, between one and two years, fostered the tendency to have the wages fixed for the term, and only occasionally did the journeymen benefit from scheduled raises during the course of the contract. The apprentices receiving pay often had escalating wages, but their long years of service and lower rate of pay placed them below the journeymen. The difficulties of examining the wages of journeymen can be illustrated in several examples from one of the more lucrative aspects of the wool business, the dyeing of finished cloth. One well-paid journeyman dyer received L12 for a year's work in 1249, and another in 1245 received 1 solidus a day and 5 solidi per cloth and also exacted from his employer the unusual provision that he would still receive his daily wage even when no work was available.[47] The second dyer, earning 1 solidus a day and not counting his bonus per cloth, would equal the first in 240 days. This second dyer worked for the master Giovanni the dyer of Castello, who in October of 1245 took a young girl as a worker in his shop. Petrina, who worked for Giovanni for six years, received in the last year her highest wages, 24 solidi for the year.[48] Giovanni paid the man working in his shop this much money in twenty-four days. In 1251, Giovanni the dyer, probably the same one, took on a boy as a journeyman in his shop and paid him 35 solidi in the fourth year.[49] These wages are more comparable to Petrina's, but in her fourth year she earned 16 solidi, less than half of the male's wage.

These examples are intended to illustrate two basic points about journeymen wages. First, age and skill counted for something. The older, experienced dyers possessed a skill that contributed real value to the cloth, and they were also capable of ruining fine cloths if things went awry. Good dyers earned high journeymen wages in most medieval cities. A young boy or girl who had just completed an apprenticeship was in no position to demand the wages of an older journeyman. Consequently, the age of the employee should be considered along with the general wage rates or particular notices of individual wages for journeymen. Second, the sex of the worker was important. Women who received formal training as apprentices seem to have been rare—in Genoa they accounted for less than 10 percent (15 of 169) of all apprenticeships.[50] Women as day laborers by contract were even rarer, but when they appeared, they earned salaries usually about half of what men earned. Women were more prominent in some trades— dyeing, spinning thread—than others, so any general statement that dyers were well rewarded needs to be qualified by realizing that women in the trade did not receive the high wages of men.

A final complication concerning wages is the time of year the masters took on journeymen. Other signs in the thirteenth century indicate that the seasonal market for labor was a reality in the urban trades. Agricultural labor was of course by definition seasonal, and no medieval town was so isolated from the countryside as to be immune from agriculture's timeless rhythms. In London, the builders' wages were highest in the peak farming months. The sea also had trading seasons, and few places in western Europe were remote enough from the ocean not to feel them. In Genoa, a stray work contract from March 1224 reveals that the wages of a *lanerius,* in this case a woolbeater, increased after the kalends (first) of August from 3½ pennies per piece to 4 pennies and remained at that rate until October 1, when the wages returned to their previous level.[51] This period of time coincided with the second principal sailing season of the calendar year, when demand for crews was high and the allure of the sea might tempt workers away from the artisan trades. The other sailing season began in April and was over by early June, so the combined seasonal demand for labor in the Mediterranean coincided exactly with the peak months of the agricultural year. In the Atlantic and North Sea regions, the winter months were even more strictly avoided, so throughout Europe, in the north and south, in the rural areas and in the manufacturing towns and ports, a parallel chronology of labor existed. Indoor labor remained possible in the winter months, and journeymen in some trades relied upon the adequate stockpiling of raw materials like wool to insure that there would be work to tide them over the winter months. The sample of 112 work contracts from Genoa reveals how the crafts coexisted with the seasonal rhythm of work in a typical port. The work contracts are spread evenly throughout the year with a modest bulge in January and a corresponding drop in February.[52] The Genoese New Year fell on Christmas, so the contracts of the last six days of December and January suggest a tendency to start them at the beginning of the year. This was the slowest time for overseas trade and perhaps provided a useful benchmark for master artisans to calculate their labor requirements. The lower wages in winter allowed masters to take advantage of what was, from their point of view, an optimal labor market. Apart from the early months of the year, the uniform distribution of contracts suggests that master artisans handled the problem of seasonal demand for labor in trade and agriculture by engaging assistants at regular intervals. The crafts offered some security in employment.

The guild statutes in general reveal little about the circumstances of the journeymen. Having passed through the rigors of apprenticeship, the day laborers bargained for employment and found it where they could, at the best terms the local market could bear. From the point of view of the masters, the journeymen and -women were but one part of a large and complex puzzle—how to recruit workers. The workers too were interested in being recruited, but they were also concerned about the length of the workday. Since they were paid by the day, they had to be concerned about what amount of labor, in terms of time, the masters expected for a daily wage—the *journée* as it was known in Paris. In that city a few guilds had a rule that succinctly described the workday of the journeymen: the valets had their vespers. As for the end of the day, the ordinances of the fullers stated, "The valets have their vespers, that is namely, that those who are hired by the day leave off work at the first ringing of vespers of Notre Dame."[53] The claspmakers, wiredrawers, and leathercurers, among others, had the same custom of relying on the bells of the cathedral or a parish church to signal the end of the workday.[54] The beginning of the workday is less certain, though, to judge from the statutes that prohibited work before dawn, shortly after sunrise seems to have been the usual starting time. As has been discussed above, some guilds permitted night work, but for the laborers hard at work since dawn, the prospect of more work into the evening must have had little appeal. The masters were by definition self-employed, and their apprentices would keep the hours of their teachers. The journeymen and their wages defined the workday, and by all signs in the thirteenth century and later, the day depended on the craft, the relative skill of the day laborer, and the nature of the labor market in the individual towns.

The masters in their guilds sometimes limited the number of apprentices a master might take on but not the number of journeymen. Perhaps masters saw a shop full of novices as a threat to local standards of production or service, or they may have feared that a master equipped with a large staff of thirteen-year-olds working hard for bed and board would be a serious threat to family enterprises in the same line of business. The difficulty in understanding this economy rests in the modern concept of child labor and the current sense that its abolition represents one of the great accomplishments of modern politics. In the central Middle Ages, no one apparently gave child labor a second thought, except for the occasional guild that drew the line at eight or ten as a minimum age. The journeymen worked in shops that had a number of boys or girls (*pueri* or *puellae*) working alongside the day laborers for meals and a place to sleep at night. These children served also to remind the journeymen that they had competition for work, especially in the unskilled trades.

A fortuitous run of four notarial acts reveals as much about one journeyman and his rise as we are likely to learn in this period. This individual portrait, placed after the evidence from the statutes and the aggregate analysis of contracts, illustrates how one person's life can confirm general trends and supply telling idiosyncrasies. On 31 October 1260, in the small northern Italian port of Ventimiglia, the fifteen-year-old Guiçardino, the son of the late Guglielmo de Matarana, made a work contract with Jacobo the tailor. Guiçardino promised to stay a year and work at tailoring (*officium sartorie*), as well as to provide "other fair services."[55] He also agreed to have his wages reduced for any time lost to illness. In return, Jacobo promised to keep Guiçardino and to pay L4s.10 for the term. Two men advised Guiçardino on his contract; he seems to have been without relatives in Ventimiglia. But he did know something about cutting cloth; this agreement was not an apprenticeship, and it contained no words on teaching or learning. The next year, on 6 November, they renewed the arrangement and changed some details. Guiçardino, a year older, dropped the patronymic and simply styled himself "de Matarana." Jacobo now called himself a *taliator*—a fair synonym. This deal was for another year to begin on 1 December and to include the same type of work, although this time the other services became "suitable" or "agreed upon"—perhaps a sign of a little bargaining.[56] Jacobo paid L5 this year and also promised to feed Guiçardino, who thus improved his lot over the previous terms. Once again the contract was curiously pessimistic about the possibility of illness; Guiçardino allowed himself to be docked, but this time Jacobo specifically agreed to keep him in sickness and in health.

Thus far this rare pair of work contracts is between the same persons. These deals were for short periods of time, but Guiçardino must have worked well in the first year. On 29 December 1262, he made plans for marriage. He accepted a dowry of L20 and the hand of Raimundina, the daughter of Nicola and Adalasia Testa de Porco (an odd name).[57] Guiçardino promised his future wife a marriage gift of L20; in practice he would retain control over this sum, but in law it belonged to Raimundina. Jacobo the tailor was present as an advisor—proof that they remained on good terms. The next notarial act, made on the same day, reveals the complicated deal actually struck.[58] Nicola and Adalasia promised to pay their future son-in-law the L20 dowry over the next five years; this installment plan provided sums close to what Guiçardino was making as a journeyman tailor. But in an even better, and so more unusual, aspect of the dowry contract, the two couples agreed to form a partnership (*societas*), to begin on the day of the marriage and last for the next four years. They all agreed to live together in Nicola's home and work at their trade, which frustratingly was not specified but presumably was tailoring. The four partners permitted themselves to take the expenses of food and clothing out of the business along the way and to split profits evenly at the end. Nicola and Adalasia put all that they had into the partnership; Guiçardino and Raimundina contributed L10, some of which must have represented what Guiçardino had managed to save over the previous two years. Jacobo the tailor was again there to counsel his former journeyman.

Because of a break in the notary Giovanni de Amandolesio's surviving work, Guiçardino slips out of the historical record, and hence his future is unknown. Perhaps he never was an apprentice as such, but by the age of fifteen, this orphan was out in the world and at work. His employer may have thought that one-year terms were the prudent course in these circumstances. In the end, Guiçardino exchanged a master for partnership with his parents-in-law and, of course, his wife. On the side, he also gained a place to live and his food and clothing. Not a bad deal. What part Jacobo played in all of this is unclear; his wife's will reveals that he had a daughter and five sons—perhaps too many responsibilities to make a permanent place for Guiçardino.[59] But Jacobo was there to see his journeyman into a new life, and presumably this berth owed something to the employer's goodwill and astuteness. No signs point to a tailors' guild in Ventimiglia. This newly created family workshop reveals even older solutions to the challenges of finding work and spouses.

The masters' collective and individual need to recruit a work force placed apprentices and journeymen into a hierarchy of labor. The market for labor by and large excluded slaves and Jews from the crafts, but for every slave in a southern European household, a poor city dweller or rural immigrant would find one less place in domestic service and therefore would increase by one the pool of apprentices and potential laborers. The exclusion of the Jews from the artisan crafts and professions is a subject that will be discussed below. Women found a place in the handicrafts, particularly in the specialized branches of the wool industry, but their lower wages acted as a check on the general level of wages and hence also affected the recruitment of male workers. David Herlihy suggests that the definition of the guild system itself contributed to the diminished role that women had in economic production.[60] The fact that guilds seldom permitted women to become masters did in the end relegate them to the least-skilled and certainly least-remunerative aspects of the trade. Even in the generally well-paid dyeing business, women received about half of what men earned.

Patriarchal habits of mind in medieval Europe affected the developing gender division of labor, which in turn defined the scope of women's work and also whether or not women would work at all in certain trades and professions.[61] The gender division of labor was of course not new in the thirteenth century. Wage labor's appearance provided men with a potential challenge to patriarchy, as well as a new type of work requiring definition in terms that suited men. The distinction between laborer and apprentice is important. The comparative rarity of women apprentices in the highly skilled trades made the passing down of knowledge from one generation to the next a monopoly for men. Male masters displayed no eagerness to train young women, and with few or no women as recognized masters, the guilds did contribute to the narrowing of opportunity for women. Given the structure of medieval crafts, fewer female apprentices meant that fewer women would have the skills necessary to bring to their families more than a subsistence wage. But for jobs that only required the ceaseless repetition of a basic manual act, like carding wool, women could slip into the work force without an apprenticeship or elaborate training. So the effect women had on recruitment of labor manifested itself in two basic ways: The disappearance of women from certain trades may have opened up more places for boys to serve as apprentices. Women, however, continued to compete as day laborers, and their low wages caused problems for unskilled men.

The masters invented the system of apprentices and journeymen, but clearly a fair amount of work continued to take place outside the cursus, especially in small towns like Ventimiglia or in disorganized trades like rockbreaking. Apprenticeship took on the appearance of fostering, though in this world of business no accepted reciprocity existed between masters and parents, and so money became involved in the relationship. Sometimes the family of the apprentice had to pay the master; in other places and instances the master offered a salary. Barter worked well for some country people who dispatched their sons and daughters to the city to learn a trade. Some rural people could supply useful payments in kind to the urban household where their child lived. The shoemaker placing his son with a weaver could offer shoes—yet this payment had less elasticity than had an equivalent payment in wheat. Payments in kind were limited to the rural families with a surplus, and money became the way to balance the equation between the value of the training to the apprentice and the benefit (if any) to the master of having this apprentice. At the end of this chapter, household production and why it required extra hands will be examined more closely; for now, it is enough to observe that apprenticeship as practiced in the thirteenth century often involved a payment one way or the other. Apprenticeship benefited from the existence of a money economy, which also accustomed the apprentice to having a cash value assigned to his or her labor. Although the chronology of life and work seems to suggest that apprenticeship should come first and hence is likely to have preceded regular wage labor for the journeymen, the sources will not support such a sweeping conclusion. Instead, on a more modest level, apprenticeship seems, in addition to being a stage of training, also to prepare a person for living by wages. Even when the parents paid or the master provided nothing but maintenance, the differences between paid and unpaid apprentices were blatant; all parties knew that some apprentices were paid and that a close reckoning of profit and costs figured into the particular ways apprentices were treated. Journeymen were already skilled and usually independent, and unless the masters had unmarried daughters, no sons, or for some reason wanted a stable of mature and often married individuals living in their households, they literally had to pay to have the journeymen live elsewhere. This analysis is a simple and straightforward explanation for wage labor's origins; it will be fleshed out by the inclusion of other considerations, but it is a start.

The next four topics in this chapter help to explain some of the special features of wage labor. Standards of production, where they existed, imposed effective work rules. Merchant guilds, in addition to posing problems for the crafts, dispensed with this system of recruiting apprentices and journeymen. Employees were not eligible to serve as guild officials, and so these posts gave the masters some special opportunities to manage their trades and professions. Finally, the hierarchy of trades had a great deal to do with wage levels, but status was more than money.

Standards of Production

Agreements on standards of production are not a usual feature of guild statutes. In chapter 2 some signs that public authorities may have imposed some regulations about prices and products on the guilds in order to protect the wider community were discussed. Masters imposed such rules on themselves in some towns, and guilds in other places thrived without de jure standards. This variability of practice helps to account for the different ways that guilds developed in various parts of Europe. The issue of standards also brings to the foreground the important question of whether guilds encouraged or stifled technological innovation. Standards may have resulted in a routinized and uninventive pattern of production, or they may have provided masters with the incentive to reduce their costs by improving efficiency and maintaining quality.

The apprenticeship system in part existed to pass on skills, and hence the ability to meet certain standards, from one generation to the next. Journeymen sometimes had the opportunity to prove that their work was in keeping with the reputation of a local craft, as when the weavers of Chartres required anyone, male or female, who wanted to become a master to display six cloths woven by his or her own hand.[62] Where the production of a masterpiece proved to be impractical, as was the case in many trades, the guild might administer a test. The fullers of Toulouse instituted a test in 1315, probably because their art was only one step in an elaborate process leading to a finished cloth, and an actual exam was the best way to ascertain skills.[63] The members of some trades, like the blacksmiths everywhere, avoided both tests and masterpieces. Indeed, these formal measurements of skill seem to have been the exception and not the rule. The examination did become a distinctive feature of the guild of university masters, who conferred on successful candidates the *ius docendi* (license to teach). These methods helped to insure some competency in the craft and were an important part of the widespread desire to maintain standards. The ordinances of the hatters of Paris provide a rare thirteenth-century example of what would become almost the universal custom in later centuries.[64] The hatters wanted the apprentices to produce a *chief d'oevre* (masterpiece). The hatters allowed themselves only one apprentice, and the point of the masterpiece was not so much to demonstrate that the apprentice was skilled in the craft, but to enable the master to engage another apprentice. At least in this example from Paris, the masters had a genuine interest in making sure that their apprentices were capable of a *chief d'oevre*. The burden of upholding standards principally fell on the masters, who were ultimately responsible for their own work, as well as for the apprentices and journeymen who worked in their shops.

The guilds of the central Middle Ages developed and used a large number of ways to establish standards of quality, and these ways naturally varied according to the kind of business. The trademark was one of the more universal methods used to identify products by the shop of origin. These trademarks helped the guild to identify masters whose work was not up to standard and also permitted customers to judge the quality of the various shops. The cotton guild of Bologna in 1288 required that no master sell a piece of cotton cloth unless it carried the master's mark, under penalty of twelve pence, half to the guild and half to the accuser. All masters had to register their marks with the guild, and they faced the heavier penalty of five solidi if they put their mark on another master's piece of cotton cloth.[65] The statutes of wool guilds across Europe reveal that masters were preoccupied with questions of quality and uniformity. That these issues were so closely tied together indicates that the craftsmen equated the reputation of their product with its uniformity among shops. A tension existed between the reputation of individual shops and the business or craft as a whole. The trademark was supposed to be a guarantee of quality, and so too were guild rules and the officials standing behind them. The wool guilds regulated the most minute details of production, from the kinds of wool to the thickness of thread and the size and weight of the cloth produced. Subsequent stages devoted to the finishing and dyeing of the cloth had similar rules. The international market for wool cloth valued products according to the town of origin, and so this kind of close regulation presumably benefited the entire wool trade.

The wool industry existed in many parts of Europe, but more specialized crafts also depended on the international network of trade. In some instances a single town might dominate a large regional market. One unusual example of this phenomenon is the guild of dicemakers (*daserii*) in Toulouse.[66] Their statutes of 1290 and 1298 do not indicate the number of dicemakers in the city, but the fact that they had enough craftsmen to form a guild devoted to this specialized business is significant. The dicemakers prohibited any of their number from importing dice from Lombardy. The emphasis was on local production, and the dicemakers of Toulouse seem to have attempted to dominate the market in Languedoc. No single town was capable of keeping a sizable guild of dicemakers at work, so an export trade was vital to this kind of business. The masters of Toulouse agreed to limit themselves to two apprentices each, and this also suggests that they were reasonably busy. The masters and their employees made a product for which the customers had an unusual concern for quality. The first item in the statutes bound the dicemakers not to manufacture any loaded, marked, or clipped dice. The masters wanted their product to have a high repute with customers, but they probably also wanted the various games played with dice to flourish. Cheating would only have hurt their business. The export market depended on the reliable and honest dice produced in the shops. The other important feature of these dice is their uniformity; the customers expected each sample of this product to be exactly the same, in fact interchangeable. The masters agreed to make dice on which the numbers one and six, five and two, and three and four were always on opposite sides of the cube, the customary rules of the game. The statutes also stipulated that no one should make dice from the bones of a horse. Customers were not in a position to determine the kind of bone for themselves, but perhaps such dice were simply judged to be unlucky, and the masters did not provide them. The question of night work has already come up in connection to quality, for the reason of sloppy work produced in poor light. The dicemakers were naturally concerned about this matter as well, and they prohibited work after vespers, except from All Saints' Day to Christmas—a time when they were busy turning out dice for presents. The ordinances of the dicemakers (*deiciers*) of Paris are not as detailed as those from Toulouse, but the Parisian rules display a similar concern for quality.[67] In Paris the masters promised not to make dice that were too heavy (loaded), or had all the same numbers, or, interestingly, were made from magnets. These dicemakers never worked at night, and their apprentices served for the long term of nine years.

The guilds involved in the supply of food also displayed a high interest in quality. André Gouron has demonstrated for all of Languedoc that city officials took an early interest in protecting public health, but the guilds as well were interested in insuring and protecting the quality of merchandise.[68] Many of the statutes relate details on the quality of raw materials used in preparing food. For example, the butchers of Florence had a rule that no meat from any animal that had died from disease should be sold to the public.[69] These butchers also agreed that two rectors of their guild should make inspections once a week to make sure the members obeyed this rule. The butchers faced the stiff fine of one hundred soldi di piccioli if they broke this rule, and the inspectors faced the same fine if they did not do their job properly. (A host of such rules attempted to protect the health of consumers, and this one also catered to the old and reasonable bias against eating tainted meat.) The butchers of Florence and other cities placed their cuts of meat in the windows so that customers would be able to shop from the street, and in public. The statutes also obligated the butchers not to mix the meat of male pigs with that from sows nor the meat of sheep with that of horses. The first distinction, based on the sex of the pig, is difficult to understand and may reflect local custom and dietary practice. The dislike of mixing meat from different sexes was widespread; in Toulouse the butchers agreed not to mix the flesh of sheep and rams.[70] Apart from these questions of taste and health, sanitation figured prominently in the statutes of victualers' guilds. One of the few rules that described a specific practice concerns the fancy bakers of Toulouse, who made sure that the meats used in their pies had been thoroughly washed in clean water.[71]

Just as explicit concern about hygiene imposed certain standards on the trades, so too did fixed prices. In London the king and the city government were active in regulating the prices and quality of basic items like bread, ale, meat, and poultry. The guilds conformed to these laws and occasionally had special rules that pertained to individual crafts. In 1274, the poulterers of London, who also sold rabbits, hares, kids, and lambs, had a detailed price list for all of their meats, and these prices took into account the changing seasons and availability of various animals.[72] Fixed seasonal prices served as a form of unambiguous standard and also allowed some competition on the basis of quality. At the Assizes of Bread and Ale, the mayor, aldermen, and officials, on behalf of the crown, made sure that these ordinances were enforced and violators were fined.

The manufacturing guilds had different methods of policing their members to make sure that standards of production were maintained. Many crafts had no obvious measure, like so many threads per pound of wool, to apply to their products. The smiths of Bologna appointed two officials, aptly called inquisitors, who were supposed to look into the work of the craft. One was responsible for the *ferris grossis*, the larger implements made from iron, the other for the *ferris minutis*.[73] If the inquisitors were satisfied with the work, they praised it before the guild; if not, they condemned the shoddy products and punished the responsible master. This procedure, a nicely balanced blend of praise and censure, relied on experienced masters to police their colleagues in the guild. The various and specialized works of the smiths required two experts, but even here the statutes' framers had to settle for the vague concept of well-done work.

The guilds primarily relied upon a system of oaths, fines, and officials, their own or those appointed by urban or royal authorities, to regulate the standards of production. This general emphasis on quality seems to have suited the masters, their employees, and customers; and some public officials encouraged the guilds to take an interest in quality. As has already been discussed, quality, particularly where some objective or numerical definition proved to be impractical, became in some cases a question of uniformity, which in turn might have fostered mediocrity and stifled innovation. In a system that emphasized cooperation among masters as a desideratum, the idea of uniformity had certain positive connotations. Uniform standards applied to finished products, not methods of production, and thus masters were free to invest capital and to tinker with ways to reduce their own costs while achieving commonly accepted results. The masters had their own secrets and arts, and the statutes as a rule did not presume to tell them *how* to do their work. The statutes never addressed the question of masters who surpassed the standards, and conceivably anyone who could have done that, while keeping costs down, would have benefited in the marketplace and perhaps prodded the guild into raising its own standards. Masters producing goods for a wider market, and the drapers of Chartres are a typical example, understood that the reputation of their wares was the most important factor in determining the price and prestige of their cloth at the fairs of Champagne. Large-scale production at the wholesale level required these masters to pool their product so that sales of large lots would be possible. The connection in this case between quality and uniformity is clear. On the local level, particularly for those masters engaged in retail trade, the incentive of the international market was lacking, but the standards of these guilds also emphasized result and not method. On balance, the freedom that masters allowed themselves to run their shops and to train their apprentices as they pleased, so long as their goods met the standards, also permitted them to experiment as they pleased.

The surviving source material contains no traces of records that would illustrate the daily lives and work of individual craftsmen in their shops.[74] Without these sources, masters remain little more than trademarks, or names on apprenticeship contracts, or lists of people who swore to support the guild. For the central Middle Ages, statutes are one of the few useful sources on the actual work of the shops, and their evidence suggests that the process of creation was left to the ingenuity of the masters and the enforced dutifulness of the apprentices and journeymen.

Merchant Guilds

Merchant guilds pose some distinctive problems that merit separate attention. Most of the examples used to illustrate aspects of guild activities come from documents that concern artisans. Within many craft guilds were rules on the conduct of retail trade and signs that some masters had transformed themselves into wealthy merchants involved in trade beyond their city walls. In a sense, all craftsmen selling to the public were merchants, but the big merchants scattered throughout some craft guilds carried on trade at a scale beyond the reach of most masters. Because any master might turn himself into a merchant, a sharp line does not separate the craft and merchant guilds. In some towns, however, merchants engaging in long-distance trade did gather together into guilds, which in turn frequently became powerful political forces. Merchant guilds contained many, if not most, of the wealthy people in town, and in some places they had the dominant voice in city government. In the next chapter the role that guilds played in the wider world of government will be examined; here the interest in the merchant guild rests in their distinctive internal structure and economic significance.

A unique set of customs for an early merchant guild comes from the Flemish town of St. Omer. These customs, redacted sometime between 1083 and 1127, and probably closer to the earlier date, reflect the heroic age of the medieval merchant, an atmosphere Henri Pirenne evoked in his many works on that subject.[75] The primary interest of this merchant guild seems to have been in their *potaciones*, or drinking parties. The emphasis on conviviality harks back to the early Germanic guilds, but this later association of merchants had clear economic roots, unlike the purely social guilds of the Carolingian age. The customs, however, do reveal a deep concern about the social aspects of this merchant guild and placed importance on harmony. Several rules go into elaborate detail about various kinds of misconduct that threatened the peace of their meetings. The merchants were concerned about their personal safety, a reasonable worry when a duel was still a lively possibility. The members devised a system of fines to punish malefactors. The merchants also established pretexts for demanding measures of wine from members, but they were generous with their drink and awarded a measure of wine every night to all of the priests of the parishes of St. Omer. The merchants had a guild hall for meetings, and they donated what was left of their corporate income for the benefit of the community, either for the gates, squares, or town fortifications or for the needs of paupers and lepers.

Some prototypical features of this merchant guild deserve notice. The merchants of St. Omer denied any help or responsibility to a trader who did not join the guild. Although mutual aid did not receive much attention in the customs, solidarity among the members clearly extended to their business lives. For example, the guild regulated the number and obligations of guarantors, and those in commerce who stood surety to agreements for one another benefited from a common sense of loyalty. The guild excluded clerics, warriors, and foreign merchants from membership, but all those who could afford to purchase a place in the guild seem to have been free to join. The customs used the word *communis* to refer to the town that benefited from the guild's donations. Whether or not St. Omer had a commune in law at this time, the town had a merchant guild that included the strongest members of the non-noble and lay population, just the type of people likely to be dominant in whatever form of government emerged in St. Omer. The guild did not provide for any apprentices or journeymen; it was an association of employers, and members were left to devise their own means of becoming merchants and recruiting assistants. Members were allowed to bring a son, nephew, or *famulus* (servant) to the meetings, and from this group the next generation of members were likely to come. In towns like St. Omer, where the merchant guild preceded any signs of craft organizations, the latter would always be in a subordinate position.

The merchant guild sometimes represented an institution like the *Calimala*, the group in Florence that engaged in the trade of rough and finished cloth and functioned, along with the *Lana* guild, as a de facto merchant guild.[76] Most merchant guildsmen were involved in a variety of finished goods and raw materials, adjusting their holdings and ventures as the market warranted. Hence the merchant guildsmen were classic middlemen, customers to the craft guilds and other merchants, producing themselves nothing but the traffic of commodities from one place to another. In the central Middle Ages, travel was expensive, difficult, and frequently dangerous. Whether by galley from Venice to Acre, or by pack animal across mountain passes, or by treacherous carts, the merchant needed an intrepid spirit. Such people, where they successfully seized the reins of city government, were not likely to form a merchant guild if they did not already have one. As Frederic Lane observed, "Venetian merchants engaged in international trade felt no need of any special organizations, such as guilds, to look after their commercial interests, for their Communal government made that its chief concern."[77]

Where some other power beyond the confines of the city claimed and exercised jurisdiction, merchants would find that forming a guild was to their advantage. Their principal aim was mutual protection, but other incentives to starting a guild were also present. Given the perils of long-distance trade, some insulation from ruinous competition was desirable. Merchant guilds did not have to worry about standards of production, but common weights and prices for important commodities were a legitimate concern. Merchant guilds did not avail themselves of an apprenticeship system in a formal sense; the capital requirements to enter the trade were too large to waste time and effort training any substantial number of people who were not needed. The job of accompanying a merchant as a servant on a voyage or trip was the best that those without means might expect. The notarial records of southern European towns contain work contracts by which a merchant hired an assistant or traveling companion. The merchant guilds did not regulate these contracts. Merchants did not share most of the basic concerns and needs of those in the craft guilds, but they had problems of their own.

The merchants' collective need for protection was immediate and related to the activities of secular rulers. As early as 1127, the merchants of St. Omer received from William Clito, Count of Flanders, complete freedom from any tolls in the county or exactions placed upon them on returning from the domains of the German emperor. The count even promised that, if he should ever make peace with his uncle Henry I of England, he would make sure that the peace included an exemption from all tolls for the merchants of St. Omer.[78] Tolls were more than vexatious; they were potentially ruinous, especially if merchants from other towns were exempt and hence gained an advantage in the wider market. Once merchants left their hometowns, they would face a bewildering array of tolls, and the farther from home, the more they needed to depend on something for protection. A merchant guild could be of some use abroad, but secular authorities, where they existed, were in a better position to come to the aid of merchants in distress. Venice, with its formidable diplomacy and ability to get charters of privilege or to make treaties with foreign rulers, performed this task for its merchants. Few city governments found themselves in equally favorable positions, and so they turned to the feudal hierarchy,

a decision with costs of its own. The communes, and even city governments in the power of a feudal lord or the king himself, existed in part
for the very purpose of gaining concessions for the merchants. The
merchant guild enabled the traders to have a body solely devoted to
their interests, and this was especially desirable in those northern
towns like Cologne where the powers of the archbishop limited the
scope of town government.

Tolls preoccupied medieval merchants. Henry I of England, in his
famous charter to the citizens of London dated 1130–1133, granted
them something particularly valuable—freedom from all customs and
tolls throughout the kingdom.[79] This privilege was part of a bundle of
rights that the burgesses of London received by virtue of their holding
Middlesex county "at farm"—for £300 a year. The burgesses were a
diverse group of men, but all of them would benefit from the toll
exemption. As the modern editors of this document noted, the assumption is "that the merchant guild comprised the burgesses who
held the borough at farm," that is, those who collectively ruled the city.
Henry II granted the citizens of Lincoln in ca. 1157 a general confirmation of their liberties as these had existed in the reigns of Edward the
Confessor, William the Conqueror, and Henry I and also confirmed
their merchant guild, which in this case included merchants from the
city and other men from the shire.[80] A writ from 1154–1160 reveals that
no one from outside Lincoln was allowed to enter the city for the
purpose of dyeing cloth or engaging in retail trade unless this individual was in the guild and contributed to the city's taxes.[81] This writ
indicates that traders from outside the city could enter the guild, and
provided that they assumed their share of the financial burden, they
might benefit from the merchant guild. In England the merchant guild
had a complicated subsequent history, particularly in the area of town
government, and is a subject that will be discussed again in the next
chapter. The merchant guild was, however, only one possible way for a
town or collection of merchants to receive privileges from the king. The
English experience had merchant guilds in some towns but not in
others, yet all were subject to the same king. This variety suggests that
local factors might have prompted the institution of a merchant guild.[82]

The internal organization and functions of the German merchant
guilds depended in the same way on the circumstances of the individual towns. Philippe Dollinger points out that the early existence of a
merchant guild in Cologne and the way it dominated the town council
served as a model for some German towns.[83] But the new towns in the

east, Lübeck and Magdeburg, also benefited as strong rulers like Frederick I and Henry of Saxony fostered commercial privileges and merchant organizations. The unique feature of the German merchant guilds is the way they combined, for the purpose of external trade in the Baltic region, into one common association, or Hanse. This body also facilitated trade in England, which recognized a single German Hanse in 1281.[84] The most important overseas stations (or *Kontore*) were in Novgorod, Bergen, London, and Bruges. The Hanse itself was not a guild but a confederation of merchant guilds, though in fact not all of the member towns had such guilds. The authority of the towns remained dominant both over the *Kontore* and the individual merchant guilds.[85] Although the Hanse was not a guild, it served to protect merchants outside their own territories, and even the strongest individual town and merchant guild, Cologne, profited from the influence of the combined towns. The individual German merchant guilds and particularly those merchants from the towns that did not develop such guilds needed this kind of mutual protection. Especially after the collapse of the Hohenstaufen empire in 1250, German secular power was in no position to bargain for favorable terms for the merchants from the imperial cities. So the Hanse demonstrates the value of the merchant guilds and also indicates why some towns were able to survive without them by the astute use of political power to protect economic interests and trade.

Merchants in the international market were in the business of moving commodities from centers of production or availability to the potential customers. These merchants above all needed protection from rapacious foreign governments, pirates, and the animosities of local producers who did not think that local manufacturers benefited from foreign trade. The cheap German hats that the cappers of London complained about came to England courtesy of the Hanse.[86] Demands for protection are as old as international trade. Associations of importers and exporters survived the medieval merchant guild, and centralized government assumed, where it was so inclined, the burden of protecting the interests of the international traders. Some states like Venice excelled in this task. The merchant guild in some places helped to bridge this gap in protection that existed from the time a centralized state was weak or nonexistent to the time it was able to pursue economic policies. In some places like London, town government filled the gap, and in other places, trade never developed enough to require a merchant guild.

The guilds organized along particular lines of business—wool, silk, banking, and the like—contained merchants whose prosperity also depended on international trade. These guilds posed different problems to government, and the issues were not simply the places and missions of amorphous trade but rather the intimate details of crafts and businesses. A merchant might ship caps one year and raisins the next, but a big entrepreneur in a wool guild was usually stuck with wool and not free to shift to some other business in order to respond to slight fluctuations in the market. The typical trader in a merchant guild was not in an easily regulated competition with fellow townsmen. Most of the ordinary concerns of guilds—questions about journeymen and apprentices, wages, standards of production, and even prices—did not worry the merchant guildsmen, who instead were usually interested in what would happen to them when they were abroad or what challenges foreigners would bring to their doorsteps. Only merchants who themselves traveled or who had agents abroad would worry about the tolls and dangers of international trade. Many small-time retailers had reason to be concerned about the effects of trade on the local market. As seen above, other guilds might approach a monarch or city government to seek protection from particular products or might agree among themselves to exclude these products from their own retail trade, but what mattered to other people only occasionally or in specific items of trade was the main and continuous business of the merchant guild. The merchant guild was, however, only one way among several for traders to manage their affairs. Where possible, they seem to have preferred to seize the reins of town government.

Guild Officials

Guild officials have repeatedly cropped up in this study. Higher authorities and the guild members held these officials responsible for the activities of the guild. The masters had varying degrees of a voice in the selection and determination of the duties of officials. The guilds were seldom democracies, and their sense of corporate identity did not obviate the need for some individuals to assume posts in the guild. These officials or officers, in contrast to the widespread use of recognizable relatives of the term *master,* had many different titles. The officials of the cloth guild of Toulouse had three Latin names: *custodes, baiuli,* and *rectores* (guardians, bailiffs, and rectors) of the guild.[87] The officials often took their titles from the tasks they performed. In some towns the expected quality of the officials became synonymous with the title of the office; in Paris the officials were frequently called *preudeshommes* (the wise or prudent men), Old French for the ubiquitous *probi homines*. In London, where Old French remained for some time the language of the law, the cordwainers had four *prodhomes*, but the lorimers made do with the more recognizable *wardeyns*.[88] The guilds of Venice had their *suprastantes* (overseers); and in Florence rectors and consuls and in Bologna *ministeriales* were the typical leading officials. The German cities displayed an equally inventive variety of German and Latin titles. Beyond the chief officials, many guilds had lesser posts—various kinds of inspectors, treasurers, and in southern Europe frequently a notary. Some large guilds that were also confraternities had a priest or chaplain supported by the members. Minor offices, excluding those for clergy, allowed even more people to participate and in some cases were stepping stones to the chief positions in the guild. Lesser officials, however, remained subordinate to the leaders of the business or profession. This discussion is mostly confined to the principal officials. The different titles for the heads of the guilds should not obscure some questions common to nearly all of the guilds—who was eligible to serve, and how were such people selected?

The masters in each guild had a monopoly on the offices. The guilds were intended to promote their members' interests, and although the guilds often matriculated or registered journeymen and apprentices, this act did not make these workers eligible for office. The masters, and whatever public or civic authority lorded over them, required a pool of people to draw upon for officials, and the masters were reluctant to let this vital part of their affairs slip through their hands. The guilds of medieval Europe had a handful of features in common. One of the most important, and revealing, is the way that masters retained control of their guild. On the next issue, however, the guilds divided into two great camps: in the first some outside authority named the officials; in the second the masters had the right to devise their own method of selection. In a few cases the masters resorted to that remarkable and tenuous practice of election. The masters had absolute power in their shops and businesses and dominated their guilds, but the question of office holding attracted the notice of others in medieval society. The clearest examples of the ways in which external authorities took an interest in guild officials are found precisely in those cities where that authority was formidable, where strong government was established or in the process of coalescing. Three cities suggest themselves for further study—Paris, London, and Venice.

That important source *Livre des métiers* by Étienne Boileau, Louis IX's *prévot* of Paris, contains the laws and customs of the guilds of Paris in the 1260s. This comprehensive source reveals the inner workings of 101 trades, some quite narrow groups with only a handful of masters in the whole city and others large associations with masters on almost every street. The customs of the first métier of the compilation, the *talemeliers* (bakers), reveal how the king treated the corporations. In this case the king gave to his own master baker the *mestrise* (overall control) of the guild.[89] The king's baker reserved the right to administer petty justice and to keep the fines that resulted from his decisions. This master baker also chose the twelve *preud'homes* who had the direct responsibility for managing the daily affairs of the guild—which in baking were invariably the size and quality of loaves of bread. This kind of arrangement suited the king: the fines of a large guild supplemented the income of members of his household. The king gave his master horseshoer the entry fines and income from administering petty justice of the *fevres* (blacksmiths) of Paris.[90] The *fevres*, however, had the right to elect six *prudhommes* of their own, and these officials were free from the *guet* (yearly tax), so the job brought more than prestige to the occupant. The smiths had favored status as a métier, even in their position as a means of financial reward to a member of the king's household.

Most other guilds had their officials appointed by the *prévot*. Free election was the exception and not the rule. The goldsmiths enjoyed the rare privilege of electing their own officials who were responsible for safeguarding the uses and customs of the craft, but these officials still had to turn the worst malefactors over to the *prévot* for punishment.[91] The goldsmiths were prestigious and wealthy, but these attributes did not bring other guilds the same privileges. The weavers of tapestries in the Saracen style, also a high-status occupation, had their officials chosen by the *prévot*.[92] In Paris there was a specialized guild of women spinning thread on small spindles, a delicate but not especially remunerative trade. This craft, however, and others like it in which women seem to have comprised almost the entire work force did not have only female officials.[93] Even in businesses where women did the work, men generally were the officials and employers. The general structure of the métiers in Paris reveals that the king, usually through his chief bureaucrat the *prévot* of Paris, controlled the selection of guild officials, all of whom took an oath to the king that they would ensure that the masters, journeymen, and apprentices observed the rules. Advantages in being a guild official still existed, and the *prévot* would often take suggestions from the masters, since he was in no position to know the trades well enough to choose the hundreds of officials who presided over them.

London does not have the same rich documentation for the thirteenth century that Étienne Boileau provided for Paris, but the surviving guild ordinances suggest a smaller degree of royal control in London. The mayor and aldermen, unlike the *prévot* of Paris, exercised authority on behalf of the city itself. The handful of guilds in London for which ordinances still exist displays some variety in the manner of choosing officials. The weavers had the right to elect their own bailiffs, but the mayor had the right to accept these officials (or not) and administer their oath.[94] The cappers' officials seem to have replaced themselves by co-optation; the lorimers elected their officials.[95] Election of guild officers was evidently common in London. Strict accountability to the city government may have made these offices onerous and unattractive. The guild officials in London were more at the mercy of the mayor than of their own members since a vigilant public authority held the officials accountable for the guild's conduct.

The doge and assemblies of Venice had one of the strictest regimes over guild officials (*suprastantes*). In Venice all of the members of the guild (*scuola*) swore an elaborate oath, enforced by the judges (*iusticiarii*), whose primary function was to control the guilds. In typical Venetian fashion, most of the guilds enjoyed the right to elect their own officials. For example, the government gave the tailors this right in 1308, but the method was widespread in the thirteenth century.[96] The three outgoing overseers of the tailors' guild selected four members, who in turn named a fifth to break ties, and these five in turn chose the three officials for the next year. The fishmongers (*pescivendoli*) had five overseers, and every September the outgoing officials chose seven electors who picked the next group of officials.[97] This rapid turnover of offices assured many masters the opportunity to serve, but again in Venice this duty seems to have been burdensome and dour. The fishmongers, as well as the other guilds of Venice, were required to go to meetings at least twice a year to have the rules read to them. They received a moderate fine for failure to attend, and the only acceptable excuses were visiting the dying and personal illness. The officials of the Venetian guilds were virtual agents of the government, a service for which they received one-third of the fines they levied on their fellow members; this must have made them unpopular with their brethren.

In towns like Florence, where the city government was changeable and guilds were more autonomous, masters selected their frequently numerous officials in complicated ways. The oil merchants had four consuls or rectors, eight councillors, a chamberlain, a notary, a messenger, two syndics, and six arbiters.[98] The oil merchants developed a complicated system of selection in which the masters from certain wards (*sestieri*) of Florence elected members from other neighborhoods to conduct a scrutiny that produced the rectors who served for six months.[99] These complex features are typical of those Italian towns that experienced political strife. In these towns masters devised methods to insure that no clique could dominate the affairs of city government or the guilds. The members of the guild insulated themselves from the actual process of selecting officials and instead relied upon a system typical of Florentine politics. The oil merchants were one of the lesser guilds (*arti minori*) and hence played a small role in communal politics. Although they acknowledged the proper jurisdiction of the commune, the oil merchants themselves regulated the internal affairs of their guild. The guilds of Bologna exercised the same autonomy, and the masters there were more inclined to elect their officials than to utilize the cumbersome system of a scrutiny. The smiths, an amalgam of various metalworking crafts, had six officials (*ministeriales*), who again served six-month terms.[100] All of the master smiths participated in the election, and their primary concern was that the successful candidates fairly represent the specialized crafts in the guild. Thus in Bologna, the masters had one of the most democratic methods of choosing officials. Their experience in guild elections was a rarity in medieval Europe. This taste of participation sometimes encouraged masters to expect some equivalent voice in town government, a desire, as will be seen in the next chapter, that had some important consequences.

The duties of guild officials involved these people in both civic affairs and the activities of their fellow masters. The turnover rate of the guild officials guaranteed that most masters would have the opportunity to experience the burdens of office and learn something about their city. Those officials whose primary tasks were to uphold standards and to inquire into complaints and disputes were in a unique position to study their craft or business and to keep abreast of how their fellow masters and competitors conducted their business. The officials had access to the shops, and on their tours of inspection, they would see most things. Natural curiosity about how people in the same line of work conducted their business might lead to the officials reexamining their own methods. The guilds fostered solidarity and frequently encouraged uniform standards; the officials, charged with enforcing the rules, also served as a potential mechanism for spreading news about innovation and better techniques, especially in the manufacturing trades. Being an official was an opportunity to learn, and perhaps these visits and intrusions in the end had a greater role than standards of production in encouraging innovation. Such officials were also powerful because they helped to define the boundary between private and public aspects of the trade.[101] Secrecy about skills and methods protected the masters from outside attention, but within their circle some loss of privacy was the price for maintaining standards of production. Those craftsmen working either in trades too small to have a guild or in new trades had an advantage over the traditional shops, at least in their ability to preserve the secrets of their trade.

Hierarchy of Guilds

Not all guilds were equal, and not all trades enjoyed the same status in the community. The concept of a hierarchy of guilds illuminates both the developing division of labor and the general social attitudes about work and its dignity, or lack of it. Several approaches to this question exist, and both regional variations and changing social responses to work argue against any static portrait of a hierarchy of guilds. The sources suggest several ways to look at what was in effect a division of labor, though contemporaries did not use that phrase. The seven great guilds of Florence (*arti maggiori*) are a classic example of how one group of guilds assumed a high level of prestige and political domination in one town.[102] Three of the big seven—the finishers and dealers of foreign cloth (*Calimala*), the importers of wool and manufacturers of local cloth (*Lana*), and the money changers and bankers (*Cambio*)—stood at the top of the *popolo* (the people). The judges and notaries, physicians and apothecaries, furriers, and big retailers and silk entrepreneurs (*Por Santa Maria*) were close behind in wealth and prestige. Wool and banks were the twin pillars of the Florentine economy, and in other towns different trades were in the dominant position. This example, however, supplies several topics for closer inspection. Medicine, the law, furs, silk, fine cloth, and money were honorable products in some eyes, more dignified than, for example, the cuts of meat and shoes produced by guilds called the *arti minori.* Wealth, in terms of the income the masters received, was often related to the quality of the product. The wealth of certain merchants and artisans was in some respects the crucial fact that set their position in the hierarchy. Wealthy entrepreneurs did not necessarily pay high wages; in some cases, as will be seen, quite the reverse occurred.

A product of any particular business derived its prestige from several factors: the value of the raw materials, the wage levels of the employees, and the quality or wealth of the customers. Wage levels are important because they suggest how the craft appealed to potential employees, as well as the ways that masters viewed their own business. The division of labor is also a part of this hierarchy. The question of women's work becomes important since women became the dominant part of the work force in some trades at the same time that they were being excluded from others. The sheer size of any guild affected its prestige; the number of masters, where available, may indicate something about the importance of the craft. Chronology also has a role; some trades were old and therefore prestigious or historically base, and others were new and had to find and defend a place for themselves. Finally, we should keep a sense of perspective on this hierarchy. Nobles by definition did not work, and they were not inclined to credit subtle distinctions among those who did. Some scholastic thinkers, pondering old questions such as whether or not a merchant could achieve salvation, produced a kind of inverse hierarchy, with merchants and money changers at the bottom. All of these possible approaches to the hierarchy of guilds require some common denominators in order to make sense of them. Length of apprenticeship and wages are good ways to introduce one type of ordering of the trades.

The statutes of the Parisian guilds and the Genoese apprenticeship contracts supply one obvious test—the length of apprenticeship where the longer the term, the more prestigious the craft. In Paris the statutes often required a standard term, but in Genoa the actual contracts show that the masters tailored the term to the age and previous experience of the apprentice. Both cities had the typical spread of terms, from four to eleven or twelve years (table 3-2). The great bulk of the Parisian trades were clustered in the middle, at eight years, and in Genoa seven years was the average term. The guilds of Paris operated in a system that sanctioned a minute division of labor; for example, three separate trades made buckles from different kinds of metal. The ordering of trades according to the years that masters thought were necessary for

Table 3-2. Length of Apprenticeship, Thirteenth Century

Years	Paris	Genoa
4	Baker, Rope, Carpenter	Draper, Spinner
5	Fur hats	Horseshoer, Barber, Cobbler, Wool, Mason
6	Hatter, Cutler, Copper buttons, Mason	Dyer, Gold threads, Tailor
7	Wool fringes, Felt hats	Turner, Smith, Carpenter, Coppersmith, Carder
8	Hatter *d'or,* Tanner, Buckles, Clasps, Locksmith, Religious artifacts (bone), Lace, Silk threads (large and small spindles), Silk cloth, Silk caps, Linen, Pins, Combs, Painter of saddles, Handles	Locksmith, Cutler, Gold foil, Butcher
9	Book snaps, Sheaths, Dice, Religious artifacts (beads and buttons)	Harnesses
10	Iron buckles, Brass buckles, Religious artifacts (amber), Silk *tissu,* Tapestries, Crucifixes, Tables, Buttons, Goldsmith	Silversmith, Armorer, Saddler, Cooper
11	Harnesses	Chestmaker
12	Copper wires, Lapidary, Trusses, Religious artifacts (coral)	

Sources: Étienne Boileau, *Livre des métiers;* Archivio di Stato di Genova, Cartolari Notarili.

Note: For clarity and brevity, a mixture of trades and products is presented. Terms of apprenticeship are statutory lengths in Paris and average lengths in Genoa.

proper training supports the idea that this hierarchy in abstract was not the same throughout medieval Europe. Paris and Genoa were quite different towns and owed their prosperity to unusual economic circumstances. Still, some useful parallels are indicated in table 3-2. Some clearly important trades are absent from one or the other column; for example, the smiths of Paris had not set a term of apprenticeship. The smiths in Genoa, with apprenticeships ranging from three to ten years, illustrate in this instance the wise ambiguity of the Parisian masters. An examination of the lengths of various apprenticeship supports the assumption that the trades on the longer end of the scale were harder to learn and hence enjoyed higher social status.

The value of raw materials is also a factor in status and can be related to the time required to learn the skill (table 3-2). Some apparent anomalies with respect to skill levels and the cost of raw materials are indicated in table 3-2. The furhatters seem out of place on the Parisian list, and certainly the term is incongruous next to the trades requiring five-year terms in Genoa. The statutes of this particular guild may not be as old as those of other guilds of the *Livre des métiers* and may reflect changed conditions in the fourteenth century.[103] The most important inconsistencies in table 3-2 are the relatively low status of the gold thread industry in Genoa and of some aspects of the silk business in Paris. Women workers predominated in both trades, and this fact is more important than the value of the raw material. Male employers bore the capital costs, and their own status may have suffered because of the sex of their work force. Both raw materials and the level of skill were factors in most cases in determining status, at least in the matter of apprenticeships. Gold- and silversmiths stand high in the rank order, as do those masters making religious artifacts from coral, an import from the Mediterranean region. Wood was a relatively humble raw material, and it did not do much for the status of simple carpenters. But the skilled hands of the joiners, the tablemakers of Paris or the chestmakers of Genoa, added considerable value to the wood and raised the status of these trades. Both cities had some trades of local significance; barrels were vital to the galleys that brought prosperity to Genoa, and only a university town like Paris would have enough trade to justify a business in book clasps.

Another useful barometer of status is whether or not the parent or guardian had to pay the master to take on an apprentice. Thirty-two of the Parisian trades had a two-tier (at least) model of apprenticeship—one term with an initial payment to the master or a longer term without such a payment. For a handful of trades, working off the premium to the master was not possible; instead, it served as an irreducible payment for entry into the craft. The hatters required of their apprentices six years of service and a fee of six livres, the mortarers six years and five livres, the painters of saddles eight years and eight livres, and the makers of religious artifacts of amber ten years and ten livres.[104] These four trades were not the most important in Paris, but they were the most difficult to enter. Twenty-nine other guilds charged an initial fee that the apprentice might work off at some rate per year, with one livre (twenty sous) the most common figure. For example, the wool guild stipulated a detailed sliding scale—four years of apprenticeship and an entry fee of eighty sous, five years and sixty sous, six years and twenty sous, or seven years and no fee.[105] A diverse group of crafts followed this procedure, which is thus not a sure guide to the status of the masters. More useful are those crafts that diverged from the standard twenty sous per year—silkweavers, sixty sous; lapidaries, fifty sous; tapestryweavers in the Saracen style, fifty sous; crucifix carvers, forty sous; and harnessmakers, thirty sous.[106] Semiprecious stones, silk, and tapestries all presume valuable raw materials. The carvers of crucifixes catered to what evidently was a lively market in Paris for religious artifacts of all types. Harnessmakers, at the luxury end of their trade, had skills that were important to the nobility. Goldsmiths provide another way to gauge the standing of their craft. They required that apprentices serve for at least ten years and also that they should know enough to earn their own living—enough to earn one hundred sous a year and the expenses of their food and drink.[107] The sum of one hundred sous is comparable to the value of the apprentices to their masters in their last year of training and certainly places this trade in the first rank.

The status of women is one exception to the emerging picture. Women spinning silk thread on large and small spindles also served long apprenticeships (eight years) and worked with a costly commodity.[108] Both groups of women were able to work off their last year of apprenticeship at the standard rate of twenty sous. Here again the standing of the trade must not be taken for the status of the worker. A note in the margin of the statutes concerning work on the small spindles records that in 1309 the trade had four masters—two women and two men—but throughout the regulations the masters used the feminine form of the noun *worker* to refer to the employees.[109] Masters and mistresses derived status from the silk business, but without data on wages, the situation of their workers remains uncertain.

The general hierarchy in Paris may be summarized as follows. The king permitted a number of trades, some quite prestigious and important, to set their own terms of apprenticeship, with or without any payment. Some other trades mentioned in their statutes signs of favored status; for example, the hatters working in peacock feathers noted that their trade catered to the churches, knights, and *haus hommes* (big men).[110] (Jean de Joinville, the biographer of Louis IX of France, has written that this modest ruler liked to wear a hat adorned with white peacock feathers.[111]) Hatters making hats from flowers, particularly roses, noted that "their trade was established to serve the gentlemen."[112] These and other indications suggest that both the quality of the raw materials and the social status of the retail customers played a large role in determining the place that a craft occupied in the hierarchy of trades and professions. The more expensive the raw materials, and the deeper the pockets of the buyer, the more likely the masters were to make a good living at the trade. Whether or not they passed some of this wealth down to the journeymen and apprentices is unknown. The premiums that parents paid to place children in particular trades are signs of some expectations. At the bottom of the hierarchy were some guilds of substantial size (like wool), some construction trades, and rag merchants. Size alone did not guarantee status. Some trades were able to claim great age as a reason for privileged status, but in Paris few masters of the 1260s were able to recall anything before the reign of Philip Augustus. The stonemasons are a notable exception; they came up with the remarkable statement that they were free from *guet* because of a privilege granted to them by Charles Martel.[113] Whether for this or some other reason, such as their own fanciful connection between Charles's epithet and the main tool of their craft, the masons felt that they were superior to the other construction trades.

As has been discussed above, the question of how the cost of raw materials affected the status of a trade depends on whether the question is considered from the perspective of employers or workers. Since the workers by definition, "on account of their poverty or wish," lacked the capital necessary for setting up their own shops, the price of raw materials had only a tangential relationship to their own sense of status.[114] Martha Howell has recently outlined an alternative way to determine a worker's labor status—"the term refers simply to the degree to which a person's role in economic production grants access to the resources of production and distribution."[115] For Howell, the worker's status hinges on this question of access to raw materials, but since the worker had no control over how the master saw fit to sell the products of a shop, distribution falls outside the matter of employee status. From one point of view this analysis, resting on the importance of the means of production, makes sense. The woman who had piles of silk or gold placed before her to turn into thread had access to a resource of production that was beyond the reach of most self-employed artisans. In an intangible way such a woman may have enjoyed higher status than those working on wool or flax, but no evidence supports this assumption. Marshall Sahlins defines a "domestic mode of production" and emphasizes three characteristics: a small labor force with a gender division of labor in place, simple technology, and finite objectives of production.[116] He also contends that this emphasis on immediate use fosters inertia and production levels below the theoretical capacity of society. Although none of these conditions (except the durable gender division of labor) hold for the Middle Ages, what Sahlins calls "a substantial degree of economic failure" in a primitive setting may also be true in this period and hence supply another test of labor status.[117] In a medieval context, failure for individual households and enterprises did not relate to the status of particular trades unless conditions drove all of the local cobblers, for example, into the streets. Tragedy for some people would not have affected the status of their trade unless their businesses were more prone than others to physical hazards or collapse of demand. Some of these real concerns may have affected the reputations of particular trades, yet as will be seen in the case of the butchers, reputation is not a clear-cut indicator of status. For journeymen as well as their employers, wages seem to be the best test of status.

Any insistence on a vision of the medieval economy as one in which idealized households were the basic unit of production neglects the early evidence for wage labor and the demographic fact that some households were incapable of meeting their labor requirements, whether because of the age of the producers, the sex or absence of children, or, paradoxically, the success of the enterprise. Some of the journeymen and most of the apprentices did join the household of the master; other journeymen maintained their own households, and this group was in the business of providing spare labor for the households that needed help. All of these apprentices and journeymen had to come from somewhere, and they were either surplus children from households producing for a market or, after the first generation, the children of wage earners.

The records on thirteenth-century wage levels are not good, but even the barest outline is a surer guide to a worker's status than is the worker's contact with someone else's raw materials. The compilation in table 3-3 of annual incomes of some Genoese journeymen in the years 1230–1256 provides such a guide. Notices of women's wages are rare, and only a few appear in the table. Some jobs did not fit into the apprenticeship scheme; service was usually an occupational dead end, and muleteers never served a training period. Being a traveling companion was for some young men the first step toward merchant status. Travel itself was a form of apprenticeship, and the *commenda* contract, in which the sedentary partner contributed all of the capital, allowed some young men with slender resources to become merchants. Genoa's market for labor had some distinctive characteristics. At times thousands of men made a living as mariners. Most of these men were pulling an oar on a galley, and some would end up as prisoners of war, slaves on the block, or lost crewmen at the bottom of the Mediterranean Sea. Their average annual wage placed them in the middle of the hierarchy. The job of mariner seems to have had no apprenticeship; in times of war the commune drafted artisans from the neighborhoods to assume places in the city's galleys. Perhaps most men growing up in Genoa had some experience at sea, and the first voyage was the best training. This trade was more dangerous than making shoes or leading mules, and the pay was good, an especially appealing fact to the unskilled or indigent. Without doubt the single largest employer in town, the galleys also helped to fix the hierarchy of labor. Trades at the higher end of the scale needed to pay more, simply to keep their journeymen from running away to sea. The exact order of the trades at the higher end of the scale is not the same as it was in Paris, but the range is similar. Smiths, armorers, and metalworkers earned high wages, as did the lucky few engaged in esoteric trades like papermaking or mixing potions.

The lower end of the wage scale for men took in some humble trades and the numerous servants. Wealthy merchants and nobles employed a fair number of men in household chores of various kinds. These servants did not work for master artisans, who could not afford the luxury. The wages of male servants were poor, but the female servants in this sample earned essentially nothing at all and were presumably counted

Table 3-3. Annual Income of Genoese Journeymen and -Women in Selected Trades, 1230–1256

Trade	Income
Men	
Smith	L18s.15
Papermaker	L16s.4
Weaver	L15
Dyer	L13s.10
Armorer	L12s.10
Miller	L12
Metalworker	L11
Apothecary	L10
Ropemaker	L8s.15
Mariner[a]	L7s.10
Horseshoer	L5s.9
Cobbler	L5
Traveling companion	L5
Muleteer	L3s.18
Cook	L3s.12
Turner	L3
Servant	L1s.14
Draper's assistant	L1s.10
Maker of spools and spindles	L1s.10
Women	
Weaver	L1
Dyer	s.15d.8
Baker's assistant	s.10
Wet nurse[b]	s.7
Servant	s.5

Source: Archivio di Stato di Genova, Cartolari Notarili.

Note: Where the wages are by the day, the work year is estimated at three hundred days. Food is occasionally added to the income at a rate of 2 pennies a day. Three hundred days is a long work year, but see argument on holidays in chapter 4.

a. Figured at two voyages per year at L3s.15 per voyage.

b. Per baby.

fortunate to have a place to stay with three square meals. The stipends of the male servants probably required that their employers feed and house them, though the contracts did not promise this. Women employees earned very little in thirteenth-century Genoa. The cloth industry and a few other trades had some opportunities for them, but it seems to be no accident that their wages in nearly all instances were below *all* male wages and not simply those of men in the same line of work. A journeyman smith earned more than fifty times the wage of a wet nurse. Even when women controlled a valuable raw material—in this case breast milk, in other instances dyes and wool—their wages did not benefit from this contact. The Genoese evidence suggests that a worker's labor status depended on the sex of the worker. Apart from this division of labor by gender, the division of labor based on the value of raw materials suggests that highly valued raw materials seem to go hand in hand with long terms of apprenticeship and high wages. The best-paid journeymen were engaged in crafts at the highest level of medieval technology. The papermaker in Genoa was working at a relatively new business, outside any guild structure, and earning high wages. Mariners had no guild and earned decent wages. The wool guild seems to have done little for the wages of women workers.

The point about access to the means of production seems most applicable to the status of masters. Unfortunately, few records shed any light on the actual business circumstances of specific masters and their shops. Master smiths in Bologna, in their efforts to regularize supplies of charcoal, attempted to ensure that no single master was in a position to monopolize essential materials or ingredients. So the masters were certainly aware that, despite the harmony of guild life, the threat of competition still existed, as well as the likely prospect that some masters would be more successful than others. One way to explore the internal dynamics of a shop is to examine partnership agreements between masters or between a master and a provider of capital. Although experienced journeymen might technically qualify as masters, they had to continue working for other masters unless they had capital.

In some cases a craftsman with no capital found a partner willing to put up the money to run a shop. The Genoese records supply a few examples of such agreements. On 5 November 1231, Bertoloto the *batifolius* and Nicola Navario concluded a partnership (*societas*) to last five years.[118] Bertoloto agreed to work at his trade, metalworking, in a house that Nicola owned and also to be responsible for putting his own brother, as well as three helpers, to work there. (Bertoloto and his brother are in a sense a household, but clearly money and work brought this group of people together.) For his part Nicola expected to learn the trade of metalworking from his partner, in effect as an apprentice, and also agreed to supply an extensive array of tools, including fourteen hammers. More importantly, Nicola placed L100 in the partnership—a sum that Bertoloto would have taken many years to save out of an average annual income of L11. Since the tools and house were separate items, the L100 must represent the capital requirements of the household—the costs of raw materials, fuel, and food for the three men and boys working there, as well as other expenses such as the tunics worth 5 solidi that each boy was to receive. According to the customary way that partners divided the profits of a *societas*, Nicola received two-thirds, and Bertoloto one-third. The partners agreed to keep the capital and profits in a box to which each had his own key, and they distributed the profits every three months. Nicola made sure that his L100 reverted to him at the end of the partnership. In exchange for training Nicola and handing over two-thirds of the profit, Bertoloto and his brother came into a well-financed and well-equipped shop, with the security of time—five years—to make a place for themselves in the Genoese market.

In settings where wage labor had as yet made little or no headway, these partnerships were probably a frequent occurrence. The capital requirements were not always as large as the case above. Eight days later two smiths also pooled their resources and talents.[119] These smiths each put in only L4. The tools and the rent, however, were probably separate expenses, so the L8 represented an initial outlay for raw materials. (The partners agreed to split the rent of the shop.) As has been seen, an apprentice smith always received a set of tools upon completing the term of training. With these tools, knowledge, and less than a year's wages, these two smiths were able to go into business for themselves. If their enterprise succeeded, they would be able to thrive as masters; for them, the biggest obstacle may have been the previous long years of training.

Partnerships from other cities reveal how an investor might simply provide capital and not plan to work at the particular trade. On 26 May 1313, the Venetians Antoniello Boldu and Fredo the dyer formed a *compagnia* to last for ten years.[120] Fredo promised to work at his art in Venice for their common profit. Antoniello agreed to contribute money as necessary but never more than L8 a year. The partners planned to employ a servant for wages (*unus famulus ad salarium*) and pay him out of the profits but not supply food and clothing. The profits were supposed to cover all of the expenses of the shop. Antoniello wanted his capital returned before the accounting of the profits, which occurred at his pleasure. Fredo promised to work hard and well, and he stipulated a huge penalty of L300 if he failed to honor his promises. An unusual document from Palermo describes a division of profits from a partnership resembling the one just recounted. Leo de Iannaccio, an active merchant and investor in Palermo, and Symanto the Jew, an entrepreneur and money changer, recorded on 27 August 1287 that they had formed a partnership about two years earlier in the silk business.[121] Leo had invested $6^1/_2$ ounces of gold, and Symanto had put the money to use. It was now time to divide the profits. Symanto acknowledged that he owed Leo 10 ounces, paid 2 on the spot, and promised to pay the remaining 8 in two installments in September. If one assumes that the 10 ounces included the original capital, then this partnership yielded about 17 percent profit a year—a respectable rate. Palermo, one of the great cosmopolitan cities of the medieval world, provides an example of harmonious and fair business relations between a Christian and a Jew—something rare in large parts of Europe.

Not enough extant partnerships exist to construct yet another hierarchy of trades, but the surviving agreements suggest some important points to consider. Capital requirements might have been formidable, as in the case of the *batifolii*, but the smiths prove that this did not always need to be so. From the point of view of the artisans attempting to join the ranks of the self-employed, their own prospects of setting up shop might have seemed the most critical aspect of their trade's status. Risks were of course present; the Parisian cobblers provide an example of a local market that was choked with former masters and journeymen eking out a living by working for others. The examples of partnership in Genoa and Venice suggest the two ways that journeymen might have become independent—find a wealthy partner or combine their own resources. These establishments became households and presumably produced for the market. But these shops were unusual households, comprised mostly of nonrelatives, and they existed because capital and markets offered these people a chance to rise through wage labor.

Thus far the evidence indicates that wages and terms of apprenticeship are good indices of status but also that cities and regions developed their own distinctive hierarchy of trades. New businesses, like the silk industry or papermaking, fit themselves into the local scheme according to the basic criteria—value of raw materials, wages, and status of customers. Despite the apparent lack of uniformity across medieval Europe, some historians have tried to discover general attitudes about specific trades. Jacques Le Goff presents an imposing list of thirty-two separate trades or professions condemned as base, and as he admits, "an exhaustive list . . . include[s] virtually all medieval professions."[122] By and large the clergy were the authors of these attitudes, and this essentially pervasive condemning of so many secular livelihoods has a tinny ring. Clergy may be found who castigated almost anything, so they provide no sure guide to widespread secular attitudes about trades. In relatively clear examples, like prostitutes and pimps, the clergy mirrored popular sentiments, but for the remaining trades more evidence is needed before concluding that one or two comments constituted a pervasive social judgment of status. Le Goff points, for example, to the status of butchers, tainted by one of the most potent of "the old taboos of primitive societies"—the blood taboo.[123] By contrast, William C. Jordan points to the "sacral" elements in the negative views of butchers. Jordan concludes that the work of the butchers resulted in "a peculiar, even suspicious regard for them in the Middle Ages."[124]

This example of one trade's ambiguous standing in the community highlights the difficulty of generalizing about amorphous concepts like labor status. As has already been seen, butchers received some attention from city officials, who were interested in this work on the grounds of sanitation and public health. These authorities were equally concerned about poulterers and fishmongers, who were also potential menaces to the health of consumers, but who never had the stigma of the butchers attached to them. The division of labor seems to have placed the onus of slaughtering on butchers alone, perhaps because their victims were large, familiar, and, in the case of horses, objects of affection. Jews would not buy meat from Christian butchers, and some Christians seem to have preferred to patronize Jewish butchers.[125] In the few places where this kind of competition affected Christian butchers, they had to accept what was for them demeaning rivalry from a group excluded from their own guild but nevertheless enjoying a higher reputation in the common business. The butchers may have had enough political clout, or were in a position to benefit from the Church's intervention, to put down their potential competitors. But they still had to deal with the way people perceived their business.

The craft of the butchers is a microcosm of the problem of social status. The butchers ranked fairly high in Genoa in terms of length of apprenticeship, and women seem to have played no role in this profession—ordinarily two signs of high prestige. Governments kept a close watch on this guild—a sign of suspicion. In Siena the butchers were the objects of continuous public complaint, and after their prominent part in a revolt in 1318, the commune outlawed their guild.[126] In Bologna the butchers served together as a company of militia, while all other citizens belonged to units organized along neighborhoods. This patriotic duty placed a more positive emphasis on the experience of the trade.[127] James B. Given found not a single butcher who was a victim of homicide in his sample of 2,434 English cases, and only a butcher and a butcher's wife appear in the ranks of the 3,492 accused.[128] If murder justifies a reputation for violence, then in this case the butchers seem slandered. Jewish butchers enjoyed higher repute in some quarters, an undoubted blow to the craft. Women were active sellers of poultry and fish, signs of the lower prestige of these businesses, yet such trades were free of the stigma Jordan and Le Goff find so important with respect to the butchers. The status of the customers ran the gamut from the richest members of society to those who could rarely afford meat, but the broad nature of the market simply focused attention on the standards and quality of the butcher shops. Finally, hunting was a noble pastime with little of the blood taboo about it and was not on a par with the slaughtering of domesticated animals. This tangled array of social attitudes often worked at cross-purposes: for every trade might be found some unsavory aspect, some critics, and a sense of pride among the people actually living by it.

Although a few tantalizing pieces of evidence are from the twelfth century (particularly from Genoa and its unique records), the sources for a history of labor are so much better from the thirteenth century that only then do the internal dynamics of the masters' strategies for recruiting labor become apparent. Wage labor seems to spring forth full-grown, but like Athena, its birth is poorly documented and hence runs the risk of appearing unremarkable. The examples drawn from many cities should not obscure the rise of regular wage labor. There was no place where the first wages were paid; instead there were the contemporary and universal problems of recruiting and training workers and a solution, wage labor, that was by no means inevitable but that fit. Masters created a system for recruiting and training labor that suited their purposes and ran their guilds through officials who wanted as little outside interference as possible. A tension existed between merchant and craft guilds, and the hierarchy of trades revealed itself in the wage levels, a new facet of the urban economy, and the social prestige of the businesses. Terms of apprenticeship and the wages of journeymen and -women have illuminated the hierarchy of trades, but the circumstances of the butchers serve as a reminder that the guilds existed and had to find a place in a wider world. Having examined the internal structure of guilds and wage labor, we will now view them in this broader context.

4

Guilds and Labor in the Wider World

Guilds and work did not exist in an economic vacuum or in a dry model in which the rest of their world consisted of things that were always equal or that came out in the wash. The ways in which the apprenticeship and journeyman system developed from the late twelfth century through the thirteenth century, as sketched in the previous chapter, can be clarified by looking at the same time span from some social perspectives. Pressures on guilds and wage labor from the outside certainly pushed the system in certain directions and cut off some possible paths. Masters were in most respects not the initiators of broad policies and pervasive attitudes, except where a functioning commune took into account the circumstances and views of employers. The power of the Church, monarchies, and aristocracies affected the new system of wage labor. And naturally these institutions were not immune from other pressures either. Investigating confraternities, social and religious attitudes about work, and the guilds and politics will be useful in analyzing this complex interplay of simultaneous changes in medieval society. The position of Jews in society and the economy serves as a common denominator here. On the premise that the treatment of minorities reveals profound features of any culture, the fate of the Jews is a touchstone that marks some characteristic features of the wider world. So we must turn to the same period that witnessed the rebirth of wages and examine a part of that story again, but this time we will look beyond the problems of fostering and employment within the household shops and the trades to find out more about the origins and the consequences of wages.

An example of how repositioning the argument yields fruitful results is to recognize that guilds were also philanthropic organizations, first to their own members and then to the wider community. Religious and charitable duties were partly an internal matter, but their primary focus was, in most ways, the next world. These spiritual concerns resulted from a guild's frequent status as a confraternity—a fact that attracted the Church's interest. A guild often possessed a strong religious character that provided a grander purpose as well as common spiritual ideals that the masters shared along with their apprentices and journeymen. To the extent that a guild was also a confraternity, relations among the workers in a trade or profession were not solely questions of the cash nexus but also involved paternalism and Durkheim's moral dimension to work. And yet, if for no other reason than that nearly all guilds were confraternities, they excluded Jews. The masters had a part in the complicated and troubled history of the treatment of Jews in medieval Europe. How the Jews should make a living involved the masters in difficult social and religious issues.

As the guilds of medieval cities became increasingly important and active in the thirteenth century, some critics began to examine the nature of work and its place in society. Others began to voice objections to monopolies, price fixing, and the barriers that some masters raised against new members. Having seen how kings and city governments intervened in the guilds, we will turn the question around and examine how some masters managed to take a decisive role in political life while others lost or never achieved it. Finally, the journeymen, in the quest for higher wages and better working conditions, were not to be silent forever.

Work and Religion

In chapter 2 we saw that the confraternity was older than the medieval guild and that many guilds may have owed their existence to the original, common religious observances of members in the same craft in either a confraternity or the parish church. Some of the same words used to describe the craft or professional guild also applied to the confraternity, and the overlapping terminology serves as a useful reminder that to disentangle the two is to engage in a modern form of analysis quite foreign to medieval attitudes about institutions. Whenever medieval people gathered together for some purpose, Christianity helped to solidify the bonds between them and to ensure that the participants in an endeavor would honor whatever they proposed to do. The use of the oath to bind people together rested on common religious practices and the high seriousness with which people viewed the oath. Swearing by Christ or the saints was more important than fines because God had his own way of dealing with oath breakers. If a guild was also a confraternity, the members had even more compelling reasons to honor their obligations to one another. People did not see a clear distinction between their roles as masters in a craft guild and as brothers or sisters in a confraternity, though occasionally the statutes of these associations reveal at least a different emphasis in the two roles. Gilles Meersseman observes that the same concepts of family, brotherhood, friendship, peace, and charity were at the bottom of so many medieval associations that the impulse to foster these values could take many forms.[1] Whatever the form of association, the father, the older brother, the close friend, or the master would still take his rightful place in a hierarchy that was again complicated by the status of women. So the same people should be expected to be in charge.

The twelfth and thirteenth centuries witnessed a rapid growth in the number of urban and rural confraternities in Europe. Organized as they were around the parish, neighborhood, or particular subject of devotion, they shared duties and observances with the religious life of guilds. Meersseman concludes that the fundamental distinction between a guild and a confraternity was that the former was primarily devoted to the material and moral interests of the members and had mutual help as the main goal. The aim of a confraternity was the *salus animarum* (the health of souls), or eternal salvation.[2] Any institution capable of performing good works fostered the spiritual health of the participants, and no medieval guild was devoid of religious or charitable concerns. These distinctions, the fruit of vast research on spirituality, remain valuable for several reasons. Meersseman does not rely on stark and artificial contrasts, and he sees a continuum of associations, many of which have the same names. Judgments about the dominant concerns in specific circumstances remain subjective and depend on incomplete sources. The rules of both guilds and confraternities owed their genesis to local needs, and at times the surviving sources do not tell the complete story. A basic rule of thumb is that virtually every guild was also a confraternity but that many of the latter were purely religious associations.

Still, something special surrounded men and women in the same trade or profession, sometimes bitter rivals or uneasy collaborators, joining together for prayer, funerals, and commemorative feasts. In Languedoc, to become a member of a guild was the same as becoming a brother or sister of its confraternity, and this applied to all levels— masters, journeymen, and apprentices.[3] The masters were the only people who controlled the guild, but the confraternity was more inclusive, though also naturally dominated by the masters who served as the officials of both. Having a soul was the prerequisite for membership in a confraternity, and this rough equality was not a feature of the craft or professional guild. Collective works of charity aided distressed guild members, but frequently the guild attended to the needs of the urban poor as well. These charitable acts brought the members face-to-face with serious social problems and their own responsibilities. Whether or not the guild had this religious dimension, and most certainly did, masters across Europe ran into rules of Christian society and had to come to terms with them. Monarchies and communes presided over a form of labor law, to the extent that they regulated the activities of guilds. The Church was an international legislator, and its rules about work were extremely important in defining the place of labor in Christian society. The Church by definition had jurisdiction over Christians, and if it needed more reason than that to take an interest in secular work, the confraternity was a natural pretext.

Finally, the connection between moral concerns and business may be made in a new way. The economist Robert Frank has proposed a model to explain why people keep commitments that seem to fly in the face of their material self-interest. The part of his argument applicable to guilds and confraternities concerns trust. He submits that people having moral sentiments do better in a market economy than people lacking them, principally because people are more disposed to trust others who have good qualities like empathy and decency.[4] In other words, those ruthlessly pursuing self-interest and its short-term rewards eventually establish a reputation for violating the moral values of the community and, hence, find themselves not welcomed as buyers and sellers. Economists and philosophers will have to decide whether or not this theory on the evolution of moral sentiments has any validity, but in this discussion of guilds is a use for this emphasis on trust and reputation. In the guild and especially in the confraternity, the masters obligated themselves to adhere to standards of proper conduct. Statutes of both institutions are replete with promises to be honest and fair. Rather than dismissing these commitments as empty pieties or self-congratulatory bows to the teachings of the Church, one can instead take the masters at their word and give them credit for recognizing, in the early phase of this new economy, that trust was not going to come easily. Efforts to codify these moral sentiments by no means abolished fraud and abuse. Yet those who violated the standards, who in effect did not recognize or accept that the guild represented a compromise on the pursuit of self-interest, suffered spiritual condemnation and immediate secular obloquy, as employers and employees shunned them.

This mechanism for enforcing and fostering commercial morality was no doubt imperfect and perhaps far from Durkheim's organic solidarity, but maybe some masters, as members of a confraternity, wanted to insure that cheaters never prospered.

No better example exists of how the wider world of the Church affected the guilds, and all those working for a living, than the Church's teaching about work on Sundays and holy days. This is a useful place to begin because this teaching extends back to early beliefs that preceded the rise of the guild and is one of the most important religious attitudes that shaped the economic environment of the central Middle Ages. Guild statutes and the rules of governments originated in a framework in which the Church had already laid down some basic precepts about licit work. The Church's rules eventually covered all of Christian society, as well as those minorities, the Jews and Muslims, dwelling within it. Guilds only represented in this context a small part of the medieval work force, but their organization made them especially accountable to the Church's teachings. At the same time, the guilds were in a better position to question these rules or to seek exceptions.

Christian attitudes about Sundays and holy days or feasts have a rich and elaborate history of their own, and work on those days is only a part of that story. The early Church had different traditions to draw upon in its effort to formulate rules on Sunday work, and by extension labor on the holy days. The Jewish tradition, revealed in the Mosaic law and later talmudic exegesis, created a strict code of conduct for the sabbath and, in particular, absolutely prohibited work. The Gospel of Matthew provides one of the most detailed accounts of Christ's response to this still-emerging teaching (12:1–8). Christ's answers to the Pharisees became a justification for abandoning the rigors of the Jewish sabbath. Sunday, now the first day of the week, became the Lord's day, and it received attention from Church councils in the late Roman state.[5] Among the many aspects of observance and devotion, work first appears in conciliar decrees of the fourth and fifth centuries. Church law prohibited servile labor on Sunday, mainly in order to encourage the laity to go to church. The Code of Justinian in the sixth century gathered together the edicts of Christian emperors on this matter.[6] The exact meaning of *servile work* remained a permanently debatable point. Roman law had its own tradition on festivals and those days on which people should not conduct business. Some continuity seems to have existed with Roman practice in this matter, and the law applied some older attitudes to the recently licit Christian holy days. Christian practice came to terms with Jewish tradition and Roman law. Later Muslim views on the *djum'a*, the day of General Assembly (Friday), required attendance at midday prayers. But apart from this obligation, the holy day was not a day of rest.[7] So Christian attitudes about work on Sunday occupied an ambiguous middle ground between Muslim and Jewish practice, and when and where Christian society came to see these differences on observing holy days, inevitable tensions resulted.

Royal and ecclesiastical legislation, supplemented by later guild statutes, reveal the subsequent history of work on Sunday and the holy days. Charlemagne, in a capitulary of 789, legislated on Sunday work and banned *opera servilia*, defined in this text as rural labor and the work of women in the cloth trades.[8] Various Anglo-Saxon codes of law prohibited work on these days and prescribed penalties for those who did. For example, the so-called laws of Edward and Guthrum (1002–1008) banned trading on Sunday, and King Aethelred's laws reiterated the usual prohibitions of servile work, business, and court sessions.[9] Canon law also continued to maintain the early teaching, and early decretal collections noted the obligation to abstain from illicit work, trade, court sessions, and the carrying out of capital sentences.[10] Local church councils reminded the laity of their Sunday duties. A council in Paris in 1212 equated servile labor with the crafts and manufactures, at this time more clearly relevant to urban society.[11] The great decretal collection of Gregory IX (1227–1241) contained a letter by this pope that provided the thirteenth-century Church with an authoritative and up-to-date list of church feasts, days (now thirty-seven in number) on which the Sunday rules applied.[12] States, cities, and guilds frequently added a patron of their own to the list, and new saints like Francis and Dominic also increased the number of local holy days. Whatever the original meaning of servile labor, probably at first concerning the lives of slaves and peasants, the Church and civil authorities had extended it to include commerce and the artisan trades. These extensions were important developments for the urban economy and the guilds, since the latter were collective bodies that could be made responsible for enforcing the rules. The fifty-two Sundays and the growing list of holy days counted for a sizable chunk of the year. All of those working for a living, a category that excludes only the nobles and the paupers, had to come to terms with these facts.

The bakers of Paris provide an interesting, if extreme, example of how one urban guild attempted to comply with the commands of the

Church. Their statutes, probably redacted in the 1260s, accepted the canonical list of holy days that Gregory IX had affirmed and added ten more, two of which honored Parisian favorites—SS. Denis and Geneviève.[13] Since in any given year at least some of the holy days fell on a Sunday, the bakers probably did not work about eighty days every year. The editors of this statute believed that the failure of the *talemeliers* to bake bread on so many days "gave rise to serious inconveniences for the feeding of the city."[14] A similar list from the statutes of the sword merchants of Bologna, dated 1283, is even longer—thirty-nine saints' days, Sundays, and Holy Week.[15] Bologna honored some saints especially important in Italy—St. Francis, St. Dominic, and Santa Catalina. These statutes did not absolutely prohibit work on those days. They banned the sale, display, and carrying of swords, but certain other activities, such as the return of purchased swords and forging, were permitted.[16] In addition the city government had the right, in time of war, to let the sword dealers work any days they wished. This provision indicates the role of political or economic necessity in determining the exact connection between work and religious practices.

Guilds did not control all urban trades and workers, but for those subject to their regulations, the guilds were a means for enforcing the rules or for obtaining collective exemptions. A typical system of fines helped to buttress a guild's authority. Secular powers and the guilds, by the thirteenth century, had created loopholes or exceptions in what was in theory a comprehensive prohibition. The Church itself had paved the way for a less rigorous interpretation of the rules. Pope Alexander III (1159–1181) had permitted servile labor on Sunday and the feasts, but only when it was for obtaining the necessities of food and clothing and when part of the proceeds went to the poor.[17] Gregory IX allowed court business on Sunday, provided that necessity or piety prompted it and that the parties agreed.[18] These exceptions created enough ambiguity for a fair amount of work on Sunday and the holy days to slip through the bans. Jacques Le Goff concludes that the Sunday restrictions did not apply to Jews, and although this was true as a general rule, local church councils occasionally tried to apply the Christian rules to the entire community, including Muslims and Jews.[19] A council in Avignon in 1209 prohibited Jews from working in public on Sundays and Christian feasts; another council in Albi in 1254 repeated this rule with the stated goal that the Jews not scandalize the Christian community by such work.[20] Large parts of Europe had few Jews or none at all; the guilds completely excluded them, and laws controlled their public behavior in other ways. Jews tended to honor their own sabbath, and if they worked on Sunday, they took business that might as easily have gone to Christian traders. These two councils did not compel Jews to honor Sunday, but by keeping their work indoors, the public behavior of a town would at least have appeared to be the same. Nothing suggests that a desire to compete with Jews produced the relaxed standards of the thirteenth century. These rules, as will be seen, are part of a complicated response to Jews at work. Instead, a plausible explanation of this change requires a look at the guilds.

The statutes of the Parisian guilds reveal that the royal servants of Louis IX, either bowing to tradition or granting new privileges, permitted many guilds to work on Sunday. The town criers, whose main job was to announce the official price of wine in the taverns and inns of Paris, normally visited each establishment twice a day, except during Lent and on Sundays, Fridays, and the eight days of the Christmas vigils when they came by once.[21] The only days on which the price of wine was not shouted out, and presumably not sold, were Good Friday and days when the king, queen, or their children happened to die. These criers worked a longer year than the bakers did; only Good Friday normally kept them from their appointed rounds. The king had an interest in fixing the price of wine in Paris, and his *prévot* allowed the criers to work virtually without restraint. Other guilds were somewhere in the middle between the bakers and the criers. The goldsmiths found a way to combine Sunday work and religious duty. They were only allowed to work on Sunday and an apostle's feast, if it did not fall on Saturday, provided that each goldsmith worked a turn in one workroom on these days.[22] Whatever the smiths earned from this labor, they deposited in a box belonging to the confraternity (*confrarie*) of the goldsmiths. All of the silver in the box went at Easter to feed the poor in the Hôtel Dieu, the principal hospice for the paupers and sick of Paris. This type of Sunday work, almost ritualistic in nature, with all of the workers in a particular shop taking turns, suggests that some scruples about the propriety of such work still existed. Pious donations assuaged those qualms. Goldsmiths could not have expected their work to be excused on the grounds of necessity or their own poverty, so they found a respectable way to put their earnings at the service of the poor.

The goldsmiths, in their regulations concerning Sunday work, serve as a reminder of the lack of a clear distinction between the confraternity and the guild. In some respects the confraternity was even more inclusive than the guild. Even if the guild in some way matriculated all of the apprentices and journeymen, the confraternity included the entire craft. The corporate sense of the guild was complex, but as a religious society, the confraternity's members followed their usual impulse to act in common. The commands of the Church to honor holy days tugged at the hearts of the members. Days off meant lost wages and work, so the masters had to calculate a way to set wages that did them as little harm as possible—hence the daily wage, a perfect way to allow for the unpaid holiday. The Church wanted people to attend services, and as members of a confraternity, the masters were obliged to foster church attendance. This goal was not incompatible with necessary work before or after prayer, realities the Church recognized and sanctioned. Masters and their employees, however, viewed the concept of necessity from different perspectives.

The masters controlled access to work in their shops. When the employer did not offer work, the day laborer had no choice but to honor the holy days. When wages were low and people lived a hand-to-mouth existence, these circumstances justified Sunday work, although they did not compel masters to offer it. Ultimately, the masters decided what was necessary or not. So, almost as an afterthought, the Church helped to define the workday for all of medieval society, not just the guilds. The idea that poverty or need was a sufficient reason to permit work on these days reflected the reality of urban life in the thirteenth century.[23] These harsh aspects of society gave the confraternity a mission that transcended religious observance and involved it in the broader urban community.

Some guild statutes betray no signs of a confraternity, and others indicate that the religious activities of the members were at the heart of corporate life. One problem that all guilds of any size faced was where to meet. The homes of the masters seem to have been too small to accommodate everyone, and medieval social attitudes tended to regard clandestine, private gatherings with suspicion. Hence, some guilds had their own hall; as has been seen, this was a custom as old as the merchant guild of St. Omer. If a guild, as a corporate and legal entity, acquired property, such an asset would naturally come to the notice of tax officials. The masters were often leery of having property in the form of a hall for this reason. Notices of guild meetings frequently refer to a church as the meeting place, as for example the money-changers and bankers' guild of Florence whose members met in the church of St. Cecilia.[24] The masters wanted their officials to make sure that candles were offered at the various altars in that church on the appropriate feasts. The guild also had masses sung in this church for the souls of deceased members. The weavers of Toulouse honored their city's patrons, the Blessed Virgin Mary and St. Stephen, by keeping oil lamps perpetually lit in the two churches of the patrons and by devoting the fines of the guild to paying for this custom.[25]

By meeting in a church, the money changers benefited from the cloak of religious respectability, and in exchange for their offerings and support, they received as well the right to meet in the church. These masters met sometimes for prayer and other times to discuss the state of their business. Probably they mixed up the two purposes from time to time; distinguishing between a collection of money changers and an assembly of men gathered to pray for departed brethren was difficult. Every guild had some social dimension, and in these centuries people were not likely to come together for any reason that did not include prayer. Holy ground was an appropriate place for such activity, and guilds took care of parish churches and the frequently beleaguered clergy who served them. Of course, parish confraternities did exist for precisely religious reasons, devoted to particular saints or religious practices. In a sense, the professional or artisan guild that met in a parish church seemed for all purposes to be a parish confraternity. This close identification was especially clear when the urban neighborhood was a center for a craft as well as a parish. Popes and canon lawyers defended both the confraternity and the parish guild, not solely on the grounds of supporting voluntary associations free from secular intrusion, but also because such groups benefited the spiritual health of the laity. Because the guild often appeared to the wider world as a confraternity, it enjoyed the protection of the Church, at least to some extent.[26]

As a confraternity, a group devoted to the common spiritual welfare of the members, the brothers (and sometimes sisters) soon found that their own security and health, spiritual or otherwise, was bound up with the fate of the outside world. The guild as a confraternity tended to follow the familiar precept of looking out for its own, or as the cutlers of Bologna expressed it, "in remedium peccatorum nostrorum" ("for curing our sins").[27] The cutlers thus paid for a mass on the second Sunday of every month in honor of their patroness St. Lucy and for the health of their own souls. The cutlers wanted a special prayer (*oratio specialis*) at the mass "so that the guild might be reformed from good to better."[28] This scene is a precious one. The cutlers paid to be instructed and improved—the hope of all those who listen to sermons. But they also expected to hear something specifically about their guild and presumably their work. The cutlers of Bologna likely acquired St. Lucy as a patroness because they met in the parish church of that saint. This was a common reason to adopt a patron saint. Other guilds chose saints whose lives were associated with the particular craft or profession. For example, the merchant guild of Valenciennes had two patrons, SS. Peter and Nicholas of Bari, both appropriate for mariners owing their prosperity to boats on the Scheldt River.[29] States, churches, families, guilds, and individuals—all tended to identify themselves with saints, whether for tangible, historical connections, proximity of relics, or even birthdays that coincided with the saint's day. Guilds and their patron saints were simply part of this broader spiritual context.

The spiritual lives of the masters and their employees brought them into the wider world in a variety of ways. Besides common prayers and other religious observances, the death of a member brought forth one of the most pervasive guild customs—the obligation to attend the funeral. The smiths of Modena, who called their guild a *fraternitas*, ordered that all brothers should be present at the funeral and burial of a deceased member (*socius*).[30] The smiths helped to transport the body to the burial site, and the statutes indicate that they were then to return to the home of the departed and to wait there for his wife and family to come back from the cemetery. This thoughtful behavior served to remind the family that the guild was not simply an association of employers but was also a support system in time of grief. The officials of the guild fined those who did not attend the funeral, a sign of the gravity of this obligation and also evidence that the trade as a whole probably closed up shop to honor the deceased. The oil merchants of Florence specifically required their members to shut their shops on the day someone died (not the day of the funeral), but only the members from the *sestiere* (neighborhood—six of these in Florence) were required to attend the funeral.[31] The barbers of Montpellier obligated themselves to go to the funerals of fellow barbers (presumably the masters), as well as the funerals of a wife, son, or daughter of a barber.[32] Since the members of the confraternity—just who they were is not always clear, but in most cases they were probably masters and their apprentices and journeymen—all participated in the funeral procession, they were part of a ritual whose purpose was to turn the body over to the Church for prayer and proper interment. Lay people present at a burial were there as mourners and observers, but in the funeral procession, their appearance served as a public reminder of the deceased's status in the community. Occasionally the officials of the guild also assumed the task of tidying up a brother's business affairs and making sure that the heirs received the proceeds.[33] Artisan wills reveal that people in the same craft or business were inclined to rely on each other as executors of wills and guardians of minors, and they also remembered each other with small legacies.[34]

Poverty and illness (unavoidable fixtures of medieval urban society) also brought the members face-to-face with the problems of their world. The Church was the instrument best prepared to respond to these problems. Although the masters had not intended their associations to be primarily charitable in nature, a guild, to the extent that it was a confraternity, developed some charitable functions. The members were the initial objects of concern. The greatest potential horror, something on the minds of all masters, was that they themselves might fall into poverty. Collapse of trade, illness, or serious accidents could reduce a master to poverty, and the guild was the obvious place to which this master could turn. Those journeymen or apprentices who fell ill or were victims of accident presumably relied upon the "in sickness and in health" clause of their contracts or the tacit assumptions of a verbal agreement, and hence they could count on their employers' help. Casual or day laborers had to turn to the Church for assistance.

The smiths of Modena worried about the possibility that anyone from their guild might become sick or poor. In their view, everyone was responsible for offering help in such circumstances. If the sick person remained in ill health for some time, the guild officials were to inform the brothers about this at their monthly meeting, "so that all should offer help and assistance, each of them as they wish"—a clear sign that, although all were obliged to help, the degree of aid remained a matter for each individual to determine.[35] These master smiths also set up a security zone for their members. Smiths traveled to procure ore, find work, and sell their wares, and they worried that they might fall sick on the road. So, in a zone that extended from the Alps to Padua and from Bologna to Parma (a good chunk of northeast Italy), the guild officials were supposed to go out and bring a sick brother home. If the brother was also indigent, the officials would transport him at the guild's expense—a comforting thought in an age when travel was always an adventure. These smiths of Modena displayed an unusual degree of solicitude about their fellow masters, but the impulse to take care of one's own was fairly typical. To try to distinguish whether this kind of assistance was a feature of the guild or the confraternity associated with it is pointless. In the minds of these masters, no such distinction existed, and the almost familial obligation of solidarity was an attribute of both faces of what was basically the same institution.

Some guilds were content to face their own problems, as well as those of their employees, and perhaps these concerns were serious enough to consume the offerings of solvent and healthy masters. But many guildsmen also recognized that poverty and sickness did not stop at their doorsteps, and as members of a confraternity, they would hear sermons about their duties to the general class of sick and miserable people and to the proverbial widows and orphans, both groups defined as the deserving poor. Giving money was naturally a feature of any guild's charitable concerns; the practice the Parisian goldsmiths followed of contributing their Sunday earnings is a case in point. Charitable uses of fines and special contributions were also common. The masons of Paris ordered that any apprentice who wanted to serve for less than six years had to contribute twenty sous to the chapel of their patron, St. Blaise.[36] In the same vein, the guilds of Toulouse donated half of the fines they collected from those who worked on holy days to the upkeep of the three bridges over the Garonne River, an obligation the city government may have imposed on them.[37] Because the Church was often responsible for these bridges, saw to their repair, and guaranteed impartial control of vital commercial routes, bridges were commonly considered to be an appropriate charity. The fullers of Lincoln donated a halfpenny each, upon the death of a brother or sister of the guild, in order "to buy bread to be given to the poor, for the soul's sake."[38] These three examples illustrate the most common forms of charitable donations by guilds or confraternities: the fabric of chapels and churches, the maintenance of clerics, and public works—bridges, city walls, and harbor moles. All of these blend into another category, hospices and those they serve, the poor, who themselves benefited as a corporate body through the establishment of almshouses or as individuals through charity received at the funerals of guild members, on holy days like Easter, or on the feast day of the patron saint of the guild. Because account books of guilds or confraternities did not survive from the central Middle Ages, the scale of these charitable activities aimed at the wider community cannot be measured. These gifts of money to worthy paupers must have made some difference to the recipients, and the masters believed, with good reason, that such charity to strangers benefited their own souls.

The most straightforward way to connect the spiritual and social concerns of the guilds with the needs of the outside world was through the product of a particular craft or profession. Some pragmatic advantages favored donating surplus commodities to the poor, as opposed to giving them money. Cash distributed to paupers was good money and represented what the economists would label a genuine-opportunity cost to the masters, who lost the chance to spend their money on something else. Stale bread was another matter; it was virtually worthless in the marketplace but still capable of bringing spiritual value to the donor and some nourishment to the recipient. A more graphic example of this phenomenon of gifts in kind concerns the butchers of Toulouse. Their statutes of 1321 reveal no special charitable policies, except the gifts to the bridges. By a later redaction of 1394, a host of detailed and bizarre rules outline the charitable concerns of the butchers.[39] Certain kinds of tainted meat, including flesh from pigs with leprous tongues and dead animals not properly slaughtered by butchers, were to be seized by guild officials and then, if edible, given to the poor. Otherwise, the officials were to throw the meat into the river. Certain other types of infractions in which the quality of the meat was not an issue, as for example tripe from an animal not slaughtered by a butcher, resulted in the meat being turned over to the poor. When the choice was between the poor and the river, the merchandise was of dubious quality with no market value. In these circumstances, that some meats were considered too foul even for the poor is remarkable, but that at least one guild passed off its refuse as a charitable donation is still noteworthy.

These examples of guild charities suggest that, as the thirteenth century progressed, the originally narrow focus on distressed members expanded to include local churches and the deserving poor. Some guilds emerged from their shells and assumed the duty of the prosperous to extend charity to the less fortunate. This capacity for giving presumably also reflects some successful business and, as will be seen, efficient preaching by the clergy. "For the wages of sin is death" ("Stipendia enim peccati mors" [Romans 6:23]) struck a fresh chord in the thirteenth century. The irony is that in part the profits of wage labor enabled the masters to be charitable and hence able to balance the accounts of their sins. Corporate giving also fostered the sense of solidarity among the masters.

André Gouron's study of guild confraternities leads him to the interesting conclusion that the opportunity to express spirituality in common fostered the fourteenth-century tendency to monopolize membership by limiting it to relatives.[40] Gouron sees the confraternity as another sign of a pervasive hostility to strangers. To the extent that the confraternity and the purely social functions of the guild tended to take up the time of artisans who also lived in common neighborhoods, some justification exists for seeing the guild as an increasingly self-contained and somewhat socially isolated institution. In the next chapter how guild membership became monopolized will be examined more closely; these changes may have had more to do with demographic pressures than they did with prayers and religious observances. But Gouron is right to focus his attention on the idea of strangers, a concept with almost no positive connotations in medieval society. In particular, the masters did not like strangers, whether they were from another town or simply fellow citizens who did not belong to the appropriate guild. Strangers represented an economic threat to the balanced status quo that masters were eager to maintain. Only the guild of university masters, no other professional guild and no craft guild at all, recognized as generally valid any standards or accomplishments in the same way that a master of arts degree was supposed to be accepted across medieval Europe. Masters could raise their eyes at a mass or funeral and see, even more completely than at a meeting of their peers, the range of people who, if not exactly their friends, were at least neighbors and nonstrangers. However, the classic stranger, at least in legal terms, was the medieval Jew, a fixture of the outside world in many regions of Europe and a potential challenge to the spiritual and economic basis of the guild.

Jews were not members of medieval guilds. Whether this was because craftsmen and professionals simply chose not to have them or because, as a confraternity, the presence of Jews would have seemed incongruous, the fact remains that Jews were on the outside. Jews were also trying to make a living, sometimes at the very businesses or skills practiced by the guildsmen, and thus were impossible to ignore. To the extent that Jews practiced a trade outside the regulations of a guild, they posed a potential economic threat, as seen in chapter 3 in the case of the butchers of Béziers. Opinions varied concerning what to do about the Jews. How Jews related to the problems of labor in the Middle Ages is a narrow but extremely important part of their history, which is separate from but intersecting with that of their Christian contemporaries. Work brought Jews and masters together, whether they wanted to be or not, and Jews were seldom in a position to prevail. A learned and revealing comment came from Robert Grosseteste, archdeacon of

Leicester from 1229 to 1232. In a letter written before he became bishop of Lincoln and in which he applauded the expulsion of the Jews from Leicester, the archdeacon observed, in R. W. Southern's eloquent paraphrase, that "Jews should be settled on the land to work with the sweat of their brow for the benefit of princes, in return for receiving a pittance for the support of their wretched lives."[41] This sort of reasoning would have pleased the guildsmen. The decisions of local and general church councils, as discussed above, ratified the tenor if not the specifics of Grosseteste's views. Attitudes about the work of the Jews developed in different directions in the thirteenth century. Clearly, Jews were expected to work apart from the Christian community and its guilds, whenever possible, but there would have to be some exceptions.

The Spanish rabbi Benjamin of Tudela traveled from his town in Spain through southern France and northern Italy on his way to the Holy Land in the 1160s. Benjamin was interested primarily in the size of the Jewish communities and their holy teachers and schools, but he occasionally gave some indication of the economic activities of the people he visited. For example, he observed a large and prosperous community of Jews in Montpellier, and thirteenth-century documents suggest that Jews managed to play some part in the overseas commerce of the town.[42] Everywhere else he visited, the groups of Jews were small or tiny, ranging from a few hundred down to the two Moroccan Jews he found in Genoa. Not until Benjamin reached Naples and Salerno did he find substantial groups of five hundred and six hundred respectively, and only when he crossed over to the Byzantine state and reached Thebes did he find a large community of two thousand inhabitants, which was famous for its silk industry.[43] Benjamin's itinerary suggests that some cities like Genoa simply excluded Jews or were so hostile as to discourage any potential immigrants. In other cities, particularly in southern France and Italy, the Jewish communities had to be engaged in some economic activities that would enable them to purchase the food necessary for survival. Some port towns may have found a use for Jews as interpreters and traveling partners, but the more sizable Jewish communities engaged in artisan manufactures or other kinds of business that brought them into direct competition with their Christian neighbors. At this point the interests of the guilds, confraternities, the Church, city governments, and princes intersected, because, when the Jews worked or employed others, they always attracted notice.

Jews were occasionally lumped together with other strangers. The makers of silk caps in Paris warned their members not to employ Jews or Lombards in any stage of manufacture.[44] These two groups posed the problem of imported techniques, possibly superior to those used in Paris, and hence raised the familiar specter of unfair competition in the guise of foreign workers. In Toulouse the dealers in secondhand clothes relied on the Jews to hawk their wares through the streets.[45] The Jews were not members of the guild, but the statutes controlled the ways that they participated in the trade. Dealers in used clothing consigned merchandise to Jews according to a standard contract: male and female Jews receiving the goods could keep them only for one week and had to return either the clothing or the sale price to the master on the following Saturday. Forcing the Jews to work on their holy day was on one level the sort of humiliation that was becoming a fixture of their lives, but it may also have been a way for the Christian masters to remove what was a galling difference between the two communities—the ways of honoring the sabbath. All guilds excluded Jews as members and by extension made the practice of trades outside their own increasingly isolated neighborhoods difficult or impossible for them, but some businesses, like used clothing and rags, brought them into what was, for the Jews, a demeaning relationship. (People in the same trade in Paris managed without the services of the Jews.[46]) The statutes of the Toulouse guild mention many of the more unsavory aspects of the business and contain rules against purchasing clothes from robbers or bordellos or acquiring garments stained with blood. The chief customers of secondhand clothing, the poor, were also the main suppliers, as were the temporarily down-at-luck who needed to raise money for food. In some places Jews served as a typical buffer between entrepreneurs and their unattractive clients, a gray area of work from which some Jews by necessity earned a living and an unavoidable reputation.

As guilds struggled to find a way to circumscribe the role that Jews could play in local economies, the questions of holy days, employment, and the exact meaning of servile labor naturally came to the foreground. On one level the masters responded to these issues in their daily business activities as they excluded Jews from access to raw materials, training, and markets. As the Church, guilds, and civil authorities in the twelfth and thirteenth centuries confined the economic life of the Jews to the unpopular and unrewarding trades, they also denied Jews the opportunity to work outside their own communities, hence making them more complete strangers. Policies toward the Jews reveal both religious attitudes and hard-headed economic judgments about potential competitors—just the sort of mixture to be expected from the medieval guild. These economic policies were only part of the complicated response of Christian Europe to Jews. The nature of the confraternity made it likely that the majority population would address the issue of Jews at work in ways that conformed to the familial and religious aspects of household production. Confraternities, so frequently associated with guilds, fostered harmony and trust within a craft or profession at the same time that they hardened the collective heart against strangers, and especially Jews. Other features of medieval society certainly encouraged the growth of anti-Semitism in these centuries. The part that the Crusades and the heightened spirituality of the age played in isolating the Jews in the midst of Christian society is not intended to be minimized here.[47] Still, for the mass of ordinary townspeople, who did not conduct pogroms or accuse the Jews of ritual murder, the most frequent point of contact with these people was in the world of work. All relations between the two groups were not hostile, but the religious character of the guilds and confraternities produced inevitable tensions. The treatment of the Jews may have represented, as Lester Little observes, the creation of a convenient group to bear the guilt of a society enduring the stresses of a commercial revolution.[48] The fate of medieval Jews was also a lesson to all those who could not work, whatever the cause or reason. The masters of the guilds and principals of the confraternities, whose primary interest was work, simply wanted them out of the way.

Attitudes about Work and Guilds

Having examined how masters and their employees developed their own institutions, we may now explore how those people outside the guild viewed these new organizations and what effects such associations had on medieval society. Social thought tended to come from the Church or at least the articulate canon lawyers and university masters who wrote about things, like money and guilds, and ideas, like work and fair prices.[49] These thinkers had much more to say about work itself than about guilds; little direct comment is made on the institutions so important to merchants and craftsmen. So attitudes on work must be found in different places, in the religious tracts and sermons of the thirteenth century, in order to gain some insights on how the rest of society viewed all of this innovative work going on in the central Middle Ages. This study will start with *work* itself because the word conjured up a variety of associations for medieval thinkers. The labor of the guild masters and their employees was only one type of work, and when their efforts are placed in a broader context, we can see how society as a whole, or at least its most educated and reflective members, noted the place of business and handicrafts in a continuum of work. Then a survey, to the limited extent possible, of the guildsmen and what they thought their place was in the wider community will follow. Some criticisms can be found of the work and practices of artisans and traders, and these views provide a litany of particular grievances against guilds.

This search for attitudes about work will begin with a few notable theologians. I have found no thinker for whom work was a central preoccupation. Instead, some of the themes at the beginning of this chapter—servile labor, work on holy days, Jews, and God as the artificer of the world—suggest some paths into systems of thought that lead to direct comment on work.[50] Theologians turned their attention to these issues, and although these writers probably do not accurately reflect the thinking of artisans, merchants, and the professions, they do provide important evidence about the Church's emerging teaching on work. The holy days and the guild confraternities provided ample grounds on which theologians could comment upon work, and so the Church produced the first universally applicable labor law in medieval Europe. Kings and city governments also legislated in this area, but the effects of such rules remained local. The Church, however, was omnipresent. The Church recognized the right of guilds to pursue their own self-interest so long as these efforts did not damage the wider community. Theologians struggled to understand the position of money and work in the world, and discussing either one seemed to be impossible without bringing the Jews into the argument.

The Franciscan scholar St. Bonaventure (1221–1274) is a typical and informed thinker on the question of work, and his writing provides a useful point of departure in order to make some sense of the connotations attached to work. Bonaventure wrote a learned treatise on the Ten Commandments, and when he came to the third, "Remember the Sabbath, and keep it holy," he revealed himself to be an astute observer of contemporary society.[51] He recognized that honoring the sabbath was a mixture of moral and ceremonial obligations that themselves neatly reflected general and specific concerns. This issue also provided the Jews with an opportunity to criticize Christians on two grounds. First, Christians said that they obeyed the Ten Commandments, but they neglected to submit to their absolute and unchanging nature—in this case the complete cessation of work. Second, and for the purposes here not so important, the Jews noted that Christians observed the sabbath on the wrong day, Sunday instead of Saturday. Bonaventure had answers for these attacks on Christian practice, but the only part of this authoritative argument that concerns the current study is work.

According to Bonaventure, God himself was the first worker, an interesting point of view, and he made the world in six days, not because he could not make it in a day or an instant if he so wanted, but in order to create the concept of duration, which helped to serve as a model for all subsequent work. And then God rested, not because he needed to, but in order to reveal the rest (*quies*) of the souls, the repose of Christ in his tomb, and the cessation of all servile labor. Bonaventure defined *opera servilia* as *opera mechanica,* and he noted in another work that he found this distinction explained in detail by Hugh of St. Victor.[52] Bonaventure, however, was the one to equate *servilia* and *mechanica*, and by doing so he went far beyond the previous, restricted definition of servile labor. His seven categories of work were: agriculture (*agricultura*); cloth manufacture, and hence the making of clothing (*lanificium*); all work in metal, stone, and wood (*fabricatio*); the victualing trades (*venatio*); the art of mixing pigments and potions (*medicina*); everything to do with shipping and the work of merchants (*navigatio*); and all forms of entertainment (*theatrica*). This standard list of work categories, inherited from classical antiquity, was now servile as opposed to the more neutral mechanical. All of these classifications of work, except the first, were capable of being organized into guilds. (The seven mechanical arts naturally paled in comparison to the seven liberal arts and were lucky to be mentioned at all.)

With his sharp eye for distinctions, Bonaventure noted that work fell into three types—the purely servile, the continuously necessary, and the completely pleasureful. The Church only prohibited servile labor on Sunday, and it permitted necessary work on the grounds of preserving life and health, basically the same reasons the popes had used in their letters. Bonaventure, however, with his emphasis on rest, considered work that pleased people to be proper on Sunday. He tolerantly believed that pleasure, resulting from games and entertainments, was an appropriate part of rest on Sunday. Those who provided these diversions were of course working, but the favorable effect of this work made it acceptable. Having defined and analyzed work, Bonaventure returned to the subject on his mind—Jewish criticisms of

Christian practices on Sunday. The commandment to keep the sabbath holy was partly a question of moral conduct as well as of ritual observance. For Bonaventure the key concept was *caritas* (for the purposes of this discussion, Christian charity), and this obligation subsumed everything else about this commandment. Charity, with all its emotional and practical consequences, excused necessary work, but it also served to distinguish what Bonaventure perceived to be the more profound appreciation of the sabbath by Christians.

What light does Bonaventure's analysis shed on attitudes toward work? On a positive note, a long time had passed since any intellectual had raised ordinary work to such a dignified position that God himself might also be the archetypical worker. Bonaventure was, as will be seen below, more positive about work and those who did it than other theologians and social critics were. Franciscan confraternities, whether associated with a guild or not, might have prompted the order's most distinguished theologian to look more closely at exactly what most people did for a living. Bonaventure's emphasis on *caritas* was another reason for the guilds to shoulder a share of the burden for those who, for whatever reason, could not work—the paupers, miserable people, the maimed, the widows, and orphans. The Jews also served as a kind of touchstone for attitudes about work. If Grosseteste had his way, the Jews would have become agricultural slaves. Bonaventure proved that charity provided ample reason for Christians to observe the holy days as they did, and the recognition of the necessity for some to work represented a good moral understanding of the day of rest. So Bonaventure's discussion suggests some fruitful lines of inquiry—the creation of the world, the third commandment and how to observe it, and the mechanical or servile arts.

St. Anthony of Padua (1195–1231) provides another early and again Franciscan view of work. Portuguese by birth, Anthony became famous not through religious tracts but by his famous and popular sermons, mostly delivered in northern Italy. The great bulk of his surviving sermons were intended for his fellow friars, and they seldom mention anything about the details of secular life. In his Sunday sermons he followed the practice of explaining the relevant passages from the Old Testament, the Gospels, and the Epistles for his theme at hand. One sermon discussed the idea that God created the world in six days.[53] For Anthony the parallel labor was the crucifixion, and the point was that Christ's sacrifice was a more difficult undertaking than creation. "As much distance as there is between saying and doing, there had been as much between creating and recreating."[54] Anthony saw the creation of the world as light and easy (*levis et facilis*) work, because God did it all by speaking; through God's words the deed was done. Even Adam was easily made (and easily fell). Christ accomplished the recreation of the world only through a difficult death. From this Anthony drew the conclusion that humankind's turning away from redemption makes the labor of the Lord in vain, and Anthony cited that remarkable verse in Isaiah, "I have labored in vain, I have spent my strength for nought and in vain."[55] Then Anthony made the crucial observation, at least for this discussion, that God had not really worked in creating the world, but through the passion God had worked to free humanity from the hand of the devil. The work of redemption was made vivid to Anthony in Christ's suffering in the garden of Gethsemane, when "his sweat was as if it were great drops of blood falling down to the ground" (Luke 22:44).

Bonaventure and Anthony would not have made much of the subtle differences between these two analyses of work. The ideas of rest and duration interested Bonaventure, and so he had no doubt that the creation of the world was indeed work. Anthony seems to have been struck by the fact that words alone accomplished creation, and he wanted to emphasize the hard work of salvation and the awful possibility that sin could render this work ineffective. Both were, however, interested in the meaning of work, and in separate ways they found work to be divinely instituted and sanctioned.

St. Thomas Aquinas (ca. 1225–1274) in his *Summa Theologica* also addressed the question "Whether God rested on the seventh day from all his work?"[56] Noting the standard observation that God produced his work without movement and labor, Aquinas offered the opinion that God cannot therefore have rested. Aquinas intended to argue against the view that God did not rest and did so in several ways. Clearly God ceased making new creatures on the seventh day, and he had also satisfied his desire for creating. These facts fit with the idea that God therefore rested.[57] Aquinas seems to be in this argument in the same place that Anthony was when looking at God's labor. Since Aquinas let stand an earlier objection that work consists of movement that in turn causes labor or work, the actual mechanics of creation remained elusive and hard to classify.

Aquinas was in no doubt that God rested on the seventh day, and he would have been hard pressed, on the basis of scripture, to conclude otherwise. The problem that all three writers faced was to define work, and the difficulty of examining it in the context of creation and God forced them to focus on some key ideas. Work and rest were clear contrasts. The old idea of servile labor, even in the expanded form Bonaventure propounded, was still strong enough to bring out the physical nature of work, in Aquinas's sense, the necessary movement. That speaking was in a vague area of work was the problem with respect to God's process of creating. But speaking also came up in more prosaic contexts, like Bonaventure's entertainments or even the sermons all three friars delivered on Sunday. Since work involved physical exertion and movement more strenuous than talking, it was easy to see work as basically servile. As Anthony observed, sweat should accompany it.

The opposite of work, rest, also helped to clarify the question. God was also the first to rest. The cessation of physical labor was divinely sanctioned, even if necessity often prompted people to work on Sunday. Rest was desirable and natural, although not available to all. Aquinas raised the point that rest was related to the satisfying of desire. He saw that work had a purpose, in fact, as many purposes as there were labors. Modern views of work that include a strong dose of what is known today as a sense of accomplishment may trace their intellectual origins to Aquinas's satisfaction of desire. Although Aquinas does not go further into this subject, and the temptation is great to read more into his analysis than is there, two more ideas seem to be implicit in his writings. First, if work was compulsory, people might rest in the sense that they would stop working, but they would be denied the opportunity to satisfy their desires. Rest without satisfaction is fitful and servile. Second, Aquinas gave all work a mental aspect, since there was a motive behind physical effort, as well as for the fortunate a goal or end to that labor. For Aquinas, desire led to movement that constituted work, and when the desire was met, the work would stop. This kind of self-regulating system functioned when people were free, and their rest consisted of both the end of exertion and the pleasure of meeting a goal.

Bonaventure, Anthony, and Aquinas ennobled work, and each one of them saw something profound and important about it. There was another side to work, where it went wrong or where it produced some kind of evil instead of good. St. Bernardino of Siena (1380–1444) was a later figure than the three already considered, and in many respects he lived in another age. Bernardino, however, was a kind of medieval historian. He had a firm grasp of ancient and medieval thought, and he mined earlier authorities like Aquinas, Alexander of Hales (ca. 1185–1245), and John Duns Scotus (ca. 1266–1308) for quotations to support his ideas. So I put forward Bernardino's analysis of work as an example of medieval thought.[58] He was certainly more competent than I am to summarize the views of his predecessors. He was also a renowned preacher with an unusual gift for reaching the laity through the practicality and vividness of his examples. In his own Siena, and in Florence where he frequently preached, Bernardino had a sophisticated audience, knowledgeable on economic matters to say the least; and the archbishop responded in kind.

Bernardino wrote a series of sermons for merchants and artisans on the subject of work. He observed that three sorts of work could be defined—some cannot be bad, like loving God; some cannot be good, like usury or fornication; and some can be either good or bad, like almsgiving or, the case at hand, trade.[59] Although Bernardino addressed his remarks to both merchants and artisans, clearly most of what he had to say related to the former. Bernardino was certain that merchants were useful to society and that they deserved to make a living. The saying of Christ contained in the Gospel of Matthew, "The worker is worthy of his hire," was cited as approving the commercial life. Bernardino noted the effort, care, work, and possible danger that characterized trade and justified its earnings.[60] He also cited the third commandment as if it had his audience in mind: "Remember, o merchant, to keep the sabbath holy."[61] So much for the good aspects of work.

Bad kinds of work relating to business and commerce existed, and Bernardino warmed to this subject, finding twenty-one examples to speak about at length. The list is worth citing as an encyclopedia of complaints, primarily against retailers, and also as an indication of the sharp practices that gave some work a bad name. The first seven concerned retail trade.[62] Nearly all master artisans also participated in retail; it was not the preserve of the pure merchant. Bernardino condemned those who bought and sold by lying, with false oaths or sophisticated words that confused honest and simple folk. Other disreputable practices revealed the sellers manipulating their wares instead of their words. Some displayed good products and sold bad ones, others simply concealed defects, and still others doctored the goods, as for example vintners who watered down their wine. I have saved for last the fifth in the list of illicit trading practices because it is the most telling. Bernardino attacked what he called evil circumventions, and he used as an example the case of merchants making conventions among themselves, which he called monopolies. When merchants decided that no one in a certain business should buy or sell except for so much or at one price, this was evil. Roman law and Christian charity condemned it. Bernardino knew that this was a frequent guild practice, in some cases the very reason for the guild's existence. He does not anywhere condemn guilds as such, but he had harsh words for all monopolies, whether they were part of a guild or not.

The next seven types of fraudulent work involved various kinds of deceit about payments.[63] Bernardino mentioned those who used false weights and measures, who did not pay on time, who did not pay in fixed terms, who broke promises, who unjustly defamed another's merchandise, and who watered down their goods, be they pepper or wool, to increase the weight and the price. In these matters Bernardino became a one-man consumer protection agency, and his audience was perhaps surprised that he knew these dodges. Once again, his fifth species of bad work merits a closer look: those who paid less than they owed deserved condemnation. Bernardino gave as his example a lapidary who buys a precious stone from a simpleton who thinks it is glass. The purchaser knows that it is worth far more but pays as if it were glass. All customers were at the mercy of the specialized knowledge of the retailers, who knew, for example, if a certain stone was glass or a sapphire or from what animal a joint of meat came. Bernardino placed the burden of honesty squarely on the shoulders of the masters and added the force of moral censure to the guild statutes covering the same ground.

The last seven examples of fraud are more heterogeneous.[64] Merchants whose work made them spend time away from home in distant lands sinned against their wives and did not go to mass. Some traveling merchants were dishonest agents for their partners back home. Some retailers were false counters and used their familiarity with numbers to deceive country people and the simple. Bernardino gave as his example here the counter who promised to pay 10 for something and then rattled off, "In the name of God and the saints 6, 7, 8, 9, 10."[65] The poor soul who could not count might discover this ruse later and return and confront the counter only to receive the same runaround. Bernardino continued to list problems, noting that some merchants clipped money, some innkeepers had devious ways to cheat their customers, and some victualers found ways to disguise rotten food and sell it for good.

Anyone listening to these twenty-one kinds of bad work would have ample reason to be suspicious the next time he or she shopped. Bernardino demonstrated that commerce tempted its practitioners into bad behavior, that the work of buying and selling posed grave moral challenges to the upright. Retailers indulging in these unethical acts had a competitive edge over the honest individuals in the same trade, and one of the tasks of guild officials was to root out the corrupt. Bernardino was appealing to the masters and traders to do something about the immoral aspects of their businesses.

Monopoly was a more difficult issue for guilds to resolve, and the Church, as seen above, had an interest in this question because of the way monopolistic practices harmed the wider community. For some guilds, to abandon monopoly would have introduced an undesirable level of competition and economic ruin for some members. Bernardino did not think that these difficulties justified a monopoly. In a sermon in Italian, Bernardino preached about the common good (*il bene comune*), and he specifically tied this idea to the guilds (*arti*).[66] Bernardino praised some trades as especially important to the common good, and he singled out the wool guild as being of the greatest usefulness to the city of Siena. The trade of shoemaking and the institution of a university (for which Bernardino invoked Bologna as a nearby example) also provided for the common good, since they fostered trade and in the case of a university added to the honor of a city. Bernardino observed that to be useful and necessary to the common good was to please God. So for the very reasons that a monopoly was evil, merchants and artisans could derive through good conduct some divine favor and a vital place in the wider world.

Although Bernardino made some points that specifically related to artisans, particularly in the matters of social utility and defective merchandise, his most detailed sermon about work did not mention relations between masters and their employees or the many possible frauds one group might commit against the other. Bernardino was interested in the work of retail trade, but he did not ponder the labor involved in producing the wares that retailers foisted on an unwary public. He did reveal that he was familiar with the labor of traveling merchants. Why Bernardino failed to talk about household production or wages in his surviving sermons is not known, but the sphere of work he preached about affected all people as potential victims and virtually all masters and merchants as possible perpetrators. But he left out the work of journeymen and apprentices.[67]

The last way to fathom the attitudes of the clergy about work is to look at the exempla of sermons. These exempla have a variety of technical meanings and uses. The exemplum is a story a preacher told to illustrate a particular theme. Christ's parables were examples of a genre already old, and medieval preachers had many thousands of edifying and relevant stories to tell in order to make their own meaning clear. The preachers also used these exempla to engage the laity in the subject at hand. In these detailed and homey stories about daily life can be seen some distilled attitudes about work. Exempla tended to have a point, and the story containing a message at least indicates something about conventional clerical views on work.

Jacques de Vitry (ca. 1160/1170–1240), from northern France, for a time bishop of Acre, historian, participant in the Fifth Crusade, and later a cardinal, was also famous because his sermons contained a rich variety of exempla. Jacques collected contemporary anecdotes and reworked folktales and stories from earlier authors, and in turn his sermons provided later writers with a great mass of material. Some of his exempla, especially in the *Sermones Vulgares*, were in sermons intended for congregations consisting of artisans, or sailors, or merchants. Thomas F. Crane and Goswin Franken collected 418 exempla from the sermons, but only a handful of these reveal any attitudes about work.[68] One exemplum is, for example, a humorous story about a man who frequented a butcher who sold cooked meats. The customer hoped that he might receive a discount, so he remarked to the butcher, "It's now seven years that I have not bought meats from anyone else but you." To this, the astonished butcher replied, "For so much time you've done this and you're still alive?"[69] This story, in a sermon for merchants, probably seemed not so funny to the butchers selling prepared meats. But it does betray a worldliness about retailing and is an example of the reality behind the usual protestations of high quality. Another story provides an instance of the kind of fraud that Bernardino of Siena later had in mind. Jacques told about an evil blacksmith, who used to insert a thorn in a horse's shoe when a pilgrim or trader brought a lame animal to his shop.[70] When the horse soon came up lame again, the blacksmith had a partner on the road out of town who would offer to buy the horse at a fraction of its worth. The blacksmith then resold the horse at a huge profit. This exemplum, in a sermon for artisans, demonstrated what a love of money could do to the soul, and Jacques noted how demons would torture the fellow in hell forever. The tale is also a sharp reminder that guild statutes were not the only means to enforce good conduct.

Although Jacques used a butcher and a blacksmith to make specific points about work, more general opinions emerge in only two stories. One is about a pauper, who by working with his own hands was able to get just enough to eat every day, with nothing remaining for the next.[71] Yet each night, much to the amazement of his more prosperous neighbors, the pauper and his wife sang and had a good time in their hut. The neighbors, envious of this peace of mind, threw a sack of money into the hut, and the pauper, now possessing some wealth, was no longer joyful but became nervous and agitated (*anxius esse et sollicitus*). In the end the pauper gave back the money. This story has many interesting aspects. The pauper worked hard and received just enough to scrimp by, yet Jacques treated this as quite normal, and it probably was. The wife's domestic labors were passed over in silence. The fancy of the well-heeled was that happiness consisted of the carefree existence of a pauper. Jacques's point, again made to merchants, was that they would be more cheerful with less wealth. He also implied that one could work hard and still be a pauper, and plenty of journeymen and day laborers could testify to that.

One final exemplum from Jacques de Vitry is an epilogue to the previous discussion about work on holy days. The story concerns those who not only worked on holy days but, when good people were at church, took the opportunity to steal from their absent neighbors.[72] Jacques tied this problem to the fate of the aged lion, now a defenseless beast and, in turn, the victim of all the animals that he had tyrannized in his prime. In the same way, these impious thieves would receive their just reward in the end. Jacques's congregation must have wondered about their own empty houses and shops during the sermon, but apart from the obvious point about work, he was also suggesting to them that those not in church, and presumably working, were suspicious characters and worth watching carefully. These exempla reveal how one talented and astute preacher used some themes about work to perk up the attention of his listeners. Jacques reveals some interesting knowledge about the give and take of the marketplace, and his testimony that poverty might go hand in hand with hard work confirms what is known about the medieval economy.

The exempla of one insightful preacher do not constitute a pervasive social attitude about work. The Middle Ages also had collectors of religious lore who put together handbooks of exempla for those preachers who delivered many sermons and whose stock of stories needed replenishing. Frederic Tubach has compiled a valuable index of exempla from a number of collections, and his 5,400 different types of stories provide a fair cross section of the genre.[73] This pool of exempla provides a means to test the drift of the sermons and writings considered here and to gain an overall impression of attitudes toward work as they formed part of a broader spectrum of social and religious views.

One should note at the outset that Tubach's list of 5,400 exempla has no notice of a story about a guild, an artisan, or a journeyman. Again, what should be made of omissions? These exempla were intended for all possible congregations of clerics, monks, nuns, peasants, and townspeople, but the absence of the guild is still important and revealing. This institution as such did not provide any grist for the preacher's mill. One story is about an apprentice; St. Nicholas helped this apprentice, who had donated money to a church, to abduct a sultan's daughter.[74] All of the exempla about masters concern the relationship between a master and servant, and two are even about a dog and his master, yet none is about a craft employee.[75] Other stories help to place these omissions in context. Eighteen exempla are about domestic servants, fifteen about peasants, sixteen about lawyers, and seven about merchants; in an additional forty, usurers are the principal characters. Although some barbers, blacksmiths, and other craftsmen figure in exempla, they are simply stock characters. Nothing about these notices brings to life some aspect of a particular trade. The collections of stories behind these exempla, therefore, provide little that related to urban work, except on the theme of usury, a sin that victimized far more people than it benefited.

I think that this poverty of relevant exempla reveals a similar problem in much medieval preaching. Except for rare people like Bernardino of Siena, preachers, and even the handbooks designed to help them, seem to have been poorly informed about and not very interested in the work of the mass of urban people. This lack of information is hard to understand, especially since many preachers must have grown up in the households of merchants and even successful artisans. Yet whatever they observed as children seems to have provided almost no stories or even metaphors for their later careers. The one exception here is usury. Still, that there are so many sermons and exempla about poverty and so few on one of its antidotes—work—is remarkable. This gap of information, or comprehension, and whatever caused it of course constitute an implicit attitude about work and the people who lived by it.

Tubach's index is more informative about work and labor, but the context of these exempla is again revealing. The only story in which the division of labor is the main theme concerns the work of monks in producing a concordance.[76] All of the exempla about work involve people in religious orders; a monk who scorns work but learns better, a monk who retires to the desert to avoid work and then repents, and a friar ordered out of church and to work.[77] Labor is also praised as the enemy of temptation.[78] Virtually every attempt to find an exemplum about secular work leads back to religious life. Even the one story that features sweat describes how the Virgin Mary collects sweat from hard-working monks and nuns.[79] Perhaps it is not surprising that handbooks of exempla contained stories that placed almost all work in the sphere of religious life, where the preachers themselves would see the point of the stories. But these handbooks were also intended to help preachers who spent most of their time addressing lay congregations. Again, nothing much from these exempla would have struck a chord with townspeople who knew something more concrete about sweat and physical labor. The clergy had good reason for thinking about work and its role in their lives; debates among the monastic orders on this subject were particularly sharp and protracted.[80]

Some preachers, like Jacques de Vitry and Bernardino of Siena, knew a great deal about the immediate circumstances of artisans and merchants. Perhaps the most direct sermons and exempla on work remained unrecorded, and some priests and friars may have talked at length about subjects like wages, apprenticeship, and the bad practices of employers. The evidence, as it survives, suggests that for every sermon on secular work there were probably a hundred on usury and that the Church was not putting forward any distinctive or prominent teaching on secular work. But the Church was not alone in this problem. As Jacques Le Goff justly observes, "It is likely that the inability of medieval heresies between the eleventh and fourteenth centuries to define a spiritual and ethical system appropriate to labor was an important cause of their failure."[81] If heretics were the only ones to fail in this regard, however, remains to be seen.

The papacy through its own law and councils, religious thinkers in a variety of genres, and to a lesser extent civil authorities and guilds in their efforts to implement the teachings of the Church—all reveal their own attitudes toward work. They do not, however, necessarily cast much light on the, as yet, unarticulated attitudes of those who did the work. Merchants, professionals, master artisans, and their employees have left behind no sure guide to their own thoughts. The folktales of the age, recorded late and perhaps having a genesis in remote antiq-uity, appear too unreliable to use with confidence as evidence for a period that was just a brief part of their own history.[82] The audience for courtly romances and epic poetry did not want to hear much about the lives of merchants, peasants, or weavers; in fact these worker groups were happy to hear tales of the lordly class. In the literature of the period are a few rare comments on labor, as when the author of *History of William Marshal* wrote these lines:

> What is it then to bear arms?
> Does one employ them as one might a harrow?
> No, it is a far more arduous labor.[83]

One might wonder how many lords were able to tell a harrow from any other agricultural implement. Still, that the profession of arms in the thirteenth century might be called an arduous labor is interesting. No one would doubt that warfare required effort. The nobility with reason also claimed that their profession demanded physical skill as well as strength. This passage might serve as evidence that the status of work had improved by this century, if the nobility wanted to join the ranks of the "laborers," but as will be seen, this assumption pushes the evi-dence too far.

This analysis of attitudes toward work can be concluded by noting the error in assuming that these ideas were changeless or that they may be fixed in time at some moment in the thirteenth century. Some models attempt to explain changes in these attitudes, or changes in a distinctive feature of medieval labor that permeated the way people worked. Georges Duby has closely investigated the genesis of the three orders—those who prayed, fought, and worked—and he ties the birth of this tripartite and functional social division to political and intellec-tual crises of the 1020s. Adalbero of Laon and Gerard of Cambrai, two bishops, formulated concepts of three orders at a time when those in Adalbero's scheme who worked (*laborant*) were identical to Gerard's farmers and peasants (*agricultores*).[84] The members of the merchant guild in nearby St. Omer would soon be a testimony to the anachronis-tic nature of these social visions with only rural workers, but later thinkers created a more capacious third order. Duby suggests several cogent reasons why this tripartite set of orders suited its age, but the important part of the argument is the insight that manual work defined the function of most people in society. Both Adalbero and Gerard clearly saw that the other two orders in society required the existence of the third. As yet, no one had much to say about the mass of serfs and peasants upon whose labors the rest of society depended, but I think that the creation of the third order was the necessary foundation for the Church's subsequently more developed interest in work.

Jacques Le Goff points to one aspect of changing attitudes toward labor. He emphasizes a change in the spiritual view of work, which he dates to the early twelfth century. This "rehabilitation of manual labor," as he calls it, originated in monastic disputes about the necessity and dignity of physical labor as part of the regimen of a spiritual life.[85] As monastic writers pondered this issue, some concluded that work was not simply Adam's curse but was instead a kind of penance and hence a means to salvation. Le Goff concludes that the Church in effect absolved labor of its post-Eden predicament, and I would add that the sermons and other writings noted earlier in this chapter were simply the means by which the Church slowly communicated this revised view of work to the laity. Monks had the Benedictine Rule before their eyes, and the specific rule on manual labor did not require it but served as a constant challenge to consider the place of work in the community. So the debate about work, at least for the monastic world, is fairly clear, yet how did a monastic dispute about work result in rehabilitating the secular labor of the rest of the world?

Le Goff seems to suggest that the Church, broadly construed, came up with the new approach as a response to the rapidly changing economic circumstances of the twelfth and thirteenth centuries.[86] The assumption by Le Goff is that the monastic dispute was a microcosm of a more pervasive problem that the Church faced: it had to come up with a more positive assessment of work or face a restive laity who might find part of its message to be irrelevant to their lives. On the surface, all of this seems plausible, and the argument does not make intellectual changes a crude result of economic developments. In this case, a monastic dispute with independent historical roots simply had a wider applicability. But in viewing all of this from the perspective of those who were working in the world, I think that the laity's presumed desire to be cheered up about their work requires a closer look. The sources coming from the Church would encourage one to believe that the laity had worries and doubts about their work and that their collective attitude was a bit apprehensive, and somewhat defensive, about the spiritual perils of a life in commerce, the professions, or the trades. Since no sources on the laity's actual views exist, it seems risky to assume that they somehow expected the Church to come up with a more positive assessment about work or that the economic changes in these centuries provoked in the workers a kind of crisis of confidence. The simple and sad fact is that the "worldview" of the laity on this question remains a mystery. Merchants, masters, and their employees produced the urban manifestation of the "commercial revolution" in the twelfth and thirteenth centuries. The evidence that comes from their side of the street reflects the necessity of work among the journeymen and apprentices and the relish with which masters and merchants created the new methods and institutions that produced sustained economic growth. If the laity is to be judged by its works, and in the absence of attitudes nothing else is available, then the sheer scope and amount of work in these centuries resulted from a mixture of coercion and necessity. This much is known, and if the payers and takers of wages did not approach their work with the same attitudes, this should not be surprising.

One final point should help to tie together the themes thus far set forth in this chapter. This issue has more to do with some of the modern attitudes about pre–Industrial Revolution work, and it is in effect a question about the history of human laziness. For some reason, later ages tended either to romanticize or to castigate the medieval laborer, and the relevant aspect of these stereotypes is the fitful quality of the work. Werner Sombart helped to canonize this view when he observed that the medieval craftsman "would work only so much as would yield him his living," and then satisfied, he would stop.[87] Sombart did not invent this vision of episodic labor. Thomas Malthus expressed similar views, but in his case only concerning the poor, in his *Essay on Population* (1798). Gertrude Himmelfarb summarizes Malthus's opinions as follows: "when they [the poor] received wages in excess of their present needs, they spent the surplus on drunkenness and dissipation," unlike tradesmen and farmers, who saved for future needs.[88] Malthus's use of the term *poor,* synonymous with the lower classes, rested on his assumption that people were "inert, sluggish, and averse from labor, unless compelled by necessity."[89] This idleness was not a particular sin of medieval people but a part of human nature, except in the tradesmen and farmers, it seems. Whether one sides with Sombart that fitful work was characteristic of only precapitalistic societies or with Malthus that these work habits were simply part of human nature (and to be changed by industrialization), both views remain impressionistic, and neither had the slightest evidence to support it. The idyllic quality of medieval work, as some believed it to be and whether true or not, became part of the baggage in the debate about how the Industrial Revolution changed the nature of work. Nothing about "Merry Old England" or wherever acknowledged the realities of work in the Middle Ages.

Not all were fooled by appearances. Adam Smith, cited earlier on the pitfalls of piecework, had also observed that "some workmen, indeed, when they can earn in four days what will maintain them through the week, will be idle the other three. This, however, is by no means the case for the greater part."[90] In this case too, Smith offered his impression, one at odds with Malthus but with just as little evidence to support it. This question—the work habits, or lack of them—is important because the attitude of working people might reveal itself in these habits, which were after all one of the principal legacies of this period. If wages and employment, as they developed in the thirteenth century, had the characteristics Malthus or Sombart ascribed to them, then the new market for labor was not very successful in disciplining workers. Hence, as Aquinas would have believed, the attitude of employees, and why not employers as well, was that people worked only until they satisfied their desires. In an era of the daily wage, paid by the week, the employees had frequent opportunities to decide whether or not to turn up for work—one of the few advantages of a hand-to-mouth existence.

That these analyses of past work habits and the presumed attitudes behind them are conjectural should be clear from the discussion thus far. If some time cards, employment records, or masters' account books were available, then constructing a reliable portrait of work habits would be possible. In the absence of these sources, one has only a few threads to tie together. The lines of inquiry developed in previous chapters suggest that looking at general attitudes or work habits is a mistake. Instead, the perspectives of apprentices, journeymen, and masters should be considered. Although all urban work was not part of the guild system, even those trades or businesses outside it had trainees, day laborers, and owners of shops or businesses, so the model is relevant to most urban work. Everything known about apprenticeship supports the conclusion that it was a hard lot and that it inculcated work habits as well as skills in those who survived it. Apprentices worked alongside their masters, and they apparently had few opportunities to shirk work, unless at the master's sufferance. Services by day and by night, inside and outside the shop; the master's right to inflict corporal punishment; the knowing provisions about runaways—

all indicate rigorous and sustained work. The apprenticeship contracts are perfect evidence at least for what the parties expected, and the masters' rights of coercion gave them an edge in avoiding disappointment about their pupils' work habits. A minority of apprentices became full-fledged masters, but the experience was not one of fitful or episodic work.

The journeymen appear at first glance to be more likely candidates for Sombart's model. Their work, rewarded with a daily wage, gave them some freedom. Wages and status also brought freedom from beatings, but the possibility of being fired was also present. The Genoese contracts reveal a stable and reliable system of employment for journeymen, one of whose more attractive features was the long terms of service. Beneath these privileged journeymen was a larger pool of casual laborers, taken on as demand warranted and discharged as easily. The masters paying for a day's work would not pay again if they were not satisfied, and even the workers by contract who promised to work diligently and well might find themselves held to these high standards. The journeymen may have experienced bouts of intense activity and seasonal layoffs, and they shared these work habits with groups as diverse as peasants and mariners. If the market for labor was tipping, as previously suggested, in favor of employers as the thirteenth century progressed, then the journeymen who satisfied their wants by working only four days in a week might not find a master willing to take them on for the next. On the days these hypothetical journeymen were at work, a master gave them the customary breaks at mealtimes and was presumably not eager to tolerate fitful labor. Bronislaw Geremek has investigated the subject of meal breaks in fourteenth-century Paris and determined that in some cases the artisans worked as many as sixteen or seventeen hours a day in the summer but no more than eleven hours in the winter. The meal and rest breaks amounted to $2^1/_2$ to $3^1/_2$ hours a day, depending on the season.[91] The artisans passed these breaks at their places of employment, so the masters set the hours and managed the breaks.

The final group to consider are the employers or masters, the most important workers, the likely inventors of what work habits there were, and the ones who set the tone for their employees. In later centuries a few signs suggest that journeymen criticized the work, and the laziness, of their masters, but for the thirteenth century no direct evidence one way or the other exists.[92] Even the most entrenched masters feared descending back into the ranks of the day laborers, and they knew also that the marketplace rewarded the ability to calculate wage rates that left behind something for themselves. Unlike apprentices or journeymen, only the employers had the luxury of making themselves dispensable, of becoming, for example, a sedentary merchant whose capital was worked by others or a master goldsmith whose shop ran smoothly in the hands of a competent son. If the end is the judge of all work and if satisfied desire counts for anything, then the real experts on rest, or even laziness, were the employers. Their attitude toward work was to leave as much of it as practicable to others, and wages, of all things, made this possible.

Politics and Dissent

Politics is not a new subject here. As discussed in chapter 2, the rise of both communes and secular monarchies decisively shaped the evolution of the medieval guild and other systems of labor, like slavery. Now, our interest is reversed: how did employers and employees take a political place in the wider community, and did the particular experiences of the professions, commerce, and the crafts have any effect outside their own sphere of activity? The political life of the thirteenth century has two sides. Much of traditional politics excluded the people considered here, or only used them as agents or sources of revenue. Political histories of the Middle Ages, outside those of the city republics of Italy and Germany, have usually allowed little or no role for the guilds, and the same, with rare exceptions, can be said of the political theorists of the period. Consequently, the search for the part that guilds may have played in politics can proceed only on two fronts—theoretical generalizations that cover western Europe and the direct experiences of some distinctive towns.

Lauro Martines suggests that, at least for the Italian cities, power was at the heart of the relationship between politics and the guilds. He argues that the urban struggle for power "offered cause enough for men to seek each other out in the name of common interest and self-interest."[93] In this view the complex and frequently bitter politics of these cities prompted merchants and craftsmen to form associations for the purpose of preserving themselves and their interests, which are not defined. Magnates (nobles) and the Church, whose bishops were at least initial contenders for power in the cities, had advantages in this struggle for power. Military and institutional experience fostered the political goals of nobles and bishops, especially when the rest of urban society remained disorganized and divided. This interpretation places much significance on the political struggle for power as the stimulus behind the formation of guilds.

A close examination of this analysis is necessary because, if it is valid, much of this book is off-the-mark. In chapter 3 the importance of wage labor and competition as sufficient causes to explain the rise of associations of employers was stressed. In the sense that masters controlled these institutions, they won in short order their struggle for power over their employees. Martines, however, is interested in guilds and the broader community, so he does not explore the internal dynamics of the crafts, trade, and professions as reasons to form guilds. Neighborhood associations, the family clans, confraternities, common rural ties, and even the communes themselves—all provided the initially powerless people a chance to claim a political role in society, and all of these alternatives seem to be more suitable bases for political action than does a common trade. In chapter 2 I stressed the largely spontaneous character of guild formation, as well as the need of craft groups to seek some legitimacy for their existence. The political vacuum of medieval Italy enabled some cities to achieve self-government at an early date, but the chronology of the commune and then the guild was not straightforward. Some towns had guilds and never experienced a free commune. By substituting "legitimacy" or "legal status" for Martines's emphasis on power, one will find that the first political acts of guilds, apparently quite modest, were in fact vital to any subsequent part that guilds might play in the struggle for power in cities across Europe. The political destiny of people who happened to be bakers or merchants was an important issue in thirteenth-century cities, but their ties along occupational lines, as well as the compelling economic benefits of these bonds, suggest that master cobblers sought out other cobblers for reasons that had far more to do with power over markets and employees than a voice in the city's affairs.

Yet Martines has certainly put his finger on the key issue—power. After all, that is the business of politics. Even in the context of the world outside the trades and employment, politics is a broad and amorphous subject, and its turf takes in everything from neighborhood feuds to the struggle between the papacy and the empire. The third order, however defined, had its own political life, as seen above, in the internal affairs of the guilds and in their relations to civic authorities. Larger political questions engaged certain urban groups, especially the judges, lawyers, and notaries whose work both expressed political ideas and helped to implement the goals of others. But matters of war and peace, dynastic ambitions, or what modern society calls the high politics of the age—these involved other urban people in a variety of ways. For example, London and Paris, vibrant economic centers with political importance, were not in the same position as say Venice and Florence to influence the destinies of their states. Where the city was in effect the state, people like the merchants of Florence might find themselves debating matters of foreign alliances—a question upon which their counterparts in Paris were most unlikely to be consulted. And, as already seen, the king of France was the most important fact of life for the métiers of Paris, but in Venice the *arti* were creatures of their own city government. The external political structure of a town and its ties to a higher authority (if one existed) must be kept in mind, because these facts shaped the political limits and opportunities of merchants and artisans.

Any analysis of political life should begin with Antony Black's recent and innovative *Guilds and Civil Society*, a book that explores this question.[94] Black's argument follows neatly on Duby's conception of the three orders, but Black has filled in the details on the third—those who worked. For Black the most distinctive and important legacy of the guild's subsequent political life is the notion of a corporate society. Guilds were one of the principal features of that society, but so too were communes, the Church, and the aristocracy. Black notes that "there was, surprisingly, no philosophy of the guild in the Middle Ages" and that the gap between "popular consciousness and learned doctrine makes it difficult to see how the practical experience of guild life affected the wider community."[95] There was also a tension between the interests of a guild and the broader concerns of a city or state. Similar problems existed between the guilds and those who worked outside such structures. So a familiar struggle took place between private and public good and between two competing notions of society, the civil and corporate. The world of the guilds was a collection of corporations, with distinct private interests and loyalties. At the same time broader allegiances, like Christian society, or local ones, like the realm or a city, were also beginning to take hold. Black sought the origins of a corporate polity—a harmonious and hierarchic society that was an amalgam of legitimate bodies like the guilds but by no means limited to them.

If the idea of a corporate society reflects the realities of medieval political life, then the guilds had some tangible part to play. Two lines of inquiry are useful to pursue. Did the internal dynamics of guild life in any way influence the politics of a city or state, and how did local circumstances affect the guilds' opportunities to find a political voice? The answers to both of these questions are in the cities and will become clear later as pairs of towns are compared and examined as models for the different forms of development. These towns originally represented something new on the political horizon, especially because some people in them began to create and control wealth. Most of these people were outside the conventional ecclesiastical and noble hierarchies; they were in fact a new community or order consisting of the people, or *peuple*, or *popolo*. Frequently seen from the outside as a common, undifferentiated horde, these people, some inside a guild and others not, had sharply defined goals and potentialities to seek power or to be a part of any political process. The rise of the *popolo* is a familiar theme in the Italian cities, but this phenomenon was not limited to Italy and was in fact a more pervasive expression of political aspirations. Since the basic political structure and ideology of medieval Europe is older than these cities, the ways in which the established order, in its varied forms, changed as a result of these new demands should be examined. Did it incorporate new groups into a revised image of civil society or subordinate them to a corporate society in which their role was to be loyal and silent?

Small cities often provide the clearest examples, and Padua and Perugia are good places to begin. Padua was a much larger and more important city than Perugia in the late thirteenth and early fourteenth centuries, but viewed from the perspectives of larger neighbors, Venice and Rome, Padua and Perugia were both places of the second rank. The communal government of Padua recognized thirty-six guilds, but only the lawyers and notaries seem to have taken a role in administration and politics.[96] J. K. Hyde concludes that "the leading Paduan citizens did not belong to the guilds," and he ties this to the fact that "commerce, manufacturing, and even finance were relatively undeveloped."[97] The people who usually ran Padua were the magnates, who drew their fortunes from the countryside, and the notaries and lawyers, who staffed and directed the bureaucracy. Perugia, the smaller of the two, had forty registered guilds in 1286.[98] The first notice of a guild in Perugia was in 1218, when a document referred to an *ars mercatorum* (the merchant guild).[99] The key political event in Perugia was the rise of the *popolo* (1256–1266), who in this city inaugurated a permanent popular regime, at the expense of the magnates. Sarah R. Blanshei describes the Perugia of about 1300 as a guild republic, in which the smaller artisan guilds were rising to the detriment of the merchant guild.[100]

Though Perugia was the less significant of the two towns, its position as a center for wool and leather industries gave some master artisans more wealth and, eventually, more political power. For a small town, Perugia also had a large and well-known guild of money changers, a trade that facilitated trade in the other goods of the town.[101] The well-entrenched magnates of Padua saw no particular craft or business rise above the rest in the city. The triumph of the *popolo* in Perugia and its quiescence in Padua have a great deal to do with the complicated story of powerful men (the popes and Ezzelino da Romano, respectively) and their ambitions. But the overall situations are comparable, and one can control for the part that guilds played. The *popolo* of Padua was not even in a position to mount a thwarted challenge to the magnates of the city. Florence is an example of a city in the second half of the thirteenth century in which the first rise of the *popolo* was met by magnates still powerful enough to fight the new regime, and the outcome remained uncertain for several decades.[102] The lesson here is that guilds were a necessary but not sufficient first step for the *popolo* to take control of city affairs. The success of the guilds naturally depended on the level of resistance they encountered, and in many places the people who controlled the countryside and its agricultural wealth, still in this century the magnates, remained powerful enough to survive. The guilds of Padua were individually unimportant, and the two most significant ones, the lawyers and notaries, were on the side of the magnates. Perugia had a substantial merchant guild and increasingly important ones in wool, leather, and money changing. In this city the lawyers and notaries had separate and distinguished guilds that stood apart from the council of guild rectors, the real organ for a craft voice in the city's politics.[103] The model for guild participation in politics that is emerging from these comparisons is that the *popolo* as a whole stood a chance of gaining power in those cities where the local economy began to be specialized in a way that benefited only a few guilds, raising their status and prosperity above the ordinary. Where guilds were numerous and roughly equivalent in wealth, the magnates were likely to retain their grip on society.

This model has a glaring exception, and perhaps it clarifies the rule. Places like Venice, Genoa, and Marseilles by definition had an active commercial life and the financial backbone to make possible the business of long-distance trade, which required a large commitment of both labor and capital. The port cities witnessed a rise of a segment of the people—the merchants who controlled as either employers or capitalists the construction, outfitting, and manning of ships. In these cities, to use a nautical metaphor, the rising tide of commerce did not lift all boats; it did not result in a political voice for all guilds. The unique circumstances of port cities gave the merchants in some places the chance to seize city government and turn it into a de facto association of the richest employers in town. So a port like Genoa had no merchant guild, but it did have, like Perugia, important leather and wool businesses. Yet the merchants in Genoa had no need to share political power with the "lesser" guilds, because the specialized local economy had created a group of people whose source of income was certainly different from the magnates of Padua but whose control of the city was basically the same. In Venice the established merchant families, already old by 1200, eventually defined themselves as noble and created one of the most durable political systems in Europe. The *popolo* would not rise in Venice.[104] The merchant oligarchy placed in the hands of the Venetian state control over the famous Arsenal and the convoy system of galleys. These were the two biggest employers in town and hence the sources of livelihoods and jobs for many ordinary Venetians.[105] Working for the state was the closest most people in Venice came to participating in the political life of their city.

Genoa may be a more typical port town, and in contrast to Venice's serenity, it has always been a model for turmoil. The Genoese merchant aristocracy managed to exclude artisans from the upper levels of communal government. The *popolo* of Genoa succeeded in installing Guglielmo Boccanegra to run the city as captain of the people in 1257, but the city chronicle reveals that as usual the authors of this sedition included some who were already powerful in the city.[106] Another disturbance in 1265 shows that the *popolo* was able to play a role in politics only when summoned to do so by one of the city's most prominent families. In this case Oberto Spinola, with support from the Doria clan and some of their rural retainers from the Scrivia Valley, engineered a coup against the Grimaldi and Fieschi families and their supporters. The authors of this part of the chronicle noted that Oberto Spinola had made a secret compact with the people—some of whom were described as not rich or good men but paupers and brawlers.[107] Whatever their origins, they were just the kind of men that Oberto Spinola wanted at his side in a tough fight, and they were in Genoese politics by invitation only. All of these families of the first rank resembled their peers who ran Venice:

they were old families, and in Genoa most of them sprang from the segment of the rural nobility that had moved into town centuries ago. Unlike the magnates of Padua, however, these Genoese and Venetian families had thrived by being actively engaged in the commercial life of their cities. Both groups in general kept the *popolo* under control. In Genoa, however, constant feuding among the elite families occasionally permitted the *popolo* to enter the fray; in Venice the elite became famous for its solidarity. No neat formula can account for this fundamental difference between the nobility of Genoa and that of Venice.[108] But the political lesson for the "people" was that the nobility, or magnates, were as equally capable of dominating the most important business in town (overseas trade) as they were of controlling the countryside. Where the nobility showed the agility necessary to take to the sea, as they did in Venice and Genoa, the guilds were most unlikely to have a political voice, except in times of great stress.

Virtually every medieval town thrived as a result of its place in the network of communications, by land or sea. Archetypical port towns are an extreme example of how the economic life of a city might come from its role in facilitating trade. For other cities, their functions as centers of government or religion affected the balance of power within the city and the people's chances of gaining a voice in their own affairs. London and Paris were cities in which many crosscurrents shaped political life. London, always the smaller of the two in the Middle Ages, is nevertheless the clearest example. It was by a large margin the first city of the realm, and from the twelfth century its rivals were increasingly distant seconds. Paris was the largest city of Capetian France, whose territories included, by the end of the thirteenth century, a number of important cities (for example, Toulouse, Marseilles, and Orleans). Both Paris and London naturally had complex histories, more and more intertwined with the monarchies that made them capitals. The small part of the story relevant to this discussion concerns the place that guilds had in city government and the influence on that system that the larger world of the monarchies wielded.

Londoners managed to play a decisive part in every crisis that the monarchy faced from the Norman Conquest through the baronial revolts of the thirteenth century. The most opportune moment in the political life of London occurred in 1191 when Prince John granted the city the right to have a commune, an event that only received some clarity when John himself became king in 1199.[109] In that year the city received the right to name its own sheriffs. Some time in the intervening period, London had gained its first mayor, Henry FitzAilwin, who served from some time in the early 1190s to 1212. Subsequent mayors were elected and served for shorter terms. A city council consisting of aldermen from the twenty-four wards of the city had existed since the early twelfth century, and at some point it became an elected body as well.[110] Guilds, by all accounts, played no role in these political successes, which resulted from the efforts of the citizens or simply the people of London. By the late thirteenth and early fourteenth centuries, however, the freedom of the city of London, the bundle of rights and obligations associated with being a citizen, had at least one strong tie to the guilds of the city. Certainly by the time of the first comprehensive records in 1309, but probably as far back as 1275, the freedom of the city could be obtained by someone in three accepted ways: by inheritance, by redemption (purchase), and by apprenticeship or servitude.[111] Admission to the freedom by redemption was the means by which foreigners attained full rights of citizenship.[112] Some Londoners born in the city received the freedom as well, but those who served their apprenticeship would find themselves entering upon freedom in a complex way.

As early as 1275, a rule mandated that the names of all apprentices should be recorded in the Chamber of the Guildhall. As already noted, later guild statutes acknowledged this requirement.[113] The surviving record of apprenticeships commenced in 1309 and noted agreements that were made in the last decade of the reign of Edward I (1272–1307). The useful feature of the recorded apprenticeships is that they provide a mixed bag of foreigners and native Londoners who were sworn to the freedom only at the end of their term. Since only a master having the freedom could have lawful apprentices, the lists in Letter Book D are also valuable because they reveal the range of trades practiced in the city.

What the existence of this source reveals about politics in London should be examined before looking at the source itself. The freedom of the city was a prerequisite for any voice in the affairs of London. Guilds were subordinate to the mayor and aldermen, and yet they had some advantages over the mass of trades without formal status. The city in effect recognized the benefits of apprenticeship and promoted the system, even for trades that apparently did not have guilds. Hence some aspects of the apprenticeship system made its extension desirable. These benefits appear to have been political ones. Apprenticeship, as a means to educate and control a work force, did not require a guild to administer it; the city government was capable of doing that. One of the most interesting features of the situation in London is that the government had legislated that all apprenticeships were to last at least seven years, and all freemen took an oath to observe this injunction.[114] In chapter 3 the length of the term was seen to be variable, and this London rule was rare. Some professions (corders, plumbers, and ironmongers) routinely required more than seven years, but all trades were stuck with the long minimum term. This kind of uniformity was desirable in London precisely because the apprenticeship had implications beyond the simple issue of appropriate training.

By granting the freedom of the city to all apprentices who completed their terms, or who paid a small fine for early entry, the city fathers were encouraging apprenticeship, but they were also using it for political purposes other than those for which it was designed. Once apprenticeship became a path to citizenship, the assurance was needed that abuses, in the guise of fictitious or short terms, would not permit undesirables to acquire status in the community. This system also benefited foreigners, mostly boys from other parts of England, whose parents could place them with London artisans and merchants and know that their sons would receive the privilege of remaining in the city and conducting a trade there. Some native Londoners did not need to serve an apprenticeship to receive the freedom, but in practice all of those whose fate was to work at a craft, whether this craft had a guild or not, were required to be apprenticed and to be registered. Rich and poor families in society were spared, for different reasons, the necessity of putting their children through this system. The great mass in the middle, however, served for a time as apprentices. The lucky children of the poor who became servants might eventually be in a position to take advantage of the freedom that was not theirs by birthright.

Even though the thirteenth-century guilds in London seem to have been politically inert, regulated apprenticeship served the community as a useful means to control access to the city and its trades, markets, and courts. Sylvia Thrupp concludes that in the early fourteenth century "crafts were for the time being acting as political clubs"; that is, they were beginning to expect a political role, at least in the wards of the city.[115] Eight guilds or companies were more important than the rest and carried greater weight in civic affairs. These eight were the mercers, grocers (pepperers), drapers, fishmongers, goldsmiths, skinners, tailors, and vintners.[116] These occupations were not the same as the *arti maggiori* of Florence. In London an international export trade was confined basically to wool and wool cloth, and no other great export industries or domestic bankers to finance these undertakings were available. The greatness of London, and hence the importance of these eight guilds, rested on the retail demand of consumers whose purchases of fish, clothing, and other necessities constituted the real strength of the local market. Six of the eight guilds (only the vintners and drapers were exceptions) drew their political and economic power, not from distant markets, but from the wholesale and retail trade of the city. Retailers dominated London, and these same guilds would not be the most important in either port or export-manufacturing cities. Men from these eight trades tended to predominate among the aldermen, who in turn basically governed London.[117] But the geographical divisions of the city—the wards—remained more important political units than the crafts. Hence political participation depended on access to the corporate rights of Londoners. Membership in a craft was one common means to acquire these privileges. Yet the crafts as such had no corporate political responsibilities except to police themselves under the watchful eyes of the mayor and aldermen.

The records of admission to the freedom of the city of London by redemption and by apprenticeship therefore provide one with a large and relatively early (1309–1312) pool of men (and a handful of women) with at least the potential to participate in politics. Unfortunately, those who took the freedom by patrimony and did not serve as apprentices do not appear on these lists. However, the sources contain a large number of names (82 of 510) for which the occupation was not stated, and some of these people may have been servants or in fact merchants in training.[118] As noted, the redemptions also included a number of Londoners who simply had not gone through the formal procedure of entering the freedom at the end of their apprenticeships, and so some mature and entrenched masters were clearly just regularizing their status. These records are not free of ambiguities, but they do provide some useful information about the sheer numerical strength of the trades and also their apparent attractiveness—the latter is especially relevant to apprenticeship.

Again, local and wholesale trade and production for the consumers in London dominated the economic life of the city (table 4-1). Three of the most important companies—the fishmongers, mercers, and drapers—were also at the top of apprenticeships. In fact the first two led all other crafts and professions (at least seventy-two in these lists) in London.[119] The other five great companies appeared more exclusive, or

Table 4-1. London Admission to Freedom by Apprenticeship, 1309–1312

Company	Number of Apprentices
Top eleven companies	
Fishmonger[a]	44
Mercer[a]	42
Chandler	31
Butcher	22
Tanner	21
Corder	14
Woodmonger, Cheesemonger	12
Glover, Draper,[a] Chaucer	11
Other great companies	
Grocer (pepperer)	4
Goldsmith	6
Skinner	4
Tailor	3
Vintner	3

Source: Sharpe, *Calendar of Letter Books,* pp. 96–179.
a. One of the great companies.

at least in these years they admitted few apprentices. The political implications of all of this cut both ways. The system in London allowed some people of very modest means to gain the freedom of the city through apprenticeship, but most of these individuals had no subsequent political say, either in their crafts or in their wards. Some of the great companies admitted large numbers of apprentices, but this was probably more a tribute to the prosperity and labor-intensive features of the trades than a sign that apprentices were seeking a political voice through their work. The city government and the trades both found using the guilds for political purposes to be convenient, but the employers in the end controlled both organizations.

The most important guilds were also not an easy path to the freedom for a different class of persons, those who paid for the privilege (table 4-2). Only the fishmongers and tailors ranked as large guilds taking in a significant number of foreigners or late registrants. One

Table 4-2. London Admission to Freedom by Redemption, 1309–1312

Company	Number of Redemptions
Top ten companies	
Baker	43
Fishmonger[a]	36
Brewer, Cook	35
Cordwainer	26
Tailor[a]	20
Furrier	19
Butcher, Chandler, Clerk	14
Other great companies	
Mercer	7
Grocer (pepperer)	4
Goldsmith[b]	2
Skinner	10
Vintner	9

Source: Sharpe, *Calendar of Letter Books*, pp. 35–96.
a. One of the great companies.
b. One goldsmith and one goldbeater.

revealing feature of tables 4-1 and 4-2 is that they do not overlap much. Eight of the top guilds by apprenticeship did not make the equivalent list for redemptions. These differences probably occurred for many reasons, not the least of which is that the lists recorded distinct groups of people—apprentices in one and established tradespeople in the other. Yet the ability to buy the freedom of the city, still not requiring the assent of the other masters in the same trade, allowed some immigrants to join even the most prestigious callings. Economic liberties were relatively easy to come by, but only a minority of former apprentices or foreigners would find themselves in the company of politically consequential leaders.

The London example is complex and instructive. In London as elsewhere, an oligarchy was in charge, and the city had by the fourteenth century wrested from the monarchy a large measure of self-rule. The corporate solidarity of the city itself remained a powerful idea, and this concept of citizenship prevented London from becoming a guild republic as Florence and Perugia at times were. Apprenticeship was too useful a means of social control to let go, and the city fathers of London took an unusually close interest in it. London's particular economic development produced, by Italian standards, a plebeian set of great companies, and so its oligarchy was still, by the early fourteenth century, not so noble or entrenched as the one in Venice.

The smooth functioning of the city government and guilds of London did not pass unchallenged. The court rolls of the mayor reveal some signs of restive trades, journeymen, and apprentices. For example, the smiths found themselves in court in January 1299, accused of conspiring to form an illicit parliament or confederacy whose purpose was, among other things, to prohibit night work because of unhealthy coal smoke.[120] The smiths managed to convince a jury that they were innocent. In March of the same year, the spurriers were also charged with prohibiting night work.[121] The spurriers had hauled violators into a church court, where they hoped that broken oaths would prove to be a useful way to enforce their rules. The parties in this case settled out of court. These same court records contain notices of disputes over apprenticeship and wages. Masters, journeymen, and apprentices took advantage of the law to bring suits about contracts before the mayor. Journeymen cordwainers complaining about a conspiracy among their masters to fix low wages were told to work well and serve their masters.[122] Juries seem to have been evenhanded on matters of apprenticeship, especially when the cases concerned disputes between masters. Citizens serving on juries had the decisive voice in settling these cases, and the mayor's court gave many citizens a chance to participate in this aspect of government. A jury heard a case in the summer of 1299 between a master tiler and a journeyman who were disputing wage rates and terms of service.[123] The journeyman had left his job, claiming that the pay was inadequate, and he tried to convince others not to work for this master. The jury found him guilty of breaking the contract and fined him. But the members of the jury were more lenient about what was in effect a one-man picket line, finding that they could not tell if he was in the habit of doing this. The mayor presided over this court, but the juries came from the wards. The laconic records reveal nothing about how these juries were composed, but the judgments followed no fixed patterns. Such a court provided a venue outside the guilds and their rules, and access to these courts benefited at least some journeymen and apprentices and let them be heard.

Paris is the best point of comparison for London. As has already been seen in the discussion of *Livre des métiers*, the French monarchy kept a strong grip on the city. In the Middle Ages, Paris never had a commune, and the king never ceded real authority to any group of citizens or guilds. Much of Parisian history derives from these basic facts. Without a commune, the métiers of Paris had the advantage of dealing directly with the king, through his principal administrative official, the *prévot* of Paris.[124] The liability inherent in this situation was that the Parisian guilds had to strike their own deals for statutes, and some professions were in a more advantageous position than others to help themselves. The métiers of Paris had no common forum or council that might have encouraged masters to think of themselves across trade lines, perhaps as some sort of corporate body.

One association brought together the different tradesmen. The "merchants of the water" ("marchands de l'eau") were a kind of merchant guild consisting of traders who were interested in free navigation up and down the Seine River.[125] This water route was vital to the city's prosperity, and other cities on it like Rouen also wanted to protect their rights. The king was the natural arbiter of any problems among his subjects, and so this group of merchants, not themselves a commune or city government, approached the monarchy for support. A *prévot* of the merchants first appears in the records in 1263, but the office may be older than that.[126] This royal official, presiding over the hall of merchants (*Parloir-aux-Bourgeois*) and the commercial affairs of the city, stood in the same relation to the traders as the *prévot* of Paris assumed with respect to the métiers. By the mid-fourteenth century some problems of jurisdiction would exist between these two officials.[127] But these bourgeois merchants had corporate interests that transcended the minute divisions of labor that characterized the Parisian métiers. The monarchy succeeded in avoiding a commune in Paris, a real victory since it ruled over so many communes in the other regions of France that it had acquired in the thirteenth century. Nevertheless, the monarchs and their servants were able to recognize the special needs of merchants engaged in regional trade and in the vital task of provisioning the city. In the thirteenth century the merchants gained royal favor and a privileged status in the city, but these concessions did not translate into any form of self-government for Paris. Any aspirations in this direction remained concealed until the 1350s and the rise of a notable *prévot* of the merchants, Étienne Marcel.

The political life in the cities considered here reveals a rich variety of experience for the merchants and artisans of medieval Europe. Local circumstances allowed the people to transform some city governments into institutions that reflected the corporate ideals of guild life. Where a monarch or some other power had its own vision of a hierarchic society, the guilds usually found themselves with no real influence or were simply invited to take a place somewhere near the bottom of the hierarchy. One contemporary political thinker, Marsiglio of Padua (1275/ 1280–1342), placed a great emphasis on citizenship and the positive ways in which people having it might govern themselves. As Antony Black observes, Marsiglio provided "a philosophy of the corporate state."[128] Marsiglio's great work *The Defender of the Peace* was in part a by-product of the debate between the empire and the papacy about their respective spheres of sovereignty. But this work, relying heavily on Aristotle's *Politics*, often treated the problems of cities and states as identical, a natural assumption for a son of Padua.[129] Marsiglio also made an eloquent appeal at the beginning of his book for his native Italy, a place "battered on all sides because of strife and almost destroyed."[130] Marsiglio's practical knowledge and scholastic training were useful for analyzing one of the oldest problems in politics—the relationship between a community and its constituent parts.

Black convincingly demonstrates that Marsiglio's view of the state is "at its very basis, corporatist."[131] Marsiglio built upon Aristotle's analysis of occupations and explained that the natural inclinations of people led them to different arts and disciplines. In turn, these social and economic divisions produced a society consisting of different "offices" or duties toward one's fellow people.[132] Marsiglio used the word *artes* for the arts (presumably mechanical in this case), but this was as close as he came to a concrete discussion of guilds and their place in the wider world. Marsiglio was no precursor of modern pluralist thought. Instead he is justifiably well known for the absolute primacy his analysis placed upon the body of citizens as a whole.[133] A narrow oligarchy kept control of Padua, and perhaps Marsiglio's knowledge of his hometown's feeble guilds helped to shape his broader ideas on a corporate society that included everyone. Ironically, the writer who looked most closely at the components of society concluded in effect that guilds would never be an adequate way for all people to express their views on laws and politics. The examples of the cities discussed above, in my opinion, prove that Marsiglio was right.

A second and even more striking irony about Marsiglio's work is that, in Black's words, "it is impossible to detect any Marsilian influence upon contemporary civic politics, and it is unlikely there was any."[134] Even in the guild republics, the system of politics excluded too many guilds, which in turn did not allow a voice for their journeymen and apprentices. Too many workers remained completely outside the guild structure. In practice, of course, some events paralleled Marsiglio's views; he would have approved of London's expansive definition of citizenship. The masters created guilds in the spirit of self-help, yet the rest of society frequently judged these institutions as enemies of the public good and not as models for organizing all of society on corporate lines. Marsiglio generalized guild values to the whole community, but this was not a step the masters were prepared to take.

A jurist who flourished just beyond the period considered here, Baldus de Ubaldis (?1327–1400), wrote on a range of issues relevant to the problems of cities, guilds, and politics. Baldus produced a cogent example of legal analysis that dissected the issues of sovereignty and legitimate authority in a more influential way than Marsiglio had. Again the idea of the public good (*utilitas publica, bonum commune*) rose to the surface.[135] Baldus recognized the two traditional sources of authority, the people and God, within the framework of types of law (*ius*)—of the people or nations (*gentium*), of nature (*naturale*), or of God (*divinum*). Like Bartolo of Sassoferrato, Baldus concluded from contemporary political realities in his native Italy that custom confers the right to bypass putative superiors. In other words, although the people had once conceded their authority to an emperor, that imperial sovereignty had lapsed de facto through desuetude, and so the people were free to exercise their own autonomy by making laws and recognizing no superior.[136] As Joseph Canning concludes, "The city replaces the emperor as the bearer of sovereignty," even if, as Baldus thought, sovereignty remained a hierarchic concept with the emperor and pope still at a higher level.[137] The key terms here are *custom* and *consent*. Custom could create rights, as Baldus noted in the cases of Venice and Genoa, which elected their own doges.[138] The consent of the people legitimized custom by long usage or expressed itself clearly in the ability to make law.

This jurisprudence has a direct bearing on guilds and employment. Baldus's de facto popular sovereignty in the city-states required that guilds have a subordinate role in relation to city governments.[139] Masters had their guilds, their officials, and the right to make statutes that were a kind of private law, but the representatives of the law, in many Italian cities the *podestà*, remained the superiors of the masters in all respects.[140] Several important facts emerge from this view of the law.

No theories of sovereignty—popular, imperial, or divine—applied to the guilds. Only if city government somehow collapsed could masters argue that a capacity to make generally applicable law had devolved on them—but this never happened. Masters remained firmly fixed in the hierarchies of the wider world. But custom and consent were expansive notions, and the newly evolved methods of recruiting and training a work force found good legal underpins in the free contracts of wage labor. The spirit of the times and the best legal thought had looked closely at contract and found consent to be a necessary ingredient. The particularism and self-promotion of the masters taxed the consent of those who were in some measure left out of the guilds.

This excursus into religion, social attitudes, and politics has helped to fill in some of the blanks surrounding the rebirth of wage labor and its early experiences. Christianity often fostered solidarity and softened the edges of coercion by bringing masters, journeymen, and apprentices into a common institution—the confraternity. Attitudes about work, mostly clerical and hence prescriptive, revealed some imperfections in this solidarity, and the attitudes themselves depended on one's position in the hierarchy of employment. Politics engaged some fortunate masters, but they had no place for employees, except as paraders and payers of excise taxes. No faith, attitude, or law challenged the new system of urban labor; hierarchy was a congenial concept, and wages were a successful way to recruit a work force.

5

Labor and Guilds in Crisis—
The Fourteenth Century

The system of urban labor described in the previous chapters was not static or uniform, and signs suggest that the pace of change across western Europe began to accelerate in the 1290s. Much of this change reflects problems in the medieval economy. In the fourteenth century a series of crises, or simple developments, had a profound effect on the customs of guilds, as well as on the considerable amount of urban work that took place outside these institutions. Guilds themselves were partly responsible for both the appearance of some problems and the ways in which societies responded to changing economic circumstances. Around 1300, astute masters recognized signs of trouble. A vast and ever-increasing literature exists on the apparent tapering off of economic growth at the end of the thirteenth century.[1] The reasons why the medieval economy began to stagnate, after a period of remarkable growth, are much debated, but the root of the problem seems to have been at the base—in agriculture. The urban aspects of this problem seem to be neglected, at least in the most recent discussions, and in this chapter I will show that the internal dynamics of urban labor affected the broader economy to a degree more significant than the percentage of the urbanized population would seem to warrant.

The first signs of trouble to be discussed here are the problems that journeymen and apprentices had in obtaining the status of self-employed masters. Journeymen discontent and changes in the terms of apprenticeship, as well as alterations in the structure of wages, help to reveal the increasingly advantageous position that the employers had in the bargaining. An important sidelight is slavery in the Mediterranean world and how in some places slaves again became a serious threat to free labor. The fourteenth-century sources also provide some solid ground for looking closely at guilds and capitalism and at the ways in which the masters stifled or advanced the development of a profit economy. The issue in this case is the degree to which the most sophisticated sectors of the economy either shifted to rural areas to escape regulation or remained thoroughly in the hands of urban laborers. New crafts and products like clocks also challenged the prevailing system of labor. Technological innovation did occur, but was this despite the guild system of education or a natural result of it? At mid-century the bubonic plague caused a demographic catastrophe in medieval Europe. This event changed in midstream the economic responses to the problems of entry to the crafts; to the balance among land, labor, and capital; to the pace of technological progress; and to the challenges of rural industry. Social protest at all levels of society increased after 1348. An examination of revolts, which frequently concerned the terms of employment, show that guilds did not everywhere maintain the consent necessary to dominate the urban economy. The fourteenth century was the crucible for creating the last and most enduring stage in the history of medieval labor.

The changes in the fourteenth century stand out more clearly in light of the previous findings about how wage labor evolved in the thirteenth century. Moving the analysis forward in time requires an occasional glance back to themes like slavery and new guilds. All of the previous layers of varnish—apprentices and journeymen, the hierarchy of trades, communes, and religion—will bring out the highlights of the fourteenth-century shocks, enabling one to ask, Why and how did wage labor and guilds survive?

The Chances of Becoming a Master

In chapter 2 the ways in which training, access to capital, and family ties helped to determine the difficult path to master status were explored, and throughout this discussion, the evidence always indicated that the experiences of men and women were quite different when the possibilities of social and career mobility were considered.[2] From the point of view of the workers, the vast problems of economic and demographic trends resolved themselves into a simple question: what were his or her chances of becoming an independent employer? This question presumes that everyone wanted to become a master. Although the secret ambitions of all journeymen will never be known, to suppose that even those who were content to work for others would have been happier if the choice were voluntary is reasonable. In turn, the masters, close students of local economies, had to weigh the consequences for themselves and their heirs of the ease of entry into their crafts and professions. In a period of sustained economic growth, both sides of the calculation had the opportunity to pursue self-interest without stepping on the toes of others. When the broad economy began to stall, the chance to become a master was more zealously guarded, and more eagerly sought. The cause-and-effect relationship needs to be considered in the reverse; perhaps restrictive practices themselves caused the economy to sour.

An initial and helpful way to approach this general question is to look at changes in guild statutes that relate to recruitment and master status. These changes obscured the earliest signs of guilds for reasons already discussed, but various fourteenth-century redactions reveal how masters responded to contemporary problems. Two special aspects of guild statutes, however, should be kept in mind. First, besides the occasional remark about the good of the trade or the general welfare, guild statutes tended to be notoriously vague about the meaning of change. In the absence of explicit motive, the historian must suggest plausible causes for these changes, yet these reasons need not reflect the actual ones. Many examples of changes in guild statutes compensate for this problem. Second, trades, regions, and cities did not experience economic downturns or stagnation in lockstep. All of the evidence should not be expected to point in the same direction, and even common problems were capable of prompting different responses.

Florentine guild statutes, because of their unusual length and frequent changes, are an exceptional source for charting policies toward new masters. The guild of the *rigattieri* (dealers in rags and used clothing) produced an unknown number of statutes before the first surviving ones of 1296.[3] This set of rules is remarkable for what it omitted—most notably, any remarks about journeymen. For our purposes the most important rule required all masters and apprentices to swear an oath to obey the statutes and the officials.[4] The oath that the apprentices took did not expire at the end of that stage of training, so all journeymen would in effect be covered by it. In 1318, the masters completely overhauled their statutes and introduced many new features. The key new aspects of the rules concern various paths to master status. The *rigattieri* allowed any blood brother of a master (that is, but illogically, only brothers sharing the same father) or any son of this brother (a nephew) to become a master without paying anything to the guild.[5] (In this rule the masters assumed that everyone knew that their own sons also entered for free.) The same free entry was extended to anyone marrying the daughter of a master, but the father of the bride was allowed to reduce the dowry by ten lire, the amount of the usual entry fine.[6] The masters did not permit any apprentices or journeymen (*laborator* in their first notice in the statutes) to buy and sell cloth outside their master's shop, except for the master's benefit. The employees were allowed to go into business for themselves (possibly as a sideline) if the master approved and if the employees paid the normal entry fine of six florins.[7] The statutes clearly indicate that journeymen and apprentices were not to have a journeyman or apprentice of their own.[8] The final set of changes from the previous rules dealt with matriculation, the right to enter the guild as a master.[9] New masters were supposed to pay the six florins, unless they were in one of the privileged categories. But, as the statutes noted, ever since 1316 new masters also had to pass five years as a journeyman or apprentice. If masters wanted to matriculate with less than five years of service, they could, but only by paying an additional six florins. The masters were so satisfied with these changes that, even though they again revised their statutes in 1324, they left these rules undisturbed.

By 1340, the *rigattieri* had combined with an allied trade, the linen merchants (*linaioli*), to form a new guild that naturally required new statutes. Some of the new rules reflect one trade's customs being adopted by the other, but some rules are also innovations. The guild extended free entry to anyone marrying the sister of a master and reduced the general entry fee to three florins.[10] The old rule about the business activities of employees took on a new form. Masters starting up a new shop were allowed to pay the entry fees of their employees whom they had set up in that shop. Here one can see that artisans might find themselves de facto heads of a shop but still the employees of masters who were beginning to look more and more like entrepreneurs.[11] A new rule specifically applying to the linen aspect of the guild concerns night work. No one was allowed to work linen by firelight (*ad lumen ignis*) under the stiff penalty of one hundred solidi.[12] The masters had two spies (*spiae*, formerly called *exploratores*), who were now responsible for enforcing this prohibition. The masters stated in more forceful terms that all factors and apprentices were under the authority of the consuls and sworn to it.[13] Finally, any brother, son, or nephew of a master who stayed (and presumably worked) in a shop had at the age of fifteen to swear obedience to the guild.[14] Since the *rigattieri* and *linaioli* are not necessarily typical trades, examining another group of changes before looking for some common motives is best.

One great Florentine guild included at the time of its first surviving statutes, 1310–1313, an amalgam of trades—the oil merchants (*oliandoli*, who gave their name to the guild), cheesemongers, dealers in salt, dealers in grain, porkbutchers, and those butchers selling dry or fresh meats and fish.[15] These trades comprised much of the business of feeding the Florentines, and in this city they probably combined for political reasons. The masters promised that they would have nothing to do with people who had not sworn to the guild.[16] In order to ensure this, the masters had to record the names of all of their sons and daughters with the guild, so that the officials might know who had not sworn. New members had to pay six florins, and a man might join along with his sons, provided that he paid six florins for each of them as well—no group rates. Children born after the master was in the guild entered for free, as did a stranger who married the daughter of a master, as long as he accepted the reduced dowry. All women, those with husbands and those without, engaging in these trades in any way were especially responsible to the consuls for the handling of their business, particularly in matters concerning money.[17] Finally, a blood brother of a master, who had remained in the same shop as his brother, might join without payment after his brother's death.[18] But if he had started up his own shop while his brother was still living, he had to swear and pay to enter the guild. This last provision did not contradict the earlier promise of free entry; the issue here was a new shop, something the masters were not prepared to concede without payment.

In 1345, the masters revised their statutes.[19] Now new masters paid ten lire instead of six florins, but those who had served in one of the trades for five years paid only two lire.[20] Sons and sons-in-law still entered freely, but the latter were under a closer eye. A prospective son-in-law had to acknowledge the reduced dowry on the day he received it or on the day he gave his wife the ring.[21] This revision dropped the complicated matter of a father entering the guild with or without his sons. The masters also changed the rules about women. Now if any woman, the daughter or wife of a master, wanted to take up the trade after the death of her father or husband, she was allowed to matriculate without payment.[22] But this favor only applied so long as she remained either a virgin after her father's death or a widow after her husband's and lived honestly. If she married, the guild canceled the matriculation, and she could not practice the trade unless she paid what new people had to pay. The masters also tightened up on their male heirs. Their sons, nephews, and grandsons, who were more than fourteen years old and who worked in a shop with a father, grandfather, or brother, were obligated for all of the contracts made by their male relatives, so long as they had matriculated in the guild and had the goods of the relative.[23] Bastards had the same obligations as sons. This rule seems to have replaced the older one about blood brothers and was, in its own terms, a powerful incentive for sons to follow their fathers in the business.

Some interesting parallels are in the changes made in these two sets of statutes, which were enacted at roughly the same time in the first half of the fourteenth century. Both guilds continue to have little to say about journeymen, and nothing in the statutes suggests that laborers not related to the current masters easily or commonly rose in status. The masters seem to have been preoccupied with their own families, particularly their sons and daughters, but also their brothers, nephews and grandsons, and, last and least, their sons-in-law. The *rigattieri* insisted that none of their employees conduct business outside the shop because the master's establishment remained the principal locus of commerce and the guild's interest. But clearly by 1340, some enterprising masters had branched out and had more than one "family workshop," and in these cases an employee was allowed to preside over the new shop, so long as the master had paid the guild. Whatever expansion in trade continued on into the 1340s appears to have been met by masters extending the scale of their businesses and not by journeymen climbing their way up in a wage economy. The *oliandoli* also came to recognize that the issue of multiple-shop ownership was important, and their rule about brothers in new shops points to the heart of the problem. Family continuity in a business was a fine theory, but the strategy of some families to expand the number of shops under their control had to be watched.

The decision of the *oliandoli* to make all heirs liable for the contracts of a deceased master helped to tie together those successful groups that were branching out across the city. Heirs bore the responsibility to fulfill the promises of a family member, and on balance this duty also presumes a fair amount of continuity in the shops. In the same way, the *rigattieri* and *linaioli* compelled their future heirs to swear to obey the rules of the guild, another clear sign that they would someday take their places as the masters of the next generation. Finally, these changes in both sets of statutes reflect a turning inward of the trades, particularly with respect to women. The two guilds subsidized marriage of daughters so long as the son-in-law practiced the trade. This method of recruiting a work force probably solved much of the labor needs not met by direct male heirs. The *oliandoli* decided to insist that their widows and daughters remain unattached, and this desire reflects the realization that the masters would not be around to select suitable husbands for these women. If these women did marry and wanted to remain in the trade, they had to pay what strangers were expected to offer, but this alone does not seem to be a powerful incentive for celibacy.

Two other aspects of these Florentine statutes are worth noting. The *rigattieri* reduced the entry fee from six to three florins, and this apparent relaxing of one barrier to entering the guild argues against the other indications of tightened rules about new members. Of course the masters knew that all of their relatives would join for free, and so the reduction may simply have been a concession to the *linaioli*, who always had a lower fee than their new partners.[24] The strong rule prohibiting night work, complete with spies to enforce it, was not a feature of the previous statutes of the linen guild. As already seen, night work was a complex subject with a variety of tensions pulling at any decision to ban it. But in this case, the rule of 1340 was clearly a new one and did not cover the ragdealers in the same guild. Changing attitudes about night work in the fourteenth century should reveal something about the state of business in particular crafts.

Overall movements of prices and wages in Florence are difficult to piece together from the fragmentary evidence. Wages for gardeners and day laborers in the construction business rose in the period 1340–1378, but whether or not the entire increase represented an improving standard of living, as opposed to an adjustment to inflation, is not clear.[25] Grain prices were also increasing rapidly from 1335 to 1352, but in the aftermath of the plague, they fell and remained at lower levels for the next fifteen or so years.[26] The real dividing line seems to be the plague; the basis for increases remains the stability of wages at low levels that characterizes the first half of the fourteenth century. Insurrections occurred among the journeymen and apprentices in the wool industry in 1343 and among the skinners in 1345.[27] This last group had a leader who was captured and executed for organizing a guild for the kinds of workers traditionally excluded from sanctioned associations. The motives behind these industrial protests remain unclear, but such troubles again suggest that workers left out of the guild still believed that organization was the answer to at least some of their problems. The masters of the guilds of Florence had the same opinion, but they used the guilds to restrict their numbers and not to foster the ambitions of journeymen and apprentices.

New statutes for the enamelers and glaziers of Paris, dated September 1309, contain signs of changes in the policies about apprentices and journeymen.[28] The masters were allowed to have only one apprentice who had to serve for not less than ten years. When the apprentice had completed half of the term, the master was permitted to take another, even if the apprentice had bought himself out of the rest of the term. Again the length of the term bears no necessary relation to the time needed to learn this craft. Apprentice enamelers were in a position to pay and hence not serve the last five years of the term. But such apprentices did not have the right to take on an apprentice of their own until ten years had passed. In addition apprentices were not allowed to practice the trade in their own households (*hostel*) until the masters had approved and sworn them to the guild. In other words these apprentices had to work as journeymen in someone else's shop for at least five years. The statutes' framers recognized that some recent masters, as of September 1309, had two or three apprentices. (This evidence indicates that the statutes represented a change in policy.) The rules stated that these masters could not take on another apprentice until the last one that was employed had completed half of the term. Over the next five years, this provision would bring all of the masters into compliance and not disrupt existing contracts. This revision indicates that the masters chose to reduce the number of apprentices across the trade and also to make sure that buying out the term did not result in some journeymen becoming masters too soon. Over the long term this revision also reduced the number of journeymen, and the masters did not appear worried about this certain outcome. The masters looking that far down the road may not have concluded that fewer journeymen would result in higher wages; if so, then this rule may be more evidence for a glut of labor. No exceptions to these new rules were allowed, not even for sons, and hence the path to master status became more difficult, at least in this one trade.

A general ordinance by Philip the Fair of France addressed itself to the familiar issue of work rules in Paris in a way that covered all of the trades. On 19 January 1322, Gilles Haquin, *prévot* of Paris, reaffirmed the decisions of the late king.[29] Some métiers of the city, using old work rules that were examined in chapter 4, declared that no one should work at night and that no one should have more than one apprentice, taken for a fixed term and at a certain price. The king had ordered, *pour le commun prouffit,* that all could now work by day and by night, as seemed best to them, and that the masters could have as many apprentices as they wished, with terms and sums left for them to decide. The common profit or benefit, easily invoked, does not explain the reasoning behind the ordinance. Bronislaw Geremek notes that in 1277 some Parisian valets complained to the king, on the grounds of their health, about long work hours.[30] The later ordinance was not a sardonic reply to the valets, but the issue of journeymen, the ones most likely to work at night and most likely to be alarmed by an influx of apprentices, is worth examining. In 1288, the dyers had extended the term of their apprenticeship from whatever was customary at the time of the *Livre des métiers* to five years, for the ostensible reason that journeymen were experiencing difficulties in finding work.[31] This solution naturally only slowed down the production of new journeymen by holding back some apprentices. All of these developments help to place the rules of 1322 in their proper context and also suggest that, once again, the new rule should be examined from the point of view of masters, journeymen, and apprentices.

Many guilds in Paris already had by 1322 the right to work at night, so in the new rule the king was simply extending this privilege, or imposing some uniformity on a confused subject. This flexibility, as well as the freedom to have as many apprentices as one needed, clearly favored the masters. More leeway on terms and fees also allowed the masters room to strike advantageous deals with parents or guardians for the services of children. Hence the common profit was clearly that of the masters. For many journeymen the ordinance spelled longer hours at work, most likely for the same pay. The number of apprentices, mostly journeymen in the making, would also increase now that the old limitation had vanished. So the consequences of the ordinance, down the road, would be a larger pool of journeymen—no advantage for them—but the immediate effects must have been to make placing children in apprenticeships in the first place easier for some parents. The last benefit makes some sense of the whole policy. If one assumes that economic conditions in Paris were tightening up in the 1320s and that the services of apprentices were the cheapest type of labor available to the masters, then opening up the system made sense. Perhaps the tangible benefits to the masters seemed modest; if so, night work had its attractions. As seen in chapter 4, however, night work cut both ways. Different masters were capable of reaching opposite views about its benefits to employers.[32] But in this case the king himself was convinced that night work was beneficial—and how would he know this? The same people who were capable of solving the employment problems of valets by keeping back apprentices might also decide that more apprentices were the solution to the problems of masters who needed more profit.

Since most changes in both Florence and Paris left alone the favored status of masters' sons, the apprentices facing real difficulties were those whose parents practiced a different craft than the one intended for them. These apprentices gained from easier entry to the trade, but the odds now weighed more heavily against the eventual opportunity to become a master. These apprentices all became journeymen, however, and this simple fact, and a problem always solved by the passage of time, should remind one not to see journeymen and apprentices as part of a static hierarchy. Instead, they represented a chronology; the real bottleneck was as usual master status.

If in some places the master's hand was becoming the stronger one in the market for labor, then some signs of this should be expected in apprenticeship contracts. The smaller sample of apprenticeship contracts, the fifty-one from Tournai dated 1264–1365, contain a few hints that masters were in a better position.[33] The eight contracts made by master weavers fall into two groups—1286–1306 and 1310–1342.[34] Two of the first four offered the apprentice the sum of seven pennies for each cloth, and the other two set the terms according "to the use and custom of the métier," presumably the same deal as the others.[35] These contracts also had short terms, two for two years and two for three years. The customs of the weavers of Tournai were to say nothing about food and clothing, but the salary of seven pennies likely removed any other obligation from the masters. The last four contracts reveal a different picture. The masters abandoned payments to the apprentices, and the terms of service were longer—on average four years. Apprentices now received food and clothing, but in one case the mother paid nine livres for this, and in the other a country father had to provide some wheat in fixed terms. This handful of contracts by itself would not sustain any sweeping conclusions but does suggest that masters were increasingly able to ask for more from their apprentices— more time, in some cases no salary, and also a payment of money or food from the parents.

Seven contracts from Tournai involve apprentices to goldsmiths. In this lucrative trade, the parents, from the first contract in 1264, had to pay the master to take on a pupil. This is what would be expected in a trade in which a master had to wait a long time for useful work from a trainee. The sums the master goldsmiths demanded varied considerably and probably depended on the age of the apprentice, a fact not recorded in these contracts, as well as the family's ability to pay. The first three of these contracts averaged a payment of fourteen livres, the last three twenty livres, with one anomalous contract for only four livres in the middle. If the middle contract is excluded, the terms of service were at the same time going down, from seven years in 1264 to four years in 1330. The higher sums and shorter terms again point to a more difficult entry into the trade, especially if the shorter apprenticeship resulted from a longer period of journeyman status or the increased age of the average apprentice.

Some changes in the Genoese apprenticeship and work contracts follow the same patterns as in Tournai. Genoa's rich records provide one of the few indices of price inflation, a problem that must be kept in mind in any study of wages.[36] Although inflation might well have been a general phenomenon in medieval Europe after 1250, its rate was not necessarily the same everywhere, so caution is in order.

It is difficult to separate out the purely monetary factors from all of the other stimulants to price increases, though these exogenous factors eventually affected the economy's monetary system.[37] The standard measure of price changes is the Fisher equation: $MV = PT$, in which M is the money supply, V the velocity or rapidity of circulation, P the general level of prices, and T the volume of transactions or real output.[38] If the equation is restated to emphasize price levels—$P = MV/T$—then the three terms on the right reveal a host of monetary, fiscal, and other factors that could account for an increase in price levels. If the other variables are held constant, an increase in M itself is the classic cause of inflation, especially when the supplies of goods, services, and outputs remain the same. The money supply may increase absolutely in two ways: a massive infusion of gold and silver into Europe or a decrease in the precious metal content of the coinage. (Relative changes in the money supply are more complex, but one relevant change, more money per capita because of depopulation, is discussed later in this chapter.) John Day has persuasively argued that another logical way to increase M, to use credit instruments as cash by endorsement or discount, was not a factor in the thirteenth or fourteenth centuries.[39] Since increases in Europe's bullion stock through mining were not large to begin with and given the inevitable wastage through wear and the export of coin and bullion to the east, there is general agreement that the supply of bullion was steady—hence M was stable.[40] Of course governments could fuel inflation and derive benefits for themselves by stretching stocks of bullion through debasement. Harry Miskimin has shown for England and France that "grain prices rose in direct proportion to debasement."[41] The other, literal, side of the coin is, as noted by Day, that "if one excludes the effects of harvest fluctuations, coinage mutations, and variations in the stock of monetary metals, the general price curve in the fourteenth and fifteenth centuries—except for the price of labor—was practically level."[42] This point about labor will be returned to again. A bullionist approach gives pride of place to M as the key to inflation and those price changes that may be attributed to it.

The other possible sources of price increases are harder to quantify and hence not easy to "plug into" the Fisher equation. If the population was increasing in an economy with a relatively rigid money supply, then the simple velocity of money, the simple frequency by which it changed hands, could contribute to price increases as more people chased the same money supply. V was not likely to decline unless people stopped spending. Warfare and its sequel, taxation, could cause shocks in spending patterns as well. Arguments based on V remain impressionistic, and most observers conclude that the velocity was usually high—a sensible view.[43] Wage labor contributed to the high velocity of money. It was after all one of the reasons for having money, and all of those silver pennies were paid and spent very quickly, especially by the journeymen. Consider T for the special case of the price of labor. Clearly if the output of labor declined, then, all things equal, the price of labor could increase. The reverse was a more familiar situation in preplague Europe; an increase in the real output of labor or, in this case, productivity could drive down the price of labor by item of output but not necessarily drive down wages for working people. The fate of these people depended on whether the output increased from technological advance or from a simple decline in real wages. Competition among masters was supposed to prevent price gouging, but the complex costs of labor probably account for the medieval preference for fixed prices and stable wage rates as the easiest ways to do business.

This theoretical look at the price of labor reveals that changes in wage rates can have many causes. Even in an economy with complete and exact records, the problem of accounting for these changes is formidable, and for the late thirteenth and early fourteenth centuries, the sources are never complete and exact. For manufacturing, the difficulties of determining typical rents, supply costs, and other aspects of overhead make it impossible to distinguish the effects of purely monetary inflation from the effects of other costs to producers, let alone changes in labor productivity, wages, and new technologies. With all of these reservations in mind, let us see what a few examples can offer on the question of wage rates. The issue of regional markets for labor is a thorny one, so places that are far apart will be examined.

Studies of the prices of two special commodities, gold and silver, and of the purchasing power of the Genoese lire money of account reveal that during the thirteenth century the price of gold per pound was steadily increasing—L48s.12d.1 in 1254, L61s.14d.3 in 1265, and L63s.3d.9 in 1291.[44] To compare silver to gold in the same years is not always possible; the equivalent price series for a pound of fine silver is L5s.10d.8 in 1253, L5s.16d.11 in 1268, and L5s.12d.4 in 1291. Silver remained virtually flat in price and hence became progressively cheaper in relation to gold. Gold, however, increased in price by 50 percent, possibly as a result of greater supplies of silver in thirteenth-century Europe and at the same time the reappearance of gold coinage, along with the lack of substantial, European gold mining. Hence gold remained an expensive import. Employers almost always paid wages in silver coins, but even these wages were probably not immune to changes in the price of gold, especially after gold was monetized in Florence and Genoa in 1252. The changes in the value of gold certainly affected the prices of a whole range of commodities that the day laborer needed to purchase in order to survive. If one assumes that the money supply is rigid and that the value of gold and silver roughly follows changes in the purchasing power of money, then the evidence from Genoa indicates some increases in prices between 1250 and 1300.

The post-1250 work and apprenticeship contracts will not support any sweeping claims about wage patterns.[45] The absolute number of these contracts seems to have declined from the level of earlier years, perhaps a sign that more labor was casual or that the expense of drawing up a formal contract was no longer tolerable. By itself, a greater reliance on labor hired at will was not necessarily a sign that the market for hired hands was becoming more favorable to the employers, but other signs suggest that this was the case. Apprenticeships, as already described, had long terms and low wages, if indeed any were offered, and journeymen had comparatively shorter terms and higher wages. Masters also had to take into account the increase in prices as reflected in the value of gold, and the changes were more palpable after 1252. Casual labor and the short-term work contracts enabled the masters to reassess wages more frequently and hence adjust to price levels and the supply of labor. The longer-term contracts usually had an incremental scale of wages, an incentive system as old as wages. Here the evidence is admittedly negative; these escalating wages did not become more common in the 1250s or after, precisely when the value of gold began to change at a rapid rate. In 1214, a six-year apprenticeship for a *filator* (threadmaker) offered wages that increased in increments of a halfpenny a day, from 2 to 4¹/₂ pennies a day over the course of the term.[46] By 1256, a five-year apprenticeship to a *lanerius* saw orderly raises by 1 penny a day, from 6 to 10 pennies a day over the term.[47] Contessa Boiasco apprenticed her son Jacobino to a *filator* for four years in 1272, and he was to receive 3 pennies a day for the first year, 3¹/₂ for the second, 4 for the third, and 5 for the fourth.[48] When Francesco de Valle Avanti apprenticed his son Antonio to a *lanerius* for four years in 1293, the master agreed to pay L5s.10 for the term, 20 solidi for the first year and 30 solidi for the remaining three.[49] These roughly similar examples suggest that wages remained flat over time, despite the changes in the value of gold. The market for labor in Genoa tipped in favor of employers toward the end of the thirteenth century. A drag at the bottom of the hierarchy of work, where the apprentices were, suffused its way through the system and certainly made matters worse for the journeymen as well.

Bronislaw Geremek has investigated wages in the construction trade at the hospice of St. Jacques in Paris. These fourteenth-century wages have no base in the previous century with which to compare, but they too reveal certain trends. Geremek also observes that salaries were rather rigid, and he suggests that customary levels of wages were the rule. Hence disputes about pay levels were rare.[50] Far from being a sign that journeymen were content with their wages, entrenched wage levels simply pushed complaints into other spheres. For example, Léo Verriest found that a Flemish artisan was imprisoned in the harsh aftermath of the battle of Courtrai (1302) simply for saying in effect that everyone should have as much as everyone else.[51] This kind of leveling comment, not rare in the later Middle Ages, makes vivid sense in the context of wage rates that do not seem to move, despite whatever was happening to prices and rents. According to Geremek, the French royal government in the 1290s began to take an interest in the issue of masters hiring away the workers of others.[52] As already seen, this was by then an old concern, but the state's role was new and in Geremek's view resulted from a desire to control wages. The principal issue about stealing or luring away another's employees was always that the mas-

Table 5-1. Daily Wage Rates of Building Craftsmen in Southern
England, 1264–1350

Period	Rate
1264–1300	3d.
1300–1304	3d.–3¹/₂d.
1304–1308	3¹/₂d.
1308–1311	3¹/₂d.–4d.
1311–1337	4d.
1337–1340	4d.–3d.
1340–1350	3d.

Source: Phelps-Brown and Hopkins, "Seven Centuries of Building Wages,"
p. 177.

ters had agreed not to compete for labor in the area of its price. In the
1290s the French state had an additional interest for its fiddling with
the silver content of the currency, a common expedient across Europe
in this decade, made the issue of the currency's value in the marketplace
a real one. Data on wheat prices adjusted for debasement suggest that
from 1315 to 1325 rigid wages were disastrous to those who needed to
buy bread.[53] One way for people to compensate for depreciated money
was to demand higher wages, but the state was opposed to this solution. Finally, in the construction trades investigated by Geremek, the
valets earned about 50 percent of what masters in the same trade
made.[54] This proportion was also part of the traditional structure of
wages and suggests that employers faced the same problems as journeymen and apprentices, as the economic growth of the previous three
centuries began to flatten out in the 1290s.

The craft wages tabulated for southern England reveal a flat wage
pattern from 1264 to 1350, with one bulge in the middle (table 5-1). In
this period the same authors examine the cost of living, as well as the
sources allow, and they produce an index of consumables that reveals
that prices fluctuated widely. The great famine of 1315–1317 (an event
with devastating consequences across much of Europe), wars, changes
in the effectiveness of taxation, as well as the ordinary rhythms of
harvests and the market for labor—all contributed to volatile prices at a
most difficult time for laborers. If the famine is used as a breakpoint

and some of the temporary extremes of prices are disregarded, then the index of consumables seems relatively flat from 1264 to the onset of the bubonic plague in 1348. From about 1310 to 1330, some sharp increases in prices occurred at the same time as wages reached their highest preplague levels.[55] These findings suggest stagnant living conditions for craftsmen, who on a more positive note were at least holding their own, but no evidence suggests any improving standard of living.[56]

These pieces of evidence from Paris, Florence, Genoa, Tournai, and England are not intended to suggest that all cities and regions of medieval Europe experienced the same changes simultaneously in the sphere of employment. The migration of workers, a subject not well documented or researched at this point, tended to ameliorate the picture in some places. For example, Richard Goldthwaite finds that foreigners accounted for 20 percent of the guildsmen in the construction trades—a clear sign of the mobility of carpenters and masons.[57] At the same time the arrival of migrant workers in the cities was spreading the problem of flat real wages. The effect that changes in the level of population had on the economy is one of the most hotly contested aspects of late medieval history. The evidence collected here reveals nothing about changes in population size, and the state of wages might have resulted from a variety of demographic circumstances. As bad as the evidence for wages is, it is better than many of the estimates of national and urban population levels. But still, the work of a variety of scholars suggests that in some places the economy reached the limits of growth in the 1290s and that the resources and technology of the medieval economy could not sustain the growth rates of the previous three centuries. If one assumes that a kind of Malthusian crisis was in the making at the end of the thirteenth century, then the problems first appeared in those areas of northern Italy and the Low Countries with the longest experience in a systematic wage economy. These problems of population pressures on wages and prices were not confined to cities and may have first appeared on the rural scene. But the cities, with their charity, wages, and apprenticeships, became the natural focal points for any economic difficulties.

Journeymen and apprentices faced these straitened circumstances at the same time that their prospects for self-employment were becoming less bright. If the period after 1348 deserves the epithet of the "Golden Age of Labor," then the previous age might be called the "Heyday of Employers." Another indication, one particularly relevant to the Spanish and Italian cities, of wage labor's place in the economy is the role of slave labor. Slavery, soon to be an important feature of European colonialism, was somewhat paradoxically never a dominant economic fact in the cities of the northern Mediterranean. Many of these cities had, however, a continuous and practical experience with the slave trade in the central Middle Ages, and this knowledge would soon find application elsewhere. But in this period, slavery represented a road not taken, and instead an apparently conscious decision was taken in favor of free labor in the countryside and in the artisan trades. A problem about slavery must be considered along with the possibilities for journeymen and apprentices. Slaves were becoming increasingly expensive in the late thirteenth and early fourteenth centuries. Given the supply of free labor and its flat wages, the rise in the price of slaves merits attention as a possible sign that the view of employment sketched here is incomplete without slaves. The reasons why slavery never really caught on in southern Europe reveal some important features of the wage economy.

The thirteenth-century Genoese notarial record contains a sufficient number of sales of slaves to permit a calculation of the average price of slaves over time. Michel Balard has investigated this problem and finds that the price increased from L4–L7 in 1239–1240 to L18–L22 around 1300.[58] He also considers the question of inflation and comes to the conclusion that silver depreciated by 28 percent and gold by 41 percent, another way of stating the more recent figures cited above and close to those price levels. By any reckoning, the price of slaves was increasing much faster than the general inflation of prices, and this points to a strong demand for slaves, though not necessarily in Genoa. The slave market was international, and although Genoa was one of the principal entrepôts of this trade, the price of slaves also reflected demand in distant places like Mamluk Egypt. The usual measure of wages helps to place these prices in perspective. The skilled weaver of the 1250s earned the price of a slave in 100 workdays. By the end of the century slaves were more expensive, and at least three times the amount of labor that was needed in 1250 was required for an artisan to buy a slave. For example, a twenty-five-year-old apprentice weaver in 1293, who did not receive any food or clothing, would have to work 540 days at 8 pennies a day to buy a slave costing L18, but a skilled worker might accomplish that feat at an unenviable pace much higher than the 1250 rate.[59] Slaves were cheap from the 1220s to the 1250s and became progressively more expensive after that time. Female slaves were nearly always more costly than male ones, but the premium the females enjoyed in the marketplace remained small. For the period 1239–1300, Balard notes that women comprised 62.9 percent and men 37.1 percent of his sample slave population.[60]

The capital requirements for slavery are thus fairly clear, but the long-term costs of maintaining slaves deserve some attention, especially since free labor also needed some minimum in order to subsist. Potential slaveowners in Genoa and elsewhere would take these expenses of slaves into account and compare them to the costs of wage labor in the market. The evidence indicates that in part the luxury appeal of having slaves operated despite any rational calculation of the economic benefits of possessing them. The majority of the female slaves were employed as servants in the households of Genoa's prominent families.[61] Poor women from the countryside, and some from the city as well, would work for nothing more than food, clothing, and a place to sleep, things that slaves required in addition to their initial purchase price. So, some of the market for slaves has more to do with questions of status than of profit. The dishonor of the slave was more tangible than the wage laborer's position of dependence. Therefore, many noble families displayed status by having female slaves from exotic places, although master artisans in the main had to be content to employ journeymen in order to reveal their place in the order of things.[62] Masters acquired apprentices for free in the marketplace, or even better, the parent or guardian paid them to take a young boy or girl into service. Most masters did not offer an apprentice any salary at all, and hence the master's only expenses were for food, clothing, and lodging—the same as for slaves. Perhaps the apprentices dined and dressed better than the slaves, perhaps not.

The cost of basic maintenance can be calculated by comparing the way that some masters paid apprentices who received food, clothing, and a daily stipend to how they paid those who received only a wage. The difference, compared over a number of cases, represents the rule-of-thumb estimate of the cost of feeding and clothing an apprentice or, by generous extension, a slave. These comparisons reveal virtually no difference between the lowest wages of day laborers and the costs of basic subsistence.[63] Some workers actually earned less than the minimum necessary to support themselves, and possibly these people remained with their families. In this wage environment, where by 1300 many hands waited for employment, the increasing capital costs of slaves must have weighed heavily in the calculations of master artisans who considered purchasing them.

The evidence on how masters used their male slaves is fragmentary. The high proportion of female slaves suggests that many were domestic servants, largely because they lived with rich families not engaged in crafts. The role of slaves in the artisan trades remained the most important source of potential difficulty for the free apprentices and journeymen who may have competed with slaves. Balard correctly proposes that the male slaves were the key to this problem and that "the needs of the Genoese artisans therefore explain the higher proportion of male slaves" owned by masters in trades in which heavy physical labor was the norm.[64] He cites a draper's will from 1296 that indicates that the master owned five male slaves, presumably employed in his business. Later guild statutes provide some information on the role that some slaves had in manufacturing. The statutes of the silk guild, redacted in 1432, state that masters were allowed to teach the art to slaves, but the slaves could never be heads of shops or officials in the guild. The slaves were permitted to work only as day laborers.[65] The masters envisioned slaves competing with free employees, but never with themselves. Statutes of the dyers' guild from 1426 make the same points. In this guild training slaves or foreigners was permissible, and they too only worked as journeymen.[66] Slavery remained important in fifteenth-century Genoa, and unfortunately, the earliest surviving guild statutes are this late.[67] In the thirteenth and fourteenth centuries, masters were likely free to use slaves as they wished.[68] By around 1300, the capital cost of L20 in an era of low wages might have seemed too much to risk in the face of disease and other uncertainties.

Genoa's experience in the slave trade was by no means unique. The merchants of Barcelona were also active acquirers of slaves in North Africa, and slaves in their city also posed some challenges to free labor.[69] The presence of Moorish slaves in Barcelona affected the organization of labor in the town and in particular apprenticeships.[70] In Barcelona the fate of Cassim, slave and caulker, mentioned in the Introduction because his labor was in effect leased for a year, serves as a reminder that alternatives to wage labor existed.[71] The editors of this notarial contract comment that times were hard for slaves in Barcelona, and the specifics of the *commenda* for Cassim are compared to one made for a cow.[72] Religious differences made continuing the practice of slavery easier, and the trade in slaves brought Barcelona into the international market, first as exporters, then as importers. Thus the factor of overseas prices entered into the local calculations of those employing slaves.

Venice too had a use for slaves in this period on the plantations of Crete and later Cyprus, and in the city itself slaves seem to have been used "mostly as domestics or concubines."[73] The slave trade of the north, centered on the Baltic and North seas, had once rivaled that of the Mediterranean region. By the late thirteenth century, however, the trade had basically collapsed, and northern journeymen and apprentices did not face competition from slaves.[74] This difference between northern and southern Europe on the question of slavery is an important one. Italians and Catalans seem to have continued to participate in the slave trade largely because of the potential profits of that business with Mamluk Egypt. Northern Europe had no ready access to this market or the sources of supply in North Africa and the northern shore of the Black Sea. But northern Europeans would show themselves capable of resuscitating the slave trade in the sixteenth century in Africa. Even in the south, where slavery was well understood and supplies of potential slaves were abundant, wage earners remained far and away the dominant form of labor in the rural and urban areas.

Slave labor in southern Europe was an option not taken, though slaves themselves continued to be an important commodity for the merchants of Barcelona and Genoa. Wage labor is certainly part of the explanation for slavery's comparative insignificance outside the sphere of domestic service. Benjamin Z. Kedar demonstrates that the Church came to accept that baptized slaves remained the property of their masters, who received from Pope Gregory IX in 1240 permission to sell slaves who had converted to Christianity.[75] Emancipations by testament or spontaneous acts of charity continued to take place. These acts reveal that spiritual and moral concerns were part of the social attitude about slavery, as were the cold calculations of profit and loss. Although the Church had in effect cleared the way for Christian slave labor to exist, employing journeymen and apprentices troubled no one's moral scruples and was apparently cheaper in the bargain. In the economic circumstances of early fourteenth-century Europe, the market for labor had tipped in favor of employers anyway, and slaves became even more of a luxury. Without the tradition of wage labor developed in the previous two centuries, southern Europe might have taken more readily to the potential of slave labor, but in fact a better system of recruiting labor was at hand, at least for as long as the supply of free people remained abundant. Perhaps some craftsmen and mariners knew that they worked because they were still cheaper than slaves—a realization that would itself explain some outbreaks of fury by employees in the fourteenth century.

Labor, Capital, and the New Crafts

Both free employees and slaves had to face competition from another source: the possibility that employers might save on the costs of labor by substituting technology, in effect capital, for wage or slave labor. That standards of production left masters free to innovate was seen in chapter 3, and a wide variety of technological improvements and completely new crafts and businesses appeared in European cities in the central Middle Ages.[76] In postplague Europe was an even greater incentive to find labor-saving devices and methods, and this motive will be examined below. At about 1300 the price of labor was not such a strong impetus to innovation. Yet new trades thrived, and their situation with respect to the guild system is instructive.

Some trades and professions existed before the dawn of the urban revival in around the year 1000. Weavers, blacksmiths, traveling merchants, and fishermen were part of the economic scene as far back as it can be examined, and these occupations often participated in the earliest guilds. Some of the "new" trades evolved out of older associations. For example, the great merchant bankers of some Italian towns had guilds that owed their existence to original groups of money changers. These guilds are usually referred to as banking guilds in English, but urban and international banking was something new in this period and, more importantly, not the professions of the founders of these guilds. In this case an older business, money changing, became more complex and carried along the institution of the guild. Other new guilds represent the growth of a business to a point at which a formal organization was desirable, especially where a guild had a political dimension as well. For example, Zurich was not a new town, nor was the trade of shopkeeping a novelty there, but only in 1336 did the shopkeepers petition the burghermeister and burghers for the right to have a guild and a common society (*ein zunft und ein gemein geselleschaft*).[77] In Zurich, a guild republic, masters benefited from having an officially sanctioned guild.[78] Other new businesses demanded that the masters adapt older skills or learn new techniques. Cloth is the clearest example of this borrowing from another trade. Western Europeans knew about wool and linen; by 1300 substantial cotton and silk industries had appeared in southern Europe and would become a durable fixture of the economy. Wool manufacture was a good school for cotton and silk, but these new materials did pose considerable challenges to the work-force's manual and mechanical skills.

Maureen Mazzaoui has investigated the growth of the Italian cotton industry, and she finds that the cotton guilds did not adopt the typical organization of the wool guilds as their model. The cotton guilds extended membership to particular groups like beaters and weavers, who were usually excluded from wool guilds, and these laborers enjoyed higher status and incomes as a result of this different guild structure.[79] These advantages did not last for long in every city because in some places the guild structure imitated the division of labor and produced several organizations representing various stages of manufacture. For example, a cotton guild in Venice was a mixed group originally, but by the end of the thirteenth century, at least three other guilds had appeared—beaters, makers of cords for bows, and makers of loom reeds.[80] In Venice, where the city government dominated the guilds, the division of large, comprehensive guilds into smaller ones might also have resulted from a desire for bureaucratic efficiency. The officials charged with overseeing the guilds favored a system that mimicked the division of labor.

The advantages that some workers had in a new craft appear to have been temporary, for sooner or later two expected changes would take place. First, the masters would assert themselves as employers and confine the direction of the guild to their number. Second, one grand guild would become, in most cities where industry flourished, a number of specialized guilds. Mazzaoui believes that this "modification of the original guild structure . . . was a response to the aspirations of subject artisans for greater control over their working conditions."[81] And further, "In despotic regimes, the formation of artisan guilds was encouraged as a means of offsetting the power of the entrepreneurial class."[82] Just who these artisans were requires a closer look. If they are considered to be masters or at least self-employed laborers working in a putting-out system, these comments help to explain the tendency toward specialized guilds. But guilds of journeymen and day laborers are another matter. The weavers and beaters, the two groups that at times had membership in the guilds, were not necessarily homogeneous. As already seen, master status depended on whether or not the artisan in question had a shop, took on employees, and trained apprentices. Perhaps day laborers enjoyed some advantages in the early days of a new craft, especially if they possessed uncommon skills. Such workers would be in a better position to bargain with the entrepreneurs in the business. Also, in the early years of a new craft's development, when the raw materials and skills to work them were hard to come by, even artisans engaged in a comparatively humble aspect of the craft might be self-employed or acceptors of raw materials consigned to them by merchants. Hence more needs to be known about the organization of new crafts on the shop level before concluding that they were more or less rigidly organized than older businesses were. Corporate society was entrenched, and in some towns participation in politics required a formal guild. These facts of life were probably decisive in the minds of masters in the new crafts, who so frequently decided, when allowed by law, to organize themselves into a guild. Even when the impulse took a long time to unfold, the habits of corporate thinking remained powerful enough to encourage the employers to conform their businesses to standard practices.

The mechanical clock is another example of how new technologies found practical applications in manufacture. Lynn Thorndike has located the invention of the clock at about 1271, but another century passed before municipal clocks became a common feature of medieval cities.[83] The social benefits of a method for determining the time were obvious. The day laborer wanted a reliable and independent means of measuring the length of the workday, merchants needed to keep appointments, and the pace of urban life required a device more trustworthy than the sundial.[84] The appearance of the mechanical clock built upon a host of minute improvements in manufacturing techniques, and for a long time clockmakers enjoyed a reputation for being the most skilled craftsmen in Europe. The first clocks were mammoth and expensive marvels—Genoa acquired its municipal clock in 1353, an event important enough to merit notice in the city chronicle.[85] The clock itself was expensive to maintain and still required constant supervision. Mass production of reliable and accurate timepieces was beyond the capabilities of medieval technology, but the earliest phase of the clock industry did draw upon the most advanced skills from a variety of crafts. As David Landes describes, the infant industry required metalworkers skilled in iron and brass, carpenters, mechanics, and repairers.[86] Smaller, portable clocks appeared in the first half of the fourteenth century, and those ornate, luxurious works involved smiths with a delicate touch in silver and other metals.[87] Landes estimates that

230 / Labor and Guilds in Crisis

"there were probably dozens of clockmakers active in Europe by the end of the fourteenth century."[88]

Clockmaking is an industry of great future significance, but one extremely small in comparison to other new crafts like cotton and silk. The small number of clockmakers scattered across Europe did not require any guild structure, and in fact the first appearance of clockmakers' guilds are very late: Paris, 1544; Nuremberg, 1565; and Blois, 1600.[89] Some clockmakers found a temporary home in an allied craft; as Landes notes, "In Augsburg [they] were part of the smiths' guild" as far back as 1368, and not until 1441 did a clockmaker "as such" enter the guild.[90] For some masters clockmaking might have been a sideline to what was their principal occupation—in this case metalworking. But for a long time even large cities had only a few clockmakers, and so the craft remained too small to have a guild even in places like Paris, which had, as previously seen, numerous guilds containing only a small number of masters. The example of Augsburg may be a typical one—masters remained in a parent guild until the industry reached a condition that required a separate organization.

This industry's slow rise has several important aspects. Technological innovation had a part in the developing division of labor. Not all new crafts owed their existence to the refinements and efficiencies of established manufactures. Clockmaking is a useful example here because it was brand-new, and in time it called forth a new wave of mechanical and metallurgical skills. Although little is known about the first generation of master clockmakers, they likely owed their education and skills to the guild system of apprenticeship, simply because that was the way artisans acquired knowledge of advanced manual techniques. Guilds incubated technological innovations and could claim some credit for these technological accomplishments. Even when the new trade was tiny, the guild continued to serve as an umbrella organization in which, for example, the clockmakers would still share many interests with their fellow smiths, who themselves turned out a bewildering array of products. The urban wage system of labor, which owed much to guild regulations, also helped to foster new trades. Wage labor tended to be mobile, an important characteristic when transferring skills from old to new trades. This mobility also helped to spread technological changes from one city to another.

New trades are the most obvious examples of a growing division of labor in medieval society. Whether or not the local cotton industry took the form of a single guild or a kind of federation of allied guilds, the important point is that new businesses added to the stock of talents in the cities. Specialization also took place within older trades, and some masters became increasingly adept at a smaller set of tasks. Guilds, as seen above, also fostered a gender division of labor as social customs dictated a large role for women in certain trades and their virtual exclusion from many others.

Economic historians have noted for a long time the efficiencies of production that result from a division of labor. The observation that specialization in turn fosters the budding-off of new trades is also a commonplace. Sometimes the formation of a new guild reveals the pace at which the gender division of labor developed. In March 1300, the royal officials of Paris established an ordinance for what was to all appearances a new trade, the manufacture of small purses from a special kind of silk in the Saracen style.[91] Tapestryweavers in this style existed, as well as various métiers of silkweavers and pursemakers, but this business of small silk purses had reached the point at which statutes and the status of a guild were desirable. The unusual feature of this guild is that the statutes list the names of the 126 women working at the craft, all silk-workers, and they also repeatedly refer only to mistresses of the trade. This business, perhaps because of the use of silk and the fine hand it required, had become a new example of women's work. In this case the gender division of labor was absolute; all of the people in the craft were women, and they now had their own set of rules.

The division of labor made itself apparent in the increasing number of separate trades found in places like fourteenth-century London and Paris. Part of this trend certainly resulted from the demands of urban life and the niches for new occupations this life provided. New trades by definition added to the gross number of possible jobs. The history of the division of labor goes back as far as work itself, and even the medieval guild is a brief part of that story. Economic development and the sheer size of markets also fostered the specialization of work, but the guild as well played a part in this process. Guilds organized production by dividing it into discrete categories and by providing appropriate work rules. These accomplishments are modest, yet they helped to institutionalize and to make permanent certain features of the division of labor. The different crafts themselves supplied the dividing lines, but perhaps more importantly, the market for labor contributed distinctions according to the age, status, and sex of the workers. The question of technological innovation will be examined again after a look at a possible impetus—the bubonic plague.

Demographic Catastrophe and Labor

The plague of 1348 had profound and immediate consequences across Europe, except for a few isolated areas in which its severity may have been less pronounced.[92] The dramatic loss of people, particularly in the densely populated cities, affected the guilds, employment, technology, and the impulse to substitute capital for labor.[93] In the aftermath of the first bout of the plague, governments and guilds were forced to deal with a radically changed economy. Where once entry to master status had been difficult and wages were low, now the ranks of masters had been thinned, and the much-debated "Golden Age of Labor" had commenced. Many old rules no longer made any sense, and the survivors found themselves in an economic world that had turned some assumptions about work on their heads. The postplague environment challenged the dynamic qualities of the guild system and wage labor. Both institutions survived, a tribute to their resiliency, yet in some respects the second half of the fourteenth century represents a watershed in the history of labor in Europe, as well as a convenient terminus for this study.

The experience of the plague called for a general response, for its effects were not limited to individual trades and neighborhoods but were broader than the scope of traditional guild activities. Some guilds on their own responded to the economic challenges of the plague. In 1349, the Florentine wool guild decided to impose production quotas on its members—all masters had a specific number of cloths they might produce per shop per year, with an upper limit of 220 cloths. John Najemy suggests that the masters hoped to maintain the price of cloth by limiting production.[94] This policy was sensible in light of the levels of mortality and the expected lower demand for cloth. But Florentine production of wool cloth increased nearly threefold from the late 1350s to the late 1360s.[95] Whether because exemptions from the quota flourished or masters cheated, the policy failed to hold down production. Even if the masters had succeeded, other towns and guilds could have devised strategies of their own that would have worked against one guild's efforts.

The scale of devastation required medieval governments to develop more in the way of a concerted policy than few had ever before attempted. The French monarchy, as previously seen, tried to control the city of Paris and to foster its prosperity and métiers. The challenge of the plague called for a more systematic approach to matters economic.

The French state did respond in a remarkable document, the Grand Ordinance of February 1351.[96] Its date alone reveals that the monarchy, in the person of King Jean II, seems to have waited until the worst of the plague was behind Paris, but the disease itself may have made a coordinated response impossible in the first few years. Problems with the English and the currency were also factors in the decision to promulgate the ordinance.[97] The king did not expressly place these rules in the context of the plague, but the ordinance several times employs the phrase *avant la mortalité* as the important benchmark of the times.[98]

The government was preoccupied with two central issues—the prices of food and wages—both natural concerns in a crisis. Signs of other worries crept in, most notably about beggars. The king wanted the friars and others preaching in Paris to remind their congregations not to give alms to those capable of working.[99] The people of Paris were to confine their charity to the blind, the handicapped, and other "miserable persons." The hospitals and almshouses of the city were allowed to give shelter to the fit for only one night. The king necessarily relied upon the Church to accomplish this intention. The clergy were responsible for guiding the laity's charitable impulses and were also the managers of the city's hospitals and almshouses. The king wanted the prelates, barons, knights, and bourgeoisie of Paris to tell their almoners that they should not give relief to these *truants*—a clear sign that the sturdy beggars were evading their social duty. The ordinance does not explain the reasoning behind this rule, but the message is clear: labor was in short supply, wages were getting out-of-hand, and hence the able-bodied were required to work.

The great bulk of the ordinance took up the question of food and covered the victualing trades in detail in order to fix their prices. The most elaborate provisions concerned the bakers, those providing the staff of life. The emphasis on prices was on their stability. The state was probably reacting to a period of wildly fluctuating prices by giving some order and predictability to the marketplace. These new prices were not fixed according to some aim of reestablishing the preplague level. Instead, they seem to reflect conditions as they existed in the winter of 1351. Prices set in the ordinance were almost invariably ceilings and not floors, and the emphasis was on no more money than a certain sum, as for example six deniers per pint of the best white wine.[100] Presumably victualers did not undercut one another's prices, since the usual rules and traditions of the métiers remained in force. The foodstuffs, besides bread, regulated by this ordinance are wine, beer, ocean and fresh-water fish, meat, poultry, eggs, and cheese, the basic larder of fourteenth-century Paris.

Prices of food appear first in the ordinance, but the government knew that it also had to do something about other prices and, naturally, wages. If the order of presentation reflects the habits of thought of the king's servants, then it supplies good evidence for some astute economic thinking. Although food shortages did not seem an immediate threat, those providing the food would be disadvantaged if only they were controlled. Some of the provisions about other trades suggest that the length of apprenticeship was not the issue it had been before the plague. The leatherworkers in cordovan and the makers of straps and belts now had apprenticeships of two years and could have as many pupils as they liked.[101] The only restriction on the strapmakers' apprentices was that they should be able to make a living at the time of their discharge. But in 1351 two years seemed to be sufficient to teach the necessary skills. Back in the 1260s this métier had required the apprentices to serve for nine years and pay sixty sous, or serve eleven years without payment.[102] Only the plague can account for this dramatic change, which again suggests that the length of the term often reveals more about the market for labor than about the actual amount of time needed to learn a trade.

The ordinances addressed the prices of other goods with the purpose of controlling their increases. The vinedressers were only allowed to pay their workers one-third more than was paid before the plague, and for other trades, like the smiths, the same proportion applied.[103] The smiths could only charge one-third more as well, and hence the masters' incomes also ran up against a ceiling. Jean II and his officials seem to have recognized that keeping wages and prices at their pre-plague levels would be impossible. At the end of the ordinance the king imposed this general rule of a one-third increase in wages on all valets working by the year, for whom no special provision existed in the specific trades.[104] The day laborers (*salaires*), paid by the day or by the piece, also had to accept the maximum of a one-third increase in their wages.[105] Since many masters faced limits on their own prices and incomes, their employees inevitably had to live with the same strictures. In order to make sure that the limits on wages were effective, the ordinances directed that no master should make a higher bid for the valets of another master.[106] This requirement buttressed the one-third limit on wage increases and also helped to maintain a uniformity of wages in the particular trades.

For one trade, the masons and their assistants, the ordinance prescribes the actual wages. From the feast of St. Martin in the winter (November 11) until Easter, the masters earned twenty-six deniers a day and their aides sixteen deniers. From Easter to the next feast of St. Martin, masters and their assistants received thirty-two deniers and twenty deniers respectively.[107] Construction wages at the hospice of St. Jacques demonstrate that the wages of masons continued to increase after the plague and the ordinance and stabilized at about seventy-two deniers in 1351–1352, where they remained until 1358.[108] The aides earned about twelve deniers a day before the plague, and their wages increased to about thirty deniers a day in 1352, at which time they leveled off for five years. The data indicate that the government was not effective in its effort to control wage increases and that the wages for masons were already out-of-date by the time the Grand Ordinance was issued. The king's wages for masons were close to the one-third principle; hence someone in the government was well informed about prevailing wages. But clearly the market for labor was even better than the one-third ceiling. Another revealing feature of this data is that the master masons maintained their roughly double salary over their assistants, and this margin was also higher than the ordinance permitted. The example of the masons casts doubt on the state's ability to enforce the rules. When prices and wages were at issue, the royal government's reach exceeded its grasp.

Two important conclusions emerge from this discussion of the Grand Ordinance, regardless of its effectiveness. First, wages markedly increased for everyone after the plague, and if the masons are a good guide, these increases involved doubling or tripling of wages, not the mere one-third increment the king attempted to impose. Second, even though the state wanted to accomplish more than it had the power to do, the crisis did force it to take a look at the economy in its most important city. Although some trades attracted appropriately specific attention, all of the métiers received a general ordinance intended for the whole city and region. The plague brought the métiers thoroughly under central authority. Corporate organization was a durable feature of Parisian life down to the revolution, but these métiers relied upon the royal government to take the lead in responding to problems about markets and wages. Robert Vivier has concluded that the Grand Ordinance was not antiguild so much as it was a frank recognition that the métiers were not doing a good enough job for Paris, especially in the fundamental area of the food supply.[109] The métiers of Paris were not going to play much of a role in the economic planning of the royal government, except as objects of control.

A final feature of the Grand Ordinance merits more attention than it received from the king. The discussion of wages in the ordinance did not distinguish the sex of the workers. Instead, the emphasis was on the traditional categories of labor—masters, valets, day laborers, and apprentices. Women served in all of these capacities and were included in the broad efforts to control prices and wages. Only three occupations in which women dominated the work force received special notice in the ordinance. These three reveal the status of women. Wet nurses taking care of children outside the home of the parents were allowed to receive fifty sous (six hundred deniers) a year and no more.[110] This provision applied to all current and future contracts, and so some women presumably had to drop back to the fifty-sous level. *Chambrières*, women taking care of cows and in service in the city, were to be paid twenty sous from the feast of St. Martin to that of St. John (winter and spring) and thirty sous for the rest of the year. Those already in service were not to leave until the end of their terms, and if they were making more than these sums, they had to return the money. These servants were earning the same amounts as the wet nurses, but in some cases the latter may have been taking care of more than one infant at a time. Finally, women called *commandarresses*, who were in the business of hiring out servants and wet nurses, functioned as labor contractors and were a kind of employment service. These women were permitted to charge fees of eighteen deniers for servants and twenty-four deniers for wet nurses. These sums had to be the same for all clients, and the *commandarresses* might claim the sum only once a year from an individual woman. Anyone hiring out the same person twice a year was to be beaten or put in the pillory.

All of the rules about *salaires* carried the stipulated fine of ten sous per infraction, and only the women who helped other women to find jobs faced the prospect of corporal punishment if they violated the ordinance—the latter, a rare and degrading penalty. This sum of ten sous weighed heavily on women and counted for 20 percent of their yearly wage. In the winter master masons were earning this yearly income of women in about twenty-five days, according to the ordinance, but in practice even less time than that was needed. The fine for infractions was the same for the mason as for the wet nurse. The most interesting feature here that reveals the status of women in the economy is the opportunity their employers had to break an existing contract legally and to impose the fixed wage on servants and wet nurses. This procedure was not a general principle in the ordinance, and chaos certainly would have ensued if the king had abrogated every employment agreement in Paris and allowed the employers to pay only the one-third premium over preplague wages. Only the women endured what seems to be the single most effective provision for enforcing the king's will. Jean II and his officials must have known this because they shied away from breaking contracts and inflicting corporal punishment in the rest of the work force, and instead they used their best weapons against the lowest-paid and politically weakest segment of the population.

Edward III of England and his Parliament were responsible for the most ambitious attempt to control the economic consequences of the plague. In 1349 the king had issued an ordinance fixing salaries and wages for all types of workers at the rate prevailing in the twentieth year of his reign, 1346/1347.[111] In the letter proclaiming the ordinance, Edward III also commanded that the many healthy beggars (*validi mendicantes*) cease asking for alms and instead go to work, on pain of imprisonment.[112] The famous Statute of Labourers, issued in 1351, contained the admission that the ordinance had been ineffective. Parliament itself complained that wages had doubled or tripled *après la pestilence*, the same experience already noted for Paris. Once again the crown, and this time Parliament, tried to set wages and payments in kind (liveries) to what they had been in 1346. Unlike the Grand Ordinance for Paris, this English statute covered the entire kingdom.

The statute first addressed the problem of rural wages, which were certainly the most pervasive system of wage labor in the country. Parliament wanted workers to be hired for the year, or some customary seasonal term, but not by the day, another sign that in this case the rural laborers found themselves in an advantageous bargaining position. All wages were to revert to what they had been in 1346/1347. The building trades again received special attention, and the statute set these wages: a master carpenter, 3 pence a day; a master mason, 4 pence a day, with the boys earning 1½ pence a day. These were basically the same wages the city of London had established for the building trades in the reign of Edward I in the previous century and were on a par with the range of wages in the first half of the fourteenth century.[113] This statute has an air of unreality about it; the effort to turn the wage clock back five years seems impractical, especially when compared to the concession of a one-third increase in wages in Paris. The statute did not neglect the issue of prices, particularly for handicraft products. This ambitious and systematic attempt to regulate prices and wages needed a means of enforcement in order to make it effective.

The Statute of Labourers required a number of specified tradesmen, like furriers and tanners, as well as "all the other workers, artisans, laborers, and all other servants not specified," to take an oath before justices and other officials to obey the wage and price rules set by king and Parliament.[114] This oath served to inform the people about the law and was also the pretext for prosecuting those who proceeded to perjure themselves and break the statute. Refusal to take the oath was itself a crime. People contravening the provisions of the statute after they had taken the oath were liable for fine, ransom, or imprisonment, according to the decision of the justices. Rural workers faced the additional punishment of some time in the stocks.[115] Parliament or the royal officials devised a strategy to encourage enforcement on the local level. The statute envisioned special justices who were to serve on commissions for laborers. These commissions, established across the kingdom from 1352 to 1359, were expected to collect fines from people who broke the law.[116] The Statute of Labourers also established an ingenious scheme for balancing these fines against normal tax revenues, the subsidies voted by Parliament. Fines levied by the justices were to be turned over to the collectors of the subsidies, "to aid the commons for the time for which the tenth and fifteenth [the subsidies] were being collected, both for the past and future."[117] The king needed money for war in France, and despite the plague, the war would continue. The commons, however, seems to have complained that paying these taxes was difficult because workers of all sorts were demanding excessive wages and hence damaging those who paid taxes. So the framers of the statute used the fines to help local communities meet the level of their assessments. This expedient certainly benefited the taxpayers and also provided an incentive for people throughout the kingdom to come forward and denounce individuals who were breaking the law.

The important question is whether or not the Statute of Labourers was effectively enforced. The English wage data gathered by Phelps-Brown and Hopkins suggest that the statute was more effective than its French counterpart. These scholars find that the average wage for building craftsmen remained at the increased postplague level of five pence a day until 1402.[118] This wage structure is certainly more stable than what Geremek has found for Paris. Bertha H. Putnam addressed the enforcement of the English statute by investigating a wide range of fiscal and legal sources. One of Putnam's most convincing arguments concerns the subsidy of 1352. That tax yielded the crown £114,767s.5d.2, of which over £10,000 came from penalties the justices of laborers and other royal officials assessed.[119] The hefty sum from fines is proof that the procedures of enforcement were successful in catching people, not necessarily that those who escaped the clutches of the law obeyed the rules on prices and wages. Putnam found a number of court records that reveal how the justices worked on the local level. The system relied on informers and local juries that were supposed to present law-breakers to the court. Employers were also able to sue their workers for recovery of excessive wages. For example, the jurors of Middlesex presented four common laborers who were charged with taking four pence a day for their work when in the past they had received only two pence.[120] The juries also supplied information about broken contracts for labor that contravened both the Statute of Labourers and the ordinary law of contract. Anyone leaving service before the end of the agreed-upon term was now committing a crime against the king.[121] As Putnam noted, these court cases supply data about wage rates and the rapid escalation that took place after the plague.[122] But the new law arrested this process.

Beginning in 1361, the justices of the peace were added to the group of officials responsible by statute for holding the line on wages.[123] These justices, usually well informed on local matters, were in a good position to uphold the law. Putnam concluded that "during the first decade [1351–1361] the wages and prices clauses were thoroughly enforced."[124] The evidence from Paris indicates that Putnam was also correct in observing that what price and wage increases occurred would have been even higher without the government's statute and legal machinery. In England the king's ability to bring hundreds of officials into the plan for enforcing the statute, as well as the local communities' incentive to cooperate in order to reduce taxes, worked in favor of moderating wage increases. The jury system also served as a watchdog on those employers who paid more than the law allowed. Some employers must have sued their employees to recover wages in order to forestall juries from presenting them for breaking the statute. Doubtless many people evaded the law, and some desperate employers paid what they needed to pay and kept their mouths shut about it.

The Iberian kingdoms provide more examples of state efforts to respond to the economic effects of the plague.[125] Pedro IV of Aragon promulgated an ordinance in 1349 for one of his domains, the county of

Catalonia and most particularly its leading city, Barcelona. Several crafts received notice as the ones demanding wage increases four or five times higher than before the plague.[126] The king established a commission to set salaries according to the just claims of the workers. If the commission could not justify the increased wages, then the workers had to go back to their old levels, under threat of corporal punishment. Workers were prohibited from forming associations for the purpose of extorting higher salaries from employers. Aragon received a more thorough and detailed set of regulations when the king and the Cortes met at Zaragoza in May 1350.[127] The new rules set wages at specific sums for such trades as the carpenters, vinedressers, and other rural workers. For workers like the smiths, fixed prices set a ceiling on incomes. The weavers and bakers were told to limit their wages to what they had been "in the past times before the plague."[128] Two other provisions, not strictly related to the question of wages, reveal that the opportunity to set rules for all workers brought forward some interesting ideas. The time from sunrise to sunset was the length of the workday for all laborers in the kingdom—a long day, especially in the summer. This rule abrogated previous customs and agreements in the specific trades. No one was allowed to hire more than twelve workers, except for those landowners employing harvesters. This rule seems unrelated to the dearth of workers, unless it was an effort to spread around what hired labor still existed, but it also provided employers with a more controlled work force. Limits on the numbers of employees were probably unrealistic to begin with, since other employers besides landowners required the services of large numbers of workers—shipowners are an obvious example. Fixed salaries prevented employers from competing on one level, but richer masters still had an advantage in the scale of their operations. The Cortes and king wanted to control this kind of competition.

Judges and local officials were supposed to enforce the law.[129] Fines, amounting to twenty days' wages for skilled labor, fell on both the workers and employers who violated the fixed pay scales.[130] The king, the local authority, and the accuser each received one-third of the fine. Aragon falls midway between the policies of the kingdoms of France and England. Flexible standards were the rule in Aragon. There no arbitrary return to preplague wages was mandated, but instead some adjustments were accepted, and more importantly, the law preserved distinctions between the daily wage and piece-rate pay. Aragon was perhaps the most realistic of the kingdoms; the king abolished these rules in 1352, ostensibly because of unspecified abuses by rural employers.[131]

In 1351 various versions of a wage-and-price policy were enacted in Castile for the different parts of the kingdom.[132] Rules for Madrid, fairly typical of the kinds of new regulations, resembled in most respects the laws of Aragon. One interesting rule, which reflects the spirit of the Grand Ordinance for Paris, concerned beggars. The king prohibited people living by manual labor from becoming beggars. Everyone was required to work, except the infirm, the aged, and those less than twelve years of age. The rules for the territory of the archbishop of Toledo described how the admonition to work would be enforced. An accuser and two witnesses were sufficient to find a person guilty of breaking the fixed-wages rule or of failing to work at all.[133] Violators received twenty lashes for the first offense, followed by forty and sixty lashes for subsequent lapses. This penalty applied to beggars and the poor. Workers could pay the stiff fine of fifty maravedis, fifty days of skilled winter wages in the archdiocese of Toledo, for the first offense. Those paying excess wages faced the same fines. The effort to control prices and wages lasted longer in Castile than it had in Aragon for the crown reaffirmed in part these regulations as late as 1369.[134]

The English law did work better than the Grand Ordinance for Paris, and the regulations of Castile remained in force longer than those of Aragon. But again, that no king or assembly chose to involve the guilds or métiers in the effort to control wages and prices is significant. Monarchies had officials to do this job for them, and the problem was more widespread than the scope of any guild. The masters found themselves with some authority to deny excessive wage increases in Paris and any at all in England, but their own prices were under the same watchful eye. The masters enjoyed the favor of the states, and the emphasis on runaway wages was as severe a problem for them as it was for the landowners needing to hire agricultural laborers. The issues of the price and supply of labor had become too serious to leave to the employers. Whatever the private jurisdictional rights of the Parisian métiers and the English guilds had been before the plague, they were now diminished. The Spanish guilds also had no part in enforcing the laws in Castile and Aragon.

Other places coped with the aftermath of the plague in a more piecemeal but perhaps more realistic manner.[135] The government of Venice, for example, had to find ways to supply its galleys with crews.

The state resorted to luring fugitives from the law back to the city, reducing the customary size of crews, and signing up boys for service at sea.[136] As Lane has pointed out, "With the population halved, the average Venetian had twice as many coins in his money-chest and was less willing to fight or submit to the hardships of life at the oar."[137] Since shipping and its allied trades were the single largest source of employment for Venetian artisans, the plague's effect on this industry reverberated through the economy. Venice's sea power suffered in an immediate way, but at least the city could count on the fact that no naval power in the Mediterranean region was immune from the shortage of crews. Apart from enticing or drafting crews, the city had to begin to find ways of turning shipping into a less labor-intensive business. Venice embarked on centuries of patient and methodical advances in ship construction that eventually resulted in a technological triumph— the galleon. Significantly, Venice did not try to solve these labor problems by slave labor, but other Mediterranean sea powers would adopt this expedient.

In most towns the issues were not as clear cut as they were in Venice. An analysis of the plague and its effects on work must take into account the conditions in the first half of the fourteenth century. Perceived changes after 1348 must withstand the challenge that their real roots were in the earlier period. A good example of the problem is the fate of the Flemish wool industry in the fourteenth century. The towns of Bruges, Ghent, and Ypres dominated the manufacture of cloth in Flanders. David Nicholas finds that the decline of the industry had its origins back in the late thirteenth and early fourteenth centuries and that several interesting signs of trouble appeared before the plague. Although mills for fulling cloth were used across Europe in the 1200s, no evidence points to their use in these three cities in the 1300s.[138] Instead, the strong guilds persisted in using their feet to treat cloth on the grounds of maintaining quality. The plague did not change this attitude. The wool masters did not invest in technological improvements of any kind, either before or after 1348, and Nicholas describes manufacturing as basically "primitive."[139] Cloth from these cities enjoyed an international reputation. Masters were naturally conservative in their reluctance to change what was once a good thing. In the fourteenth century they paid a heavy price for this failure to innovate, but, after all, at least they had something from which to decline.

The troubles of the cloth manufacturers in Bruges, Ghent, and Ypres illuminate other aspects of the pre- and postplague scene. International competition in wool cloth was a constant of life in these centuries, and improved transport compounded the problems that local producers faced. Places with closer supplies of wool, as for example England, or at least with access to high quality wool, accompanied by a willingness to move into the luxury end of the business when necessary, as in Florence, had advantages that the Flemings could do little or nothing to counteract. The cloth of these three Flemish cities also experienced the compliment of imitation, particularly in the surrounding smaller towns and villages of Flanders. In Bruges the manufacturers "concentrated on keeping the rural industry strictly local and on preventing the manufacture of cloth which might be sold as that of Bruges."[140] Hostility to rural industry dated from around 1300, and in this case Bruges compelled its smaller neighbors to comply with the ban. In Ghent all clothmaking in a five-mile radius around the city was prohibited, and a similar three-mile rule existed in Ypres.[141] These provisions were enforced, with varying results, throughout the fourteenth century. The most dramatic measure these cities took was to launch punitive expeditions into the countryside to confiscate or destroy looms. Ghent engaged in this effort in 1358, 1359, and 1363, and in the last campaign the weavers and fullers themselves participated.[142] The problem of competition outside the urban guilds was already old by 1348 and remained serious after the plague. Local politics also had a part in this matter. The count of Flanders, Louis of Male (1346–1384), steered a middle course between favoring the smaller towns and villages and ruining the three largest cities of his domain.[143] At this level of politics, the relationships Flanders had with the kings of France and England also influenced such mundane but vital matters as the supply of raw wool.

The economic history of the wool industry in Flanders reveals guilds and labor caught up in events beyond their control. Rural industry and international competition contributed to declining wages for textile workers throughout the fourteenth century.[144] If the problems in Flanders inevitably resulted from external pressures and internal stagnation, then the decline itself obscures the consequences of the dreadful population losses of the plague years. Even the radical change in the number of people did not inaugurate a golden age of labor in Flanders, except perhaps for those lucky enough to emigrate. Urban guilds tried to enhance their own prospects by attacking rural industry, but rural townspeople and villagers were capable of finding allies of their own, occasionally the count of Flanders, to defend their right to make a living. Even these smaller centers of production failed to establish themselves as the leaders of a restored wool industry, and they were not any more innovative than the big cities.

In order to reach some conclusions about the ways in which technological progress and the supply of labor were connected, one needs to keep in mind a sense of the chronologies of the pace of invention and the rise of wage labor. For some scholars the real technological revolution of the Middle Ages took place long before the plague.[145] Technology continued to develop after the epidemic, perhaps even at a faster pace, but this development would have more to do with the internal dynamics of technological progress than with the plague or the supply of labor in any form. Carlo Cipolla suggests that the "scarcity of labor" after 1348 was too facile an explanation for subsequent advances in the mechanics of production.[146] Instead, he wonders why western Europe was so receptive to change, and he concludes, "We do not know." The question is a good one because it draws attention to the fact that inventiveness must find a favorable social climate in order to have any effect. The mechanical clock is an example of a happy fit between technological advances and the social need to know the time of day. But can a different answer to Cipolla's question be found?

The work of Lynn White, Jr., and others has proved beyond doubt that the Middle Ages witnessed considerable technological progress. From the horse collar and the fulling mill to eyeglasses and the clock, the ingenuity of medieval people was extraordinary, perhaps not in contemporary terms, but certainly when compared to the modest achievements of classical antiquity. Therefore the question concerns the relative pace of technological change, not its absence. After the plague a host of inventions and improvements in existing techniques took place, but was this simply more of the same? Certainly examples exist of what the economists call factor substitution, in this case the increased reliance on one factor of production, capital, in order to replace another, labor. In Venice a change in the kind of shipping that resulted in greater reliance on the cog as opposed to the labor-intensive galley provides the clearest example of this phenomenon; so too does the invention of movable type a century after the plague. The sailing vessels and the printing press both suggest that factor substitution was not a sudden and dramatic response to the plague. Another way of looking at factor substitution is to concede Cipolla's point that the per capita wealth of western Europe increased after the deaths of 1348–1349. The evidence concerning the Parisian masons indicates that this new wealth, in the form of higher wages as well as simple inheritances, was as badly distributed as before the plague. Considerable amounts of capital were wasted or abandoned as masters, journeymen, and apprentices took years of training to their graves and as whole villages disappeared back into scrub. But still, enough wealth survived to be passed on, even if much of it ended up consumed rather than invested. Enough remained to make some factor substitution practical—but not necessarily desirable.

Cipolla is also surely right that factor substitution is more than a simple change in the supply of labor. White proposes that "by the early fourteenth century, then, Europe not only showed an unmatched dynamism in technology: it also arrived at a technological attitude toward problem solving."[147] White is impressed with the amount of technology Europe borrowed from other places and then improved, and he accounts for this "amazing openness of the medieval European mind" by appealing to culture, specifically the Christian ethos.[148] Religion encouraged compassion, but the case that benevolence toward working people fostered the development of labor-saving devices is not convincing.[149] Positive attitudes about work did result, as already noted, from God's own creation and rest, but work also remained one of the penalties to humankind's sinful nature and an obvious sign of ignoble status.[150] The strong emphasis on work in early monasticism did not remain the dominant theme. The evolution from "to work is to pray" to the more refined "to pray is to work" is a problem for those who look to the cultural climate alone to explain the effective use of technology. White concedes that no real connection between science and technology in the Middle Ages existed. So where religion might have had its greatest impact on technology, in the universities, little or no interest in the mechanical problems of artisans appeared.

Why were Europeans so receptive to technological change and foreign borrowings? This debate can be moved forward by asking, Whose minds were open? Anonymous tinkerers were responsible for much of medieval technological progress in the artisan trades. Their very anonymity has made pinning down the date or even the locale of inventions like eyeglasses, the mechanical clock, the compass, or the use of waterpower in manufacturing impossible.[151] Borrowings complicate this task of attribution, and in some cases the search is for the person who brought back from the East something as intangible as an idea. Craftsmen and merchants had the open minds, and the institutions of the guild and wage labor are the aspects of the cultural climate that can account for the technological advances under review. The emphasis here is on "can." Cipolla's response is a weighty caution. Nevertheless, the case for merchants and artisans leading the way in technology, both before and after the plague, is a strong one. Intellectuals of the thirteenth and fourteenth centuries, of course themselves almost invariably university masters and hence guildsmen, seem to have invented nothing of practical value. Some interesting ideas, Roger Bacon's come to mind, remained unnoticed in manuscripts and haunt only modern scholars. Characteristically, the foremost scholar of medieval technology, Lynn White, Jr., ends his classic study with the invention that university masters most eagerly sought—the perpetual motion machine.[152] The problem of perpetual motion was esoteric, and medieval science did not provide answers to weavers who were looking for a better loom. Medieval travelers were a heterogeneous lot, but apart from a few hearty souls like Jacques de Vitry, scholars, unlike their modern successors, were not notable travelers outside the ambit of the universities and church councils. By inclination not interested in artisan manufacturing or in traveling to distant lands in search of good ideas, the university masters are not candidates for the open minds being sought in this discussion. Even though some of these masters may have come from craft or merchant families, their most revealing contact with these groups probably came in "town and gown" confrontations, or even in the occasional sack of a university.

So if the professionally educated are excluded, the merchants and artisans, in or out of a guild, emerge as the most open-minded members of society. To some, guild statutes portray a dreary world of conformity, but the more positive aspects of guild life, already noted here in various contexts, reveal a system of education and a pride in craftsmenship conducive to technological progress. A good idea, creative or borrowed, required an institutional framework to fix the advance and not allow it to remain the secret of a particular shop or merchant. The anonymity of medieval inventions suggests that nothing stayed a secret for long in this world and that too many people quickly adopted better methods and tools for the primacy of the originator to last for long or in the end to have any real significance. The Venetian state, precocious in many areas, began to grant ten-year patents for inventions in 1474.[153] More than five centuries of increasingly effective patents and copyrights have obscured the medieval craft world in which such rights did not exist, where, to the contrary, people were obliged to open up their shops to guild inspection and where theft of technology was part of the ordinary practice of business. Where good ideas were free, open minds reaped rewards.

Marc Bloch suggested an hypothesis, which Pierre Dockès has recently refined, that, although originally intended to explain the rise of the water mill and the end of rural slavery, nonetheless may be applicable to the problem of urban technological innovation in this later period.[154] In brief, this hypothesis states that technological change results from changes in the ways that people exploit labor. The argument is that changes in social structure, in this case the system of labor, in turn produce a new balance of power in which some people have an incentive to foster technological improvements and, perhaps more importantly, have the power to coerce the adoption of new methods. The rise of wage labor certainly counts as a profound change in the history of labor, and it should also count as a fundamental technological improvement, if "technology" can stand for something as incorporeal, or at least nonmechanical, as wage labor. On one level the path of analysis seems conventional; this hypothesis simply infers that once again the self-interest of employers would result in factor substitution and technological progress. But a more attractive and fruitful possibility exists—that technological progress itself can be coerced. Masters were able to enforce work rules and methods in their shops, and so they could make their employees adopt new techniques. The masters might as easily have stifled innovation. But a new use for Bloch's hypothesis can be seen if one keeps in mind that wage labor was a type of invention and that masters seized it with alacrity in an age that witnessed a myriad of technological advances. In the thirteenth and early fourteenth centuries, perhaps wages, with their possibilities of coercion in the market for labor and in the shop, let loose the whirlwind of technological change. How did this happen? The masters succeeded not only by making the journeymen use new methods, or by substituting new machines for the journeymen, but also by dominating the new relationship between the payers and takers of wages. This change in the social structure made the wage earners the valuable means by which technology paid.

Wage labor also allowed people to move around within a city or from one to another. In the years of labor shortage after 1348, when cities were even more underpopulated in relative terms than the countryside and less able to generate growth in the numbers of inhabitants, the mobility of labor kept the cities alive and circulated technological knowledge across Europe. The entrenched masters had themselves established urban wage labor, and as they made joining their own ranks more difficult, they made more people reliant on the system, not as a stage of a working life, but as a permanent condition of earning wages. Again, an open mind was a valuable commodity for those who wanted something more than a life of wages. This receptivity to different ideas might easily have become for some a life of crime or beggary. Not everyone was temperamentally inclined to accept as permanent the conditions set by the employers.[155] And no one could guarantee that an enthusiasm for change would be limited to technology.

Guilds, Labor, and Protest

A vast literature and debate exist for the social revolts of the fourteenth century, and recent anniversaries of the Ciompi Revolt in Florence (1378) and the Peasants' Revolt in England (1381) have added fuel to the fire.[156] The most recent phase of the controversies has deprecated generalization and called for prosopographical analysis of participants and a close scrutiny of local politics. This problem of balancing generalizations against the bewildering array of local evidence is not a new one for this study. It is fitting to conclude by once again striking a balance between these claims and by seeking a productive basis for comparisons. These revolts also provide a means to test the usefulness of the perspective on guilds and labor put forward in this study.

Michel Mollat and Philippe Wolff stress the popular element in social revolt, but they do not claim that such a feature is part of all revolts.[157] They conclude that general economic trends are important to understanding social protest and that a pent-up desire existed for broader participation in the affairs of cities and the emerging nation states.[158] Having observed that "the spirit of system is in history a dangerous temptation," Mollat and Wolff nevertheless proceed to offer an analysis based on the familiar notions of *structure et conjoncture*.[159] This form of analysis stresses demographic movements after the plague, prices, and finally the specific events, the local triggers that determine the timing and particular nature of revolts. The model for looking at history as composed of timeless and slowly changing features that individuals can do little or nothing to effect has not found favor with all historians. As seen time and again in this study, no reason exists, even in the case of an event as pervasive as the plague, for assuming that its effects were experienced to the same degree across Europe. Guilds and the institution of wage labor do not neatly fit into Mollat and Wolff's interpretation; these institutions are not as permanent and timeless as geography, as durable as the family, or as ephemeral as the pace of daily events. Organizations put together by human hands and mutable enough to take into account local problems and ingenious solutions are certainly slippery historical subjects, but they deserve a place in any analysis of the revolts in postplague Europe. Mollat and Wolff neglect to do this in their synthesis.

Guilds and wage labor are a useful means to explore some common features of these revolts—despite the lofty structures and conjunctures of the synthesizers and the variety of local experience. Once again, the histories of labor and social protest intersect only along a narrow range of issues. Some fresh aspects of both topics become apparent if the two are considered together. Some of the findings of this study have a direct bearing on the level and quality of forms of social protest after the plague. First, this study has noted signs of discontent in thirteenth-century cities and endemic troubles about politics and money in medieval cities once they again appeared on the scene in a meaningful way in the eleventh century. If one concedes the scale and numbers of revolts after 1348, one should still keep in mind that the accumulated experience and grievances of previous centuries mattered. Second, finding enough documents to analyze the social status and wealth of members of mass movements in the fourteenth century is not always possible. In some cities the surviving source material can support detailed investigation, as it has for a revolt in Brunswick in 1374 and the disturbances up to and including the Ciompi Revolt in Florence.[160] For other places finding out much about participants in revolts has not been possible.[161] Guilds were to some extent vertical social and economic groups and included masters with different amounts of wealth and political ambitions. Consequently, guilds as such are not necessarily the best place to look for batches of protestors. Yet sometimes overriding common interests of masters, journeymen, day laborers, and apprentices are more revealing. The concerns of those who paid salaries and taught skills were not the same as for those who lived by a daily wage or wanted to learn a craft. Although locating rebels individually might not be possible, some useful distinctions can be made along lines of employment.

Telling the story of dozens of fourteenth-century revolts in order to recapitulate Mollat and Wolff's work is not necessary. A few well-known examples will illustrate the place of employment in the movements of social protest. The problem of agricultural employment is outside the scope of this work, but the coincidence of urban and rural revolt will raise the issues of migrant labor and industries outside the cities. The Jacquerie in the upper basin of the Seine River in 1358 was almost exclusively a rural revolt, and its causes have much to do with the political situation in France after the English captured Jean II at the battle of Poitiers in 1356. Raymond Cazelles usefully points out the role that rural artisans took in the Jacquerie. By looking at the letters of remission issued after the revolt, Cazelles concludes that "there were more rural artisans than peasants" involved in the troubles.[162] Perhaps the artisans were less likely to be slaughtered during the course of the revolt or astute enough to seek pardons as soon as practicable. This observation makes sense of the rallying cry of the Jacquerie: "Laissons tout aller et soyons tous maitres" ("Let all go as it will and may everyone be masters").[163] By burning chateaux and attacking nobles, the participants in the Jacquerie vented their anger on society's masters, but the rural artisans may also have been saying, "Let everyone be self-employed." The desire to be a master is in a technical sense a curious request in the small towns and villages of the Seine Valley, where the métiers were weak or nonexistent, so the call was not likely to be one for master status and the perquisites of a guild. Instead, this revolt provides a bit of precious evidence for the rejection of the employer-employee relationship.

Before the Jacquerie occurred in the countryside, Paris experienced its own disorders. The same power vacuum resulting from the king's imprisonment provided the elites of Paris with the chance to extract their city government from the clutches of royal authority and to behave like members of a commune. Étienne Marcel, coming from an elite family and connected by marriage and fraternal ties to other prominent families, was *prévot* of the merchants and hence the leader of the upper bourgeoisie and superintendent of the métiers of Paris.[164] The confusion in central authority and his own ambition freed Marcel from his role as the crown's representative and allowed him to act independently. The prevailing interpretations of the events in Paris emphasize the political struggles between Marcel and the merchants of Paris on the one hand and between the Dauphin, various contenders for power, and the nobility on the other. The interest here is more sharply focused on the way Marcel was able to galvanize the artisans of the métiers into participating for the first time in the political life of their city. In January 1357, Marcel and others "made all the *menestreux* [men of the métiers] stop work" and arm themselves.[165] This general strike gave Marcel the leverage he needed to seize the reins of government in Paris. Another instance of the métiers' necessary support in sheer numbers occurred on 22 February 1358, when a crowd of about three thousand armed men, *tous les mestiers*, led by Marcel broke into the royal palace and forced the Dauphin to wear the colors of the revolt.[166] These men did not launch a successful national revolution that would ensure their immortality (as was the case for the stormers of the Bastille), so nothing is known about their individual circumstances or which crafts may have been more enthusiastic than others.

The *Grandes Chroniques* record a curious incident on the same day. The crowd that stormed the palace murdered the marshals of Champagne and Normandy. That same evening, a group described as *povres varles* (poor valets, journeymen) picked up from the courtyard of the palace the bodies of the nobles and put them in a cart.[167] The valets then dragged the cart through the streets of Paris to the church of St. Catherine, where they left the bodies. This episode is worth recounting because of what the valets did next. They took a mantle from one of the corpses as their salary (*pour leur salaire*) for having brought the bodies there. And then the valets left. They had worked, behaved well, and expected to be paid. The symbolic taking of the mantle vividly struck the chronicler Pierre d'Orgemont, not only because of the fate of the two nobles, but perhaps also because the valets had taken what they wanted in stripping a noble and then walked away. This behavior was not typical of wage laborers in Paris.

The political struggle for authority in France brought some artisans into political action, but what they hoped to gain from their efforts remains unclear. Marcel could rouse people by attacking the abuses of royal agents, and the requisitions of goods from merchants and masters were particularly hated.[168] A functioning commune had appeared, cutting across the fine lines of the numerous métiers, and this organization would have attracted masters, the ones in the best position to afford arming themselves. By the spring of 1358, Marcel was even emulating the Jacques by sending out bands of armed Parisians, again of unknown composition, to attack the noble fortresses and chateaux surrounding the city.[169] But in the end the cry that all should be masters had a different ring in Parisian ears. Marcel abandoned the rural revolt to its grisly fate and was himself assassinated at the end of July for reasons apparently unconnected to the course of the revolt. By the end of the year the Dauphin was installed in Paris, and the people escaped retribution for their foray into questions that would be settled for the foreseeable future without their advice.

Mollat and Wolff invoke the Grand Ordinance of February 1351 as part of the background to the Jacquerie, but, whether because it was not enforced or still suited employers, the regulations on prices and wages seem not to have been an issue that left traces in the record.[170] The Grand Ordinance had strengthened the hand of the merchants' association in Paris and perhaps indirectly paved the way for a *prévot* to assume leadership in default of other authority.[171] Marcel was the representative of the merchants and masters, and the cross section of citizens who participated in city or guild affairs was, even in the summer of 1358, extremely limited.[172] The urban journeymen and apprentices, without a voice in the métiers and too poor to be the victims of requisitions, did not heed the call to become masters.

The Florentine revolt of the Ciompi in 1378 is the classic example of an insurrection in which guilds and the desire to have them were decisive issues. Once again local political circumstances, in this case a war with the papacy in which an interdict caused some difficulties for Florentine trade, as well as the postplague economic scene in which a local wool industry experienced the same competition affecting wool centers across Europe, provide the backdrop for understanding the pace of events in Florence during the summer of 1378.[173] As previously seen, Florence had a commune in which membership in a guild was a prerequisite for any chance to partake in political life. The wealthy entrepreneurs of the *Lana* and *Calimala* guilds controlled the wool industry by dominating the *sottoposti*, the organizers of production outside the great shops and the middlemen in much of the putting-out system. These *sottoposti* were regulated by, but not members of, the wool guilds. Below the *sottoposti* were the true Ciompi who gave their name to the revolt—the thousands who lived by wages, mainly for the city's biggest employer, the various stages in the manufacture of wool cloth. In July of 1378, after months of factional disturbances in the city, an enormous crowd of *sottoposti* and Ciompi presented itself in the square in front of the town hall and demanded a guild of their own. These people seized the government on 22 July and installed one of their own, a woolcomber named Michele di Lando, as the standard-bearer of justice, the chief executive of the city. A special committee (*balia*) of thirty-two, empowered to reform the state, quickly authorized three new guilds, the necessary vehicles for the rebels to take a legitimate place in government. Two of these guilds, the dyers and the shirtmakers, gave some *sottoposti* and small shop owners what they wanted, but the third guild, the Ciompi, included thousands of ordinary wage earners and raised them up to the level of the members of the other guilds.

The motives behind the demand for these three new guilds have generated considerable debate. The ideological views of the *sottoposti* and Ciompi took form in the desire to have guilds, but was this a traditional Florentine image of a corporate society simply taken up by those excluded in the past, or a failure to come up with a program more relevant to the economic needs of petty entrepreneurs and wage earners?[174] Samuel Cohn's observation that "the Florentine Ciompi did not simply copy the corporate forms and structures of their masters" gains force not only when the sheer size of the Ciompi guild is taken into account but also by realizing it was a guild of nonmasters.[175] This last was by no means a traditional idea. When the views of the rebels finally found a hearing in the Palazzo della Signoria, it is not surprising that the new regime tried to impose production quotas on the wool factories in order to bolster employment or that the owners responded by what amounted to a lockout in August. Those scholars who have criticized the Ciompi for having an insufficiently "proletarian" program, or simply for the crude effort to mimic their betters, or for having no program at all seem to have neglected the fact that the guild, especially in Florence, was an association of employers. When the Ciompi had a guild for a couple of months, they stood the definition of a guild on its head. Far from revealing themselves to be in the thrall of cultural hegemony about guilds or incapable of formulating an ideological program of their own, the Ciompi brought the vision of corporate society to its logical conclusion—a guild for everyone, a short step away from the state.

The Ciompi guild was the first to go. A complex set of events just before and after 1 September—an even more radical plot to seize power, Michele di Lando's betrayal of his supporters, and a traditional oligarchy finally willing to bury old splits—conspired to bring about the end of the *balia* of thirty-two and the suppression of the Ciompi guild. The dyers and shirtmakers acquiesced for the price of their own survival; the oligarchy got rid of them in 1382. In the end the major guilds reasserted their power over the commune, and things reverted to what they had been before the revolt, with a more vigilant eye on the malcontents among the Ciompi.[176] The revolt failed for the usual reasons in this period: the entrenched guilds and powerful leaders in the city commanded the resources necessary for the adroit use of force, once they again closed ranks. The failure of the Ciompi is less surprising than its temporary success and what it reveals about the aspirations of wage earners to be, in a fundamental way, their own masters.

The English Peasants' Revolt of 1381, by its scope and diverse elements, seems to defy a general analysis.[177] Although its name suggests that it was a rural revolt, the contemporaneous disturbances in many cities argue against what one scholar has called "the false dichotomy between town and countryside."[178] Once again national issues and politics, in this case the Poll Tax and the course and cost of the war with France, account for some specific grievances and the timing of the revolt. The best account of what one group of rebels wanted comes from the peasants that Wat Tyler led to London, and their demands exclusively concerned questions of land tenure in the countryside. The urban participants in London, described as "commoners" and "the poor favoring the rustics," are mostly an anonymous crowd.[179] Documents emanating from the suppression of the revolt reveal that a few men of higher status with personal grievances of their own also took part in the June disturbances in London.[180] Where the surviving sources permit a closer inspection of the rebels, the usual mixed bag emerges. In Canterbury "disaffected and underprivileged artisans and petty tradesmen" were a prime source of trouble; in York "craftsmen and commoners" led the way.[181] R. B. Dobson finds drapers, mercers, tailors, and butchers involved in the revolt in Beverley, and he concludes that the rebels probably included people from "all of the forty or more craft guilds" in the city.[182] The local studies have revealed that the guilds did not serve as vehicles for social protest or provide any organizational basis for seizing power in any English town.

Although the Poll Tax and its collectors were resented, the Statute of Labourers was apparently not mentioned anywhere and was not an issue that seems to have prompted the revolt. William Langland's lines on the worker who "curses the king and all his council for enforcing laws to vex laborers" may echo some continuing resentment about the Statute of Labourers from a less than sympathetic source.[183] At the Cambridge Parliament in 1388, the Commons (a very different group than the rebels of 1381) asked for more labor legislation and in particular for the abolition of guilds and fraternities.[184] Perhaps by 1388 continuing low-level disturbances prompted the members of Parliament to be suspicious of any possible source of sedition, but they gave the guilds more credit for initiative than they deserved. Employer and employees are hard to distinguish in these urban revolts, as in the others. The narrative evidence suggests that particularly in London some journeymen and apprentices figured prominently as sympathizers with their rural counterparts, the peasantry. Why these people found the arrival of the peasants in London to be a pretext for insurrection is not revealed in the accounts of the uprising.

The chronicler Jean Froissart, providing the fullest and most colorful explanation of peasant motives, quoted the priest John Ball in these famous words: "Good people, things cannot go right in England and never will, until goods are held in common and there are no more villeins and gentlefolk, but we are all one and the same. In what way are those whom we call lords greater masters than ourselves?"[185] The word *master* again appears, this time in a thoroughly rural setting and very much in the spirit of the Jacquerie of 1358. But journeymen and apprentices had escaped villeinage. Although the urban workers may have cheered on their rural counterparts in these efforts to escape bondage, the word *master* had a different connotation in London or York. Guilds were not likely to figure in any revolt against masters of any kind. Thus, that English guilds are absent from accounts of the revolt is not surprising. Even as tools of repression, the guilds were a poor means when compared to the other instruments at the royal government's disposal.

This survey of late fourteenth-century revolts reveals a pattern of failure everywhere. Peasants, journeymen, and apprentices were not equipped to seize and hold power; the forces at the beckoning of kings, nobles, and urban elites were sometimes slow to coalesce but in the end proved sufficient to carry the day for established authority. Guilds were frequently caught in the middle of these struggles and were almost invariably powerless to join the forces of insurrection or reaction. Individual masters might take sides or provide critical help to one side or another, but the problems of kingdoms and cities were beyond the ability of a particular guild to solve. Even where some form of guild-dominated city government exercised real authority, the interests of the masters and the diversity of guilds represented in government worked against any swift and effective action. In a political sense these revolts reveal that time was passing the guilds by. The guilds, communes, monarchies, and estates did not exist to foster the hopes of journeymen and apprentices. Workers sometimes joined together to promote their own self-interest, but these shadowy organizations only appear in the records of efforts to deny their petitions or to suppress their associations. Lacking any institutional base for political or economic action, the wage earners and pupils were reduced to being part of the crowd. Only in Florence were the wage earners successful in forming a guild, but once again that accomplishment is measured in weeks. The wage earners learned that their economic subordination meant political impotence, and their disgust with the system in the end only sharpened the instruments of repression.

Conclusion

Even though the Roman system of labor and colleges failed to survive the collapse of the empire in the west, Roman experience remains a valuable point of comparison for the Middle Ages. Although the most common fate of the medieval economy is to serve as a prelude to some analysis of the early modern period or the Industrial Revolution, the late ancient and medieval economies are also good and yet neglected subjects for comparative history. For example, this study has noted several instances in which parallel solutions to the same problem, which have often been mistaken for signs of continuity, instead highlight the essential features of labor and employer organizations. Roman law on contracts was sophisticated, and the rebirth of wage labor in the eleventh and twelfth centuries took place at a time when people also revered the idea of contract. In some places Roman law helped medieval people to express the forms of contract, but the break with ancient practice had been so sharp as to reveal two distinct historical experiments. Roman colleges had some pagan and then Christian religious practices that perhaps added a moral tone to work, but no voices were raised against slavery in manufacturing. The triumph of wage labor meant the demise of slavery in medieval Europe. In this regard the cities became islands of personal freedom, even as they also harbored neighborhoods of extremely poor people working at dismal subsistence wages.

If Rome reminds one of the possibilities of the slave system, the medieval rural economy should indicate that coercion might take many forms. In the Middle Ages cities offered an escape from serfdom, and even in towns where the nobility took up residence and flourished, no signs have been found of compulsory labor services being translated to the urban handicrafts and trade. Havens of refuge for runaway serfs, the cities did not take up lordship as a means to acquire and coerce labor. The urban need for labor in the twelfth and thirteenth centuries was more *regular* than serfdom, as it had evolved, could provide. So for a time the gulf between the urban and rural economies was a great one—until the rural landlords followed suit and began to rely more upon wage labor, sharecropping, and tenants.

This study is not the place to tie the rural economy to urban wage labor and guilds, but one line of inquiry is worth noting here. The recent controversy between Robert Brenner and his many critics about agrarian class structure, coercion, and the development of capitalism in late medieval Europe has generally been conducted without reference to the cities.[1] The participants in the "Brenner debate" have chosen to omit wage labor, and only Brenner himself recognizes its significance, though he has pushed its effects into the later Middle Ages, past the urban origins witnessed here.[2] The first wages may actually have been paid in the countryside, but regular wage labor by contract, regulated first by the guilds and then by the commune or the state, is an urban innovation. The consequences of this development, so fundamental to the evolution of capitalism in Europe, should encourage historians of labor in later periods to acknowledge the true beginnings of their subject.[3]

Another potential line of inquiry concerns the tension between co-operation and self-interest and the degree to which classical market theories explain the earliest phase of the wage economy. Robert Frank has suggested that apparently irrational behavior, at least in terms of what a conventional self-interest model would predict, can result from emotional commitments to unopportunistic ideals. If, as Frank contends, being motivated by emotions is often a long-term benefit to material (and presumably moral) self-interest, then the medieval economy should provide a good case study for one early solution to the problem of self-interest and cooperation.[4]

Many aspects of the guild encouraged masters to deal fairly with one another, their employees, and the public. This emphasis on fairness in the market was also an important part of shared religious values in the guild or the confraternity. Did employers, and employees as well, actually engage in selfless or unopportunistic conduct on the grounds of some emotional commitment to a concept of fairness? Individual motive tends to elude historians except in those rare cases when the sources explicitly reveal it. A careful analysis of employment contracts across Europe might corroborate the Genoese evidence on paternalism, the use of slaves, and wages for women. In these matters the role of emotional or religious attitudes seems to be critical for understanding the personal bonds between employer and employee, opinions about the morality of slavery, and the place of women in the economy. Research on these topics demands the balanced perspective already noted and can only benefit from an approach that ignores the standard specializations of social and economic history.

People in the central Middle Ages reinvented the institutions of wage labor and guilds because they found unfettered competition for workers, markets, and raw materials less desirable than cooperation. A desire to face the uncertainties of the world in solidarity with other employers expressed a collective self-interest that understood the long-term benefits of mutual support. This system held some people back and allowed mediocrities to survive, but the masters reckoned these costs as worth the general assurance that most of them wanted—security. Medieval employers were not the first or last to exchange a little liberty for some order and predictability in the markets, and guilds embodied their compromise—a durable one in historical and economic terms. This solidarity among employers in the same line of work or business, combined with the natural limits of household pro-duction, summoned forth wage labor, another novelty in the urban setting and one with an even longer sequel. What appears to modern eyes as natural and unexceptional was once new, and I have tried to evoke the time and place in which wage labor and guilds were exciting experiments. Although in some places monarchies or town governments prodded the masters to form guilds or quickly and permanently dominated them both, most of these organizations were the spontaneous creations of their members and hence reflect, however faintly, the original reasons for their invention.

This study has run the risk of exaggerating the effects of guilds and particularly of wage labor on the medieval economy. These innovations took place in an economy and society that remained overwhelmingly agrarian. In the countryside no craft or professional guilds existed, but a system of casual wage labor with traditions of its own could be found. But again, the ahistorical modern sense of wage labor's inevitability has belittled the other possible outcomes and the great variety of experiments that occurred in organizing a way for some to provide employment to the many. Choices about piecerate or a daily wage, the role of women in a craft, the exclusion of religious minorities from the guild, and the ways of recruiting and educating a work force laid the foundations for subsequent economic development but also ruled out certain possible paths. Critical decisions about these matters made in the twelfth and thirteenth centuries had ramifications far beyond the medieval period.

The study of labor offers excellent opportunities for integrating the histories of women, men, and children in the Middle Ages. The gender division of labor demands a balanced perspective, and this means that one must keep in mind the issues of age and skill. Some distinct changes for men and women are incomprehensible without the experience of the other. The wage economy reflected broader bias and hence, in modern terms, denied equal opportunity to women and wasted half the potential of society. Prevented from learning certain skills and offered only low wages, women were perhaps more open to alternatives to the system. Sofia and her sisters were an example of this phenomenon, and closer scrutiny of the records should uncover more cases of women who found a path to economic independence. This much the wage economy offered them, an opportunity not fully realized even in this century.

The history of the division of labor continued on after the fourteenth century, and the modern, bewildering variety of occupations would stun even the Parisian masters. Yet they would recognize the continuum from apprentice to journeyman or casual laborer in today's society as in theirs, not as a static hierarchy, but as a kind of sieve designed to keep some back and as something that can be measured in human life spans. A small minority progressed through the stages to self-employment where it was practicable, but wage labor always required that most could and should not. The Genoese masters would be surprised to see so many women and so few children at work today at trades and professions they had dominated, yet they would find the wage differentials between men and women doing the same work to be eerily familiar.

The history of wage labor and guilds should not be pigeonholed as either social or economic history. The connections that guilds had in some places to local politics and everywhere to more pervasive influences like confraternities and religious views on work also demand that work be placed in the context of intellectual and church history as well. Since these subjects help to explain some distinctive features of the system of labor in regions and particular cities, scholars working in other fields may find that questions about wages and labor will yield fruitful insights. Studies of medieval technology have broken the ground here and not neglected the crucial links between labor and technological innovation. The Black Death and its consequences provide another setting in which labor history and broader social and economic changes have already attracted notice. Wage labor and guilds survived the calamity of the bubonic plague—a tribute to their hardiness and adaptability. In this light the end of the ancient economy represented a sharper break in the history of labor than did the death of one-third of Europe's people. This fact reminds one that arguments based only on the supply of labor need to take into account the social and intellectual framework in which employers make their choices. The employers in this study, masters needing more hands than their families could provide, should not bear the onus of their fifteenth- and sixteenth-century successors, and beyond. In other words, the stagnation at the end of the system, if indeed that describes it, should not be read back into the period covered by this study.

Masters in the medieval guilds took the first stab at solving the problems of competition, efficiency, and distribution of power in an economy. They usually found themselves caught in the middle between entrenched authority and their own employees. They were not always asked to choose sides, but when they did, they almost never aligned with their workers against those who were, in terms of power or wealth, their betters. The much-lamented gulf between employer and employee is as old as wages and remains as unbridgeable as it was on the first day of the relationship.

I have argued that the most enduring legacy of the medieval guild is wage labor and its rules, but economic corporatism, vocational education, and solidarity among employers on the one hand and employees on the other rank not far behind wages as important bequests. The sources for this study preserve the names and circumstances of too few people when compared to the anonymous millions who toiled away in the centuries that mark the elaboration of the system. These general findings therefore rest upon a collective experience that is mostly irretrievable in individual cases; behind every guild statute and apprenticeship contract there must have been quite a story.

A final example illustrates this point. On 1 March 1348, a Genoese woman named Castella placed her nephew Jacobo as an apprentice with Andrea the tailor.[5] In this case the master promised to pay his apprentice L16 over the five-year term according to a sliding scale that began at L2 a year and finished at L5. What makes this ordinary contract remarkable is that it occurred at the same time that the bubonic plague was devastating Genoa. The notary Guidotto de Bracelli recorded it in the midst of his other work: mostly wills (which he was writing at two or three a day), the estate inventories of the dead, and work contracts. Life contracted to its basics in these first grim weeks of the plague. Yet even then, work continued, and the changes in the ways people agreed to work, something new in the past three centuries, remained essential even in the worst of times.

Notes

All classical works cited are in the Loeb series, unless otherwise noted, and all translations are my own, unless otherwise noted.

Abbreviations

ASG	Archivio di Stato di Genova.
CN	Cartolari Notarili.
CT	Pharr, *The Theodosian Code and Novels and the Sirmondian Constitutions.*
Digest	*Corpus Iuris Civilis,* vol. I, *Digesta.*
MGH	*Monumenta Germaniae Historica.*
PL	Migne, *Patrologia Latina.*
Variae	Mommsen, Cassiodori Senatoris, *Variae,* in *MGH, Auctorum Antiquissiorum* (Berlin, 1894).

Introduction

1. Contract is one of the principal themes in Bloch's classic *Feudal Society;* see especially the concluding remarks, pp. 450–452.

2. Thrupp, "The Gilds," pp. 230–280; pp. 624–635, for excellent bibliography. Though the subject matter is similar, my analysis, methods, and conclusions differ fundamentally from Thrupp's.

3. Black, *Guilds and Civil Society,* p. 233, but with the caveat that the debt is an unfair one.

4. Durkheim, *De la division du travail social,* p. viii. The standard English translation by George Simpson suppresses the style and imagery of the original French, which is cited here.

5. Ibid., pp. 327–336.

6. Ibid., p. xxxiv, for panacea; p. xxxvi and chapter 3, on organic solidarity and the division of labor.

7. Ibid., pp. 390–406, chapter 5 and conclusion. For an interpretation that emphasizes the coercive aspects of the division of labor, see Rueschemeyer, *Power and the Division of Labour,* especially explicit on pp. 190–191.

8. Verriest, *Les luttes sociales,* p. 6.

9. Madurell-Marimon and Sanz, *Comandas comerciales barcelonesas,* p. 151.

Chapter 1

1. Waltzing, *Étude historique sur les corporations,* 1:334–341. Waltzing's work remains valuable, despite the harsh views of Ruggini in "Le associazioni pro-

fessionali," p. 60. Ruggini's work provides an exhaustive bibliography but only goes beyond Waltzing's in the section on the eastern half of the empire (pp. 97–112).

2. Plutarch, *Life of Numa,* 17; and Waltzing, *Étude historique sur les corporations,* 1:62–63.

3. Livy, I.18–21, discusses the reign of Numa.

4. Waltzing, *Étude historique sur les corporations,* 1:65.

5. Plutarch, *Life of Numa,* 17.

6. *Digest* XLVII.22.4 (Gaius). See also Waltzing, *Étude historique sur les corporations,* 1:79.

7. Waltzing, *Étude historique sur les corporations,* 1:72.

8. Waltzing, *Étude historique sur les corporations,* 1:104–105, for discussion of relevant passages in Cassius Dio.

9. Suetonius, *Life of Julius Caesar,* 42: "Cuncta collegia praeter antiquitus constituta distraxit."

10. Suetonius, *Life of Augustus,* 32: "ad nullius non facinoris societatem coibant" (Graves translation).

11. *Digest* XLVII.22.3 (Marcian).

12. Arrangio-Ruiz, *Fontes Iuris Antejustiniani,* pt. 3, Lex Collegii Lanuvini: "Quib [us coire co] venire collegium (que) habere liceat," a senatus consulto from 133–136 A.D.

13. *Annales* XIV, 17, p. 305 (Teubner): "collegiaque quae contra leges instituerant, dissoluta."

14. Meiggs, *Roman Ostia,* pp. 311–336, for discussion of colleges; and Waltzing, *Étude historique sur les corporations,* 1:169–170, for Pompeii.

15. Pliny, *Letters,* X, 33, 34, "collegium fabrorum"—presumably carpenters; and Waltzing, *Étude historique sur les corporations,* 1:124.

16. *Digest* XL.3.1 (Ulpian); XXXIV.5.20 (Paulus); also II.4.10.4 (Ulpian).

17. See Meiggs, *Roman Ostia,* for uses of inscriptions found in Ostia.

18. *Digest* X.4.7.3 (Ulpian).

19. *Digest* XIX.2.13.1 (Ulpian).

20. *Digest* III.4.1 (Gaius).

21. *De collegiis et corporibus* in *Digest* XLVII.22.

22. *Digest* XXVII.1.17.6 (Callistratus).

23. *Digest* L.4.9 (Paulus), on merchants; L.5.10 (Paulus), on measurers. See Rickman, *The Corn Supply of Ancient Rome,* pp. 88–91, for the special problems of this trade.

24. For Marcus Aurelius, *Digest* L.6.12 (Callistratus); and for Pertinax, *Digest* L.6.13 (Callistratus).

25. *Digest* XLVII.22.1.2 (Marcian).

26. Meiggs, *Roman Ostia,* p. 321.

27. Waltzing, *Étude historique sur les corporations,* 2:49.

28. *Digest* L.6.6.4 (Callistratus).

29. *Scriptores Historiae Augustae,* 33.2, Life of Severus Alexander.

30. Meiggs, *Roman Ostia,* p. 313.

31. Waltzing, *Étude historique sur les corporations,* 1:199.

32. Waltzing, *Étude historique sur les corporations,* 1:425–439.

33. Waltzing, *Étude historique sur les corporations,* 1:346–347.

34. Waltzing, *Étude historique sur les corporations,* 1:383–425, for detailed discussion of the various officials of the colleges.

35. Meiggs, *Roman Ostia,* p. 323.

36. Waltzing, *Étude historique sur les corporations,* 1:184–185, confirmed by Ruggini, "Le associazioni professionali," p. 123. See also the argument of Crook, *Law and Life of Rome,* pp. 179–180 and 200; apprenticeship existed under Rome, but the examples concern slaves, an important distinction here. See *Digest* XIX.2, for *locati-conducti,* and *Institutes* III.24.4, for the clearest explanation in Roman law that work was a species of rent because it received a wage or rent (*merces*) and not a price (*pretium*).

37. Westermann, "Apprentice System in Roman Egypt"; contracts explained on pp. 297–298.

38. Ibid., for examples of slave apprentices.

39. Jones, *The Later Roman Empire,* 2:834–841.

40. *CT* XIV, 3.1.

41. *CT* XIV, 3.12.

42. *CT* XIV, 3.2.

43. *CT* XIV, 3.3.

44. *CT* XIV, 3.5.

45. *CT* XIV, 3.8.

46. *CT* XIV, 3.10.

47. *CT* XIV, 3.11.

48. *CT* XIV, 4.1.

49. *CT* XIV, 4.4.

50. *CT* XIV, 8.1.

51. *CT* XIV, 7.1.

52. *CT* XIV, 4.3.

53. *CT* XIV, 4.4.

54. *CT* XIV, 6.1 and 3.

55. *CT* XIV, 6.3.

56. Liebeschuetz, *Antioch,* p. 29.

57. Ibid.

58. Ibid., p. 221.

59. Ibid., p. 222.

60. Ibid.

61. Ibid., pp. 222–223.

62. Waltzing, *Étude historique sur les corporations,* 2:479.

63. Waltzing, *Étude historique sur les corporations,* 2:483.

64. Waltzing, *Étude historique sur les corporations,* 2:484.

65. Orsted, *Roman Imperial Economy,* p. 17.

66. Mrozek, "Die Goldbergwerke," pp. 102–105.

67. De Ste Croix, *The Class Struggle,* p. 192—a conclusion valid for the Principate as well as the late empire. The legions and the bureaucracy seem to me to be important exceptions.

68. Williams, *Diocletian and the Roman Recovery,* pp. 128–132; pp. 224–227, for the extract from the edict. See also the discussion of fourth-century wages in Mickwitz, "Geld und Wirtschaft im römischen Reich," pp. 132–142. Mickwitz was mostly interested in the issue of inflation, but he did note that the day labor system in Egypt had disappeared by the end of the fourth century (p. 134). More research in the papyri may reveal an earlier, regular wage pool of laborers in Egypt.

69. Rostovtzeff, *History of the Roman Empire,* p. 178.

70. Grierson, "Commerce in the Dark Ages," pp. 131–132.

71. Duby, *The Early Growth of the European Economy,* pp. 48–54.

72. *Variae,* XII, X, 28: "Propter sterilitatem quoque praesentis temporibus."

73. *MGH, Leges* V, cap. 64, p. 189.

74. *Variae,* III, 11, VIII, 11.

75. *Variae,* IV, 25.

76. *Variae,* II, 4.

77. *Variae,* II, 26.

78. *Variae,* IV, 5.

79. *MGH, Epistolae II, Gregorii I Papae Registrvm Epistolarvm,* ed. Hartmann, IX, 113.

80. Ibid., IX, 200.

81. Monti, *Le corporazioni,* p. 158.

82. Isidore of Seville, *Etymologiarvm sive Originvm,* bk. IX, iv, 29: "Est enim sordidissimum genus hominum patre incerto progenitum. Privati sunt extranei ab officiis publicis." Solmi thought that this passage reveals that in Isidore's eyes the *collegiati* were, like slaves, condemned to a penal existence (*L'Amministrazione finanzaria,* p. 162).

83. *MGH, Scriptorum Rerum Merovingicarum,* Gregorii Episcopi Turonensis, tom. I, bk. VII, 4, p. 336.

84. Dopsch, *Foundations of European Civilization,* p. 336.

85. Duby, *The Early Growth of the European Economy,* pp. 50–51, for his use of the work of Marcel Mauss.

86. Tacitus, *Germania,* 13. See Loeb edition (London, 1963; reprint, 1914), pp. 282–283, on *comitatus.*

87. See Ducange, *Glossarium mediae et infimae latinitatis.*

88. *MGH, Legum II, Capitularia Regum Francorum,* tom. I, p. 51: "De sacramentis per gildonia invicem coniurantibus, ut nemo facere praesumat." For more on the "Coniuratio" as a type of social organization, see Oexle, "Conjuratio und Gilde," especially pp. 212–213, where the author summarizes his argument that oath taking represents a strand of continuity between the ancient and medieval societies; but Oexle also stresses the changes in the social meaning of the oath.

89. *MGH, Legum IV, Liber Papiensis Karoli Magni,* p. 61: "nixa conspiracione."

90. Hincmar of Rheims, *Capitula Synodica,* in *PL,* vol. 125, cols. 773–778; col. 777, for *gildonia.*

91. Grierson, "Money and Coinage under Charlemagne," p. 536.

92. Ibid., pp. 535–536.

93. Murray, *Reason and Society,* pp. 37–38.

94. Attenborough, *Earliest English Kings,* The Laws of Ine, cap. 16, pp. 40–41.

95. Whitelock, *English Historical Documents,* p. 400.

96. Herlihy, *Medieval Households,* pp. 44–48, for discussion of the *Sippe* and *fara*—two terms that illustrate that no neat or agreed-upon formula for defining kinship existed in the early Middle Ages, or among its students today.

97. Attenborough, *Earliest English Kings,* p. 77.

98. VI Athelstan 8.6, in Attenborough, *Earliest English Kings,* p. 165, and in Whitelock, *English Historical Documents,* p. 426.

99. Whitelock, *English Historical Documents,* pp. 603–604.

100. Ibid., pp. 605–607.

101. Ibid., p. 606.

102. Solmi, *L'Amministrazione finanzaria,* pp. 20–27, for document; pp. 139–165, for lengthy discussion of *ministeria.* See Monti, *Le corporazioni,* pp. 168–

172, for discussion; pp. 219–222, for excerpts from document. See also Lopez and Raymond, *Medieval Trade*, pp. 59–60, for discussion of this document. Solmi thought considerable continuity existed through Roman, Lombard, and twelfth-century guilds.

103. Hartmann, *Zur Wirtschaftsgeschichte Italiens*, p. 125.

104. Monti, *Le corporazioni*, p. 217.

105. Ibid., p. 166. See Toubert, *Les structures du latium médiéval*, p. 674, for a similar conclusion; he is emphatic that the *scholae* were not guilds. For an argument in favor of some continuity, see Racine, "Associations de marchands et associations de métiers."

106. Hartmann, *Zur Wirtschaftsgeschichte Italiens*, p. 40.

107. Stöckle, *Spätromische und byzantinische Zünfte*, pp. 8–11. But, as an example of the kind of confusion noted above, Ostrogorsky concludes that "Byzantine corporations are genetically related to the Roman *collegia*, but differ from these in many respects and resemble typical medieval guild organizations" (*History of the Byzantine State*, p. 254).

108. English translation here is by Boak, "The Book of the Prefect." For a good bibliography on this text, see Vryonis, "Demokratia and Eleventh Century Guilds," pp. 293–294.

109. Lopez, "Silk Industry."

110. Boak, "The Book of the Prefect," p. 616.

111. Ibid., p. 615.

112. Ibid., p. 616.

113. Ibid., p. 614. See also Stöckle, *Spätromische und byzantinische Zünfte*, p. 138, on liturgies.

114. Boak, "The Book of the Prefect," p. 609.

115. Vryonis, "Demokratia and Eleventh Century Guilds," pp. 289–314.

116. Boak, "The Book of the Prefect," p. 603.

117. Kazhdan and Epstein, *Change in Byzantine Culture*, p. 52. As these scholars also noted, even the eleventh-century evidence for any lingering effects of *The Book of the Prefect* is not good.

118. Goitein, *A Mediterranean Society*, 4:5.

119. Claude Cahen, *Encyclopaedia of Islam*, 2:961–965, "*futuwwa.*"

120. Lapidus, *Muslim Cities*, p. 101.

121. See, for example, Karl Marx, *Deutsche Ideologie*, vol. 3 of *Marx Engels Werke* (Berlin, 1962), pp. 22–27. Marx, however, was more interested in the end of his feudalism than its beginnings—see Schlomo Avineri, *The Social and Political Thought of Karl Marx* (Cambridge, 1968), pp. 154–156. See Dockès, *Medieval Slavery and Liberation*, p. 91, for an effort to salvage the feudal mode of production, at least for the rural scene.

Chapter 2

1. The literature on the economic expansion of the central Middle Ages is enormous. See, for example, Lopez, *The Commercial Revolution*; Cipolla, *Before the Industrial Revolution*; and Duby, *The Early Growth of the European Economy*, for three summaries that have become standard accounts.

2. An exception is migrant agricultural labor—certainly known in the Carolingian period. See Dockès, *Medieval Slavery and Liberation*, p. 97, where he notes that these people worked in exchange for room and board.

3. Strait, *Cologne in the Twelfth Century,* and Jakobs, "Bruderschaft und Gemeinde."

4. Ennen and Eckertz, *Quellen zur Geschichte der Stadt Köln,* pp. 329–330.

5. Boos, *Quellen zur Geschichte der Stadt Worms,* p. 50. An English translation of this document is in David Herlihy, *Medieval Culture and Society* (New York, 1968), p. 185.

6. Gouron, *La réglementation des métiers,* p. 37.

7. See Skinner, *The Foundations of Modern Political Thought,* pp. 3–22, and Martines, *Power and Imagination,* pp. 7–61, for two accounts of the rise of the communes.

8. Vercauteren, *Actes des comtes de Flandre,* pp. 293–299. Vercauteren described this charter as being made famous through the work of Henri Pirenne and Charles Verlinden.

9. Readily available details on these problems can be found in the following: Galbert of Bruges, *The Murder of Charles the Good,* pp. 193–194, for the swearing of the commune of Bruges, 27 March 1127; Dhondt, "Les solidarités médiévales," p. 541, for the commune; and Benton, *Self and Society in Medieval France,* pp. 145–190, for background and an account of the revolt in Laon in 1112.

10. Vercauteren, *Actes des comtes de Flandre,* p. 295: "Omnes qui gildam eorum habent, et ad illam pertinent et infra cingulam ville sue manent liberos omnes a teloneo facio." For more on the merchant guild, see chapter 3.

11. Galbert of Bruges, *The Murder of Charles the Good.*

12. Vercauteren, *Actes des comtes de Flandre,* p. 132.

13. See Munz, *Frederick Barbarossa.* The theory of a great design need not be accepted in order to appreciate the important role Pavia played in the emperor's strategy in northern Italy, as in the Council of Pavia in 1160 (pp. 216–219).

14. Solmi, *L'Amministrazione finanziaria,* pp. 271–273, for document; pp. 157–160, for discussion.

15. Ibid., pp. 269–271, for charter of Frederick I for Pavia.

16. Ibid., pp. 160–165.

17. The London guilds commonly used the term *misterium.* See below.

18. Riley, *Munimenta Gildhallae Londoniensis,* vol. 2, pt. 1. See as examples Ordinances of the Lorimers, p. 78, 45 Henry III.

19. Douglas and Greenaway, *English Historical Documents,* pp. 1014–1015; and Riley, *Munimenta Gildhallae Londoniensis,* 2:33, for original Latin.

20. Douglas and Greenaway, *English Historical Documents,* p. 1014; and from Riley, *Munimenta Gildhallae Londoniensis,* 2:33: "Henricus, dei gratia, Rex Anglie, Dux Normanniae et Aquitanniae, et Comes Andegaviae, Episcopis, Justiciariis, Vicecomitibus, Baronibus, ministris, et omnibus fidelibus suis Londoniarum, salutem. Sciatis me concessisse. . . ."

21. Douglas and Greenaway, *English Historical Documents,* pp. 1013–1014; and Riley, *Munimenta Gildhallae Londoniensis,* 2:29–32.

22. Riley, *Munimenta Gildhallae Londoniensis,* 2:48.

23. Douglas and Greenaway, *English Historical Documents,* p. 1039, for Lincoln guild; pp. 1043–1044, for Winchester guild; p. 1042, for Oxford charter.

24. Gouron, *La réglementation des métiers.*

25. Reyerson, *Business, Banking, and Finance,* for background on Montpellier. Gouron carefully analyzes and puts to rest the notion that Roman colleges might have survived from late antiquity, in places like Narbonne, into the Middle Ages; see his *La réglementation des métiers,* pp. 19–36.

26. Gouron, *La réglementation des métiers*, p. 39, for tanners and dyers; p. 54, for consuls in Toulouse and Montpellier.

27. Gouron, *La réglementation des métiers*, pp. 58 and 64, for Toulouse. For some instances of the role of the consuls over employment, see Castaing-Sicard, "Contrat de travail et louage d'ouvrage dans la vie toulousaine."

28. Gouron, *La réglementation des métiers*, p. 64. Boissonade, *Essai sur l'organisation du travail*, looks at the problems of millers and secular authority (pp. 111–129).

29. Gouron, *La réglementation des métiers*, p. 175.

30. For a careful and complete look at the expenses of mills, see Brown, *In the Shadow of Florence*, pp. 111–114. This work deals with paper mills and their operation.

31. Gouron, *La réglementation des métiers*, p. 174. This document is edited in Limouzin-LaMothe, *La commune de Toulouse*, pp. 358–361. The consuls noted that men and women might be innkeepers.

32. See the now classic formulation in Duby, *The Three Orders*, especially pp. 308–321, for how this model in part adapted itself to the rise of towns. See also Michaud-Quantin, *Universitas*, pp. 147–166, for use of the word *commune* and its relation to the rise of towns.

33. Marri, *Statuti dell'arte del Cambio di Firenze*.

34. For some recent comment on notaries, see Abulafia, *The Two Italies*, pp. 6–24; Epstein, *Wills and Wealth*, pp. 5–24 and passim; and Pryor, *Business Contracts*, pp. 16–17 and 20–23. The Italian series *Studi storici sul notariato italiano* is also useful.

35. See Clanchy, *From Memory to Written Record*.

36. Lopez, *The Commercial Revolution*.

37. See Postan, "The Chronology of Labour Services," in his *Essays on Medieval Agriculture*, pp. 89–106.

38. ASG, CN, cart. n. 14, 357r bis, Maestro Salmone notary.

39. ASG, CN, cart. n. 4, 34r, Oberto Scriba de Mercato notary.

40. Pryor wrote that in Marseilles the apprenticeship contract seems to have been "completely unregulated by statute"; see his *Business Contracts*, p. 111.

41. Salatiele, *Ars Notariae*, p. 165. For a thorough study of formularies and how they may illuminate apprenticeship in Bologna, see Greci, "Il contratto di apprendistato," pp. 151–167.

42. For more on apprentices, see chapter 3.

43. Salatiele, *Ars Notariae*, p. 278—a form of contract closely resembling the *locatio-conductio rei* (see chapter 1). An even more detailed formulary, known as the *Aurora*, by Rolandino Passageri explains work contracts (*locatio-conductio operarum*) and offers the subtle point that a wage (*merces*) is paid according to the estimate of the value of a person's use; see Rolandino, *Svmma*, p. 115r.

44. ASG, CN, cart. n. 14, 327r, Maestro Salmone notary: "matutino sancti andree usque sero secundum consuetudinem laneriorum."

45. For more on feast days, see chapter 4.

46. The first is in Chiaudano, *Oberto Scriba de Mercato*, document no. 126.

47. Bizzari, *Imbreviature notarili I*, document no. 324, p. 131.

48. Bizzari, *Imbreviature notarili II*, document no. 210, p. 117.

49. Gouron, *La réglementation des métiers*, pp. 121–122.

50. ASG, CN, cart. n. 18, pt. II, 322v, Matteo de Predono notary.

51. ASG, CN, cart. n. 22, 42v, Bonovassallo de Maiori notary.

52. ASG, CN, cart. n. 18, pt. II, 322v, Matteo de Predono notary.

53. ASG, CN, cart. n. 22, 122v, Bonovassallo de Maiori notary.

54. See *Annales Ianuenses,* vol. III, under year 1244.

55. For a catalog of published documents on the crusade of Louis IX, see Byrne, *Genoese Shipping,* pp. 3–4.

56. Hall-Cole, Krueger, Renert, and Reynolds, *Giovanni di Guiberto,* document no. 1123. ASG, CN, cart. n. 14, 352v–353r, for ad exstendendum folium in 1226.

57. ASG, CN, cart. n. 22, 42r–v, Bonovassallo de Maiori notary.

58. For some ideas on the medieval idea of contract and its broad significance, see Bloch, *Feudal Society,* pp. 450–451.

59. Salatiele, *Ars Notariae,* p. 278.

60. Numerous examples of land sales are in the records known as the Ravenna papyri. See Tjäder, *Die Nichtliterarischen Lateinischen Papyri Italiens,* vols. 1 and 2. In volume 2 is a detailed and typical land sale in Ravenna dated 616–619 that betrays the influence of Roman law and the idea of contract (text and commentary, 2:126–138).

61. For some comments on the various kinds of fostering patterns in medieval society, see Goody, *Family and Marriage in Europe,* pp. 68–75.

62. Chiaudano and Moresco, *Il cartolare di Giovanni Scriba,* document no. 1035.

63. Ibid., supplement, vol. 2, no. 3, p. 259.

64. ASG, Notai Ignoti, busta 1, no. 33, document I, Oberto Scriba de Mercato notary.

65. ASG, CN, cart. n. 4, 31r, Oberto Scriba de Mercato notary (1214); cart. n. 14, 150v, Maestro Salmone notary (1226).

66. Gaudenzi, *Statuti delle società,* 2:406.

67. Bizzari, *Imbreviature notarili II,* document no. 86, pp. 51–52.

68. Blancard, *Documents inédits sur le commerce de Marseille,* no. 699, p. 155.

69. Ibid., no. 849, pp. 221–222.

70. Ibid., no. 423, p. 33; and Pryor, *Business Contracts,* p. 112.

71. Archives Départmentales de L'Hérault, Serie BB 1, Notes Jean Grimaud de l'an 1293, 80v. I am grateful to Kathryn Reyerson for a microfilm copy of this cartulary.

72. Verriest, *Les luttes sociales,* p. 49.

73. Ibid., p. 8.

74. Ibid., p. 55: "as us et as coustumes dou mestier."

75. Ibid., p. 49: "si come sen enfant." This, however, was in return for a payment of twelve livres for the first year.

76. Lombardo, *Documenti,* no. 89.

77. Krueger and Reynolds, *Lanfranco,* no. 219, for the earliest work.

78. Many examples of a fixed salary for dyers can be found: ASG, CN, cart. n. 21, pt. I, 203r–v (1251); cart. n. 18, pt. II, 346r (1249).

79. ASG, Magistrato delle Arti, busta 178, fascie 23, for the statutes of the dyers' guild.

80. Besta and Barni, *Liber Consuetudinum Mediolani,* pp. 132–133. See Violante, *La società milanese,* pp. 41–70, on the economic development of Milan and the contribution of the merchants.

81. See Skinner, *The Foundations of Modern Political Thought,* pp. 62–65, and also Canning, *Baldus de Ubaldis,* pp. 96–97, for more on Bartolo and the idea of popular or civic sovereignty.

82. Black, *Guilds and Civil Society,* pp. 16–23.

83. For more on the Fieschi family, see Sisto, *Genova nel duecento*.

84. Black, *Guilds and Civil Society*, p. 21. Black emphasizes a Germanic tradition that permitted people to form a guild on their own initiative. The Anglo-Saxon and Carolingian precedents discussed here in chapter 1 do not support this view.

85. Ibid., p. 17.

86. Gaudenzi, *Statuti delle società*, 2:265–281. For background on Bologna and its guilds, see Pini, *Città, comuni, e corporazioni*, pp. 219–258.

87. Gaudenzi, *Statuti delle società*, 2:279: "donec discordia esset inter societates Mercatorum et Pellipariorum et societatem Sartorum."

88. Ibid., pp. 221–245.

89. Ibid., see pp. 224–225, on ten-year rule for a voice in guild affairs.

90. The classic work on medieval slavery remains Verlinden, *L'Esclavage dans l'Europe médiévale*.

91. Mickwitz also stressed the independent origins of northern guilds. See his *Die Kartellfunktionen der Zünfte*, p. 233.

92. Ennen and Eckertz, *Quellen zur Geschichte der Stadt Köln*, pp. 335–338. The statutes define the *pannatores* as "qui suos pannos incidunt."

93. Ibid., p. 335: "jura nostra de domo Civium et de officialibus de Richir-zegheide." See Strait, *Cologne in the Twelfth Century*, pp. 70–71, for more on the *Richerzecheit* of Cologne. This group was originally an eating club of guild masters, but by 1179–1182 the members were regulating guilds on an official basis.

94. Ennen and Eckertz, *Quellen zur Geschichte der Stadt Köln*, p. 336.

95. Ibid., p. 338.

96. Riley, *Munimenta Gildhallae Londoniensis*, 2:101–104, 54 Henry III.

97. Ibid., p. 101: "pro utilitate et commoditate pauperum illius officii cum multi sunt."

98. Ibid., pp. 102–103: "capellas falsas a partibus transmarinis ad civitatem adduxerint . . . ad maximum detrimentum totius populi regni."

99. Aclocque, *Les corporations, l'industrie et le commerce à Chartres*, pp. 11–12: "de me officia sua tenebant et per manum mean tenendum institui."

100. Ibid., pp. 327–336: "par le tesmoin que nous avons apris d'anciennes genz." Note that the ordinances are in Old French, a parallel here to the German, but not the Italian, guilds of the thirteenth century.

101. Ibid., p. 330.

102. Ibid., p. 332 and passim.

103. Murray, *Reason and Society*, p. 322; this is a general theme discussed throughout the book, as is the idea of merit.

104. For more on these protests, see chapter 5.

105. Little, *Religious Poverty and the Profit Economy*, pp. 113–120. See also Grundmann, *Religiöse Bewegungen*, pp. 72–91.

106. On the legitimization of the Humiliati, see Bolton, "Innocent III's Treatment of the Humiliati."

107. Zanoni, *Gli Humiliati*, p. 154.

108. Grundmann, *Religiöse Bewegungen*, p. 160.

109. Little, *Religious Poverty and the Profit Economy*, p. 118. Little makes this point about the fustian workers, who he says never became organized; now see Mazzaoui, *The Italian Cotton Industry*.

110. Grundmann, *Religiöse Bewegungen*, p. 159.

111. Bolton, "Innocent III's Treatment of the Humiliati," p. 76.

112. ASG, CN, cart. n. 18, pt. II, 313r, Matteo de Predono notary.

113. ASG, CN, cart. n. 21, pt. I, 52v, Matteo de Predono notary.

114. I know of only one more such apprenticeship, a weaver named Resonata: ASG, CN, cart. n. 14, 287v–288r, Maestro Salmone notary.

115. Lopez, "Le origini dell'arte della lana," in his *Studi*, p. 158, for inventory.

116. ASG, CN, cart. n. 11, 142r, Lantelmo notary.

117. Mannucci, "Delle società genovesi d'arti e mestieri"; this document is on pp. 286–289.

118. Zanoni, *Gli Humiliati*, p. 305.

119. Gaudenzi, *Statuti delle società*, 2:299.

120. Zanoni, *Gli Humiliati*, p. 171.

121. Little, *Religious Poverty and the Profit Economy*, p. 119.

122. Michaud-Quantin, *Universitas*, p. 195 and passim.

123. Mickwitz, *Die Kartellfunktionen der Zünfte*, pp. 9–10.

124. Ibid., p. 161.

125. Ibid., pp. 163–164. In the end, this continuity of monopolistic practices convinced Mickwitz that some continuity must exist from the ancient to the medieval guild (p. 234).

126. Ibid., pp. 163–164.

Chapter 3

1. Walter Jackson Bate, *John Keats* (Cambridge, Mass., 1972), p. 31.

2. Gaudenzi, *Statuti delle società*, 2:269: "parvus discipulus minor X annis." Aclocque mentions six-year-old apprentices in Chartres but supplies no examples; see her *Les corporations, l'industrie et le commerce à Chartres*, p. 27.

3. Gaudenzi, *Statuti delle società*, 2:346.

4. Epstein, "Labour in Thirteenth-Century Genoa," p. 128.

5. For some of the many examples of this practice, see Gaudenzi, *Statuti delle società*, 2:302, in the wool guild of Bologna.

6. Ibid., pp. 232–233. Shoemakers put their sons in the guild at age fourteen (p. 255).

7. Aclocque, *Les corporations, l'industrie et le commerce à Chartres*, p. 332, for statutes of the *bourgeoisie de la rivière*.

8. Epstein, *Wills and Wealth*, pp. 133–134.

9. Gaudenzi, *Statuti delle società*, 2:231. The smiths of Bologna allowed themselves only two apprentices, with no limit on sons.

10. Riley, *Munimenta Gildhallae Londoniensis*, 2:78.

11. De Lespinasse and Bonnardot, *Les métiers et corporations de la ville de Paris: Le Livre des Métiers d'Etienne Boileau*, p. 58 (hereafter cited as *Livre des métiers*). For more on apprenticeship in Paris, see Fagniez, *Études sur l'industrie et la classe industrielle*, pp. 55–74; most of the evidence is from the fourteenth century, and no notarial records exist to provide runs of contracts.

12. Gaudenzi, *Statuti delle società*, 2:270, for tailors; 2:406, for weavers.

13. De Lespinasse and Bonnardot, *Livre des métiers*, p. 46.

14. Epstein, "Labour in Thirteenth-Century Genoa," p. 128.

15. Mulholland, *Early Gild Records of Toulouse*, p. 45: "Prudens et Sapiens."

16. See below for more on standards of production.

17. Gaudenzi, *Statuti delle società*, 2:270, on tailors requiring a *carta*; the *fornitori spadarum* had a notary of the guild, for this purpose among others (2:337).

18. Riley, *Munimenta Gildhallae Londoniensis,* 2:93–94.

19. ASG, CN, cart. n. 18, pt. II, 213r, Bonovassallo de Maiori notary (20 November 1245): "docendi ut mos est . . . docere diligenter de arte mea lignaminorum quam exercio prout melius scivero."

20. ASG, CN, cart. n. 55, pt. II, 57v, Angelino de Sigestro notary (20 October 1292).

21. ASG, CN, cart. n. 18, pt. II, 212r, Bonovassallo de Maiori notary (8 November 1245).

22. ASG, Notai Ignoti, busta 10, 107A, Lanfranco Cazano notary.

23. Gaudenzi, *Statuti delle società,* 2:231, for smiths; 2:333–334, for *fornitori spadarum.*

24. De Lespinasse and Bonnardot, *Livre des métiers,* p. 181.

25. Epstein, "Labour in Thirteenth-Century Genoa," p. 126.

26. ASG, CN, cart. n. 31, pt. I, 5r, Matteo de Predono notary (17 January 1248).

27. The statutes of the tailors' guild in Verona reveal that all of the masters paid something to their apprentices twice a year. See Simeoni, *Gli antichi statuti delle arti veronesi,* statuti, IV, p. 292.

28. ASG, CN, cart. n. 14, 381r, Maestro Salmone notary (9 December 1231).

29. For example, see ASG, CN, cart. n. 31, pt. I, 83r, Matteo de Predono notary (23 January 1251).

30. Several examples from 1293 are in ASG, Notai Ignoti, busta 10, 107A, Lanfranco Cazano notary.

31. De Lespinasse and Bonnardot, *Livre des métiers,* p. 115.

32. Riley, *Munimenta Gildhallae Londoniensis,* 2:99–100.

33. Ibid., p. 100.

34. Ibid., p. 99.

35. Ibid., p. 100.

36. See note 14.

37. De Lespinasse and Bonnardot, *Livre des métiers,* p. 189.

38. See chapter 5 for more on social protest and revolt after the plague.

39. Adam Smith, *The Wealth of Nations,* pp. 81–82.

40. Ibid., p. 82.

41. Phelps-Brown and Hopkins, "Seven Centuries of Building Wages," and "Seven Centuries of the Prices of Consumables."

42. Phelps-Brown and Hopkins, "Seven Centuries of Building Wages," pp. 174–176.

43. Ibid., p. 177.

44. Ibid., p. 176.

45. Phelps-Brown and Hopkins, "Seven Centuries of the Prices of Consumables," p. 193.

46. Epstein, "Labour in Thirteenth-Century Genoa."

47. ASG, CN, cart. n. 18, pt. II, 346r, Tomasso de San Lorenzo notary (1 September 1249); 163r, Bartolomeo de Fornari notary (26 November 1245).

48. Ibid., 191v, Bartolomeo de Fornari notary (8 October 1245).

49. ASG, CN, cart. n. 31, pt. I, 138v, Matteo de Predono notary (23 May 1251).

50. Epstein, "Labour in Thirteenth-Century Genoa," pp. 130–133.

51. ASG, CN, cart. n. 14, 180r, Maestro Salmone notary.

52. Epstein, "Labour in Thirteenth-Century Genoa," p. 126.

53. De Lespinasse and Bonnardot, *Livre des métiers,* p. 108: "Li vallet ont leur

vesprées: c'est a savoir, que cil sont loué a journée lessent oevre au premier cop des vespres Nostre Dame."

54. Ibid., p. 82, claspmakers; p. 54, wiredrawers; p. 190, leathercurers.

55. Balletto, *Atti rogati a Ventimiglia*, p. 290: "alia servicia decencia."

56. Ibid., pp. 401–402: "alia servicia convenientia."

57. Ibid., p. 481.

58. Ibid., pp. 482–483.

59. Ibid., pp. 529–530.

60. Herlihy, *Medieval Households*, p. 101. Shahar, *The Fourth Estate*, p. 203: "Those periods of institutionalization were detrimental to women."

61. For a summary of various theories on the connection between patriarchy and the division of labor, see Sokoloff, *Between Money and Love*, a study of women's work in modern industrial society.

62. Aclocque, *Les corporations, l'industrie et le commerce à Chartres*, p. 332.

63. Gouron, *La réglementation des métiers*, p. 251.

64. De Lespinasse and Bonnardot, *Livre des métiers*, p. 175.

65. Gaudenzi, *Statuti delle società*, 2:403.

66. For what follows, see Mulholland, *Early Gild Records of Toulouse*, pp. 34–40, statutes of the *taxillii*.

67. De Lespinasse and Bonnardot, *Livre des métiers*, pp. 149–151.

68. Gouron, *La réglementation des métiers*.

69. For what follows, see Castellani, "Il più antico statuto dell'arte degli oliandoli," p. 191. In Florence the butchers were in the guild of the oil merchants.

70. Mulholland, *Early Gild Records of Toulouse*, p. 67.

71. Ibid., p. 55.

72. Riley, *Munimenta Gildhallae Londoniensis*, 2:82–83.

73. Gaudenzi, *Statuti delle società*, 2:239.

74. But see below on artisan partnerships.

75. Espinas and Pirenne, "Les coutumes de la gilde marchande de Saint Omer," for statutes of the guild.

76. For some summary comments on the major guilds of Florence, see Dören, *Italienische Wirtschaftsgeschichte*, pp. 272–273 and passim, and his classic study of the wool industry and guilds, *Die Florentiner Wollentuchindustrie*.

77. Lane, *Venice*, p. 104.

78. Vercauteren, *Actes des comtes de Flandre*, pp. 295–296.

79. Douglas and Greenaway, *English Historical Documents*, pp. 1012–1013. Gross's *The Gild Merchant* remains the only general treatment but should be used with caution.

80. Douglas and Greenaway, *English Historical Documents*, p. 1038.

81. Ibid., p. 1039.

82. Reynolds, *History of English Medieval Towns*, pp. 81–83.

83. Dollinger, *The German Hanse*, p. 14.

84. Ibid., pp. 39–40.

85. Ibid., pp. 61–64.

86. Riley, *Munimenta Gildhallae Londoniensis*, 2:102–103.

87. Mulholland, *Early Gild Records of Toulouse*, p. 13.

88. Riley, *Munimenta Gildhallae Londoniensis*, 2:84, cordwainers; 2:79, lorimers.

89. De Lespinasse and Bonnardot, *Livre des métiers*, p. 7.

90. Ibid., pp. 38–39.

91. Ibid., p. 34.

92. Ibid., p. 103.

93. Ibid., p. 72.

94. Riley, *Munimenta Gildhallae Londoniensis,* 2:126.

95. Ibid., p. 102, cappers; p. 79, lorimers.

96. Monticolo, *I capitolari delle arti veneziane,* pp. 18–19, tailors. For a more detailed analysis of Venetian guilds, see Romano, *Patricians and Popolani,* pp. 65–72, especially p. 66, where he describes these guilds as "hierarchic and oligarchic."

97. Ibid., pp. 67–70.

98. Castellani, "Il più antico statuto dell'arte degli oliandoli," p. 151.

99. Ibid., pp. 152–153.

100. Gaudenzi, *Statuti delle società,* 2:224.

101. For more on secrecy as one way to defend privacy, see Bok, *Secrets,* pp. 9–24.

102. Becker, *Florence in Transition,* pp. 105–110, 118–119, and passim.

103. De Lespinasse and Bonnardot, *Livre des métiers,* p. 206.

104. Ibid., p. 175, hatters; p. 88, mortarers; p. 171, painters of saddles; p. 61, makers of religious artifacts.

105. Ibid., p. 94.

106. Ibid., p. 61, lapidaries; p. 78, silkweavers; p. 102, tapestryweavers; p. 127, crucifix carvers; p. 181, harnessmakers.

107. Ibid., p. 33.

108. Ibid., p. 68, large spindles; p. 70, small spindles.

109. Ibid., p. 72. Some Parisian trades blatantly excluded women and occasionally gave reasons: the tapestryweavers claimed that "the métier is too laborious" ("le mestier qui est trop greveus" [p. 102]), and the lapidaries felt that "their métier is very subtle" ("leur mestier est moult soutif" [p. 62]).

110. Ibid., p. 205.

111. M. R. B. Shaw, *Joinville and Villehardouin: Chronicles of the Crusades* (Harmondsworth, 1963), p. 177.

112. De Lespinasse and Bonnardot, *Livre des métiers,* p. 199: "il fut establi pour servir les gentiuz houmes."

113. Ibid., p. 91. *Guet* was the duty or tax of night watch.

114. De Lespinasse and Bonnardot, *Livre des métiers,* p. 115.

115. Howell, *Women, Production, and Patriarchy,* pp. 23–24.

116. Sahlins, *Stone Age Economics,* p. 87.

117. Ibid., p. 67.

118. ASG, CN, cart. n. 14, 333v–334r, Maestro Salmone notary.

119. Ibid., 340r (13 November 1231).

120. Tiepolo, *Domenico Prete di S. Maurizio,* pp. 228–229.

121. Bugarella, *Le imbreviature del notaio Adamo de Citella,* p. 238.

122. See Le Goff, "Licit and Illicit Trades in the Medieval West," in his *Time, Work and Culture,* p. 59.

123. Ibid.

124. Jordan, "Meat Market of Béziers," pp. 37 and 41.

125. The problem of the Jewish butcher is the principal subject of Jordan's article.

126. Bowsky, *Siena under the Nine,* pp. 210–211.

127. Gaudenzi, *Statuti delle società,* 1:363–376, for the status of the butchers; the rules present a mix of details on the butchers as a guild and as a company of militia.

128. Given, *Society and Homicide*, pp. 87 and 93. By contrast, thirty-eight millers and their wives were accused.

Chapter 4

1. Meersseman, *Ordo Fraternitatis*, 1:7.

2. Ibid., 1:8.

3. Gouron, *La réglementation des métiers*, p. 362.

4. Frank, *Passions within Reason*, pp. 66–67.

5. For references to early Church councils, see Naz, *Dictionaire de Droit Canonique*, vol. 4, cols. 1227–1230, "Dimanche."

6. See *Corpus Iuris Civilis, Codex Iustinianus*, III, 12, "De Feriis," for legislation of the Christian emperors; and *Digest* II.12, on holidays, adjournments, and various other times, according to the classical jurists.

7. See *Encyclopaedia of Islam*, shorter version, pp. 92–93, for rules and practices on the *djum'a* and for other notices of work on Muslim holy days. See Goitein, "Le culte du vendredi musulman," for background on Muslim practices. Goitein noted the perilous overlaps—Jews shopped for their sabbath on the Muslim day of assembly; Christians worked and prepared for Sunday on Saturday—that were all sources of potential tension (p. 492).

8. *MGH, Legum* I, *Capitulare Ecclesiasticum*, tom. I, cap. 80, p. 66.

9. Whitelock, Brett, and Brooke, *Councils and Synods*, p. 310, for laws of Edward and Guthrum; p. 369, for laws of Aethelred.

10. For references to work by Burchard of Worms and Ivo of Chartres, see *Corpus Iuris Canonici*, Pars Secunda, Decretalium Collectiones, *Decretals of Gregory IX*, lib. II, tit. IX, "De Feriis," col. 270. I searched Gratian, *Corpus Iuris Canonici*, Pars Prior, Decretum Magistri Gratiani, without result.

11. Mansi, *Sacrorum Conciliorum*, Council of Paris, 1212, col. 843, extended older definition: "opera servilia seu fabrilia."

12. See note 8, *Decretals of Gregory IX*, lib. II, tit. IX, cap. 5, cols. 272–273. Holy days included Christmas; feasts of St. Stephen, John the Evangelist, the Holy Innocents, and St. Silvester; the Circumcision; Epiphany; the seven days of Holy Week; Pentecost with the two following days; the nativity of John the Baptist; all of the feasts of the Virgin and the Twelve Apostles, especially Peter and Paul, and feasts of St. Lawrence, St. Michael, and All Saints.

13. De Lespinasse and Bonnardot, *Livre des métiers*, pp. 8–9. On the dating and administrative significance of Étienne Boileau's career, see Jordan, *Louis IX*, pp. 171–181.

14. De Lespinasse and Bonnardot, *Livre des métiers*, p. 8.

15. Gaudenzi, *Statuti delle società*, 2:343.

16. Ibid., p. 334.

17. *Decretals of Gregory IX*, lib. II, tit. IX, cap. 3.

18. Ibid., cap. 5.

19. See Le Goff, "Licit and Illicit Trades in the Medieval West," in his *Time, Work and Culture*, p. 301 (in notes). For comments on Muslim work on Sundays in Christian Valencia, see Burns, *Islam under the Crusaders*, p. 90.

20. Grayzel, *The Church and the Jews*, p. 305, for the Council of Avignon in 1209, and p. 337, for the example from the Council of Albi in 1254.

21. De Lespinasse and Bonnardot, *Livre des métiers,* p. 23.

22. Ibid., p. 33: "Nus Orfevres ne puet ouvrir sa forge au jour d'apostele, se ele n'eschiet au samedi." For more on the confraternities in Paris, see Fagniez, *Études sur l'industrie et la classe industrielle,* pp. 33–42; he notes that the confraternities allowed strangers (that is, people not in the trade or craft) to join (p. 34).

23. See, in general, Mollat, *The Poor in the Middle Ages,* pp. 117–190.

24. Marri, *Statuti dell'arte del Cambio di Firenze,* pp. 36–37.

25. Mulholland, *Early Gild Records of Toulouse,* p. 21.

26. See chapter 2.

27. Gaudenzi, *Statuti delle società,* 2:412. See also Gouron, *La réglementation des métiers,* p. 351; St. Lucy was the patroness of the tailors in Albi.

28. Gaudenzi, *Statuti delle società,* 2:412: "ut dicta sotietas de bono in melius reformetur."

29. Meersseman, *Ordo Fraternitatis,* 1:193. Across Europe, St. Nicholas was a prized patron for mariners, merchants, and fishermen.

30. Franchini, *Lo statuto della corporazione dei fabbri,* p. 45. See Huntington and Metcalf, *Celebrations of Death,* pp. 1–34, for a useful survey of funerals and the meaning of ritual.

31. Castellani, "Il più antico statuto dell'arte degli oliandoli," p. 185. The statutes of the rag merchants of Florence (1296) assumed that the death and burial of a member took place on the same day; see Sartini, *Statuti dell'arte dei rigattieri,* p. 12.

32. Gouron, *La réglementation des métiers,* p. 353. In Verona those tailors not obligated to attend the funeral were supposed to stop their work until their brothers returned from the burial; see Simeoni, *Gli antichi statuti delle arti veronesi,* p. 291.

33. Franchini, *Lo statuto della corporazione dei fabbri,* p. 50.

34. Epstein, *Wills and Wealth,* pp. 133–134, for some information on the wills of artisans.

35. Franchini, *Lo statuto della corporazione dei fabbri,* p. 50: "ita quod omnes prebeant auxilium et iuvamen quilibet prout volunt."

36. De Lespinasse and Bonnardot, *Livre des métiers,* p. 88.

37. Mulholland, *Early Gild Records of Toulouse,* pp. 65–66; and also Gouron, *La réglementation des métiers,* p. 390. For more on the connection between charity and bridges in Germany, see Maschke, "Die Brücke im Mittelalter."

38. Toulmin Smith, *English Gilds,* p. 180, statutes of 1297.

39. Gouron, *La réglementation des métiers,* pp. 399–401, for edition of the statutes of 1394.

40. Ibid., p. 364. In Durkheim's terms, this solidarity, rooted in the family and religion, was mechanical rather than organic.

41. Southern, *Robert Grosseteste,* p. 249.

42. Adler, *The Itinerary of Benjamin of Tudela,* p. 30. For activities of Jews in Marseilles, see Blancard, *Documents inédits sur le commerce de Marseille,* nos. 697, 1025, and passim. For good general comments on this issue, see Ashtor, "The Jews in the Mediterranean Trade."

43. Adler, *The Itinerary of Benjamin of Tudela,* p. 5, Genoa; p. 8, Naples and Salerno; p. 10, Thebes.

44. De Lespinasse and Bonnardot, *Livre des métiers,* p. 84.

45. Mulholland, *Early Gild Records of Toulouse,* p. 45.

46. De Lespinasse and Bonnardot, *Livre des métiers,* p. 151.

47. See Chazan, *European Jewry and the First Crusade*, pp. 27–37 and 50–60.

48. Little, *Religious Poverty and the Profit Economy*, pp. 56–57.

49. One fine example of this work is Baldwin's *Masters, Princes, and Merchants*, which contains a valuable analysis of the views of one thinker, an individual who was, however, somewhat remote from the realities of the commercial life (pp. 261–311).

50. See Ovitt, *The Restoration of Perfection*, pp. 57–70, for a close look at commentaries on Genesis from Philo to Aquinas.

51. For what follows, see *De Decem Praeceptis, Collatio* IV, in *Opera Omnia*, 5:519–522.

52. In the *De Reductione artium ad theologiam*, in *Opera Omnia*, 5:319, Bonaventure's source, Hugh of St. Victor, discussed the mechanical arts of his *Eruditiones Didascalicae, PL*, vol. 176, cols. 760–763. For Hugh, the seven mechanical arts were the handmaidens that Mercury accepted as a dowry from Philology. For more on the mechanical arts in ancient and medieval thought, see Ovitt, *The Restoration of Perfection*, pp. 107–126.

53. Locatelli, *S. Antonii Patavii Sermones Dominicales et in Solemnitatibus*, pp. 182–183, the sermon Dominica IV post Pascham.

54. Ibid., p. 182: "Quanta distantia est inter dicere et facere, tanta fuit inter creare et recreare."

55. Ibid., for the King James translation of Isaiah 49:4: "In vacuum laboravi sine causa, et vane fortitudinem meam consumpsi."

56. Aquinas, *Summa Theologica*, q. 73, art. 2, p. 542: "Utrum Deus septima die requievit ab omni opere suo."

57. Ibid., with the important phrases for the two types of rest being "pro cessatione ab operibus" and "pro impletione desiderii."

58. This example takes into account Kirshner's stipulations that Bernardino was not an economist and hence that one should be wary of distorting the preacher's religious purpose; see Kirshner, "Reading Bernardino's Sermon on the Public Debt," especially pp. 562–563. In the same collection, Delcorno's "L'*ars predicandi* di Bernardino da Siena" is also filled with pertinent insights on these sermons as historical sources.

59. Bernardino of Siena, *Opera Omnia*, sermo XXXIII, Dominica quarta in Quadragesima, pp. 140–169; p. 140: "De mercationibus et artificibus in generali, et de conditionibus licitis et illicitis earumdem." Bernardino credits Alexander of Hales with these three distinctions. A similar sermon in Italian (Tuscan) is on merchants, artisans, and their work; see Bargellini, *San Bernardino da Siena*, pp. 860–893.

60. Bernardino of Siena, *Opera Omnia*, sermo XXXIII, p. 142.

61. Ibid., p. 147: "Momento, o mercator, ut diem sabbati sanctifices."

62. Ibid., for selling by lying; pp. 151–155, for other illicit retail trading practices.

63. Ibid., pp. 155–158.

64. Ibid., pp. 158–161.

65. Ibid., p. 159: "Al nome di Dio e de li sancti 6, 7, 8, 9, 10." This is one of the few slips into Italian in these Latin sermons, but Bernardino probably delivered them in the vernacular. In the Italian sermon, the sequence in written numbers is "1, 2, 3, 5, 7, 8, 10, 13, 14, 17, 19 and 20"; see Bargellini, *San Bernardino da Siena*, p. 880.

66. Bargellini, *San Bernardino da Siena*, pp. 887–888.

67. Spicciani claims that Bernardino was well informed about the wages of workers ("La povertà 'involuntaria'," p. 817), but his principal reference, Cannarozzi's *San Bernardino da Siena,* does not seem to me to sustain this conclusion. Sermons on contracts invariably turn into discourses on usury. One sermon that specifically addresses the question of wages only concerns the servants of the commune—another instance of fraud against the public good. See Cannarozzi, *San Bernardino da Siena,* vol. 5, sermon XLV, p. 15.

68. *Sermones Vulgares* in Crane, *The Exempla or Illustrative Stories;* and *Sermones Communes* in Franken, *Die Exempla des Jacob von Vitry.* For some comments on the exempla as historical sources, see Murray, "Confession as a Historical Source," especially pp. 291–297.

69. Crane, *The Exempla or Illustrative Stories,* exemplum CLXII, p. 70: "Jam sunt vii anni quod ab alio carnes non comparavi a vobis." Ille valde ammirans respondit: "Tanto tempore hoc fecisti et adhuc vives?"

70. Ibid., exemplum CXCIII, pp. 80–81.

71. Ibid., exemplum LXVI, pp. 27–28.

72. Ibid., exemplum CLXXXIV, pp. 77–78.

73. Tubach, *Index Exemplorum.* Tubach cataloged and cross-indexed these exempla by types, moral lessons, and characters.

74. Ibid., n. 3472.

75. Ibid., n. 1700 and 1702, on dogs.

76. Ibid., n. 2970.

77. Ibid., n. 5386, 5385, 5384.

78. Ibid., n. 2969.

79. Ibid., n. 5114.

80. John Van Engen explores the early phase of this subject in his "Theophilus Presbyter and Rupert of Deutz."

81. See Le Goff, "Trades and Professions as Represented in Confessor's Manuals," in his *Time, Work and Culture,* p. 110.

82. Hence this explains my caution on the use of exempla and my preference for those from an author like Jacques de Vitry. His are datable and often original to him, or at least the first written notice.

83. Quoted in Duby, *William Marshal,* p. 55.

84. Duby, *The Three Orders,* p. 51, Adalbero; pp. 40–42, Gerard.

85. See Le Goff, "Trades and Professions as Represented in Confessor's Manuals," in his *Time, Work and Culture,* pp. 114–115. For a similar argument, see Ovitt, *The Restoration of Perfection,* p. 163, where the case for secularized labor is unconvincing.

86. See Le Goff, "Trades and Professions as Represented in Confessor's Manuals," in his *Time, Work and Culture,* p. 112, for as close as he comes to an explanation.

87. See Sombart, *The Quintessence of Capitalism,* p. 16, where the case rests on an anecdote from Goethe. Some modern anthropological research in fact supports this view of intermittent labor in hunter-gatherer and primitive agricultural societies (Sahlins, *Stone Age Economics,* pp. 17–35), but why this pattern should apply in medieval Europe is not clear.

88. Himmelfarb, *The Idea of Poverty,* p. 106.

89. Quoted in ibid., p. 107.

90. Adam Smith, *The Wealth of Nations,* p. 81.

91. Geremek, *Le salariat,* p. 81; pp. 80–82, general discussion of meal breaks.

92. For example, a medievalist would yearn for the rich level of detail in Darnton's "Workers Revolt: The Great Cat Massacre of the Rue Saint-Severin" in his *The Great Cat Massacre*, pp. 75–104.

93. Martines, *Power and Imagination*, p. 39.

94. Michaud-Quantin's *Universitas* is also fundamental here.

95. Black, *Guilds and Civil Society*, pp. 76 and 84.

96. Hyde, *Padua in the Age of Dante*, p. 311, number of guilds; p. 178, on lawyers and notaries.

97. Ibid., pp. 178 and 193.

98. Blanshei, "Perugia, 1260–1340," p. 67.

99. Ibid., p. 16.

100. Ibid., p. 58.

101. Lane and Mueller, *Money and Banking*, p. 85.

102. This subject of magnates is addressed in detail in Najemy, *Corporatism and Consensus*, pp. 10–47.

103. Blanshei, "Perugia, 1260–1340," p. 17.

104. Richard Mackenney explains the absence of popular uprisings in Venice on three counts: the government promoted the *arti*, the noble and guild interests did not threaten one another, and the state gave the guilds the security of good law and fair courts. (His second point remains to be proved.) See his *Tradesmen and Traders*, p. 4 and more emphatically on p. 29. See also Romano, *Patricians and Popolani*, pp. 4–8, for other views on conflict and stability that emphasize local geography and the economy.

105. On the Arsenal, see Lane, *Venetian Ships and Shipbuilders*, pp. 129–145, where the information is more detailed for the fourteenth and subsequent centuries, but government was probably the single biggest employer in town as early as the founding of the Arsenal in 1104.

106. *Annales Ianuenses*, IV:25–26.

107. Ibid., IV:71–72.

108. Every conceivable explanation for these differences has been put forward. The most convincing one relies on the role of vertical social ties, especially in Genoa. See Diane Owens Hughes, "Kinsmen and Neighbors in Medieval Genoa," in Miskimin, Herlihy, and Udovitch, *The Medieval City*, pp. 95–111.

109. Brooke and Keir, *London, 800–1216*, pp. 46–47 and 49–50.

110. Ibid., pp. 245–252.

111. Sharpe, *Calendar of Letter Books*, pp. ii–ix.

112. But they were not the only ones to become citizens through redemption. Also, by 1312, foreigners needed the permission of citizens in the same trade to enter the freedom; see Thrupp, *The Merchant Class*, p. 70.

113. Sharpe, *Calendar of Letter Books*, p. viii.

114. Ibid., p. ix; pp. 195–196, for oath.

115. Thrupp, *The Merchant Class*, p. 70.

116. Ibid., p. 6.

117. Ibid., p. 65. Thrupp call the aldermen an oligarchy, and the mayor was always an alderman.

118. The unknowns account for the differences between these figures and those of Thomas in *Calendar of Pleas*, pp. xxxii–xxxv.

119. The total depends on the overlap of some French and English trade names and on some ambiguous trades.

120. Thomas, *Calendar of Early Mayor's Court Rolls*, pp. 33–34.

121. Ibid., p. 52. Dragging citizens into church courts on these matters was also illegal.

122. Ibid., p. 149; the year was 1303.

123. Ibid., pp. 40–41.

124. Cazelles, *Nouvelle histoire de Paris*, pp. 177–183. See Fagniez, *Études sur l'industrie et la classe industrielle*, pp. 51–54, for the minimal role the métiers had in politics.

125. Cazelles, *Nouvelle histoire de Paris*, pp. 197–201.

126. Ibid., p. 208.

127. Ibid., p. 213; also see chapter 5 in this book.

128. Black, *Guilds and Civil Society*, p. 86.

129. Gewirth, *Marsilius of Padua*, p. 6.

130. Ibid., p. 4, for the translation of "propter litem laceratum est undique, quasi solutum." See Previté-Orton, *The Defensor Pacis*, p. 2, for this Latin quote.

131. Black, *Guilds and Civil Society*, p. 89. But this corporatism was not confined to the guilds, and the "people" as a corporate entity is a kind of legal fiction—hence caution on Marsiglio as a proponent of the sovereignty of the people (Wilks, "Corporatism and Representation," pp. 253–258).

132. Wilks, "Corporatism and Representation," pp. 253–258, and Previté-Orton, *The Defensor Pacis*, p. 27, for the *artes et disciplinae* as *officia*, with support from Aristotle for a "natural" division of labor.

133. A point also emphasized by Skinner, *The Foundations of Modern Political Thought*, pp. 60–66. Marsiglio had noted the duty of those people in groups and communities to be charitable toward one another, and after all, material support was at the core of a guild's reason for existing.

134. Black, *Guilds and Civil Society*, p. 95.

135. Canning, *Baldus de Ubaldis*, p. 90.

136. Ibid., pp. 113–114.

137. Ibid., p. 116.

138. Ibid., p. 117.

139. Ibid., p. 138.

140. Ibid., p. 258, for this Latin citation from Baldus: "Vlterius nota quod collegia artium et artifices licet habeant proprios iudices tamen nihilominus possunt conveniri sub potestate, et quod potestas dicitur superior non solum artium sed artificum et etiam prepositorum ipsorum."

Chapter 5

1. All of the standard texts now take this position, buttressed by recent local studies. See, for example, Postan, *The Medieval Economy and Society*, pp. 35–39.

2. The special circumstances of women at work have now been addressed at length in a new book that appeared too late to receive justice here; see David Herlihy, *Opera Muliebria: Women and Work in Medieval Europe* (New York, 1990).

3. Sartini, *Statuti dell'arte dei rigattieri*. For a comprehensive study of one Florentine guild, the construction trade, for which unfortunately no early set of statutes exists, see Goldthwaite, *The Building of Renaissance Florence*, pp. 249–272.

4. Sartini, *Statuti dell'arte dei rigattieri*, p. 14.

5. Ibid., p. 58.

6. Ibid., p. 76.

7. Ibid., p. 77.

8. Ibid., p. 80.

9. Ibid., p. 82.

10. Ibid., p. 218. From 1296 to 1340, the value of the florin in soldi di piccioli actually increased from forty-one soldi to about sixty-three soldi, so the decline in the fee is even more pronounced; see Goldthwaite, *The Building of Renaissance Florence*, p. 429.

11. Sartini, *Statuti dell'arte dei rigattieri*, pp. 219–220. Roberto Greci has also concluded, by a different route, that becoming a master in fourteenth-century Bologna was harder than in previous centuries; for this scholar a process of pro-letarianization explains the obstacles to joining the ranks of the employers; see his "Il contratto di apprendistato," especially pp. 93–95.

12. Sartini, *Statuti dell'arte dei rigattieri*, p. 221. This fine was not in the linen statutes of 1318. The text has one hundred solidi; this must be in error.

13. Ibid., p. 245.

14. Ibid., pp. 248–249.

15. Castellani, "Il più antico statuto dell'arte degli oliandoli."

16. Ibid., p. 164.

17. Ibid., p. 173.

18. Ibid., p. 194.

19. Morandini, *Statuti delle arti degli oliandoli*. This edition contains the earlier Italian statutes but is criticized by Castellani, whose work was used in this study instead.

20. Ibid., p. 113.

21. On the various stages of betrothal in Florence, see Klapisch-Zuber, "Zacharias, or the Ousted Father: Nuptial Rites in Tuscany between Giotto and the Council of Trent," in her *Women, Family, and Ritual*, pp. 178–212.

22. Morandini, *Statuti delle arti degli oliandoli*, p. 114.

23. Ibid., p. 172.

24. Sartini, *Statuti dell'arte dei rigattieri*, p. 172.

25. Cohn, *The Laboring Classes*, p. 138. Cohn relies on de la Roncière, who demonstrates that wages more than doubled for master builders (*Florence*, table 54, 1:295) and for the laborers (1:346). For a good analysis of the problems of deter-mining real and nominal wage rates, see Goldthwaite, *The Building of Renaissance Florence*, pp. 317–342.

26. Cohn, *The Laboring Classes*, p. 138.

27. Ibid., p. 139.

28. Fagniez, *Documents relatifs à l'histoire de l'industrie*, 2:21.

29. De Lespinasse, *Les métiers et corporations*, 1:1.

30. Geremek, *Le salariat*, pp. 103–106.

31. Ibid., p. 122, for the request of the dyers in 1288. For omission in earlier statutes, see de Lespinasse and Bonnardot, *Livre des métiers*, p. 112.

32. See details about pinmakers, chapter 4.

33. Verriest, *Les luttes sociales*, pp. 4–139.

34. Ibid., excluding for the time being the postplague contracts; for reasons, see below.

35. Ibid., n. 7, 19 June 1288, p. 55: "as us et as coustumes dou mestier."

36. See chapter 3; typical Genoese wages of the mid-thirteenth century are listed in table 3-3.

37. Miskimin, *Money, Prices, and Foreign Exchange*, pp. 1–13, for a good analysis of this problem.

38. Ibid., pp. 26–28, for an application of the Fisher equation to a real economy.

39. See Day, "Late Medieval Price Movements and the 'Crisis of Feudalism,'" in his *The Medieval Market Economy*, p. 95 and passim. Here the author translates his own article from *Annales E.S.C.* (1979): 305–318.

40. Ibid. Spufford, *Money*, pp. 339–363 and passim, emphasizes the periodic bullion shortages in Europe, but the thirteenth and most of the fourteenth centuries witnessed ample silver supplies—another sign that *M* was stable, at least relative to the population.

41. Miskimin, *Money, Prices, and Foreign Exchange*, p. 83; pp. 73–83, general discussion. See also Spufford, *Money*, pp. 289–314, for a fine analysis of debasement across Europe.

42. Day, "Late Medieval Price Movements and the 'Crisis of Feudalism,'" in his *The Medieval Market Economy*, p. 102.

43. Miskimin, *Money, Prices, and Foreign Exchange*, p. 13.

44. For gold and silver prices, see Felloni and Pesce, *Le monete genovesi*, pp. 223–224. The authors recalculated the purchasing power of the Genoese lira over these years and reached the same results (p. 296). Early fourteen-century inflation was much worse.

45. For a fuller treatment of the following, see Epstein, "Labour in Thirteenth-Century Genoa."

46. ASG, CN, cart. n. 4, 7v, Oberto Scriba de Mercato notary.

47. ASG, CN, cart. n. 31, pt. I, 234v–235r, Matteo de Predono notary.

48. ASG, CN, cart. n. 55, pt. II, 10r, Bonovassallo de Maiori notary.

49. ASG, Notai Ignoti, busta 10, 4v, Lanfranco Cazano notary.

50. Geremek, *Le salariat*, p. 107. Although Geremek's wage statistics only begin in 1340, they do reveal that in the years immediately preceding the plague of 1348 wages were flat or in a slight decline (graph, p. 123). De la Roncière rightly emphasizes that master masons were paid according to their skills and that considerable variation existed in the wages they commanded (*Florence*, 1:285–290 and 340–341).

51. Verriest, *Les luttes sociales*, p. 11: "Dist que ceskuns devroit d'avoir autant d'avoir li une que li autre."

52. Geremek, *Le salariat*, pp. 131–132.

53. Miskimin, *Money, Prices, and Foreign Exchange*, p. 74, table.

54. Geremek, *Le salariat*, p. 90. Master builders were a rare example of "masters" working for a wage—in their case the employers whose records survive were states (fortifications and palaces) and the Church. Hence Goldthwaite's caution against using construction wages as typical industrial wages is sound, and the seasonal nature of this trade is also a difficulty; see his *The Building of Renaissance Florence*, pp. 322–324 and 331.

55. Phelps-Brown and Hopkins, "Seven Centuries of the Prices of Consumables," pp. 184 and 193.

56. Miskimin's calculations (see note 53) again show that real wages in England did not rise enough during the famines, so "stagnation" might be too rosy a description for the plight of English wage earners.

57. See Goldthwaite, *The Building of Renaissance Florence*, pp. 259–260, where he notes that some of those listed as foreigners may have been sons of foreigners—still evidence for migration. For a fine case study of migration, see Sprandel, "Die Ausbreitung des deutschen Handwerks." Sprandel finds increased migra-

tion in the fourteenth century, first to Paris and later to the provinces (p. 78); all of this moving about also spread German technology, particularly for cloth (p. 100).

58. Balard, "Rémarques sur les esclaves," p. 660. I rely here on my study, "Labour in Thirteenth-Century Genoa," pp. 133–137.

59. ASG, Notai Ignoti, busta 10, 107A, 3v–4r, Lanfranco Cazano notary.

60. Balard, "Rémarques sur les esclaves," p. 650.

61. Epstein, *Wills and Wealth*, pp. 189–192.

62. Orlando Patterson has written extensively on the connection between the status and honor of the master as they related to the dishonor of the slaves; see his *Slavery and Social Death*, pp. 79–94.

63. Epstein, "Labour in Thirteenth-Century Genoa," pp. 135–136.

64. Balard, "Rémarques sur les esclaves," p. 652.

65. *Mostra de le antiche stoffe genovesi del secolo XIV al secolo XIX* (Genoa, 1941), p. 110, the "laboratores ad iornatam."

66. ASG, Magistrato delle Arti, busta 178, fascie 23, folio 10r.

67. For slavery of fifteenth-century Genoa, see Gioffrè's *Il mercato degli schiavi*, a book that demonstrates the vivid connection between this slave world, now extended to the Canary Islands, and what was in store for the Caribbean. For general comments, see Heers, *Esclaves et domestiques au Moyen Age*.

68. Unlike the situation in Bologna; see chapter 2.

69. See Dufourq, *L'Espagne catalane et le Maghrib*, and Miret Y Sans, "L'esclavitud en Cataluña."

70. See Bonnassie, *La organizacion del trabajo en Barcelona*.

71. Madurell-Marimon and Sanz, *Comandas comerciales barcelonesas*, p. 151.

72. Ibid., p. 116.

73. Lane, *Venice*, pp. 132–133.

74. The most thorough analyses of the decline of northern European slavery are Verlinden, *L'Esclavage dans l'Europe médiévale*, 1:729–747 (for France), and Karras, *Slavery and Society in Medieval Scandinavia* (for Scandinavia). In the latter work, one of the author's major conclusions is that "the availability of other forms of labor—both tenants and hired workers—was probably the major factor in the end of slavery in Sweden as in other Scandinavian countries" (p. 153).

75. Kedar, *Crusade and Mission*, pp. 148–151.

76. On the scope of technological change, see White, *Medieval Technology and Social Change*.

77. Staatsarchiv Canton Zürich, Zürich, Stadt und Landschaft: Zunftwesen, Zünfte S1336–1784, A.73.2, first document under Safran. This document is edited in Schnyder, *Quellen zur Zürcher Zunftsgeschichte*, 1:25–27.

78. The revolution of Rudolf Brun occurred in June 1336, and the shopkeepers, who formed the nucleus of what became Zurich's prestigious Saffran guild, wanted to take a place in the new regime; see Gyr, *Züricher Zunft-Historien*, pp. 25–30 and 184–209.

79. Mazzaoui, *The Italian Cotton Industry*, pp. 107–122, greatly compresses the argument here.

80. Ibid., p. 108.

81. Ibid., p. 109.

82. Ibid.

83. Thorndike, "The Invention of the Mechanical Clock."

84. For more, see Epstein, "Business Cycles and the Sense of Time."

85. Stella, *Annales Genuenses*, vol. 17, pt. 2, p. 153.

86. Landes, *Revolution in Time,* pp. 78–79.

87. Ibid., pp. 80–81.

88. Ibid., p. 81.

89. Ibid., p. 439.

90. Ibid.

91. De Lespinasse, *Les métiers et corporations,* 3:9–10.

92. For several good accounts of the plague, see Ziegler, *The Black Death,* and Carpentier, "Autour de la peste noire."

93. Yet generalizations about the plague always require caution. For Ghent, plague year 1368 was the real disaster, and little evidence of vacant or unrented housing exists before that date; see Nicholas, *The Metamorphosis of a Medieval City,* p. 24. In Siena, by contrast, signs of a housing surplus appear from the autumn of 1348 to February 1350, but not afterward; see Bowsky, "The Impact of the Black Death," p. 32.

94. Najemy, "*Audiant Omnes Artes,*" pp. 70–71.

95. Ibid., p. 71. The price of cloth depended on its style and quality, and the annual profits of some wool producers were still high after the plague and the attempt to limit production; see Hoshino, "La produzione laniera nel trecento a Firenze," pp. 53 and 56.

96. De Lespinasse, *Les métiers et corporations,* 1:2–44.

97. Vivier, "La Grande Ordonnance"; pp. 205–206, for the background of the ordinance.

98. Evidence also suggests that food prices were particularly high in 1351, another reason for the ordinance; see Delachenal, *Les Grandes Chroniques de France,* pp. 32–33.

99. De Lespinasse, *Les métiers et corporations,* 1:3.

100. Ibid., p. 9.

101. Ibid., pp. 23–24.

102. De Lespinasse and Bonnardot, *Livre des métiers,* p. 181.

103. De Lespinasse, *Les métiers et corporations,* 1:27, for vinedressers (*vignerons*); 1:32, for smiths (*fevres*).

104. Ibid., p. 39.

105. Ibid., p. 40.

106. Ibid., p. 37.

107. Ibid., p. 34.

108. Geremek, *Le salariat,* p. 123.

109. Vivier, "La Grande Ordonnance," p. 206.

110. De Lespinasse, *Les métiers et corporations,* 1:31, for these three occupations.

111. Ordinance and statute in Putnam, *The Enforcement of the Statute of Labourers,* pp. 8–11 in appendix, for ordinance; pp. 12–17 in appendix, for statute. A full English translation is in Dobson, *The Peasants' Revolt of 1381,* pp. 63–68. Text of statute was checked against *Statutes of the Realm,* vol. 1 (London, 1810), pp. 311–313, but cited for convenience from Putnam.

112. Putnam, *The Enforcement of the Statute of Labourers,* p. 11 in appendix.

113. See chapter 3 for the details of the thirteenth-century regulations.

114. Putnam, *The Enforcement of the Statute of Labourers,* p. 14 in appendix: "touz autres ouerours, artificiers, et laborers, et touz autres seruantz nient especifiez, soient sermentez."

115. Ibid., p. 14 in appendix.

116. Ibid., p. 15 in appendix.

117. Ibid., p. 16 in appendix: "en eide de la commune pur temps qe les disme et quinzisme courgent, auxibien pur tout le temps passe come pur le temps auenir."

118. Phelps-Brown and Hopkins, "Seven Centuries of Building Wages," p. 177.

119. Putnam, *The Enforcement of the Statute of Labourers,* pp. 128–129 in appendix. For a closer look at local enforcement, see Clark, "Medieval Labor Law."

120. Putnam, *The Enforcement of the Statute of Labourers,* p. 408 in appendix.

121. Many cases of this exist, including, for example, ibid., p. 409 in appendix, again for Middlesex.

122. Ibid., p. 75.

123. Ibid., p. 25.

124. Ibid., p. 221.

125. For background on the plague in Spain and Portugal, see Callico, "La peste negra."

126. Verlinden, "La grande peste," p. 113.

127. Ibid., pp. 119–120, for this and the following.

128. Ibid., p. 125: "en los tiempos passados ante de la mortalidat."

129. Ibid., p. 126.

130. Ibid., p. 119, fine of twenty sous for carpenters earning twelve pence a day plus their food.

131. Ibid., p. 127.

132. Ibid., pp. 128–129, for this and the following on Castile. See also Callico, "La peste negra," pp. 86–87, for the problems in Castile where workers "demandaran tan grandes precios et soldadas et jornales."

133. Verlinden, "La grande peste," p. 133.

134. Ibid., p. 137.

135. And some did not. Siena, Orvieto, and Pisa had price and wage laws, but Perugia and Florence did not; see Bowsky, "The Impact of the Black Death," p. 30.

136. Lane, *Venice,* pp. 169–170. Reinhold C. Mueller has estimated that Venice suffered a 50 percent drop in population in 1348–1349, down from its medieval high of 110,000–120,000; see his "Peste e demografia," pp. 94–95.

137. Lane, *Venice,* p. 175.

138. Nicholas, *Town and Countryside,* pp. 78–79.

139. Ibid., p. 79.

140. Ibid., p. 198.

141. Ibid., pp. 77 and 198, Bruges; p. 198, Ghent; and p. 99, Ypres.

142. Ibid., pp. 209–210.

143. Ibid., pp. 204–215; Louis's efforts involved a long and complicated struggle.

144. Ibid., p. 80. Other evidence suggests that some wages outside the textile industry sharply increased after the plague; see Blockmans, "The Social and Economic Effects," p. 848, for agricultural workers in Holland; p. 849, for construction wages in Ghent.

145. See, for example, White, *Medieval Technology and Social Change,* on agriculture and on the question of mechanical power, explicit on p. 79.

146. Cipolla, *Before the Industrial Revolution,* pp. 173–174. For a more positive argument based on labor scarcity, admittedly in a different context, see Kolchin, *Unfree Labor,* pp. 16–19.

147. See White, "Cultural Climates and Technological Advance," in his *Medieval Religion and Technology*.

148. Ibid., p. 230. A problem concerning the Christian ethos and the differences in technological progress between the Roman west and the Greek east is not satisfactorily resolved by White.

149. Ibid., p. 237.

150. Ibid., p. 241.

151. Carus-Wilson, "An Industrial Revolution of the Thirteenth Century."

152. White, *Medieval Technology and Social Change*, pp. 129–134.

153. Lane, *Venice*, p. 320. Bok emphasizes that patents imply open use, not secrecy, and this protection of an inventor's rights for a limited time seems in keeping with the ethos of the guild system (*Secrets*, p. 140).

154. Bloch, "Les inventions médiévales," in his *Mélanges historiques*, pp. 822–832; and Dockès, *Medieval Slavery and Liberation*, pp. 175–178.

155. Geremek, *Les marginaux parisiens*, pp. 320 and 341, for astute comments.

156. For England, see Hilton and Aston, *The English Rising of 1381*; and for Florence, *Il tumulto dei Ciompi*.

157. Mollat and Wolff, *Ongles blues*, p. 7.

158. Ibid., pp. 271–316.

159. Ibid., p. 274.

160. For Brunswick, see Rotz, "Investigating Urban Uprisings," where the author summarizes his work on a number of cities. For Florence, a recent survey is Samuel K. Cohn, Jr., "Florentine Insurrections, 1342–1385, in Comparative Perspective," in Hilton and Aston, *The English Rising of 1381*, pp. 143–164.

161. Note this comment on some city archives: "abundant enough to provoke interesting questions but too fragmentary to provide much in the way of conclusive answers" (R. B. Dobson, "The Risings in York, Beverley, and Scarborough, 1380–1381," in Hilton and Aston, *The English Rising of 1381*, p. 114).

162. R. Cazelles, "The Jacquerie," in Hilton and Aston, *The English Rising of 1381*, p. 76.

163. Quoted in Mollat and Wolff, *Ongles blues*, p. 128.

164. Ibid., p. 119.

165. Delachenal, *Les Grandes Chroniques de France*, p. 96: "firent cesser tous menestreux d'ouvrer"; he explained in note that Marcel and his associates caused a work stoppage.

166. Ibid., pp. 148–149.

167. Ibid., p. 152.

168. Mollat and Wolff, *Ongles blues*, p. 120.

169. Ibid., p. 126; and R. Cazelles, "The Jacquerie," in Hilton and Aston, *The English Rising of 1381*, p. 78.

170. Mollat and Wolff, *Ongles blues*, p. 128.

171. Vivier, "La Grande Ordonnance," p. 212.

172. Geremek, *Les marginaux parisiens*, p. 320, for comments on the political indifference of the "underclasses."

173. See Gene Brucker, "The Ciompi Revolt," in Rubinstein, *Florentine Studies*, pp. 314–356. On the interdict, see Trexler, *Republican Florence under the Interdict*; also, Samuel K. Cohn, Jr., "Florentine Insurrections, 1342–1385, in Comparative Perspective," in Hilton and Aston, *The English Rising of 1381*. The most complete narrative of the events remains Rodolico's *I Ciompi*.

174. Najemy, in his *"Audiant Omnes Artes,"* argues that the Ciompi Revolt took place "within the historic framework of Florentine corporatism" (p. 61); but the Ciompi guild itself was the antithesis of typical Florentine guilds.

175. Samuel K. Cohn, Jr., "Florentine Insurrections, 1342–1385, in Comparative Perspective," in Hilton and Aston, *The English Rising of 1381*, p. 154, taking on the views of G. Brucker.

176. Well documented by Cohn, *The Laboring Classes*.

177. The fullest treatment is Hilton's *Bondmen Made Free*.

178. A. F. Butcher, "English Urban Society and the Revolt of 1381," in Hilton and Aston, *The English Rising of 1381*, p. 85.

179. Most of the relevant sources are collected with a fine commentary in Dobson's *The Peasants' Revolt of 1381*; descriptions in this text are by the *Anonimalle Chronicle*, p. 156, and Thomas Walsingham, p. 168.

180. Dobson, *The Peasants' Revolt of 1381*, pp. 226–228, a good example of a London brewer with an axe of his own to grind.

181. For Canterbury, see A. F. Butcher, "English Urban Society and the Revolt of 1381," in Hilton and Aston, *The English Rising of 1381*, p. 110. For York, see R. B. Dobson, "The Risings in York, Beverley, and Scarborough, 1380–1381," in Hilton and Aston, *The English Rising of 1381*, p. 121.

182. R. B. Dobson, "The Risings in York, Beverley, and Scarborough, 1380–1381," in Hilton and Aston, *The English Rising of 1381*, p. 130.

183. Skeat, *Piers the Plowman*, B text, p. 222: "And thanne curseth he the kynge. and all his conseille after, suche lawes to loke. laborers to greue."

184. J. A. Tuck, "Nobles, Commons and the Great Revolt of 1381," in Hilton and Aston, *The English Rising of 1381*, p. 209. This atmosphere of suspicion prompted an investigation that produced a notable source—The English Guild Returns of 1389. See Toulmin Smith, *English Gilds*, and Westlake, *The Parish Gilds of Mediaeval England*.

185. *Froissart: Chronicles*, trans. G. Brereton (New York, 1978), p. 212.

Conclusion

1. Aston and Philpin in *The Brenner Debate* conveniently gather together the original articles from *Past and Present*, 1976–1982.

2. Aston and Philpin, *The Brenner Debate*, pp. 33, 229, and 292.

3. See, for example, Schultz, *Handwerksgesellen und Lohnarbeiter*, for a close study of wage labor and guilds in Colmar, Basel, Freiburg, and Strasbourg. This book picks up the histories in the aftermath of the plague, but the sources do not seem to reveal anything about the central Middle Ages—a defect the author does not remedy by comparisons to other cities.

4. Frank, *Passions within Reason*, pp. 254–255, for summary of this "friendly amendment" to the self-interest model.

5. ASG, CN, cart. n. 332, pt. I, 172 r, Guidotto de Bracelli notary.

Bibliography

Manuscripts

Genoa
Archivio di Stato di Genova
 Cartolari Notarili (The cartularies are cataloged by traditional and often erroneous attributions.)

Cart. N. 4	Lanfranco et al.
Cart. N. 5	Lanfranco, Raimundo Medico, et al.
Cart. N. 7	Pietro Rufo et al.
Cart. N. 11	Giovanni Enrico de Porta
Cart. N. 14	Maestro Salmone
Cart. N. 18 pt. II	Giannino de Predono
Cart. N. 21 pt. I	Palodino de Sexto
Cart. N. 22	Palodino de Sexto
Cart. N. 31 pt. I	Matteo de Predono
Cart. N. 54	Oberto de Langeto
Cart. N. 55 pt. I	Azone de Clavica
Cart. N. 55 pt. II	Azone de Clavica
Cart. N. 86	Giovanni de Corsio
Cart. N. 332 pt. I	Guidotto de Bracelli

 For a partial catalog of these manuscripts, see Ministero dell'Interno, Pubblicazioni degli Archivi di Stato, *Archivio di Stato di Genova: Cartolari notarili genovesi*, Vols. 22 and 41, Rome, 1956 and 1961.

 Notai Ignoti
  Busta 1, 3, 7, 10
 Sezione Manoscritti
  Manoscritto N. 102, *Diversorum Notariorum*
 Magistrato delle Arti
  Busta 178

Montpellier
Archives Départmentales de L'Hérault
 Serie BB 1, Notes Jean Grimaud de l'an 1293

Zurich
Staatsarchiv Canton Zürich
 Zürich, Stadt und Landschaft: Zunftwesen, Zünfte S1336–1784, A.73.2

Primary Sources

Adler, Marcus. *The Itinerary of Benjamin of Tudela*. London, 1907.
Annales Ianuenses, Annali genovesi di Caffaro e de' suoi continuatori. Vol. I, *Fonti per la storia d'Italia*, N. 11, 1099–1173. Edited by Luigi Tommaso Belgrano. Genoa, 1890. Vol. II, *Fonti per la storia d'Italia*, N. 12, 1174–1224. Edited by Luigi Tommaso Belgrano and Cesare Imperiale di Sant'Angelo. Genoa, 1901. Vol. III, *Fonti per la storia d'Italia*, N. 13, 1225–1250. Edited by Cesare Imperiale di Sant'Angelo. Rome, 1923. Vol. IV, *Fonti per la storia d'Italia*, N. 14, 1251–1279. Edited by Cesare Imperiale di Sant'Angelo. Rome, 1926. Vol. V, *Fonti per la storia d'Italia*, N. 14 bis, 1280–1293. Edited by Cesare Imperiale di Sant'Angelo. Rome, 1929.
Aquinas, Thomas. *Summa Theologica*. Rome, 1923.
Arrangio-Ruiz, Vicenzo. *Fontes Iuris Antejustiniani*. Pt. 3. Florence, 1969.
Attenborough, F. L. *The Laws of the Earliest English Kings*. Cambridge, 1922.
Balletto, Laura. *Atti rogati a Ventimiglia da Giovanni da Amandolesio dal 1258 al 1264*. Bordighera, 1985.
Bargellini, Piero, ed. *San Bernardino da Siena: Le prediche volgari*. Milan, 1936.
Benton, John F. *Self and Society in Medieval France: The Memoirs of Abbot Guibert of Nogent*. New York, 1970.
Bernardino of Siena. *Opera Omnia*. Vol. 4, *Quadragesimale de Evangelio Aeterno, Sermones XXVII–LII*. Florence, 1956.
Besta, Enrico, and Gian Luigi Barni. *Liber Consuetudinum Mediolani*. Milan, 1949.
Bizzari, Dina. *Imbreviature notarili I. Liber imbreviaturarum Appulliesis notarii comunis Senarum*. Turin, 1934.
———. *Imbreviature notarili II. Liber imbreviaturarum ildibrandini notarii*. Turin, 1938.
Blancard, Louis. *Documents inédits sur le commerce de Marseille au Moyen Age*. Marseille, 1884.
Boak, A. E. R. "The Book of the Prefect." *Journal of Economic and Business History* 1 (1928–1929): 597–619.
Bonaventure, St. *Opera Omnia*. Florence, 1891.
Boos, Heinrich. *Quellen zur Geschichte der Stadt Worms*. Vol. 1. Berlin, 1886.
Bugarella, Pietro. *Le imbreviature del notaio Adamo de Citella a Palermo (Primo Registro 1286–1287)*. Rome, 1981.
Cannarozzi, Ciro, ed. *San Bernardino da Siena: Le prediche volgari*. Vols. 4 and 5. Florence, 1940.
Castellani, Arrigo. "Il più antico statuto dell'arte degli oliandoli di Firenze." *Saggi di linguistica e filologia italiana e romanza (1946–1976)* 2 (1976): 141–252.
Chiaudano, Mario. *Oberto Scriba de Mercato (1186)*. Turin, 1940.
Chiaudano, Mario, and Mattia Moresco. *Il cartolare di Giovanni Scriba*. 2 vols. Rome, 1935.
Corpus Iuris Canonici. Graz, Austria, 1955.
Crane, Thomas F. *The Exempla or Illustrative Stories from the Sermones Vulgares of Jacques de Vitry*. London, 1890.
Delachenal, R., ed. *Les Grandes Chroniques de France: Chronique des règnes Jean II et Charles V*. Vol. I. Paris, 1910.
de Lespinasse, René. *Les métiers et corporations de la ville de Paris*. Tom. 1, *XIV–*

XVIIIe siècle: Ordinances Générales. Paris, 1886. Tom. 3, *XIVe–XVIIIe siècle: Tissus, etoffes, vêtement.* Paris, 1897.

de Lespinasse, René, and F. Bonnardot. *Les métiers et corporations de la ville de Paris: Le Livre des Métiers d'Etienne Boileau.* Paris, 1879.

Dobson, R. B. *The Peasants' Revolt of 1381.* London, 1970.

Douglas, David C., and George Greenaway. *English Historical Documents, 1042–1189.* London, 1981.

Ennen, Leonard, and G. Eckertz. *Quellen zur Geschichte der Stadt Köln.* Vol. 1. Cologne, 1860.

Fagniez, Gustave. *Documents relatifs à l'histoire de l'industrie e du commerce en France.* Vol. 1. Paris, 1898. Vol. 2. Paris, 1900.

Franchini, Vittorio. *Lo statuto della corporazione dei fabbri del 1244: Contribuito alla storia della organizzazione del lavoro in Modena nel secolo XIII.* Modena, 1914.

Franken, Goswin. *Die Exempla des Jacob von Vitry.* Munich, 1914.

Galbert of Bruges. *The Murder of Charles the Good.* Translated by James Bruce Ross. New York, 1967.

Gaudenzi, Augusto. *Statuti delle società del popolo di Bologna.* Vol. 1, *Società delle armi.* Vol. 2, *Società delle arti.* Rome, 1896.

Gewirth, Alan. *Marsilius of Padua: The Defender of Peace.* New York, 1956.

Gregory of Tours. *Monumenta Germaniae Historica. Scriptorum Rerum Merovingicarum,* tom. I.

Hall-Cole, Margaret W., Hilmar C. Krueger, R. G. Renert, and Robert Reynolds. *Giovanni di Guiberto.* Turin, 1939.

Hincmar of Rheims. *Capitula Synodica. Patrologia Latina,* vol. 125.

Hugh of St. Victor. *Eruditiones Didascalicae. Patrologia Latina,* vol. 176.

Isidore of Seville. *Etymologiarvm sive Originvm.* Edited by W. Lindsay. Oxford, 1911.

Krueger, Hilmar C., and Robert Reynolds. *Lanfranco.* Genoa, 1951–1953.

Limouzin-LaMothe, R. *La commune de Toulouse et les sources de son histoire (1120–1249).* Paris, 1932.

Locatelli, Antonio Maria, ed. *S. Antonii Patavii Sermones Dominicales et in Solemnitatibus.* Padua, 1895.

Lombardo, A. *Documenti della colonia veneziana de Creta.* Turin, 1942.

Madurell-Marimon, José-Maria, and Arcadio Garcia Sanz. *Comandas comerciales barcelonesas de la baja edad media.* Barcelona, 1973.

Mannucci, Francesco L. "Delle società genovesi d'arti e mestieri durante il secolo XIII." *Giornale storico e letterario della Ligure* 6 (1905): 241–305.

Mansi, J. D. *Sacrorum Conciliorum.* Vol. 22.

Marri, Giulia C., ed. *Statuti dell'arte del Cambio di Firenze (1299–1316).* Florence, 1955.

Monticolo, Giovanni. *I capitolari delle arti veneziane. Fonti per la storia d'Italia,* vol. 26. Rome, 1926.

Monumenta Germaniae Historica. Legum I, Capitulare Ecclesiasticum.

———. *Legum II, Capitularia Regum Francorum.*

———. *Legum IV, Liber Papiensis Karoli Magni.*

Morandini, Francesco, ed. *Statuti delle arti degli oliandoli e pizzicagnoli e dei beccai di Firenze (1318–1346).* Florence, 1961.

Mulholland, Mary. *Early Gild Records of Toulouse.* New York, 1941.

Pharr, Clyde. *The Theodosian Code and Novels and the Sirmondian Constitutions.* Princeton, N.J., 1952.

Previté-Orton, Charles, ed. *The Defensor Pacis of Marsilius of Padua.* Cambridge, 1928.

Riley, Henry Thomas, ed. *Munimenta Gildhallae Londoniensis.* 3 vols. London, 1860.

Rolandino Passageri (Rolandinus Bononiensis). *Svmma Totivs Artis Notariae.* Venice, 1546; anastatic reproduction, Bologna, 1977.

Salatiele. *Ars Notariae.* Edited by G. Orlandelli. Milan, 1961.

Sancassani, Giulio. *Le Imbreviature del notaio Oltremarino da Castello a Verona 1244.* Rome, 1982.

Sartini, Ferdinando, ed. *Statuti dell'arte dei rigattieri e linaioli di Firenze.* Florence, 1940.

Schnyder, W., ed. *Quellen zur Zürcher Zunftsgeschichte.* Vol. 1. Zurich, 1936.

Sharpe, Reginald. *Calendar of Letter Books of the City of London, Letter Book D circa A.D. 1309–1314.* London, 1902.

Simeoni, Luigi. *Gli antichi statuti delle arti veronesi.* Venice, 1914.

Skeat, Walter W. *The Vision of William Concerning Piers the Plowman.* 2 vols. London, 1886.

Smith, Toulmin. *English Gilds.* London, 1870.

Solmi, Arrigo. *L'Amministrazione finanzaria del Regno italico nell'alto medio evo.* Pavia, 1932.

Stella, Giorgio. *Annales Genuenses.* Edited by Giovanna Petti Balbi. Bologna, 1975.

Thomas, A. H. *Calendar of Early Mayor's Court Rolls.* Cambridge, 1924.

———. *Calendar of Pleas and Memoranda Rolls.* Cambridge, 1929.

Tiepolo, Maria Francesca. *Domenico Prete di S. Maurizio: Notaio in Venezia, 1309–1316.* Venice, 1970.

Tjäder, Jan-Olof. *Die Nichtliterarischen Lateinischen Papyri Italiens aus der Zeit 445–700.* Vol. 1. Uppsala, 1955. Vol. 2. Stockholm, 1982.

Tubach, Frederic C. *Index Exemplorum: A Handbook of Medieval Religious Tales.* Folklore Fellows Communications N. 204. Helsinki, 1969.

Vercauteren, Fernand. *Actes des comtes de Flandre, 1071–1128.* Brussels, 1938.

Verriest, Léo. *Les luttes sociales et le contrat d'apprentissage à Tournai jusqu'en 1424.* Académie Royale de Belgique, Classe des Lettres et des Sciences morales et politiques et Classe des beaux-Arts. Vol. 9. Brussels, 1912.

Whitelock, Dorothy. *English Historical Documents I, c500–1042.* London, 1979.

Whitelock, D., M. Brett, and C. N. L. Brooke. *Councils and Synods with Other Documents Relating to the English Church.* Vol. 1. Oxford, 1981.

Secondary Works

Abulafia, David. *The Two Italies: Economic Relations between the Norman Kingdom of Sicily and the Northern Communes.* Cambridge, 1977.

Aclocque, Geneviève. *Les corporations, l'industrie et le commerce à Chartres du XIe siècle à la révolution.* Paris, 1917.

Airaldi, Gabriella. *Genova e la Liguria nel medioevo.* Turin, 1986.

Ashtor, Eliyahu. "The Jews in the Mediterranean Trade in the Later Middle Ages." *Hebrew Union College Annual* 55 (1984): 159–178.

Aston, T. H., and C. H. E. Philpin, eds. *The Brenner Debate: Agrarian Class*

Structure and Economic Development in Pre-Industrial Europe. Cambridge, 1985.

Balard, Michel. "Rémarques sur les esclaves à Gênes dans la seconde moitié du XIIIᵉ siècle." *École Française de Rome, Mélanges d'archéologie et d'histoire* 80 (1968): 627–680.

Baldwin, John. *Masters, Princes, and Merchants: The Social Views of Peter the Chanter and His Circle.* Princeton, N.J., 1970.

Balletto, Laura. "I lavoratori nei cantieri navali (Liguria, secc. XII–XV)." In *Artigiani e salariati: Il mondo del lavoro nell'Italia dei secoli XII–XV,* pp. 103–153. Pistoia, 1984.

Barron, Caroline M. "The 'Golden Age' of Women in Medieval London." *Reading Medieval Studies* 15 (1990): 35–58.

Becker, Marvin. *Florence in Transition.* Vol. 1, *The Decline of the Commune.* Baltimore, 1967.

Black, Antony. *Guilds and Civil Society in European Thought from the Twelfth Century to the Present.* Ithaca, N.Y., 1984.

Blanshei, Sarah R. "Perugia, 1260–1340: Conflict and Change in a Medieval Italian Urban Society." *Transactions of the American Philosophical Society* 66, pt. 2 (1976): 1–128.

Bloch, Marc. *Feudal Society.* Translated by L. Manyon. Chicago, 1961.

———. *Mélanges historiques.* Paris, 1966.

Blockmans, W. P. "The Social and Economic Effects of the Plague in the Low Countries, 1349–1500." *Revue belge de philologie et d'histoire* 58 (1980): 833–863.

Boissonade, Prosper. *Essai sur l'organisation du travail en Poitou depuis le XIe siècle jusqu'en à la révolution.* Paris, 1900.

Bok, Sissela. *Secrets: On the Ethics of Concealment and Revelation.* New York, 1982.

Bolton, Brenda. "Innocent III's Treatment of the Humiliati." *Studies in Church History* (1972): 73–82.

Bonnassie, Pierre. *La organizacion del trabajo en Barcelona a fines del siglo XV.* Barcelona, 1975.

Bowsky, William M. "The Impact of the Black Death upon Sienese Government and Society." *Speculum* 39 (1964): 1–34.

———. *Siena under the Nine, 1287–1355.* Berkeley, Calif., 1981.

Bremond, Claude, Jacques Le Goff, and Jean-Claude Schmitt. "*L'Exemplum.*" Turnhout, Belgium, 1982.

Brentano, Robert. *Rome before Avignon: A Social History of Thirteenth-Century Rome.* New York, 1974.

Brooke, Christopher, and Gillian Keir. *London, 800–1216: The Shaping of a City.* Berkeley, Calif., 1975.

Brown, Judith. *In the Shadow of Florence: Provincial Society in Renaissance Pescia.* New York, 1982.

Burns, Robert I. *Islam under the Crusaders: Colonial Survival in the Thirteenth Century Kingdom of Valencia.* Princeton, N.J., 1973.

Byrne, Eugene. *Genoese Shipping in the Twelfth and Thirteenth Centuries.* Cambridge, Mass., 1930.

Callico, Jaime Sobriqués. "La peste negra en la peninsula ibérica." *Annuario de estudios medievales* 7 (1971): 67–102.

Canning, Joseph. *The Political Thought of Baldus de Ubaldis.* Cambridge, 1987.
Carpentier, Elizabeth. "Autour de la peste noire: Famines et épidémies dans l'histoire de XIV siècle." *Annales E.S.C.* 27 (1962): 1062–1092.
Carus-Wilson, E., ed. *Essays in Economic History.* Vol. 2. New York, 1962.
――――. "An Industrial Revolution of the Thirteenth Century." *Economic History Review* 11 (1940): 39–60.
Castaing-Sicard, Mireille. "Contrat de travail et louage d'ouvrage dans la vie toulousaine des XIIe et XIIIe siècles." In *Recueil de mémoires et travaux publié par la Société d'histoire du droit et des institutions des anciens pays de droit écrit,* vol. 4, pp. 83–89. 1958.
Cazelles, Raymond. *Nouvelle histoire de Paris: De la fin du règne de Philippe Auguste à la mort de Charles V, 1223–1380.* Paris, 1972.
Chazan, Robert. *European Jewry and the First Crusade.* Berkeley, Calif., 1987.
Cipolla, Carlo. *Before the Industrial Revolution: European Society and Economy, 1000–1700.* New York, 1976.
――――. *Clocks and Culture, 1300–1700.* New York, 1977.
Clanchy, M. T. *From Memory to Written Record: England, 1066–1307.* Cambridge, Mass., 1979.
Clarke, Elaine. "Medieval Labor Law and the English Local Courts." *American Journal of Legal History* 27 (1983): 330–353.
Cohn, Samuel K., Jr. *The Laboring Classes in Renaissance Florence.* New York, 1980.
Coornaert, Émile. *Les corporations en France avant 1789.* Paris, 1941.
Crook, John. *Law and Life of Rome.* Ithaca, N.Y., 1967.
Darnton, Robert. *The Great Cat Massacre.* New York, 1984.
Day, John. *The Medieval Market Economy.* Oxford, 1987.
de la Roncière, Charles. *Florence: Centre économique regionale au XIV siècle.* 5 vols. Aix-en-Provence, 1977.
Delcorno, Carlo. "L'*ars predicandi* di Bernardino da Siena." In *Atti del simposio internazionale cateriniano-bernardiniano,* edited by Domenico Maffei and Paolo Nardi, pp. 419–449. Siena, 1982.
de Roover, Raymond. *The Rise and Decline of the Medici Bank, 1397–1494.* Cambridge, Mass., 1963.
de Ste Croix, G. E. M. *The Class Struggle in the Ancient Greek World.* London, 1981.
Dhondt, J. "Les solidarités médiévales: Une société en transition, la Flandre en 1127–1128." *Annales E.S.C.* 12 (1957): 529–560.
Didier, P. "Les contrats de travail en Bourgogne au XIV et XV siècles d'après les archives notaires." *Revue historique de droit français et étranger* 50 (1972): 13–69.
Dini, Bruno. "I lavoratori dell'arte della lana a Firenze nel XIV e XV secolo." In *Artigiani e salariati: Il mondo del lavoro nell'Italia dei secoli XII–XV,* pp. 27–68. Pistoia, 1984.
Dixon, E. "Craftswomen in the *Livre des Métiers.*" *Economics Journal* 5 (1895): 209–228.
Dockès, Pierre. *Medieval Slavery and Liberation.* Chicago, 1982.
Dollinger, Philippe. *The German Hanse.* Translated by D. S. Ault and S. H. Steinberg. Stanford, Calif., 1970.
Dopsch, Alfons. *The Economic and Social Foundations of European Civilization.* London, 1937.

Dören, Alfred. *Die Florentiner Wollentuchindustrie.* Stuttgart, 1901.

———. *Italienische Wirtschaftsgeschichte.* Jena, 1934.

Duby, Georges. *The Early Growth of the European Economy.* Translated by Howard B. Clarke. Ithaca, N.Y., 1974.

———. *The Three Orders: Feudal Society Imagined.* Translated by A. Goldhammer. Chicago, 1980.

———. *William Marshal: The Flower of Chivalry.* Translated by Richard Hower. New York, 1985.

Dufourq, Charles-Emmanuel. *L'Espagne catalane et le Maghrib aux XIIIe et XIVe siècles.* Paris, 1966.

Durkheim, Émile. *De la division du travail social.* Paris, 1930.

Epstein, Steven A. "Business Cycles and the Sense of Time in Medieval Genoa." *Business History Review* 62 (1988): 238–260.

———. "Labour in Thirteenth-Century Genoa." *Mediterranean Historical Review* 3 (1988): 114–140.

———. *Wills and Wealth in Medieval Genoa, 1150–1250.* Cambridge, Mass., 1984.

Espinas, G., and H. Pirenne. "Les coutumes de la gilde marchande de Saint Omer." *Le Moyen Age* 5 (1901): 186–196.

Fagniez, Gustave. *Études sur l'industrie et la classe industrielle à Paris au XIII et au XIV siècle.* Paris, 1877.

Fanfani, Amintore. *Saggi di storia economica italiana.* Milan, 1936.

Felloni, Giuseppe, and G. Pesce. *Le monete genovesi: Storia, arte, ed economia delle monete di Genova dal 1139 al 1814.* Genoa, 1975.

Finley, M. I. *Ancient Slavery and Modern Ideology.* New York, 1980.

Frank, Robert H. *Passions within Reason: The Strategic Role of the Emotions.* New York, 1988.

Geremek, Bronislaw. *Les marginaux parisiens aux XIVe et XVe siècles.* Paris, 1976.

———. *Le salariat dans l'artisanat parisien aux XIIIe–XIVe siècles.* Paris, 1968.

Gioffrè, Domenico. *Il mercato degli schiavi a Genova nel secolo XV.* Genoa, 1971.

Given, James B. *Society and Homicide in Thirteenth-Century England.* Stanford, Calif., 1977.

Goitein, S. D. "Le culte du vendredi musulman: Son arrière plan social et économique." *Annales E.S.C.* 13 (1958): 488–500.

———. *A Mediterranean Society: The Jewish Communities of the Arab World as Portrayed in the Documents of the Cairo Geniza.* Vol. 1, *Economic Foundations.* Berkeley, Calif., 1967. Vol. 4, *Daily Life.* Berkeley, Calif., 1983. Vol. 5, *The Individual.* Berkeley, Calif., 1988.

Goldthwaite, Richard A. *The Building of Renaissance Florence.* Baltimore, 1980.

Goody, Jack. *The Development of the Family and Marriage in Europe.* Cambridge, 1983.

Gouron, André. *La réglementation des métiers en Languedoc au moyen âge.* Paris, 1958.

Grayzel, Solomon. *The Church and the Jews in the XIIIth Century.* New York, 1966.

Greci, Roberto. "Il contratto di apprendistato nelle corporazioni bolognesi (XIII–XIV sec.)." *Atti e memorie: Deputazione di storia per le provincie di Romagne* 27 (1976): 145–178 and (1977): 61–106.

Grierson, Philip. "Commerce in the Dark Ages: A Critique of the Evidence." *Transactions of the Royal Historical Society,* 5th ser. 9 (1959): 123–140.

————. "Money and Coinage under Charlemagne." In *Karl der Grosse*, edited by W. Braunfels, vol. 1, pp. 501–536. Dusseldorf, 1965.

Gross, Charles. *The Gild Merchant*. Oxford, 1890.

Grundmann, Herbert. *Religiöse Bewegungen im Mittelalter*. Hildesheim, 1961.

Gyr, Salomon. *Züricher Zunft-Historien*. Zurich, 1929.

Hanawalt, Barbara, ed. *Women and Work in Preindustrial Europe*. Bloomington, Ind., 1986.

Hartmann, Ludo M. *Zur Wirtschaftsgeschichte Italiens im frühen Mittelalter*. Gotha, 1904.

Heers, Jacques. *Esclaves et domestiques au Moyen Age dans la monde mediterranée*. Paris, 1981.

Herlihy, David. *Medieval Households*. Cambridge, Mass., 1985.

————. *Pisa in the Early Renaissance: A Study of Urban Growth*. New Haven, Conn., 1958.

Hessel, Alfred. *Geschichte der Stadt Bologna von 1116 bis 1280*. Berlin, 1910.

Hilton, Rodney H. *Bondmen Made Free: Medieval Peasant Movements and the English Rising of 1381*. London, 1973.

Hilton, R. H., and T. H. Aston, eds. *The English Rising of 1381*. Cambridge, 1984.

Himmelfarb, Gertrude. *The Idea of Poverty: England in the Early Industrial Age*. New York, 1983.

Hoshino, Hidetoshi. "La produzione laniera nel trecento a Firenze." In *Il tumulto dei Ciompi: Un momento di storia fiorentina ed europea*, pp. 41–58. Florence, 1981.

Howell, Martha. *Women, Production, and Patriarchy in Late Medieval Cities*. Chicago, 1986.

Huntington, Richard, and Peter Metcalf. *Celebrations of Death: The Anthropology of Mortuary Ritual*. Cambridge, 1979.

Hyde, J. K. *Padua in the Age of Dante*. New York, 1966.

Il tumulto dei Ciompi: Un momento di storia fiorentina ed europea. Florence, 1981.

Jakobs, Hermann. "Bruderschaft und Gemeinde: Köln im 12. Jahrhundert." In *Gilden und Zünfte*, edited by B. Schwineköper, pp. 281–309. Sigmaringen, 1985.

Jones, A. H. M. *The Later Roman Empire, 284–602*. 2 vols. Oxford, 1964.

Jordan, William C. *Louis IX and the Challenge of the Crusade*. Princeton, N.J., 1979.

————. "Problems of the Meat Market of Béziers, 1240–1247." *Revue des études juives* 135 (1976): 31–49.

Jordan, W. C., B. McNab, and T. F. Ruiz, eds. *Order and Innovation in the Middle Ages: Essays in Honor of Joseph R. Strayer*. Princeton, N.J., 1976.

Karras, Ruth Mazo. *Slavery and Society in Medieval Scandinavia*. New Haven, Conn., 1988.

Kazhdan, A. P., and A. W. Epstein. *Change in Byzantine Culture in the Eleventh and Twelfth Centuries*. Berkeley, Calif., 1985.

Kedar, Benjamin Z. *Crusade and Mission*. Princeton, N.J., 1984.

Kirshner, Julius. "Reading Bernardino's Sermon on the Public Debt." In *Atti del simposio internazionale cateriniano-bernardiniano*, edited by Domenico Maffei and Paolo Nardi, pp. 547–622. Siena, 1982.

Klapisch-Zuber, Christiane. *Women, Family, and Ritual in Renaissance Italy*. Chicago, 1985.

Kolchin, Peter. *Unfree Labor: American Slavery and Russian Serfdom*. Cambridge, Mass., 1987.

Landes, David S. *Revolution in Time: Clocks and the Making of the Modern World*. Cambridge, Mass., 1983.

Lane, Frederic C. *Venetian Ships and Shipbuilders of the Renaissance*. Baltimore, 1934.

————. *Venice: A Maritime Republic*. Baltimore, 1973.

Lane, F. C., and R. C. Mueller. *Money and Banking in Medieval and Renaissance Venice*. Baltimore, 1985.

Lapidus, Ira. *Muslim Cities in the Later Middle Ages*. Cambridge, Mass., 1967.

Le Goff, Jacques. *Time, Work and Culture in the Middle Ages*. Translated by A. Goldhammer. Chicago, 1980.

Liebeschuetz, J. *Antioch: City and Imperial Administration in the Later Roman Empire*. Oxford, 1972.

Little, Lester K. *Liberty, Charity, Fraternity: Lay Religious Confraternities at Bergamo in the Age of the Commune*. Bergamo, Italy, and Northampton, Mass., 1988.

————. *Religious Poverty and the Profit Economy in Medieval Europe*. Ithaca, N.Y., 1978.

Lopez, Robert S. *The Commerical Revolution of the Middle Ages, 950–1301*. Cambridge, 1976.

————. "Silk Industry in the Byzantine Empire." *Speculum* 20 (1945): 1–42.

————. *Studi sull'economia genovese nel medio evo*. Turin, 1936.

Lopez, R. S., and I. W. Raymond. *Medieval Trade in the Mediterranean World*. New York, 1955.

Mackenney, Richard. *Tradesmen and Traders: The World of the Guilds in Venice and Europe, c.1250–c.1650*. Totowa, N.J., 1987.

Maffei, Domenico, and Paolo Nardi, eds. *Atti del simposio internazionale cateriniano-bernardiniano*. Siena, 1982.

Martines, Lauro. *Power and Imagination: City States in Renaissance Italy*. New York, 1979.

Maschke, Erich. "Die Brücke im Mittelalter." *Historische Zeitschrift* 224 (1977): 265–292.

Mazzaoui, Maureen F. *The Italian Cotton Industry in the Later Middle Ages, 1100–1600*. Cambridge, 1981.

Meersseman, Gilles. *Ordo Fraternitatis: Confraternite e pietà dei laici nel medioevo*. 3 vols. Rome, 1977.

Meiggs, Russell. *Roman Ostia*. Oxford, 1973.

Michaud-Quantin, Pierre. *Universitas: Espressions du mouvement communautaire dans le Moyen Age latin*. Paris, 1970.

Mickwitz, Gunnar. "Geld und Wirtschaft im römischen Reich des vierten Jahrhunderts n. Chr." *Societas Scientiarum Fennica, Commentationes humanarum litterarum* 4, no. 2 (1932): 132–142.

————. *Die Kartellfunktionen der Zünfte und ihre Bedeutung bei der Enstehung des Zunftwesens*. Helsinki, 1936.

Miret Y Sans, Joaquin. "L'esclavitud en Cataluña en los ultimos tiempos de la Edad Media." *Revue Hispanique* 41 (1917): 1–109.

Miskimin, Harry A. *Money, Prices, and Foreign Exchange in Fourteenth Century France*. New Haven, Conn., 1963.

Miskimin, H. A., D. Herlihy, and A. L. Udovitch. *The Medieval City.* New Haven, Conn., 1977.

Mollat, Michel. *The Poor in the Middle Ages.* Translated by A. Goldhammer. New Haven, Conn., 1980.

Mollat, Michel, and Philippe Wolff. *Ongles blues: Jacques et Ciompi.* Paris, 1970.

Monti, Gennaro Maria. *Le corporazioni nell'evo antico e nell'alto medio evo.* Bari, 1934.

Mrozek, Stanislaw. "Die Goldbergwerke im römischen Dazien." *ANRW* 6 (1977): 95–109.

Mueller, Reinhold C. "Peste e demografia." In *Venezia e la peste 1348/1797,* pp. 93–95. Venice, 1979.

Muir, Edward. *Civic Ritual in Renaissance Venice.* Princeton, N.J., 1981.

Munz, Peter. *Frederick Barbarossa.* London, 1969.

Murray, Alexander. "Confession as a Historical Source in the Thirteenth Century." In *The Writing of History in the Middle Ages,* edited by R. H. C. Davies and J. M. Wallace-Hadrill, pp. 275–322. Oxford, 1981.

————. *Reason and Society in the Middle Ages.* Oxford, 1978.

Najemy, John M. "*Audiant Omnes Artes:* Corporate Origins of the Ciompi Revolution." In *Il tumulto dei Ciompi: Un momento di storia fiorentina ed europea,* pp. 59–93. Florence, 1981.

————. *Corporatism and Consensus in Florentine Electoral Politics, 1280–1400.* Chapel Hill, N.C., 1982.

Nicholas, David. *The Metamorphosis of a Medieval City: Ghent in the Age of the Arteveldes, 1302–1390.* Lincoln, Nebr., 1987.

————. *Town and Countryside in Fourteenth Century Flanders.* Bruges, Belgium, 1971.

Oexle, Otto G. "Conjuratio und Gilde im frühen Mittelalter: Ein Beitrag zum Problem der sozialgeschichtlichen Kontinuität zwischen Antike und Mittelalter." In *Gilden und Zünfte,* edited by B. Schwineköper, pp. 151–213. Sigmaringen, 1985.

Orsted, Peter. *Roman Imperial Economy and Romanization.* Copenhagen, 1985.

Ostrogorsky, George. *History of the Byzantine State.* New Brunswick, N.J., 1969.

Ovitt, George, Jr. *The Restoration of Perfection: Labor and Technology in Medieval Culture.* New Brunswick, N.J., 1987.

Patterson, Orlando. *Slavery and Social Death.* Cambridge, Mass., 1982.

Phelps-Brown, E. H., and Sheila Hopkins. "Seven Centuries of Building Wages." In *Essays in Economic History,* edited by E. Carus-Wilson, vol. 2, pp. 168–178. New York, 1962.

————. "Seven Centuries of the Prices of Consumables, Compared with Builders' Wage-Rates." In *Essays in Economic History,* edited by E. Carus-Wilson, vol. 2, pp. 179–196. New York, 1962.

Philipps, William D., Jr. *Slavery from Roman Times to the Early Transatlantic Trade.* Minneapolis, 1985.

Pini, Antonio Ivan. *Città, comuni, e corporazioni nel medioevo italiano.* Bologna, 1986.

————. "La ripartizione topografica degli artigiani a Bologna nel 1294: Un esempio di demografia sociale." In *Artigiani e salariati: Il mondo del lavoro nell'Italia dei secoli XII–XV,* pp. 189–224. Pistoia, 1984.

Pirenne, Henri. *Les villes et les institutions urbaines.* 2 vols. Paris, 1939.

Postan, Michael M. *Essays on Medieval Agriculture and General Problems of the Medieval Economy.* Cambridge, 1973.

————. *The Medieval Economy and Society: An Economic History of Britain, 1000–1500.* London, 1972.

Pryor, John H. *Business Contracts of Medieval Provence: Selected Notulae from the Cartulary of Giraud Amalric of Marseilles, 1248.* Toronto, 1981.

Putnam, Bertha H. *The Enforcement of the Statute of Labourers.* New York, 1908.

Racine, P. "Associations de marchands et associations de métiers en Italie de 600 à 1200." In *Gilden und Zünfte,* edited by B. Schwineköper, pp. 127–149. Sigmaringen, 1985.

Reyerson, Kathryn. *Business, Banking, and Finance in Medieval Montpellier.* Toronto, 1985.

Reynolds, Susan. *An Introduction to the History of English Medieval Towns.* Oxford, 1970.

Rickman, Geoffrey. *The Corn Supply of Ancient Rome.* Oxford, 1980.

Rodolico, Niccolo. *I Ciompi: Una pagina di storia del proletariato operaio.* Florence, 1945.

Romano, Dennis. *Patricians and Popolani: The Social Foundations of the Venetian Renaissance State.* Baltimore, 1987.

Rorabaugh, W. J. *The Craft Apprentice: From Franklin to the Machine Age in America.* Oxford, 1986.

Rostovtzeff, M. *The Social and Economic History of the Roman Empire.* Oxford, 1957.

Rotz, Rhiman. "Investigating Urban Uprisings with Examples from Hanseatic Towns, 1374–1416." In *Order and Innovation in the Middle Ages: Essays in Honor of Joseph R. Strayer,* edited by W. C. Jordan, B. McNab, and T. F. Ruiz, pp. 215–233. Princeton, N.J., 1976.

Rubinstein, N., ed. *Florentine Studies.* London, 1968.

Rueschemeyer, Dietrich. *Power and the Division of Labour.* Stanford, Calif., 1986.

Ruggini, Lellia C. "Le associazioni professionali nel mondo romano-bizantino." In *settimane* 17, *Artigianato e tecnica nella società dell'alto medioevo occidentale,* pp. 59–193. Spoleto, 1971.

Sahlins, Marshall. *Stone Age Economics.* Chicago, 1972.

Schmitt, Jean-Claude. *Precher d'exemples: Récits de predicateurs du Moyen Age.* Paris, 1985.

Schultz, Knut. *Handwerksgesellen und Lohnarbeiter: Untersuchungen zur oberrheinischen und oberdeutschen Stadtgeschichte des 14. bis 17. Jahrhunderts.* Sigmaringen, 1985.

Schwineköper, B., ed. *Gilden und Zünfte.* Sigmaringen, 1985.

Shahar, Shulamith. *The Fourth Estate: A History of Women in the Middle Ages.* Translated by C. Galai. New York, 1983.

Sisto, Alessandra. *Genova nel duecento: Il capitolo di San Lorenzo.* Genoa, 1979.

Skinner, Quentin. *The Foundations of Modern Political Thought.* Vol. 1, *The Renaissance.* Cambridge, 1978.

Smith, Adam. *The Wealth of Nations.* New York, 1937.

Sokoloff, Natalie J. *Between Money and Love: The Dialectics of Women's Home and Market Work.* Boulder, Colo., 1980.

Sombart, Werner. *The Quintessence of Capitalism.* Translated by M. Epstein. New York, 1915.

Southern, R. W. *Robert Grosseteste.* Oxford, 1986.

Spicciani, Amleto. "La povertà 'involuntaria' e le sue cause economiche nel pensiero e nella predicazione di Bernardino da Siena." In *Atti del simposio internazionale cateriniano-bernardiniano,* edited by Domenico Maffei and Paolo Nardi, pp. 811–834. Siena, 1982.

―――. "Solidarietà, previdenza e assistenza per gli artigiani nell'Italia medievale (secoli XII–XV)." In *Artigiani e salariati: Il mondo del lavoro nell'Italia dei secoli XII–XV,* pp. 293–343. Pistoia, 1984.

Sprandel, Rolf. "Die Ausbreitung des deutschen Handwerks im mittelalterlichen Frankreich." *Vierteljahrschrift für Sozial und Wirtschaftsgeschichte* 51 (1964): 66–100.

Spufford, Peter. *Money and Its Use in Medieval Europe.* Cambridge, 1988.

Stöckle, Albert. *Spätromische und byzantinische Zünfte.* Leipzig, 1911.

Strait, Paul. *Cologne in the Twelfth Century.* Gainesville, Fla., 1974.

Thorndike, Lynn. "The Invention of the Mechanical Clock about 1271 A.D." *Speculum* 16 (1941): 242–243.

Thrupp, Sylvia. "The Gilds." In *Cambridge Economic History of Europe,* vol. 3, pp. 230–280, 624–635. Cambridge, 1963.

―――. *The Merchant Class of Medieval London.* Ann Arbor, Mich., 1962.

Toubert, Pierre. *Les structures du latium médiéval.* Rome, 1973.

Trexler, Richard. *Republican Florence under the Interdict.* Leiden, Netherlands, 1974.

Van Engen, John. "Theophilus Presbyter and Rupert of Deutz: The Manual Arts and Benedictine Theology in the Early Twelfth Century." *Viator* 11 (1980): 147–163.

Venezia e la peste 1348/1797. Venice, 1979.

Verlinden, Charles. *L'Esclavage dans l'Europe médiévale.* Tom. 1. Bruges, Belgium, 1955. Tom. 2. Ghent, Belgium, 1977.

―――. "La grande peste de 1348 en Espagne: Contribution à l'étude de ses conséquences économiques et sociales." *Revue belge de philologie et d'histoire* 17 (1938): 103–146.

Violante, Cinzio. *La società milanese nell'età precomunale.* Bari, 1953.

Vitale, Vito. *Il comune del podestà a Genova.* Milan, 1951.

Vivier, Robert. "La Grande Ordonnance de février 1351: Les mesures anti-corporatives et la liberté du travail." *Revue Historique* 138 (1921): 201–214.

Vryonis, Speros. "Demokratia and Eleventh Century Guilds." *Dumbarton Oaks Papers* 17 (1963): 287–314.

Waltzing, Jean-Pierre. *Étude historique sur les corporations professionelles chez les romains.* 4 vols. Louvain, Belgium, 1895.

Westermann, W. L. "Apprenticeship Contracts and the Apprentice System in Roman Egypt." *Classical Philology* 9 (1914): 295–315.

Westlake, H. F. *The Parish Gilds of Mediaeval England.* London, 1919.

White, Lynn, Jr. *Medieval Religion and Technology.* Berkeley, Calif., 1978.

―――. *Medieval Technology and Social Change.* Oxford, 1962.

Wilks, Michael. "Corporatism and Representation in the *Defensor Pacis.*" *Studia Gratiana* 15 (1972): 253–292.

Williams, Stephen. *Diocletian and the Roman Recovery.* New York, 1985.

Zanoni, Luigi. *Gli Humiliati nel loro rapporti con l'eresia, l'industria della lana ed i communi nei secoli XII e XIII.* Milan, 1911.

Ziegler, Philip. *The Black Death.* New York, 1969.

Index

Abbotsbury, 41
Adalbero of Laon, 185
Agricultura, 174
Albi, 161, 277 (n. 27)
Alexander III, pope, 160
Alfred, king of Wessex, 39
Amisscere, 85
Anomie, 7
Anthony of Padua, St., 175–176
Antioch, 24–25, 31
Anti-Semitism, 172. *See also* Jews
Antoninus Pius, Roman emperor, 17
Apprenticeship, 65–67, 103–111, 123–125,
  188–189, 219, 224, 272 (n. 2); Roman,
  19–20, 23, 265 (n. 36); in Genoa, 75–76,
  108–111, 141–143; in Marseilles, 76; in
  Siena, 76; in Bologna, 76, 83–85, 269
  (n. 41); in Montpellier, 76–77; in
  Tournai, 77–78, 216–217; in Crete, 78;
  in London, 106, 197–202; in Paris, 106–
  107, 125, 141–144, 214–215, 234, 272
  (n. 11); in Verona, 273 (n. 27)
Aragon, 239–241
Arcadius, Roman emperor, 23
Aristotle, 204, 281 (n. 2)
Armorers: in Genoa, 70–71
Arras, 56
Ars, 32, 72, 204
Artificium dies, 18
Arti maggiori, 140
Arts: mechanical, 278 (n. 52)
Athelstan, 40
Attenborough, F. L., 39
Augsburg, 230
Augustus, Roman emperor, 13
Avignon, 161

Bakers: Roman, 21, 22; in Antioch, 24; in
  Naples, 32; in Toulouse, 60; in Paris,
  137, 160–161
Balard, Michel, 223, 224

Baldus de Ubaldis, 205
Ball, John, 255
Barbers, 165
Barcelona, 9, 225, 240
Bartolo of Sassoferrato, 81, 205
Batifolii: in Genoa, 70, 72, 149–150
Bedwyn, 41
Belisarius, 28
Benedictine Rule, 186
Benjamin of Tudela, 170
Bergen, 134
Beverley, 254
Béziers, 169
Bithynia, 14–15
Black, Antony, 6, 81, 204
Blanshei, Sarah R., 193
Bloch, Marc, 73, 247
Blois, 230
Boccanegra, Guglielmo, 195
Boileau, Étienne, 137–138, 142
Bologna, 66, 76, 82–86, 108, 136, 161,
  166, 178, 180
Bonaventure, St., 173–175
Book of Customs, 58, 87–89
Book of the Prefect, 45–47
Brenner, Robert, 258
Brewing, 41
Bruderschaft, 86
Bruges, 55, 242–243
Brun, Rudolf, 284 (n. 78)
Brunswick, 249
Butchers, 127–128, 152–153, 168, 181
Byzantium, 44–47, 170

Cahen, Claude, 48
Cairo, 47
Calimala, 131, 252
Callistratus, 17
Cambio, 62, 163
Cambridge, 40–41
Canning, Joseph, 205

(